CHINA
AND
THE CHINESE

CHINA
AND
THE CHINESE

A GENERAL DESCRIPTION OF
THE COUNTRY AND ITS INHABITANTS: ITS CIVILIZATION
AND FORM OF GOVERNMENT; ITS RELIGIOUS AND
SOCIAL INSTITUTIONS; ITS INTERCOURSE WITH OTHER
NATIONS;
AND ITS

PRESENT CONDITION AND PROSPECTS

BY THE REV. JOHN L. NEVIUS

TEN YEARS A MISSIONARY IN CHINA

WITH A MAP AND ILLUSTRATIONS.

GYAN

Published by

Gyan Publishing House
5, Ansari Road
Daryaganj, New Delhi-110002
Phone: 011-47034999, 9811692060
E-mail: books@gyanbooks.com

Distribution Network
gyanbooks.com
India, USA, Canada, UK, Australia, France

ISBN : 978-81-212-3237-1 (PB)
First Published, 1869

2nd Impression 2020

Printed at: Gyan Press, Delhi.

China and the Chinese
Author: John L. Nevius

CHINA

AND

THE CHINESE:

A GENERAL DESCRIPTION OF

THE COUNTRY AND ITS INHABITANTS; ITS CIVILIZATION AND FORM OF GOVERNMENT; ITS RELIGIOUS AND SOCIAL INSTITUTIONS; ITS INTERCOURSE WITH OTHER NATIONS;

AND ITS

PRESENT CONDITION AND PROSPECTS.

BY THE REV. JOHN L. NEVIUS,

TEN YEARS A MISSIONARY IN CHINA.

WITH A MAP AND ILLUSTRATIONS.

NEW YORK:

HARPER & BROTHERS, PUBLISHERS,

FRANKLIN SQUARE.

1869.

To My Wife,

HELEN S. COAN NEVIUS,

EVER MY MOST

JUDICIOUS COUNSELLOR AND EFFICIENT HELPER,

THIS VOLUME IS INSCRIBED.

PREFACE.

OUR new relations with China, her practical nearness to us, and more especially the late visit of the Chinese Embassy, have served to awaken a new interest in that Empire. Seldom have two parties been suddenly brought together, who had before so thoroughly misunderstood each other as have we and the Chinese. I have been asked by intelligent scholars in China—"Do you have schools in your country?" When they discover that we, whom they have been accustomed to regard as barbarians, give evidence of some degree of mental culture, and are acquainted with their language and literature, the question naturally arises in their minds—"Do they obtain their education in China; or may they not have schools in their own country?" When told that institutions of learning are common with us, the inference is very apt to be—"Then the people of your honorable nation are also acquainted with the books of Confucius;" supposing that wherever throughout the world there are schools, the text-books must of course be the Chinese Classics, as few of them have a conception of a system of instruction derived from any other source.

This ignorance of other countries is truly remarkable; but hardly more so than that which exists among Western nations with reference to the Chinese. I have been asked by educated men in the United States—"Are not the

Chinese a remarkably dull and uninteresting people? Are they susceptible of feelings of affection and gratitude? Are you able to develop their intellectual and moral perceptions; and have any of them really become true and reliable Christians?"

The erroneous views which we mutually entertain of each other are due to a want of reliable information; and this want has resulted from our wide separation, and our infrequent and imperfect intercourse.

Now that China—which we have heretofore thought of as situated in the extreme East, and shut off from us by the intervening nations of Europe and Asia—has become our next neighbor on the West, it is very important that we become better acquainted with its inhabitants, and that we and they should cultivate that mutual respect and sympathy which ought to characterize two great nations whose interests and destinies are in the future to be so closely united.

To promote this desirable end is the principal object of this book; and if it should in any good degree subserve so important a purpose it will require no apology for its publication.

It has been my design to give a general description of China and the Chinese, rather than detailed information on particular subjects, having special reference to the religious condition and wants of the people, and the character and results of the labors of missionaries.

While making occasional use of other works on China, I have depended, for the most part, on my own observations and experiences during ten years of familiar intercourse with all classes of the people, and in different parts of the Empire.

Most of the contents of the chapters relating to the prevalent religions and superstitions are taken from letters which I prepared while in China, which were published in "The Home and Foreign Record" and the "Foreign Missionary."

In quoting from the Chinese Classics in the third chapter, I have generally adopted the excellent translation made by Dr. Legge of Hong-kong.

I have been careful not to make statements of facts without their being well authenticated; and I believe that the opinions advanced in this book will accord in the main with those of other persons who have had the same opportunities for observation.

JOHN L. NEVIUS.

OVID, N. Y., August, 1868.

CONTENTS.

CHAPTER IV.

COMPETITIVE EXAMINATIONS AND SCHOOLS.

CHAPTER V.

THE CONSTITUTION OF THE CHINESE GOVERNMENT.

CHAPTER VI.

THE RELIGIONS OF CHINA.

CHAPTER VII.

BUDDHISM.

CHAPTER VIII.

BUDDHISM—CONTINUED.

CHAPTER IX.

TAUISM.

CHAPTER X.

NATIONAL RELIGIOUS RITES AND BELIEFS.

CHAPTER XI.

MUTUAL RELATIONS AND INFLUENCES OF THE RELIGIOUS SYSTEMS OF CHINA.

CHAPTER XIV.

THE LANGUAGES OF CHINA.

CHAPTER XV.

BENEVOLENT INSTITUTIONS OF CHINA.

CHAPTER XVI.

THE MORAL TRACT LITERATURE OF CHINA.

CHAPTER XVII.

SOCIAL CUSTOMS, ETC.

CHAPTER XXI.

MISSIONARY LIFE IN CHINA.

CHAPTER XXII.

DIFFERENT METHODS AND AGENCIES EMPLOYED IN MISSIONARY WORK.

CHAPTER XXIII.

RESULTS OF MISSIONARY WORK.

ILLUSTRATIONS.

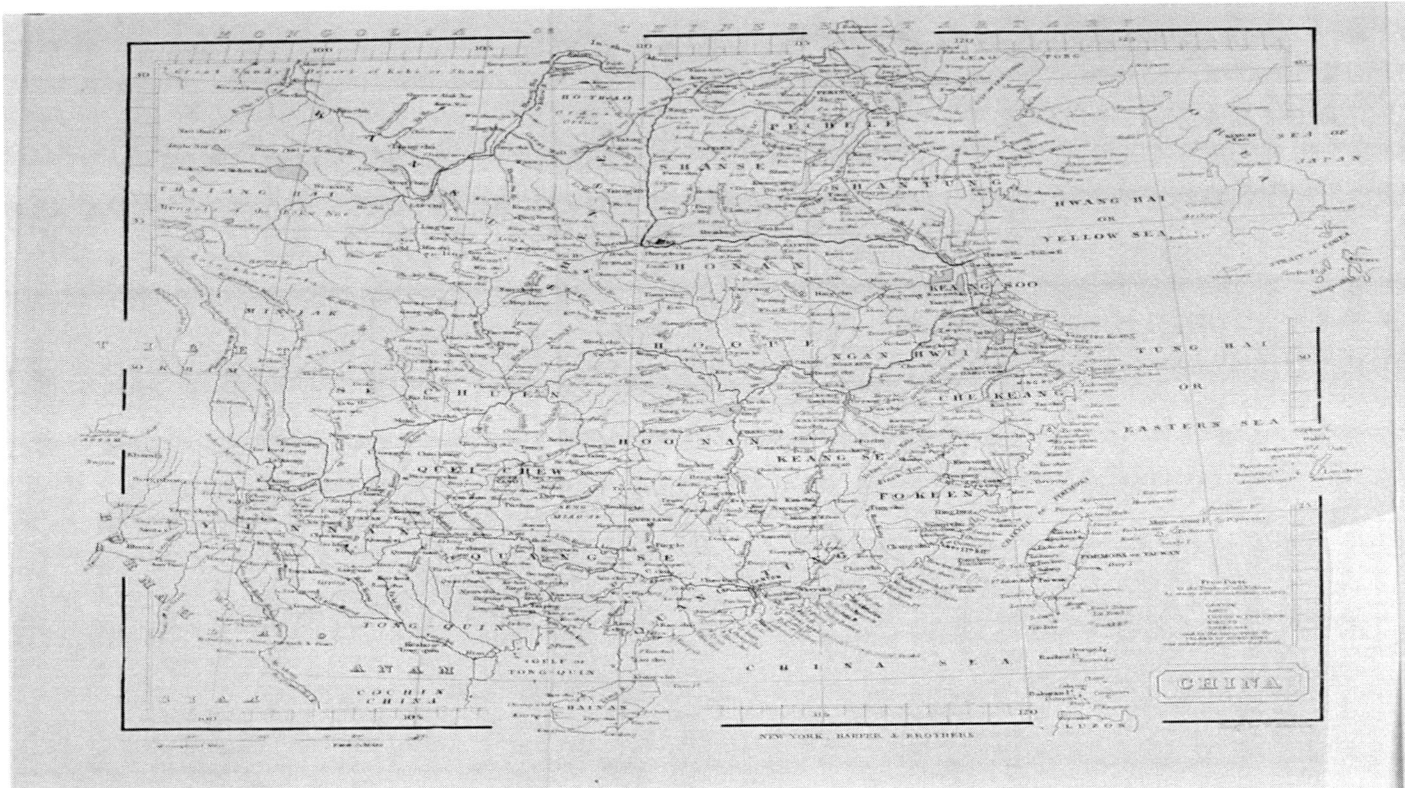
CHINA
MONGOLIA
CHINESE TARTARY
LEAO TONG
PECHELE
SHANSE
SHANTUNG
HONAN
KEANG SOO
HOOPE
NGAN HWUI
CHE KEANG
SE CHUEN
HOO NAN
KEANG SE
FOKEEN
QUEI CHEW
YUNNAN
QUANG SE
TONG QUIN
ANAM
COCHIN CHINA
GULF OF TONG QUIN
HAINAN
LUZON
FORMOSA or TAIWAN
SEA OF JAPAN
HWANG HAI OR YELLOW SEA
TUNG HAI OR EASTERN SEA
CHINA SEA
TIBET
NEW YORK, HARPER & BROTHERS

CHINA AND THE CHINESE.

CHAPTER I.

GENERAL VIEW OF THE CHINESE EMPIRE.

The word China not Known by the Chinese.—The Names they Use to Designate their Country.—General Resemblance of China to the United States: in Position, Form, Climate, Productions, Natural and Artificial Divisions, and in Area.—Description of the Walled Cities of China.—The Population of the Empire.—Peculiarities of Climate, and their Connection with the Monsoons.—Rivers and Natural Scenery.

THE word China is at present unknown in the empire which we call by that name. It was no doubt introduced in the West from the nations of Central Asia, who in speaking of the Chinese use the terms Jin, Chin, Sin, Sinæ, and Sinistæ. These names were probably derived from the powerful Tsin family, which held sway over the north-western part of China as early as 770 B.C.; and obtained the government of the whole empire 250 years B.C. The early prominence of this name in that part of the country which was first reached by the routes of Western traders strongly confirms the view now generally adopted by commentators, that the Chinese are specifically referred to in the forty-ninth chapter of Isaiah—"Behold, these shall come from far; and lo, these from the North and from the West: and these from the land of Sinim."

The names which the Chinese use in speaking of themselves are various. The most common one is *Chung Kwoh*,

"Middle Kingdom;" the term "middle" signifying not only that they are the geographical centre of the world, but also the centre of light and civilization. Another name is *Chung Hwa-Kwoh*—"Middle Flowery Kingdom;" "flowery" presenting the idea of beautiful, cultivated, refined. The terms *Tien-Hwa-Kwoh* and *Tien-Chao*—"Heavenly Flowery Kingdom," and "Heavenly Dynasty"—are sometimes used, the word "heavenly" presenting the Chinese idea that the empire is established by the authority of heaven, and that the Emperor rules by divine right. This title has given rise to the contemptuous epithet applied to this race by Europeans—"The Celestials." They also speak of themselves as "*Tien-hia*"—"Under Heaven"—that is, "the world." The particular title of the reigning dynasty is often used, as at present *Ta-Tsing-Kwoh*, the "Kingdom of the Great Tsin Dynasty."

In giving a correct general idea of China to Western nations, I can not, perhaps, do better than to institute a comparison between it and the United States, to which it bears a striking resemblance. It occupies the same position in the Eastern Hemisphere that the United States does in the Western. Its line of sea-coast on the Pacific resembles that of the United States on the Atlantic, not only in length but also in contour. Being found within almost the same parallels of latitude, it embraces the same varieties of climate and productions. A river as grand as the Mississippi, flowing east, divides the empire into two nearly equal parts, which are often designated as "North of the River," and "South of the River." It passes through an immense and fertile valley, and is supplied by numerous tributaries having their rise in mountain ranges on either side, and also in the Himalayas on the west.

The area of China proper is about the same as that of the organized states of the American Union. The resemblance holds also in the artificial divisions. While our country is divided into more than thirty states, China is divided into eighteen provinces; this division furnishing still another name for the empire, in common use, *Shih-pah-seng*—"The Eighteen Provinces." These provinces are on an average about twice as large as our states. As our states are divided into counties, so each province has about ten divisions, called *Fu*; and each *Fu* is again divided into about an equal number of *Hien*. These divisions and subdivisions of the provinces are generally translated in English departments, or prefectures, and districts. In this work I shall use the Chinese terms and their English equivalents interchangeably. The above-mentioned divisions and subdivisions are much larger than our corresponding counties and townships. While the empire has its capital at Pekin, so each province, Fu and Hien, has its capital or seat of civil power, in which the officers exercising jurisdiction over it reside. While our national name, United States, covers not only the states, but the comparatively sparsely-populated territories, so the Chinese Empire includes, in addition to the eighteen provinces, or China proper, Manchuria, Mongolia, Sungaria, Eastern Turkistan, Koko-nor, and Thibet. The most of these territories belonged originally to the present Tartar rulers of China, and after the subjugation of the eighteen provinces were united with them in the same empire. The whole circumference of the empire is about 12,000 miles, and the whole area about 5,000,000 of square miles—nearly twice that of the United States, exclusive of the lately-acquired Russian Possessions. When we speak of China without specifications we refer to the eighteen provinces exclusively, which include the vast proportion of the population, wealth, and intelligence of the empire.

Here the parallel between the United States and China ceases, and in nearly every point of comparison we have a decided contrast. The capitals of the different divisions of the empire are all walled cities. These form a striking feature of the country. There are important distinctions between the cities of the third class, most of which are designated by the character *Hien*, a few by the character *Cheo*, and a few by the character *Ting*, which need not here be particularly described. Though varying considerably in size, these different cities present nearly the same uniform appearance. They are surrounded by walls from twenty to thirty-five feet in height, and are entered by large arched gateways, which open into the principal streets, and are shut and barred at night. These walls are from twenty to twenty-five feet thick at the base, and somewhat narrower at the top. The outside is of solid masonry from two to four feet thick, built of hewn stone, or bricks backed with earth, broken tiles, etc. There is generally a lighter stone facing on the inside. The outside is surmounted by a parapet with embrasures, generally built of brick. The circumferences of the provincial cities vary from eight to fifteen English miles; those of the *Fu* cities from four to ten; and those of the *Hien* cities from two or three to five. Some of the larger and more important cities contain a smaller one, with its separate walls, enclosed within the larger outside wall. This is the Tartar or military city. It is occupied exclusively by Tartars with their families, forming a colony or garrison, and numbering generally a few tens of thousands, including military officers of different grades. In times of insurrection and rebellion the Emperor depends principally upon these Tartar colonies to hold possession of the cities where they are stationed. In such emergencies the inhabitants of these enclosed Tartar cities, knowing that their lives and the lives of their families are at stake, sometimes defend themselves with great desperation.

The provincial capitals contain an average population of about 1,000,000 inhabitants, the *Fu* cities from 100,000 or less to 600,000 or 800,000, while the cities of the third class, which are much more numerous, generally contain several tens of thousands. The most of these towns of different classes have outgrown their walls, and you sometimes find one-fourth or even one-third of the inhabitants living in the suburbs, which in some cases extend three or four miles outside the walls in different directions. Property is less valuable in these suburbs, not only because it is removed from the busi-

PART OF THE WALL OF PEKIN.

ness parts of the city, but also because it is more liable to be destroyed in times of anarchy and rebellion.

All the names to be found on our largest maps of China are the names of walled cities, and many of those of the third class are not down for want of space. The whole number in the aggregate is over 1700. Supposing them to have an average circumference of four miles each, the whole length of wall such as has been described would be 6800 miles, nearly one-third the circumference of the globe. If we add to this the 1500 miles of continuous wall separating China from Chinese Tartary in the North, it will swell the estimate to more than 8000 miles.

The above engraving of a part of the wall of Pekin will give a very good idea of the appearance of Chinese cities generally, as seen in the distance, with their watch-towers and guard-houses, and the moat outside the wall. The camels represented in the engraving are very rarely seen in the south of China. The reader may in imagination substitute in their place pack-mules and donkeys for most of the cities of Northern China, and men bearing burdens and sedans for the cities of the South.

From the number and size of the cities of China it might be inferred that they contain the great proportion of the inhabitants of the empire. This is, however, by no means the case. The Chinese are mainly an agricultural people, and live for the most part in the almost innumerable villages which everywhere dot its fertile plains. You seldom see a detached or isolated farm-house. The country people live in towns and hamlets for the sake of society and mutual protection. Most of the cities, even the smaller ones, have thousands of these villages under their jurisdiction. In the more populous parts of China you will generally find, within a circumference of three or four miles radius, from one hundred and fifty to two hundred of these villages, some of the larger of them rivalling the smaller walled cities in population and wealth.

It is not strange that the question respecting the population of China has excited a great deal of interest. The most reliable information we have on this subject is the Chinese census of 1812, which there is no good reason for discrediting. This census estimates the population of the eighteen provinces at 360,000,000. Should we adopt these figures as reliable, we must regard the actual number of the present inhabitants of China as not far from 400,000,000.

The mere statement of this number fails to convey to the mind a clear conception of the reality which it expresses. A better idea of the population may be obtained by comparison. The one nation of China contains nearly one-third of the whole human race. Its inhabitants are about equal in number to those of all the kingdoms of Europe and of North and South America combined. Any one of the more populous of the eighteen provinces contains a population nearly equal to that of the largest nations of Europe or of the United States. These statements seem incredible at first sight, but a little consideration will show that there is in them no inherent improbability, while personal observation and inquiry tend to confirm their truth.

The Chinese census, above referred to, only gives an average population of about three hundred persons to the square mile, while that of England and Belgium is greater. Now perhaps no country in the world is more fertile and capable of supporting a dense population than China. Every available spot of ground is brought under cultivation, and nearly all the land is made use of to provide food for man, pasture-fields being almost unknown. The masses of China eat very little animal food. What they do eat is mostly pork and fowls, the raising of which requires little or no waste of ground. The comparatively few horses and cattle and sheep which are found in the country are kept in stables, or graze upon the hill-tops, or are tethered by the sides of canals. Taking these facts into consideration, that an extended and exceedingly fertile country, under the highest state of cultivation, is taxed to its utmost capacity to supply the wants of a frugal and industrious people, and the statement that it contains as dense a population as three hundred to the square mile need excite no wonder or incredulity.

An independent proximate estimate of the population of China may be made from the basis of its cities. A few years since, nineteen contiguous cities were visited by two missionaries from Ningpo. One of these contained 300,000 inhabitants; ten of them from 50,000 to 100,000; and eight from 10,000 to 20,000. The average population would be about 60,000 each. If this tour had extended a few days' journey to the north, it would have included the cities Shao-hing and Hang-chau, the former containing about 800,000 and the latter 1,000,000 inhabitants, which would have raised the average not a little. Taking 60,000, however, as the average for the cities of the Chekiang province, and reducing the general average of the empire from 60,000 to 40,000, we will have for the cities of China alone 68,000,000. But we find under the jurisdiction of each city a number of large villages rivalling it in population. If we assume that the larger unwalled towns, to the number of one-tenth of the whole, contain double the population of the cities, we will have for the population of the cities and a small fraction of the unwalled towns 200,000,000. Regarding the almost innumerable villages as containing only the same population as the cities, and a few of the larger villages, and we reach the result of 400,000,000, for the whole population. This estimate makes no pretensions to accuracy, but is intended to show how consistent the Chinese census is with facts, and how difficult it would be to fix upon any lower figures.

Every thing you see in China conveys the same impression of a country overburdened with a population which swarms about you wherever you go. The fields are everywhere full of laborers; in the mountainous districts you will see scores of terraces, rising one above another to the height of 500 or 1000 feet, and the hills cultivated in many places to their very tops. Pedestrians are everywhere seen in the roads and by-paths, the rivers and numerous canals are filled with boats, and a great variety of busy artisans ply their crafts in the noisy streets of the cities and villages.

The peculiarities of climate along the Chinese coast are due in a great measure to the northern and southern monsoons, the former prevailing with more or less uniformity during the winter and the latter during the summer months. These winds give a greater degree of heat in summer and of cold in winter than is experienced in the United States in corresponding latitudes. At Ningpo, situated in latitude thirty-one—about that of New Orleans—large quantities of ice are secured in the winter for summer use. It is, however, seldom more than an inch in thickness. In this part of China snow not unfrequently falls to the depth of six or eight inches, and the hills are sometimes covered with it for weeks in succession. In the northern provinces the winters are very severe. In the vicinity of Pekin, not only are the canals and rivers closed during the winter, but all commerce by sea is suspended during two or three months; while in the summer that part of China is very warm, producing sweet potatoes, peaches, and grapes in abundance. The period of the change of the monsoon, when the two opposite currents are struggling with each other, is marked by a great fall of rain, and by the cyclones which are so much dreaded by mariners on the Chinese coast. The southern monsoon gradually loses its force in passing northward, and is not very marked above thirty or thirty-two degrees of latitude, though its influence is decidedly felt in July and August. With the exception of the summer months, the climate of the northern coast of China is remarkably dry; that of the southern coast is damp most of the year, especially during the months of May, June, and July.

In different parts of the country almost every variety of climate may be found, hot or cold, moist or dry, salubrious or malarious. The ports which until recently have been exclusively occupied as places of residence by Europeans have unfortunately been among the most insalubrious of the empire, not so much from the enervating effects of their southerly latitudes as from their local miasmatic influences, being situated in the rice-producing districts, and surrounded more or less by stagnant water during the summer months. Under the treaty of 1860, which opened new ports in the north and the interior, we have access to climates which will compare favorably with most parts of our own country.

The eighteen provinces present every conceivable variety of landscape—comprising valleys and alluvial plains, high table-lands, and regions noted for wild and picturesque mountain scenery. It is finely watered by numerous rivers. To say nothing of streams of less note, the River Yiang-ts flows through its entire length from west to east, and, receiving many tributaries from the northern and southern provinces, bears on its bosom the commerce of more than 150,000,000 of people. It passes through a very rich and populous region, and presents to the traveller natural scenery of varied beauty, and numerous unfamiliar objects curious and picturesque.

Several ports on this river are now open to foreign commerce, and vessels drawing more than twenty feet of water and from two hundred and fifty to three hundred feet long, are clearing from the port of Han-kao, six hundred miles in the interior, for London, Liverpool, and New York.

In the front of the accompanying engraving, and opposite the large city Wu-chang, which is seen on the opposite side of the "Great River" in the distance, is the site of the foreign settlement in Han-kow. Han-kow being a kind of suburb of Wu-chang, and having no wall around it, is not found on any of the maps of China; though it has a population probably not less than 300,000. In the map accompanying this book the name of the city is incorrectly spelled Vu-chang.

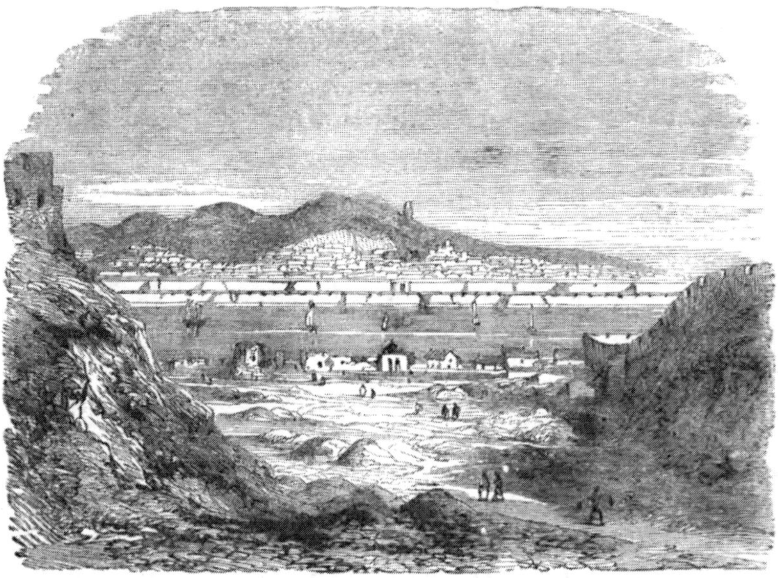

WU-CHANG.

CHAPTER II.

GENERAL VIEW OF THE COUNTRY AND ITS INHABITANTS—CONTINUED.

Travelling.—Roads.—Streets.— Canals.— Boats.— Sculls.—Mud-slides.— Sedans or Kiau-ts.—Burden-bearers.—Beasts of Burden.—Mule-litters.—Productions of the Soil.—Different Varieties of Teas.—Vegetables.—Fruits.—Implements.—The Threshing-floors of Scripture.—The use of Fertilizers.—Style of Architecture and Materials used.—Fire-walls in Cities.—No Stoves in Northern Houses.—Artisans.—Business Men.—Order and General Prosperity.

THE modes of travelling vary greatly in different parts of the empire. In many of the provinces, especially along the coast and in the south, canals take the place, for the most part, of roads. The great Imperial Canal, stretching from Hang-chau, in Central China, to Pekin, a distance of six hundred miles, is often referred to by writers on China as one of the greatest of public works in any country, and as a striking evidence of the wisdom of the government and vast resources of the empire. This, however, is but one of the main arteries of canal communication, and its length is insignificant in comparison with the aggregate length of the other canals of the empire. I have no doubt that its length is equalled, if not exceeded, by that of the canals within the jurisdiction of some of the individual departmental or *Fu* cities. In the vicinity of Ningpo the country is supplied with a complete net-work of them, often intersecting each other at distances of one or two miles, or less. Farmers frequently have short branch canals running off to their houses, and the farm-boat takes the place of the farm-cart or wagon. Heavy-loaded passage and freight boats are seen plying in every direction. The ordinary rate of charge for passage, at the highest estimate, would be less than one-half of a cent per mile. A boat manned by two persons, and of such size that ten Chinamen think they can sleep comfortably in it, may be chartered for one dollar a day, and will accomplish within the twenty-four hours a distance of from forty to seventy or more miles.

In sections of the country where canals are so numerous the roads are simply foot-paths, sometimes hardly wide enough for persons to meet without one of them stepping off the flag-stones, by which they are almost invariably paved. These roads or paths are found running along the banks of the ca-

CANAL SCENE NEAR SOO-CHOW.

nals, or winding about among the unfenced fields. In Central and Southern China the streets of the cities are not much wider than the paths in the country, their width varying from five to ten or fifteen feet.

The canals are generally from twenty to forty or fifty feet in width. The boats in them are from four to eight feet wide, and from twenty to thirty or more in length. They are propelled for the most part by a scull of a peculiar construction, by which the strength of the boatman is applied most effectively and economically.

This scull is seldom straight, has generally a broad blade, and turns upon a pivot in the stern. The upper end of it is attached to the bottom of the boat by a rope which the boatman seizes with his right hand, the left being laid on the scull handle. These boats in different parts of the empire present an almost endless variety. A traveller in crossing a river and hiring one in the canal on the opposite side is often surprised to see the marked change in the construction and style, not only of the boat, but of all its appointments.

While sculls are justly preferred in most parts of China, sweeps or oars are occasionally seen.

Among the numerous kinds of boats in different places, there is one belonging exclusively to the city of Shao-hing, but sometimes found hundreds of miles away from home, which merits a special reference. It is called by the natives *Kyiah-wo-jun*—"Foot-propelled boat." It resembles a canoe, and is made to carry one passenger with a little baggage. The hull is generally decorated with landscape paintings. A thick, bent bamboo matting covers the top, and while it protects the traveller from sun and rain, obliges him to keep a recumbent position except when one of the mats is removed. The boatman sitting in the stern, which is only about a foot and a half wide, and bracing his back against a board, propels his little craft in a very peculiar way with a foot-oar, and guides it with a paddle.

It is so crank that the passenger must be careful in moving for fear of upsetting it. This may be called the dispatch-boat of China. One boatman will sometimes ply the oar for sixteen or more hours with very little intermission, changing constantly from one foot to the other. I have known one of them to stop for a moment at an eating-house, procure a bowl of rice and one of vegetables, resume his seat, put the two bowls on one hand, the two chop-sticks in the other, one foot on the oar, and the paddle under his arm to steer by, and so proceed on his journey and enjoy his dinner at the same time. In the rivers are larger boats, while the junks will compare in carrying capacity with our sea-going vessels.

In the Che-kiang province, in passing through the canals from one elevation to another, use is made of *mud-slides*, which take the place of locks in our own country. On either side of this slide, or inclined plane, is a windlass with large cables of twisted bamboo. A noose on the end of the cable is placed round the stern of the boat on either side, and from twenty to

TRADING JUNK.

forty men turn the windlasses. The boat is gradually drawn up the inclined plane, is poised for a moment on the top, then the bow droops, and it slides down the other side into the water, sometimes with a velocity which occasions serious accidents.

The bridges crossing the canals are very numerous. Generally stone abutments approach each other from opposite sides, leaving a vacant space between them of about twelve feet which is covered by heavy stone slabs. Arched bridges, however, and some of them very beautiful, are frequently seen spanning the canals and smaller rivers. Boats are often tracked or towed by the boatmen on shore, and sails are hoisted when the wind is favorable.

In the coast provinces of Central and Southern China, where canals are so numerous, vehicles and beasts of burden and draught are almost unknown. In the mountainous districts passengers and goods are carried by men, passengers in a sedan or palanquin by two men, and baggage and freight by single coolies, the burden being divided and suspended from the opposite ends of a strong elastic pole, the middle of which rests upon the shoulder. Two sedan-bearers will carry a man of ordinary size, with twenty or thirty pounds of baggage, twenty miles in a day; and a coolie, with more than one hundred and fifty pounds burden, will perform the same journey, though requiring a little more time. The hardy mountaineers, whose muscles have been developed by years of this kind of labor, will carry a burden five or ten miles in a day weighing more than three hundred pounds.

MODE OF CARRYING BURDENS BY ONE PERSON.

TWO MEN CARRYING A PRESENT OF A LARGE JAR OF SPIRITS.

GENTLEMAN RIDING IN A SEDAN, WITH SERVANT ON FOOT.

The above engravings illustrate the three modes of carrying burdens so common in China. The last one represents the sedan and its attendants when just about to start, or when the bearers are about so set the sedan down. The third bearer is an extra one or relay, who walks by the side of the sedan, takes his turn in carrying it, and assists in placing it upon the shoulders of the other two, and in putting it down. The attendant in a long gown is the gentleman's body-servant, who carries and presents his employer's cards, and waits upon him as he has occasion to require his services. When the bearers are in motion, they take a long rapid stride, which carries them about four and a half miles an hour. When there are but two of them they generally stop every mile or two. They employ these few moments of rest in smoking, chatting, and perhaps taking a glass of wine. When the traveller is in a hurry he often adds "*wine money*," which accelerates his progress greatly.

When the burden to be carried is very heavy, such as large stones, logs, etc., it is divided and distributed by larger and smaller poles, so as to be borne by ten, fifteen, twenty, or more men.

In those portions of the empire where canals are impracticable, as is the case in a large part of the province of Shantung, beasts of burden are numerous, principally mules and donkeys, which are imported from Manchuria in large droves. On the plains a rude kind of cart is used; and in the more mountainous districts goods are carried on pack-mules and donkeys, and passengers in mule-litters. The mules used for the latter purpose are very fine, and will walk in a long summer's day from fifty to sixty miles, the drivers keeping pace with them. In the north of China the streets of the cities are wide enough to admit the passage of wheeled vehicles.

The productions of China, as before intimated, are similar to those of the United States. Sugar-cane is grown in large quantities in the southern provinces; rice and tobacco and cotton in the southern and central; winter wheat, millet, and sorghum in the central and northern; and maize or Indian corn in all the provinces. Sorghum is called in this country the Chinese sugar-cane, though as far as I can learn it is not used for its saccharine properties in any part of the empire.

Rice is the great staple for food in the south, and millet in the north. The cotton produced in the south supplies the vast proportion of the population with clothing; and it is all spun and woven by the women, the Chinese being entirely ignorant of modern machinery of every kind. Tea is produced in the central and southern provinces. The differences in the varieties are due partly to the soil and climate of different localities; partly to the time when the leaf is plucked; but principally to the mode of curing or preparing it for the foreign market.

The vegetables of China are numerous, including many varieties with which we are not familiar. The sweet potato is found in all the provinces. The Irish potato has been until recently unknown, and is now little valued by the natives. Carrots, turnips, leeks, and garlic are very common, also cucumbers, water-melons, and musk-melons. Peas are cultivated to some extent, and beans in great varieties and large quantities. In the north of China beans take the place of oats with us, as the principal hearty food for horses, mules, and donkeys. They are always cooked, and animals like them, and thrive on them wonderfully.

The fruits are similar to those of the United States, but most varieties are decidedly inferior. Grapes, peaches, and apricots in the north, and oranges and bananas in the south, will compare favorably with the same fruits in our own country.

Agricultural implements, as also those of every other kind, are exceedingly rude and primitive. The fields are ploughed in the south by a single bullock or water-buffalo, and by bullocks, mules, and donkeys in the north, where these three animals are not unfrequently seen harnessed together three abreast, with occasionally a horse by way of variety.

In the north you see threshing-floors, resembling those spoken of in the Old Testament. A little spot of ground near

CART DRAWN BY BULLOCKS, OR MULES, OR HORSES, OR BY THESE DIFFERENT ANIMALS TOGETHER.

the house is, just before harvest, hardened and packed, and looks not unlike a cement floor. The sheaves of grain are brought hither on the backs of mules and donkeys. The heads of the sheaves are cut off with a large straw-knife, and the grain is trodden out by donkeys or beaten out by flails, and the chaff being thrown up with a shovel, is blown away by the wind. I have never seen a barn in any part of China. The

IRRIGATION BY MEANS OF AN ENDLESS CHAIN-PUMP.

straw is stacked or stored away in some vacant loft, and is soon disposed of for provender and fuel.

Great care is taken throughout the empire to preserve every thing which can be used to enrich the soil. Every city and village contributes its quota of fertilizing material, which the countrymen apply for and generally purchase. This custom, although of incalculable use in adding to the productiveness of the soil, is an intolerable nuisance to the foreign residents.

When the farmers have little else to do, the sediment of the canals is scooped out and spread over the land, and the canals in this way are kept from filling up. A great deal of manual labor is expended on a small area. In different provinces irrigation is practiced to a large extent.

The style of architecture in China is rather solid and substantial than beautiful, and seems to us heavy and gloomy. Houses have sometimes two stories, though usually but one. They are built of stone, or wood, or brick, according to the cheapness of these articles in different places, and the preference of the builder. The floors are generally cement or earth. The windows are of lattice-work, upon which is pasted white paper, which requires to be renewed frequently. The dwellings of the rich and the temples are exceedingly costly, and sometimes elaborately ornamented with wood and stone carvings and paintings. The most of these houses are made up of different buildings, separated by open courts. An outer wall, which often entirely conceals the street, at the same time shuts out the outside world from the inmates. In cities a group of buildings is often protected from fire by extending the wall between them and the adjoining ones several feet above the houses. Cities are often saved from general conflagrations by these fire-walls. The want of pure air in the cities is compensated in part by free ventilation in the houses. The people are not particular to have the doors and windows tight, and the doors, excepting the one on the street, are generally open, at least in the day-time.

There are no stoves or fire-places even in the north of China, where the winters are severe. To keep the hands and feet warm, brass and earthen foot-stoves are used, and a delicate little hand-stove which gentlemen and ladies carry in their sleeves. In the colder latitudes a raised platform, or dais, is built in the room, of brick and stone, under which a fire is kindled, a chimney carrying off the smoke. The whole substance of this dais becomes heated, and retains its warmth for several hours. This is the almost universal bed of the north of China. It radiates very little heat, however, into the room. The people keep themselves warm by the use of additional clothing.

In the winter, furs, which are largely imported from Manchuria, are much worn by the more wealthy classes.

A traveller on visiting China will probably be struck with

FISHING WITH CORMORANTS.

the industrious character of the people and the variety of their occupations. Of the out-door laborers, in addition to the farmers, who form a large proportion of the population, the fishermen are also very numerous. Some of them pursue their calling along the sea-coast, and some in the inland lakes, rivers, and canals. Almost every conceivable means of taking fish is made use of—hooks, spears, the drag-net or seine, the scoop-net, the cast-net, the lift-net, the gill-net and others.

In many parts of Southern China fish are captured by means of cormorants, which swim under water in pursuit of their prey with great rapidity. They are prevented by a string or ring placed round their throats from swallowing the large fish. These they are trained to yield up to their master, who always follows them in a small boat or on a raft, and generally makes use of a long bamboo pole, with the heavier end of which he pushes his raft, while he directs and controls the movements of the birds with the other.

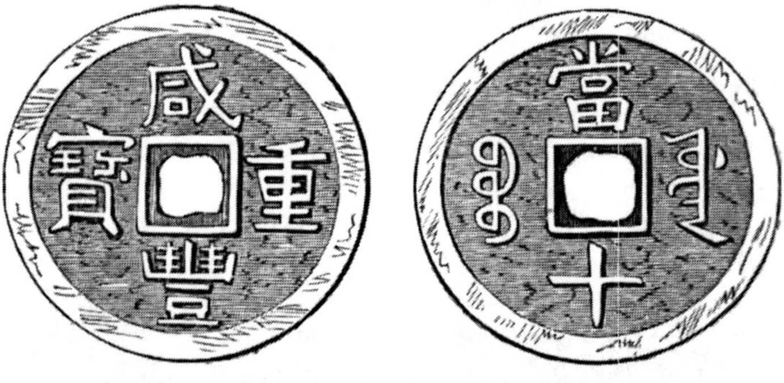

Obverse. Reverse.

FAC-SIMILE OF CASH COINED BY THE LAST EMPEROR, HIEN-FUNG, who reigned from 1851–61, representing ten common cash.

Among their artisans they number carpenters, masons, tailors, shoemakers, workers in iron and brass, and silversmiths and goldsmiths, who can imitate almost any article of foreign manufacture; also workmen in bamboo, carvers, idolmakers, needle manufacturers, barbers, hair-dressers, etc., etc.

Business men sell almost every kind of goods and commodities wholesale and retail. Silk stores, fur stores, and jewelry stores present a fine display of showy and costly goods. Money-changing shops will give you silver by weight for the copper coin of the country, or the reverse, or, for an equivalent, their bank bills, redeemable any time either in silver or copper coin.

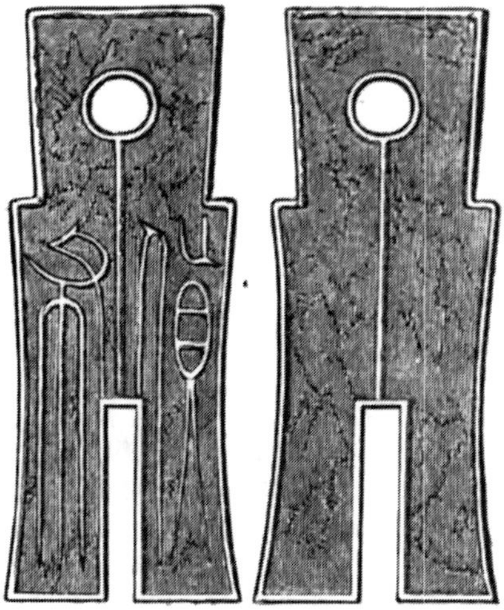

Obverse. Reverse.

FAC-SIMILE OF ANCIENT COIN, COINED DURING THE HAN DYNASTY, ABOUT A.D. 9.

Drug stores, with signs covered with golden letters, each striving to be more dazzling than the rest, advertise to furnish every thing in the Chinese *materia medica* which can be drawn from the resources of the eighteen provinces and foreign kingdoms. The names and titles on these sign-boards are the most pretentious and grandiloquent that can well be imagined.

As a general thing quiet and contentment are manifest, and the people seem industrious and happy.

In the streets of the cities and villages you will see men elegantly dressed and with polished manners. Large fortunes are amassed very much in the same way and by the same means as in our own country. The wealth of the rich is invested in lands or houses, or employed as capital in trade or banking, or is lent out on good security, and often at a high rate of interest.

Even a general and superficial view like that which has been attempted in the preceding pages, is sufficient to show that this is a country of no small degree of civilization and refinement, in which law and order prevail, and where a well-organized government gives at least some good degree of protection to the persons and property of its citizens.

CHAPTER III.

CONFUCIUS AND CONFUCIANISM.

The Relation of Confucianism to the Chinese Civilization.—The name Confucius.—His Character and Mode of Life.—The Manner in which he is regarded by the Chinese.—His own Estimate of himself.—Not the Originator of a new System, but the Propounder and Perpetuator of an Ancient one.—The Confucian Classics.—General Description of their Contents.—The Five Relations of Life.—The Five Virtues.—The political or governmental Feature of Confucianism.—Importance of Self-government and Culture.—General Estimate of Confucius and his System.

IF I have succeeded in presenting in the previous chapters a just and life-like view of the extensive territories, vast population, and immense resources and wealth of the Chinese empire, and the general prosperity, happiness, and refinement of its inhabitants, I trust a desire has been excited in the mind of the reader to know this remarkable people more intimately, and to inquire into the sources of their prosperity, the peculiarities of their culture and civilization, and the stable foundations upon which their government and institutions have so long rested.

No doubt the character and prosperity of the Chinese are due, more than to any other cause, and to all other causes combined, to that system of teachings which is called Confucianism.

The man who has given his name to this system is the only one of his race who has achieved a world-wide reputation, and this he has done in a truer and more literal sense than any other uninspired teacher, his fame extending over larger territories and vaster populations. He was born in the province of Shantung, and the department of Yin-chau, B.C. 551. His family name was Kung, and his most commonly used given name Chong-ni. He was generally called by his disciples Kung-fu-ts, or "The teacher Kung." This title was Latinized by the Jesuit missionaries, giving us the word Confucius, which has now become current among Western nations.

His parents were respectable, though poor. He manifested a taste for study when very young, and became a teacher at the age of twenty-two. His character as a learned man soon drew toward him a large number of admiring and devoted disciples. He was repeatedly applied to by the petty princes who ruled the small kingdoms, into which China was at that time divided, to take office and assist in the administration of government, and remarkable accounts are given of the salutary measures he introduced, and the beneficial results which followed. He was, however, so little a courtier, and his morality and theories of government and political economy were of so severe a type, that he generally remained but a short time in a place, his presence either becoming distasteful to his employers, or his sense of justice and propriety being shocked by constantly beholding what he could neither approve, or reform.

Much of his long life was spent in journeying from province to province, vainly endeavoring to reform the abuses of the times, giving instruction to his followers, and prosecuting his studies. Greatly neglected and imperfectly appreciated during his life, his people have, since his death, gone to the opposite extreme of exaggerating his merits and exalting him "above all that is called God or is worshiped," almost ascribing to him perfection of virtue and omniscience, in opposition to his clear and repeated acknowledgments of imperfections and ignorance.

His own estimate of himself is probably very near the truth, perhaps erring a little on the side of modesty and depreciation. He says: "The sage and the man of perfect virtue—how dare I rank myself with them? It may simply be said of me, that I strive to become such without satiety, and to teach others without weariness. In letters I am perhaps equal to other men; but the character of the superior man, carrying out in his conduct what he professes, is what I have not yet attained to. The leaving virtue without proper cultivation; the not thoroughly discussing what is learned; not being able to move toward righteousness of which a knowledge is gained; and not being able to change what is not good —these are the things which occasion me solicitude. I am not one who was born in the possession of knowledge; I am one who is fond of antiquity, and earnest in seeking it there. A transmitter, and not a maker, believing in and loving the ancients."

As is frankly stated by himself, he was not the originator of any new doctrine or system of doctrines, but simply the expounder and perpetuator of the teachings of the sages who preceded him. At that early period he was already looking back into antiquity and endeavoring to save its works from oblivion.

We may infer from his example that a want of originality, and a servile following of old forms and usages, was a characteristic of his race more than two thousand years ago; a peculiarity which his teachings and example have served to render still more extreme and confirmed.

The fact that Confucius made no marked advance on the knowledge of his predecessors, but was always referring to the golden age of the past, is calculated to produce a profound impression as to the moral and intellectual culture of those who laid the foundations of the Chinese civilization more than three thousand years ago. Confucius, then, was rather the exponent and embodiment of the Chinese culture than the originator of it.

The Chinese classics, in which the Confucian system is found, comprise what are called the Wu-king and the S-shu—"The Five Classics and the Four Books." The former, with one exception, existed before the time of Confucius, and are frequently referred to in his teachings. They are the Shu-king, the most ancient historical work in China; the S-king, or "Book of Odes;" the Yih-king, or "Book of Changes" (an abstruse and incomprehensible system of philosophy, ontology, etc.); the Li-kyi, or "Book of Rites and Ceremonies," and the Chuen-tsew, "Spring and Autumn"—the last being a historical work written by Confucius himself, and covering a period of a few hundred years before his time. It is called Spring and Autumn, because the commendations and examples presented in it for imitation are supposed to be life-giving like spring, and the criticisms and rebukes withering like autumn.

Of the Four Books, the first and most important is that which contains the sayings and teachings of Confucius himself as recorded by his disciples after his death. The second contains the teachings of Mencius, a celebrated philosopher who lived about two hundred years after the time of Confucius. The other two works, called the "Great Learning" and the "Doctrine of the Mean," are considerably smaller than the preceding, with which they are associated as a part of the Four Books, though they really originated before the time of Confucius, and are found in the "Book of Rites." These books are emphatically and almost exclusively the text-books in all the schools of China, and are regarded as the *summum bonum* of knowledge and literary excellence. They have moulded the minds and characters of the Chinese race, and are the ultimate standard to which all moral, governmental, historical, and religious questions are referred.

The contents of these books may be represented in general as made up of ethics, history, political economy, biography, and poetry. The religious element is almost entirely wanting. It is distinctly stated by the disciples of Confucius that he did not discourse on the gods. Silence on this subject was probably not owing to any contempt for or disregard of it, but to ignorance. Confucius professed to teach positive truth, in opposition to what is vague, uncertain, and inferential; and when he could not speak clearly and authoritatively he chose not to speak at all. When asked by one of his disciples about death, his sad answer was—"Imperfectly acquainted with life, how can I know of death?"

C

A correct general idea of his system may be obtained from the Five Relations, which form the basis of it, and the Five Virtues, which were the subject of his most frequent conversations. The Five Relations are those subsisting between emperor and officer, father and son, husband and wife, older and younger brothers, and friends.

The principles and duties connected with the first relation present, as they are developed and explained, the Chinese system of government and political economy, which forms a large part of Confucius's teachings. The principles underlying this relation are often referred to, and illustrated and enforced by references to ancient history, and the lives and examples of the renowned rulers of antiquity.

The next three relations belong to the family, which is justly regarded as the true foundation of the State. Here are to be inculcated lessons of respect, obedience, and regard for law. Here habits of subjection to lawful authority are formed which fit the individual for being a good citizen. This idea is clearly brought out in the Confucian analects: "There are few who, being filial and fraternal, are fond of offending against their superiors. There have been none who, not liking to offend their superiors, have been fond of stirring up confusion."

Filial piety stands first in the category of human duties, and is an important part of the religion of the Chinese. Disrespect or disobedience to parents is sometimes punished with death. No stigma which could be attached to the character of a Chinaman is more dreaded than that of *Puh-hiao*—"undutiful." Children in their earlier years are required to be respectful, dutiful, and retiring; when their parents are advanced in life they are expected to reverence and cherish them, to anticipate all their wants, and strive in every way to please them; and, when parents are dead, to worship and sacrifice to them. Men are exhorted to avoid intemperance and vice, lest they injure or debase the bodies derived from their parents. It is regarded as one of the strongest motives to a virtuous and honorable life to avoid disgracing and offending departed ancestors, and to live in such a manner as to reflect honor upon them. Respect for parents is also regarded as naturally connected with and leading to reverence for the Emperor, who is the Great Father of his people as well as the Son of Heaven.

The relation between husband and wife is not largely dwelt upon. Woman has an inferior position allotted to her, and is the servant rather than the companion of her husband. The duties of brethren are expressed in the oft-repeated maxim—"*Hiung ai, ti kin*"—"The elder is to love, the younger is to respect."

There remains the wider relation subsisting between friends, which it is unnecessary to dwell upon. These Five Relations cover the whole sphere of human duties. The relation between God and man is neglected and unknown, while almost divine honors are awarded to the Emperor and to ancestors.

The Five Virtues of the Confucian system are *Jen*, *Yi*, *Li*, *Cu*, and *Sin*—"Benevolence," "Righteousness," "Propriety," "Knowledge," and "Faith."

It is worthy of remark that in this system, as in the Christian, *Jen*, or Benevolence, stands first and foremost. Of this virtue and excellence Confucius seems to have had so high a conception or ideal that he did not regard any contemporaries, and but few of the ancient worthies, to have fully attained to it. The following is his definition of it. When asked by one of his disciples, "Is there one word which may serve as a rule of practice for all one's life?" his answer was, "What you do not want done to yourself do not do to others." This one word, for the government of the whole life, is "all the law" of the Confucian system, and is, to say the least, the nearest approximation to the Golden Rule of our Saviour which has ever been reached by any ancient sage. It is simply this rule in the negative form, having for its object rather the deterring of men from doing evil than the inciting them to do good. In another paragraph of Confucius's teachings he seems almost to have grasped the idea of the positive side of this precept. "When one cultivates to the utmost the principles of his nature, and exercises them on the principle of reciprocity, he is not far from the path. What you do not like when done to yourself do not to others. In the way of the superior man there are four things, to not one of which have I as yet attained. To serve my father as I would require my son to serve me; to this I have not attained. To serve my prince as I would require my minister to serve me; to this I have not attained. To serve my elder brother as I would require my younger brother to serve me; to this I have not attained. To set the example in behaving to a friend as I would require him to behave to me; to this I have not attained."

The next virtue is *Righteousness*, which is defined, that which *ought* to be done. The appeal here made is not to any written code of law, but to the human conscience, the law written on the heart. It will at once be seen how comprehensive this principle is, relating to every act or deed of which the conscience says it is right; it ought to be done.

The next virtue, *Propriety*—outward forms and ceremonies—brings to view a characteristic feature of this system. Every inward state of feeling is supposed to have a proper outward expression. While the inner feeling naturally gives rise to its external manifestation, so the habitual cultivation of the outward forms of propriety tends to foster and develop the inner virtue.

There are also certain forms or rules of propriety and conduct which should regulate the intercourse between men in different ranks and positions in society, and which naturally and necessarily belong to certain times, circumstances, and occasions.

These rules of propriety are regarded as the great balance-wheel which gives harmony and unity to society, or as one of the chief corner-stones on which society and government rest, and without which mutual understanding and respect would give place to confusion, lawlessness, and anarchy.

Confucius devoted much of his attention to the study of the rites and ceremonies of different kingdoms and states, and the importance which he attached to this matter has had much to do in developing and stereotyping those inflexible formalities and minute conventionalities which are everywhere seen in social and public life.

Knowledge relates to general learning and intelligence, but especially to a knowledge of men, a knowledge of one's self, and practical wisdom in dealing with others. For those who are in high positions, and are required to influence and govern others, Confucius insists upon a life of severe study, close and patient observation, and mature thought.

In addition to the careful culture of the affections, the conscience, the outward behavior, and the intellect, sincerity of heart and truthfulness are specially insisted upon as essential. The character *Sin* is used both to represent faith and truthfulness, the ground of faith. In speaking of self-culture and self-restraint, the difficulties of controlling the "unruly member" have not been forgotten. It is to be regretted that in a few instances Confucius illustrates this difficulty in his own experience, thus weakening the force of his teachings, and confirming the statement that he had not been able to reach his own standard.

While Confucius refers to the sages of the past as the authors of his system, he rests its authority upon the verdict of conscience, and it was to this that he constantly appealed. He sought to interpret rightly and to follow carefully the suggestions and intimations of man's moral nature. This characteristic feature of Confucius has so impressed itself upon the Chinese mind, that nothing is more common, even in the familiar language of the masses, than appeals to the fixed principle of right and true doctrine as attested by conscience.

The ultimate object of Confucius's teachings is the promotion of good government; and the instruction of his disciples relates principally to their preparation for successfully influencing and controlling others. He did not seek this end by devising the best code of laws for restraining and coercing the inhabitants of the empire, but by pointing out rules and principles for self-government and culture. He relied on moral and not physical force, on example and instruction rather than law and punishment. He believed that if the rulers cultivated virtue the people would revere, obey, and imitate them. His beautiful though, perhaps, Utopian conception of a perfect government was one in which the ruler sways the minds of his people by illustrating in his own person the perfection of virtue, and thus sits still and looks abroad upon a peaceful and happy state.

In addition to the failure of Confucius to live up to his standard of sincerity, which has been referred to above, it is further to be regretted that, in adopting the views and following the examples of those who preceded him, he sanctioned and encouraged the worship of gods and ancestors, the pride and self-conceit of his nation, and the doctrine of revenge, as allowable and obligatory in the one case of a son whose father has been murdered.

To reproach Confucius, however, for these defects, and because his system, though excellent in many respects, is manifestly imperfect, is to find fault with him for being human. Would it not be unreasonable to expect him to approach nearer to the Christian standard of truth and worship than he has? While he was not and did not aspire to be great as a metaphysician or logician, he was rather the practical philosopher, thoroughly versed in the knowledge of his times; a close observer of men, earnest, sincere, and retiring in his spirit, and desiring to benefit his race, and to teach the truth. It is, perhaps, not too much to say of him that the system of ethics and morality which he taught is the purest which has ever originated in the history of the world independent of the divine revelation in the Bible, and that he has exerted a greater influence for good upon our race than any other uninspired sage of antiquity.

CHAPTER IV.

COMPETITIVE EXAMINATIONS AND SCHOOLS.

The Chinese Idea of the Qualifications of Officers.—Origin of the Competitive Examinations.—Classes of Persons excluded.—Two preparatory Examinations.—Examination for conferring the first Degree.—For conferring the second Degree.—Third Degree.—Corresponding Military Examinations.—Various Advantages secured by the Literary Examinations.—The Position and Influence of Literary Men.—Character of Chinese Schools.—Pupils commit to Memory whole Books without understanding their Meaning.

THE earnestness and zeal with which Confucius taught were the natural result of his strong conviction that the general happiness and prosperity of the people, and the stability of the government, could only spring from the principles of truth and righteousness, apprehended by and operative in the minds of the people generally, and especially of the ruling classes. All his teachings had more or less a political or governmental reference.

This supreme importance of securing wise and virtuous rulers was acknowledged by the Chinese from an early period, and the sources of intellectual and moral culture were supposed to be found almost exclusively in the ancient classics. The desire to bring the influences of these works to bear upon the education of civil rulers, and their better preparation for the performance of their official functions, became more and more prominent, and resulted about one thousand years ago in the establishment of a system of Competitive Literary Examinations, which has been modified and improved during successive ages, and has become one of the most remarkable and powerful organizations which the world has ever known.

Through and by these competitive examinations, persons from almost every condition in life may rise to the highest positions of honor and influence in the empire.

There are, however, four classes, who, with their posterity for three generations, are excluded from them; namely, the children of prostitutes, public play-actors, executioners, the inferior grades of the servants or attendants of mandarins, and jailers. It is supposed that the immediate descendants of these classes, whatever their intellectual qualifications might be, would be destitute of those moral qualities which should be possessed by good rulers. All persons whatever are prohibited from attending these examinations within three years after the death of a father or mother; as the strife for honor and preferment, and the close application which is necessary to success, are deemed inconsistent with those feelings of filial piety which should occupy the mind during the period of mourning for a deceased parent.

A minute account of the details of this system of examinations, and its workings, though it might be interesting to a few, would be tiresome to the general reader. Only a sketch or outline will be attempted in this chapter.

According to the theory of the Chinese government, all its civil officers must be literary graduates of the second or third degree. The first degree is conferred in the *Fu* cities, the second in the provincial capitals, and the third in Pekin, the national capital.

Two preparatory examinations are required of the undergraduates before they are allowed to compete for the first degree. The first of these is the examination of the scholars of each *Hien* by the district magistrate. The next is the examination of all the scholars under the jurisdiction of a *Fu* city by the prefect of that city. These two preparatory examinations need not be specially described, as they differ very little from the next following. No degree is conferred, but those who stand highest on the roll in these examinations are very apt to be among the successful competitors in the next one.

The first degree is conferred, not by the local officer, the prefect, but by literary chancellors, or imperial commissioners, sent from the capital for that purpose. In the crowds which now throng the streets of the *Fu* city, every city and village, and almost every hamlet in the prefecture is represented. Each of these aspirants after literary honors has already filed with a clerk of the district magistrate of the *Hien* city to which he belongs a paper containing the name of his father, grandfather, and principal teacher, and also the name of his neighbors on the right hand and on the left, together with his own name, age, stature, complexion, etc. This paper must be signed by well-known securities, who are literary graduates. The existence of this document furnishes a strong motive, if such be needed, to secure good behavior, and in case of infringement of rules, or other criminality, is of great use in finding the offender and bringing him to justice. As the whole number of the scholars attending these examinations ranges in different cities from 3000 to 6000 or more, the examination hall can not contain all at one time, and the scholars from different *Hien* are admitted together. No individual is allowed to enter unless the literary graduate who is his security is present in person to answer for him when his name is called. When admitted, each person is assigned to his place or seat. The competitors are not allowed to take in with them any books or helps to composition, but only writing materials and a little food.

LITERARY UNDER-GRADUATE, OR STUDENT.

When all the arrangements are completed, themes are announced for two prose essays and one poem, and each individual scholar proceeds at once to his work. The themes are taken from the Four Books, being generally some utterance of Confucius or Mencius. Each candidate is supposed to be familiar with the meaning, connection, and scope of these themes, and with the rules and regulations which are to guide him in his impromptu compositions.

The essays required must be completed before night, and the hall emptied. The name of each competitor is written on one corner of his composition, the paper is folded over and pasted so as to conceal it, and it is not discovered until the essay has been examined and its merits decided upon.

This examination is repeated at least once. If an individual fails to complete his work within the prescribed time, or violates any of the rules, he is not permitted to enter the hall the next time, and so the number of competitors is diminished.

Those whose essays and poems are adjudged to be the best are required to pass another examination, consisting of writing from memory from a book well known in China, and called the "Sacred Edict." This must be done with perfect accuracy. After this the names of the successful competitors are announced.

The number is very small compared to the whole. They receive the first degree, called *Siu-tsai*—"Beautiful Ability."

The examinations for the second degree are held triennially in each of the provincial capitals. The presiding officers are two persons of high rank and literary merit, commissioned from Pekin. The graduates of the first degree, who assemble from different parts of the province, generally number from 5000 to 8000. The more wealthy are accompanied by servants, and many others by relatives and friends, who avail themselves of this opportunity of visiting the provincial capital.

The large examination halls in the provincial cities contain accommodations for near 10,000 competitors. Each person is supplied with a little cell or compartment. The students take in with them their bedding and food, as they are required to stay in the hall two days. Servants and friends are parted from them at the door. When the arrangements are complete the doors are shut, and no ingress or egress is allowed until the time allotted to the composition of the essays has expired. The whole number inside the examination walls, including officers, examiners, assistants, servants, etc., is generally from 10,000 to 12,000.

Themes are announced from the Four Books for three prose essays and one poem. When the compositions are finished they first pass into the hands of a class of examiners whose business it is to see whether they are free from glaring defects and conform to the general rules of the examination. If they pass this ordeal, they are then copied in red ink by a company of scribes. This is done to prevent the examiners from recognizing the handwriting of any of the competitors. Another class of assistants carefully compares the original manuscript with the copy, character by character, to see that no mistake has been made in transcribing.

The copies are now examined by another company of scholars, and those compositions whose literary character is good receive a round red mark, without which they pass no further. The manuscripts which survive this sifting process reach the hands of the chief examiners, and those of the highest literary excellence are selected from them. On the morning of the third day the gates are opened, and those who have finished their work and come out first are greeted as they emerge from their confinement with the firing of guns and the best music which China affords. After an intermission of only one day the candidates enter the hall again for a similar examination, except that in this case the themes for the prose essays and the poem are taken from the Five Classics instead of the Four Books. After another day's intermission a third examination is held. The subjects given out are in this case miscellaneous.

The commissioners decide upon the worthy competitors in

view of the results of these three examinations, having vowed before heaven, in a temple within the enclosure, to deal justly and honestly. The proportion of the successful candidates to the whole number is about one to a hundred. They receive the second degree, called *Kyu-jin*—" Promoted (or advanced) Men."

Notwithstanding all the precautions which are taken to prevent collusion and favoritism, there are methods, which need not be described here, by which the examining officers are said to be sometimes bribed and corrupted. Still, the system of examinations could hardly be more thoroughly elaborated and systematized, and few pass through this ordeal without being possessed of more than ordinary ability.

The tax of these examinations upon the physical strength of those who take part in them is very great. Many come home exhausted and depressed. Some are taken ill and die in the hall. In such cases the body is removed over the back wall, as the taking it out openly through the front door would be regarded as an evil omen, and an unnecessary interference with the formal and invariable routine of the exercises.

It is unnecessary to describe in detail the higher examinations through which *Kyu-jin* are advanced to the third degree. This examination is conducted in the national capital, and is also held triennially. The graduates of the second degree from the different provinces are assisted by a certain sum of money from the imperial treasury, to be used for defraying their travelling expenses. Two or three hundred persons receive the third degree at every examination. They are then eligible to office, and are either retained in the capital or sent out to occupy official positions in the provinces.

There is also a system of military examinations, formed after the model of those which have been described. In them the relative merits of different competitors are determined by lifting heavy weights, bending bows of different degrees of strength, shooting arrows at a target, shooting from horseback, and occasionally the shooting at a mark with fire-arms.

Nothing in connection with the present customs of this nation more strikingly illustrates their disposition to adhere to old stereotyped forms and usages, when they are palpably obsolete and useless, than these military exercises.

MILITARY CANDIDATES COMPETING WITH BOW AND ARROW.

A principal part of the military examinations consists in shooting at a mark with a bow and arrow from horseback. The horse runs in a trench about two feet deep, so that he can not endanger his rider by moving out of a perfectly straight line; the arrow is discharged into or at a bundle of straw, about two feet in diameter, and about four feet distant from the trench. The horse is led into one end of the trench by a groom, and started by a stroke of his whip, if he needs it, and is often received at the other end by another groom. The few horses found in the south of China are obtained and used almost exclusively for this military exercise.

It is not difficult to understand how the literary examinations exert a powerful influence on the whole empire. The preparation and selection of educated men, familiarized with the history, government, political economy, literature, and ethics of the nation, is by no means the only advantage derived from them, though it is the primary and principal one. A powerful stimulus is given to literary pursuits, which is the principal cause of the establishment of schools. Were literature cultivated only from the love of it, and for its own sake, the case would be different. Persons of almost every class, and in almost every station in life, make an effort to send their boys to school with the hope that they may distinguish themselves, be advanced to high positions in the State, and reflect honor on their families. The great proportion of them, in the course of three, four, or five years, find that much study is a weariness to the flesh, give up their hopes of literary preferment, and many of them, having learned to write a good hand, acquired the knowledge of a few characters, and a smattering of learning, become clerks in stores, and afterward business men.

Of those who compete for literary honors a very small proportion are successful in attaining even the first degree, though some strive for it for a life-time. These unsuccessful candidates, and the graduates of the first and second degrees, form the important class of literary men scattered throughout the empire. Most of them devote themselves wholly to study. They are the readers and writers of the country; the men of influence and the formers of public opinion. Many of them are as learned as their more fortunate brethren, who may have a more ready talent for off-hand composition, or larger purses, or friends at court.

Having studied the same text-books, and been trained under the influence of one general system, they have a homogeneous culture; and being uniformly distributed among the provinces, and mingling daily with their less cultivated friends and neighbors, they impress themselves upon and mould the masses, and render the whole population homogeneous.

The large proportion of this class are comparatively poor,

and their services may be obtained for a very small remuneration. They are employed to teach the village schools. Rich families in different neighborhoods often assist in keeping up the school for the credit of the village, and opportunities for obtaining a Chinese education are thus brought within the reach of all.

Graduates of the first and second degrees generally have the charge of more advanced pupils, and command higher wages, and many are engaged as tutors in private families. They are also employed as scribes or copyists, and to write letters, family histories and genealogies, indictments for law-suits, etc.

In the larger cities schools are established by the government, and in many places free schools are supported by wealthy individuals, but these institutions do not seem to be popular, and are not flourishing.

The manner in which the schools of China are conducted is peculiar, and worthy of special notice. The text-books are the Chinese classics, or elementary and preparatory books for beginners introductory to them. There is no occasion for the complaint so often heard with us, that the teacher wishes to introduce a new book, for theirs are nearly all two thousand years old, and few have any idea of their being changed for the next two thousand years. These books are all written in the book-language, as different from the vernacular as Latin is from English. Every word in this written language has its independent and arbitrary representative or symbol, so that there are as many different characters as there are words. The beginner, then, instead of learning an alphabet as with us, commences learning these characters or words separately, each of which has its own sound or name. The first object is to learn the name, without any reference to the meaning. At first, perhaps ten of them, more or less, are learned in a day. By degrees the pupil becomes familiar with the most common ones, and is then introduced to the Chinese classics—the sayings of Confucius, for instance. He learns a few lines for a lesson, the teacher giving to him the names of the characters which have not been met with before.

No attention as yet is given to the meaning. The object is simply to become familiar with the names of the individual characters and to commit the sentences to memory, just as a boy might be required to commit to memory a paragraph of Virgil, repeating every word accurately, without the slightest idea of the meaning or of the structure of the language. In this way thousands of these arbitrary symbols are learned, and book after book committed to memory before the first attempt is made at explanation.

Another feature, which is still more singular, is that the pupils study out loud, and all separately, without being organized into classes. Each boy, after being helped in learning the names of the unfamiliar characters in his task—which may be shorter or longer, a few sentences for the smaller boys and a page for the larger—shouts it out from his desk at the top of his voice, over and over, until he can repeat it without looking on the book. I suppose the object or design of this singular custom is to make use both of the voice and the ear, in order to make a stronger impression upon the memory.

This method has the additional advantage of keeping the boys at work better than they could be by a silent mental effort; of letting the teacher know when they are flagging (in which case he raps on his desk, and they burst out again in full chorus); of exercising and developing the lungs and vocal organs, and cultivating a habit of mental abstraction.

In the course of a few years the teacher begins to explain the books which have been memorized. In the mean time, however, the pupil has almost unconsciously obtained a considerable insight into the language, from its points of coincidence with his vernacular, and the hints which he has picked up from the conversations of teachers and advanced pupils.

From the beginning, lessons are taken every day in writing; first on transparent paper over a copy, afterward by imitation, commencing with large characters, and diminishing the size gradually. A fine hand is much admired; and as the characters are very numerous, and some of them very elaborate, it is common for persons to employ a portion of the time during their whole life-time in improving their penmanship.

When boys have reached the age of twelve or fourteen they commence writing literary compositions. The style and character of these is determined by that which prevails in the literary examinations. The object is not to bring out any new ideas, but to follow in the track of the orthodox commentators, and observe strictly prescribed rules. The essays are a kind of literary mosaic, composed of ethical axioms, historical references, obscure allusions, and hints, poetical, biographical, and historical, with which their memories are stored; while they almost unconsciously fall into the style and forms of expression with which their minds have become familiar in the course of their *memoriter* studies.

It will readily be seen that the Chinese system of education, while it develops and stores the memory to an unprecedented extent, discourages and precludes all freedom of thought and originality.

The characters and relations of the different languages of China, which have necessarily been referred to in connection with schools, are treated of more fully in the fourteenth chapter.

CHAPTER V.

THE CONSTITUTION OF THE CHINESE GOVERNMENT.

The Chinese Government patriarchal.—Titles of the Emperor.—The Throne not strictly Hereditary.—Relations of the Emperor to his Officers.—The Cabinet.—The General Council.—The Six Boards.—Different Courts and the Censorate.—The Imperial Academy.—Provincial Governments.—The Civil Code.—Practical Workings of the Chinese Government.—Restraints brought to bear upon the Emperor, Officers, and People.—The People sometimes assert and demand their Rights.—Insurrections and Rebellions.—Republicanism of China.—Village Elders.—Private Redress.—Family Feuds.

THE Chinese government is one of the great wonders of history. It presents to us to-day the same character which it possessed, in the germ at least, more than three thousand years ago, and which it has retained ever since, during a period which covers the authentic history of the world.

A prominent English writer,* in speaking of the Chinese executive system, characterizes it "as at once the most gigantic and the most minutely organized that the world has ever seen."

The character of the government is patriarchal. It assumed its present form at a very early period, when the Chinese race was divided into petty kingdoms and principalities. As the empire grew in territory and population the fundamental idea was retained, the system of government being expanded and modified to suit the conditions of the growing state.

The most common titles of the Emperor are *Hwang-Shang*—

* Thomas Taylor Meadows, Chinese interpreter in Her Majesty's civil service, and author of "The Chinese and their Rebellions," published in London by Smith, Eldin, & Co.

"The August Lofty One," and *Tien-Tsz*—"The Son of Heaven." He exercises supreme control over the whole empire, because Heaven has empowered and required him to do so. His patriarchal character, while it confers on him absolute sovereignty, imposes also the obligation to treat his people with leniency, sympathy, and love. He lives in unapproachable grandeur, and is never seen except by members of his own family and high state officers. "Nothing is omitted which can add to the dignity and sacredness of his person or character. Almost every thing used by him or in his service is tabooed from the common people, and distinguished by some peculiar mark or color, so as to keep up the impression of awe with which he is regarded, and which is so powerful an auxiliary to his throne. The outward gate of the palace must always be passed on foot, and the paved entrance-walk leading up to it can only be used by him. The vacant throne, or even a screen of yellow silk thrown over a chair, is worshiped equally with his actual presence, and a dispatch is received in the provinces with incense and prostration."*

The throne is not strictly and necessarily hereditary, though the son of the Emperor generally succeeds to it. The Emperor appoints his successor, but it is supposed that, in doing so, he will have supreme regard for the best good of his subjects, and will be governed by the will of Heaven, indicated by the conferring of regal gifts, and by providential circumstances pointing out the individual whom Heaven has chosen.

In governing so large a realm it is found necessary for the Emperor to delegate his authority to numerous officers, who are regarded as his agents and representatives in carrying out the imperial will. What they do the Emperor does through them. The recognized patriarchal character of the government is seen in the familiar expressions of the people, particularly at times when they consider themselves injured or aggrieved by their officers, when they are apt to say—"A strange way for parents to treat their children."

* Williams's "Middle Kingdom."

The government of China is constituted as follows:

1. "The Cabinet * consists of four principal and two joint assistant chancellors, half of them Manchus and half Chinese. Their duties, according to the imperial statutes, are to deliberate on the government of the empire, proclaim abroad the imperial pleasure, regulate the canons of State, together with the whole administration of the balance of power, thus aiding the Emperor in directing the affairs of State." Subordinate to these six chancellors are six grades of officers, amounting in all to upward of two hundred persons. The first chancellor in the list acts as premier.

2. "The General Council is composed of princes of the blood, chancellors of the Cabinet, the presidents and vice-presidents of the Six Boards, and chief officers of all the other courts in the capital. Its duties are to write imperial edicts and decisions, and determine such things as are of importance to the army and nation, in order to aid the sovereign in regulating the machinery of affairs." It is principally by means of this council that the Emperor and his immediate advisers become acquainted with and control those who are engaged in different departments of the government at the capital and in the provinces.

"The principal executive bodies in the capital under these two councils are the *Luh-pu*, or Six Boards, which are departments of long standing in the government, having been modelled on much the same plan during the ancient dynasties. At the head of each board are two presidents, called *Shang-shu*, and four vice-presidents, called *Shi-lang*, alternately a Tartar and a Chinese; and over three of them—those of revenue, war, and punishment—are placed superintendents, who are frequently members of the Cabinet. Sometimes the president of one board is superintendent of another. There are

* Most of the contents of the few pages which immediately follow are abridged from Williams's "Middle Kingdom," and the quotations are also from the same author. Persons who wish to obtain minute and reliable information about China should possess themselves of this truly invaluable work.

three subordinate grades of officers in each board, who may be called directors, under-secretaries, and controllers, with a great number of minor clerks, and their appropriate departments for conducting the details of the general and peculiar business coming under the cognizance of the board, the whole being arranged and subordinated in the most business-like style. The details of all the departments in the general and

A CHINESE CIVIL OFFICER IN FULL DRESS.

provincial governments are regulated to the minutest matter in the same manner. For instance, each board has a different style of envelope in which to send its dispatches, and the papers in the offices are filed away in them."

The following sentence from Mr. Meadows's book—"The Rebellions of China"—will give the reader his views with reference to the business-like and methodical character of the

Chinese mind and institutions: "As, however, all public business is, as a general rule, more methodically and systematically conducted in China than in England, so we find," etc.

3. "The first of the Six Boards is the Board of Civil Office, which regulates the distribution of officers over the empire. Its business is divided into four kinds, attended to by four different bureaus.

4. "The Board of Revenue attends to the census, the levying and collecting of duties, and the public granaries, etc. It is divided into fourteen departments.

5. "The Board of Rites has for its object the determining of rites and ceremonies for state occasions, and for the intercourse of officers in the provinces. Subordinate to this is a Board of Music."

The other three boards are the Board of War, the Board of Punishment, and the Board of Public Works.

9. "The Court of the Government of Foreigners, or the colonial office, has reference to colonies and dependencies, and intercourse with foreign nations.

10. "The Censorate is intrusted with the duty of exposing errors and crimes in every department of the government, and sometimes censors do not shrink from the dangerous task of criticising or exposing the conduct of the Emperor himself. Special censors are placed over each board, and also over provincial officers.

11. "The Court of Representation receives memorials and appeals from the provinces and presents them before the Cabinet.

12. "The Court of Judicature has the duty of adjusting all the different courts in the empire, and forms the nearest approach to a Supreme Court, though the cases brought before it are mostly criminal. When the crimes involve life, this court, with the Court of Representation and Censorate, unite to form one court; and if the judges are not unanimous in their decisions they must report their reasons to the Emperor, who will pass judgment upon them.

13. "The Imperial Academy is intrusted with the duty of drawing up governmental documents, histories, and other works. Its chief officers take the lead of the various classes, and excite their exertions to advance in learning, in order to prepare them for employments and fit them for attending upon the sovereign. . . . . Its chief officers are two presidents, or senior members, who are usually appointed for life after a long course of study. . . . . Subordinate to the two senior members are four grades of officers, five in each grade, together with an unlimited number of senior graduates, each forming a sort of college, whose duties are to prepare all works published under governmental sanction. These persons are subject from time to time to fresh examinations, and are liable to lose their degrees, or be altogether dismissed from office, if found faulty or deficient." It is regarded as a high distinction by the Chinese to be a member of this academy, and its objects, organization, and high literary character reflect great honor on the Chinese government.

It is impossible to descend into detail in speaking of the provincial governments, or even to mention individually the many classes of officers of different grades who are commissioned and sent from the capital to the provinces and territories. The whole business of the government is thoroughly and effectively systematized, and its influence is felt in every remote city, hamlet, and family. Records are kept of all matters of importance. The *Pekin Gazette* is published daily, giving an account of the transactions of the General Council and other important matters of State.

As the Constitution of the government has been long since fixed on a basis laid thousands of years ago, so the laws of China, which form the basis of the present code, originated with the writer Li-Kwei, who lived about 2000 years ago. Additions, alterations, and improvements have been made from that time to this. These laws are now classified into General, Civil, Fiscal, Ritual, Military, and Criminal. They were republished in 1830 in twenty-eight volumes, the whole being divided into four hundred and thirty-six sections. A writer in the *Edinburgh Review*, in an article on "Stanton's Translation of the Chinese Code," gives the following estimate of it:—"When we turn from the ravings of the Zendavesta or Puranas to the tone of sense and business in this Chinese collection, it is like passing from darkness to light, from the drivellings of dotage to the exercise of an improved understanding; and, redundant and minute as these laws are in many particulars, we scarcely know one European code that is nearly so freed from intricacy, bigotry, and fiction."

The Chinese are frequently charged with barbarity and cruelty in the establishment and administration of their laws. Dr. Williams's testimony on this point, than whom we can not have a more competent or reliable witness, is as follows:—"Sheer cruelty, except in cases of treason against the Emperor, can not be charged against this code as a whole; though many of the laws seem to be designed to operate chiefly *in terrorem*, and the penalty is placed higher than the punishment really intended to be inflicted, that the Emperor may have scope for mercy, or, as he says, for 'leniency beyond the bounds of law.' Some officers are lenient, others severe; the people in some provinces are industrious and peaceable, in others turbulent and averse to quiet occupations, so that one is likely to form a juster idea of the administration of the empire by looking at the results as seen in the general aspects of society, and judging of the tree by its fruits, than by drawing inferences applicable to the whole machine of State from particular instances of oppression and insubordination, as is so frequently the case with travellers and writers."

With this general view of the Constitution and laws of the empire, and the plan of education and literary examinations described in a former chapter, we may now glance at the practical workings of the whole system.

The Emperor is held in check by the Constitution and laws of the empire; a sense of his responsibility, the constant watch, influence, and advice of his chief officers, and the consciousness that he too is amenable to public opinion, and that a gross violation of his trust would weaken his influence over his péople, and might cost him his throne. Some of the Emperors of China have been men of high character and great executive ability, worthy of the position which they have occupied; others have been weak and inefficient, bearing the name and the insignia of royalty, while the government has been administered by other hands; and others have united a powerful will with a vicious nature, and brought ruin upon themselves and their people.

Officers are restrained from great excesses, extortion, and injustice by the fear of the people, who know their rights, and sometimes assert them; by superior officers and censors, who exercise watch and surveillance over them; and also by inferior officers, who are waiting anxiously for their removal, that they may be advanced to occupy their places. The danger of popular and ambitious rulers gaining too much influence over the people, or forming combinations against the State with others with whom they are associated, is in a great degree prevented by their constant removal from one part of the empire to another, which matter is carefully attended to by the Board of Civil Office at Pekin. Officers in the provinces are seldom permitted to remain in one place more than three or four years. They are never sent to exercise their functions in their native districts, nor are they allowed to marry within the bounds of their jurisdiction.

Literary men, both under-graduates and graduates of the first and second degrees, occupy an intermediate position between the officers and people, and are an important and powerful auxiliary to the government. They are bound to it by the hope of becoming officers under it. They are also, for the most part, in thorough sympathy with it, being imbued with the spirit of Confucianism, and regarding the government as the embodiment of the wisdom of their ancient sages. Their influence over their uninformed and uncultivated neighbors tends to promote respect for their rulers and obedience to the laws.

The restraints brought to bear upon the people, in addition to their sense of right and their regard for their own reputation and their own interests, are the severity of their laws, the absolute authority of their rulers, and their liability to extortion, often practiced by officers and underlings whenever the people give occasion for it by petty crimes, misdemeanors, and insubordination. When disaffected from real or imaginary causes, they are prevented in a great measure from insurrectionary combinations, not only by the careful watch of their officers, but by the isolation of different parts of the empire, and the impossibility of ready communication and co-operation between the inhabitants of the various provinces on account of the differences in their spoken languages.

But in extreme cases of injustice and oppression the people are not without the means of redress, and they know when and how to use them. Though docile and yielding to a fault, neighborhoods and districts sometimes rise in a body in open rebellion against the local authorities, and assert and maintain their rights. When an officer is notoriously avaricious, exacting, and unjust, the people have a right to presume that he is acting in opposition to the wishes and instructions of his sovereign. Smarting under the effect of some fresh act of oppression, they sometimes rise in a body, and march to the office of the obnoxious magistrate, not as petitioners, but as plaintiffs and accusers. It is not uncommon on such occasions for the magistrate, laying aside his dignity of office, to come out and treat in person with the leaders or spokesmen of the movement, hearing patiently their complaints and giving satisfactory promises of amendment and redress, after which the people go back quietly to their homes. If the officer is grievously in fault, this is almost sure to be the result. Otherwise this case of maladministration would probably be reported to the capital, and the officer be summoned to appear before the Emperor, with the danger of losing his office, if not his life.

Sometimes the officer, with or without sufficient cause, refuses to entertain the complaint of the people, and insists on their submitting to his authority, and is supported by his superiors. In such an event a body of soldiers is sent, if necessary, to quell the disturbance, the life of one or more of the leaders is perhaps sacrificed to vindicate the majesty of the laws, and the people succumb to superior force and necessity.

When injustice and corruption are general, as is the case at the present time, local insurrections become frequent. Different bodies of malcontents unite in forming serious rebellions; the people consider themselves absolved from their allegiance, refuse to recognize the Emperor as the heaven-sent ruler and tranquilizer of his people, and all things tend to anarchy and disintegration. Thus the Chinese government rests ultimately upon the will of the people. Their sympathy and support are lost by a departure from the recognized principles of the government, and he who would reassure them, and tranquilize the empire, must give evidence of his ability and sincerity, and go back and build again on the old foundations.

Notwithstanding the Chinese government has been represented as an unlimited monarchy and as an absolute despotism, it will be seen from the foregoing statements that some decidedly republican ideas prevail, and that the people have a good degree of personal liberty. Chinese scholars often speak in terms of the highest admiration of the government of the United States. The character of Washington is also much admired by them, and a worthy panegyric has been written on it by one of their prominent men.

It is a fact worthy of special mention in this connection that the Chinese are allowed to choose from among themselves their own "elders" who form a kind of *imperium in imperio*, and attend to and relieve the officers of the Emperor of a great deal of business. Many petty differences, misunderstandings, and quarrels are referred to the elders for arbitration, and thus the expense, demoralization, scandal, and embittered feelings of a lawsuit are often avoided. The officers sometimes influence the people indirectly and quietly through the elders, and on the other hand, measures originating in the will of the people are commended to the attention of the officers by the elders.

Sometimes the elders fail to satisfy and harmonize parties at variance, and the two factions prefer to settle their difficulties themselves; in other words, to "fight it out," and the authorities allow them to do so. This liberty is granted when the quarrel is personal or local, and not calculated to endanger the interests of the community at large or weaken the authority of the officers, and when the questions involved are confused and perplexing. The magistrates often take "hush-money," from both parties, and at the same time avoid any further trouble in the matter. A family will sometimes gather together its relatives, friends, and sympathizers, and persons hired for the purpose, together constituting a decidedly formidable company, and unexpectedly make their appearance at the house of a person with whom they are at variance, armed with spears and clubs, and demand redress. The attacked party, particularly if he is in the wrong, and without the sympathy and support of friends and neighbors, is very apt to yield and to accept the terms imposed. These demonstrations do not generally proceed further than to make a *show* of violence.

Blustering, reckless, and unprincipled foreigners are sometimes hired in the vicinity of the open ports to take a part in these intimidating expeditions, and missionaries have been inveigled into the same business by professed *friends* or *inquirers*, by means of the specious plea of going as "peace-makers." Sometimes the foreigner is invited to pay a friendly visit, without suspecting the real motive of his host, who makes his own representations with regard to the visit to his neighbors.

A few years since a large landholder, about fifty miles

from Ningpo, was visited by an armed company of the farmers who tilled his land. They demanded from him a higher percentage of the proceeds of the soil. The rich man, having many servants in his establishment, resisted force with force. The laborers soon returned with a larger party, and the defendant employed additional assistance. This soon grew to be a serious affair. The house of the landholder assumed the appearance of a besieged fortress, and the movement that of a small rebellion. The authorities, for some reason or other, determined not to interfere. The contest continued for weeks, if not months. The result in this case was, that the laborers were obliged to succumb, and the successful landholder received a letter of commendation from Pekin, and an honorary title.

The people being associated in large families, and exceedingly clannish, family feuds sometimes become very bitter, and are perpetuated from generation to generation. This is especially the case in the southern part of China, where the inhabitants are more passionate and turbulent.

The above facts are referred to to show the practical workings of the Chinese government, and illustrate its imperfections as well as excellences.

CHAPTER VI.

THE RELIGIONS OF CHINA.

Importance of the Study of the Religions of China.—The threefold Division of their Religions by the Chinese.—The words Religion and Sect used in a modified Sense.—Different Modes of understanding and applying the Chinese Classification.—The Plan adopted in this Book.

In order to a right understanding of the Chinese character and civilization, some knowledge of the systems of idolatry which prevail in the empire, and of the religious beliefs of the people, is absolutely necessary. It is no easy matter to give a satisfactory classification and representation of these religious systems. So diverse, multiplied, and confused are the doctrines of belief, that it is difficult for any one to give an intelligible account of his own creed or that of others. Perhaps the best classification is that adopted by the Chinese, who always speak of their religious systems as three, namely, *Ju-Kiau*, *Sih-Kiau*, and *Tau-Kiau.*

The word *kiau* is generally used as a verb, and means "to teach." As a noun, it means a "system of teaching." It is the nearest equivalent the Chinese language affords to our word *religion*, though it is much more general in its meaning, and may be applied to a system of teachings which has no religious element whatever.

It must be borne in mind that when we use the terms religion and sect in connection with the Chinese, we do it in a new and modified sense. Our word religion always suggests the idea of God and his worship, and also a future state of blessedness as the object of religious faith and the end of a religious life, while its associations are spiritual and heavenly. The word *kiau*, however, does not necessarily bring up to the

Chinese mind any of the suggestions and associations which the word religion does to ours. Again, while there are three systems of teachings, the Chinese are not, strictly speaking, divided into different sects. These systems are not regarded as rival and antagonistic, but co-ordinate and supplementary, and the people make use of them together, giving to each more or less importance or prominence, according to their preferences or fancies.

Sih-Kiau and *Tau-Kiau* may be literally translated Buddhism and Tauism, and present two distinct systems, the origins, authors, histories, and peculiarities of which may be fully and clearly represented.

The first term, *Ju-Kiau*, is more vague and indefinite in its meaning and application, and is differently understood by different persons.

The literal translation of the character *Ju* is "scholar," "literary," etc., and *Ju-Kiau* is sometimes called the "Religion of the Learned." But the most prominent and important of the forms of worship prescribed by the *Ju-Kiau* are practiced as much by the common people as by scholars, and, in fact, are adopted by the people universally. It is evident, then, that the term "Religion of the Learned," as a translation for *Ju-Kiau*, is inadmissible.

The *Ju-Kiau* is sometimes represented as the "State Religion." The principal objection to this term is that it would be calculated to give a wrong impression, as it would have to be used in a new and unauthorized sense, there being no religion in China which is specially sanctioned and upheld by the State. There are peculiar rites and forms of worship practiced exclusively by officers, because they are regarded as specially appropriate to them as officers. In addition to these official rites, they, with their families, adopt very much the same forms of belief and worship that the common people do.

The *Ju-Kiau* is most commonly, and I think with most reason, regarded both by native and foreign writers as synonymous with the teachings of Confucius or Confucianism. Some would use this term in a more limited, and others in a more general sense—the former confining it strictly to the teachings of Confucius, and the latter giving it a new and wider signification, and associating with it those national idolatrous usages and rites which do not naturally belong to Buddhism or Tauism. The objections to the use of this word are, that in the former sense it is not comprehensive enough, and in the latter it is so comprehensive as to be inappropriate, attributing to the Chinese sage doctrines and practices which originated long after his time, and are strikingly inconsistent with his teachings.

I presume that the Chinese classification of their three systems of teaching was more appropriate and accurate in former times than it is at present, the forms of idolatrous worship having greatly multiplied, and the three systems having become modified and intertwined in their mutual acting and reacting upon each other.

Each of the above translations of the Chinese term *Ju-Kiau* expresses some prominent feature or peculiarity of it, but gives only a partial and incomplete view, and is thus calculated more or less to mislead.

In this book I have determined, thinking this course the freest from objections, to regard the *Ju-Kiau* as synonymous with Confucianism; this word being taken, in its strict and limited sense, as referring to the system of ethics, political economy, and ancient religious rites taught by Confucius and his predecessors. This first system having been treated of briefly in the third and following chapters, I will take up the other two, Buddhism and Tauism, in the chapters which immediately follow, and afterward in additional chapters present various forms of belief and worship which are naturally associated with or have grown out of these religious systems individually, or have resulted from them conjointly.

Chronologically, Tauism should come next in order, but

Buddhism takes the precedence of it, in its position and influence in the empire, and accordingly occupies the second place in the Chinese enumeration.

Other minor sects of religionists, which have not exercised a decided and permanent influence on the Chinese race as a whole, need not be particularly mentioned.

Such, however, is the prominence of Mohammedanism in some parts of the empire as to require a special reference. It is said to have been introduced into China a short time after the death of Mohammed. A few adherents of this sect are now found in every part of the empire. Occasional mosques are seen in the Eastern provinces. There is one small one in Ningpo; and a few years since I found a rather imposing one in Hang-chow, and an interesting class of persons connected with it. In the north-western part of the empire there are large Mohammedan communities, and in some places they are said to form one-third of the population. Dr. Williams states that "early in the last century the whole number in the country was computed to be half a million."

They practice circumcision; observe nominally one day in seven as a day of rest; proscribe the use of swine's flesh; bear decided testimony against idolatry; and, like the Jews, keep themselves in a great measure separate from the rest of the population.

They regard Mohammed as the great and unrivalled Prophet of Heaven, while they assign to Jesus a lower rank, with Abraham, Moses, and David.

They have relaxed a good deal in the strictness of their religious observances, and they conform to some of the idolatrous rites of the other religious sects.

When I met them in Hang-chow they treated me with the greatest cordiality, invited me to examine their mosque and to attend their services, referring with evident delight to the fact that we worship the same God and Creator of all, in opposition to the prevailing Chinese idolatry. I could not help feeling, in that distant land full of idols and heathen temples, that, notwithstanding our wide and irreconcilable differences, this was indeed one strong bond of sympathy.

The Jews and Roman Catholics of China will be particularly referred to in the latter part of this book.

CHAPTER VII.

BUDDHISM.

Introduction of Buddhism into China.—Its reputed Founder.—Different Orders of Buddhist Divinities.—Peculiarities of Buddhism as it exists in different Countries.—Popular Traditions relating to Buddha.—Doctrines and Religious Rites of Buddhism.—Descriptions of Buddhist Temples.—Construction of Images.—Particular Description of Temples and Idol Worship at Hang-chow.—Buddhist Priests.—Organization of the Monasteries.—Hermits living in Huts or Caves.—Priests confined in Sealed Rooms or Cells.—Acquiring of Merit by Proxy.—Buddhist Nunneries.

BUDDHISM is emphatically the religion of China, and of the whole of Eastern Asia. It was introduced into China about the year 60 of the Christian era. At that time the Emperor Ming-ti sent an embassy to the West to seek for religious teachers. Some suppose that this embassy was suggested by a dream, and others by a saying of Confucius — "In the West there are great sages." It is not improbable that a rumor of Him who was "born King of the Jews" may have reached the extreme of Eastern Asia, and had something to do with this movement. However this may have been, the expedition starting from China on this important errand proceeded as far as India, and there met with Buddhist priests, and learned from them of their deity Buddha, their sacred books, and the doctrine of a future state, and a way of escape from sin and its consequences. Supposing they had gained their object, they returned home with this new god and new religion of the Hindoos. This was the introduction of Buddhism into the East.

The name of the reputed founder of this sect is *Shakyamuni*, who is supposed to have lived in the 7th century B.C., or earlier. By a life of contemplation, meritorious works, and self-imposed austerities, he reached the condition of Buddha, that of "complete knowledge." The term in Chinese is *Fuh*. Above and beyond this is a higher degree of development or attainment, called *Nirvana*, which is the highest condition to which mortals can attain, and of which their nature is capable. Here consciousness, personality, and all wishes and desires are lost in an ideal existence, and all relations and intercourse with the material world cease. Buddha, denying himself the pleasures of this superior unconscious state, pauses on the confines of it to give exercise to his benevolence in instructing and elevating men.

There is an inferior grade of divinities which have not yet reached the condition of Buddha, and are called *Poosa*. They are still imperfect in knowledge and virtue, though far in advance of ordinary men. As they are nearer mankind in the scale of being, they are supposed to be in closer sympathy with him, more intimately acquainted with his circumstances, and more approachable. For this reason they are most worshiped by the people.

Buddhism has assumed different forms in different countries. A distinction is made between Southern Buddhism as it is found in Ceylon, Burmah, and Siam, and Northern, as found in Thibet and China. The religious books of Northern Buddhism are in Sanscrit, or are translations from Sanscrit. Those of Southern Buddhism are in Pali, a language of more recent origin. The Northern Buddhists have also added books, legends, and deities which are not known elsewhere.

In Thibet this system is connected with a religious hierarchy, exercising political power, at the head of which is the Grand Lama, who is regarded as the incarnation of Buddha. When the Grand Lama dies, the priests fix upon some infant into whose body the spirit of the deceased lama is supposed to have passed, and the infant becomes the next Grand Lama.

In China no such religious hierarchy has been tolerated, and Buddhism exists without lamas. The Buddhism of Mongolia partakes of the character of that of Thibet. That of Corea,

Japan, and Cochin China has evidently been copied from China.

With these general statements, I will confine myself strictly to Buddhism in China, speaking of its practical aspects as it is believed and practiced by the people at present, and is incorporated with their religious and social life.

The popular traditions of the Chinese relating to Buddha are of that marvellous character calculated to work upon the imagination and blind faith of an ignorant people. He is represented as having been born in a regal palace, an heir to luxury and power, which had no charms to attract him. It is believed that, on his appearance in the world, a halo of glory encircled him, which was visible throughout all the surrounding country, and the earth around him spontaneously produced a profusion of lotus flowers. One of the first acts which he performed was that of walking seventeen steps toward the North, South, East and West, with one hand pointing toward heaven and the other toward the earth, declaring, in a loud voice—"In heaven and earth there is not another greater than I." Many accounts are given of his remarkable strength and natural endowments, so exceedingly overwrought that they might be expected to excite the suspicion of the most credulous. He left his home at an early age to lead the life of a recluse, and, after years of self-imposed austerity, attained to the perfection of virtue and ascended to heaven as a god, leaving many remarkable proofs of his superhuman power.

The distinctive characteristics of the Buddhist system are a belief in a benevolent deity, associated with inferior ones, whose special object and care it is to save men from sin and its consequences, and also the doctrine of the transmigration of souls, and the efficacy of good works. In accordance with these doctrines, the religious or idolatrous rites of Buddhism consist in prayers to these gods, works of merit and austerity, and provision for the anticipated wants of the spirit in Hades, and also for deceased relatives and friends.

Temples erected to the worship of this deity are found in

every part of the empire, and are numerous, costly, and imposing. We see in China the same disposition manifested by other nations of the past, to perform idolatrous ceremonies in "high places." The theory of Buddhism requires its temples to be built in retired situations among the hills, for the sake of the quiet and seclusion which such places afford. Accordingly, most of the buildings connected with this sect which are not erected in cities and towns for the convenience of the inhabitants, are found in the most beautiful and romantic situations which the country affords. The largest of them are, to a certain extent, built on a common fixed plan, which may be described as follows:

They are composed of several separate buildings in a line directly back of the front one. If the nature of the ground admits of it, each building in the rear rises several feet above the one before it, and is reached by a flight of stone steps. The paths leading to these temples are often disposed with much taste and art, winding through beautiful groves of pine and bamboo, over fine arched bridges, along luxuriant hedges and fish-ponds, and affording oftentimes beautiful views of natural scenery.

Entering the wide front door of the first building, you see before you a large image in a sitting posture, its face bearing the expression of a contemptuous smile. This idol is called *Mi leh-fuh;* its office is to guard the entrance to the temple, and it is smiling at the foolishness of mankind who spend their lives in the vain pursuit of worldly pleasures. Immediately behind this image, and facing the back opening or door, is a standing figure, dressed in mail from head to foot, and holding in the hand a large battle-club. This image is called *Wei-to Poo-sah,* and is regarded as the guardian deity of the temple, protecting it from evil spirits, thieves, etc. The spacious interior of this, as well as the other buildings, is undivided by partitions or upper floors; the roof is supported by numerous large pillars. Besides the two images in the middle above described, there are four others, called the *Sz-kin-kang,*

GATE-WAY OF BUDDHIST TEMPLE NEAR CANTON.

or "Four Golden Heroes." They are very large, and in a standing posture, two being on each side of the building. One, holding a large umbrella in his hands, is called *To wen tien hwang*, or "The All-hearing Heaven King," and it is said that when he spreads his umbrella it darkens heaven and earth. The one with a large guitar is called *Tsang chang tien hwang*, or "Add-length Heaven King," probably with reference to his power of conferring longevity. He is supposed to awe and subdue evil spirits and demons by touching the chords of his instrument. One, holding in his hand a sword, and having a fearful countenance, is called *Chi kwoh tien hwang*, or "Grasp-empire Heaven King." The remaining one, who is represented as holding in his hands a dragon, and trampling under his feet snakes and reptiles, is called the *Kwang muh tien hwang*, or "Clear-eyed Heaven King." These four gods are regarded as the protectors of the people generally, and particularly of those who believe in Fuh.

The second building is larger than the first, generally about seventy feet deep, ninety feet wide, and forty or fifty feet high, though sometimes larger. It is called the "Great, Glorious, Precious Temple." Its chief deities are three large images of Fuh, called the Past, the Future, and the Present Fuh; also the "Three Precious Ones." They are situated in the middle of the building, in a line facing the front door, and are represented as sitting on large high pedestals, surrounded by lotus flowers. In front of these immense images, which are generally about twenty feet high, is a tablet inscribed to the Emperor, no doubt to secure his favor to the sect. On the two sides of this building may be seen either the eighteen *Lo-han*, persons who are supposed to be absorbed into Fuh; or the twenty-eight *Sing-sin*, which represent different stars. All these are human figures about as large as life. Immediately in front of the three large images of Fuh is generally seen a standing veiled image of *Kwan-shi-yin Poo-sah*, one of the principal Buddhist deities, which is represented as a young virgin, and is executed in the best style of Chinese art. This

THE THREE PRECIOUS ONES.

goddess is supposed to have appeared on the earth at different times, and in different forms and characters. She is worshiped as the *Sung-ts neang-neang*, or "Conferrer of Sons;" the "Thousand-handed *Kwan-yin*," the "Seven-faced *Kwan-yin*," and also as a male deity of the same name. The "Conferrer of Sons" is generally represented with a child in her arms. This female deity is the one in which the Roman Catholics have recognized such a strong resemblance to the Virgin Mary as to attribute its existence to Satanic agency. It is evident that the natives are in a measure acquainted with this dislike of the Romanists, as it is reported among the people that they "hate *Kwan-shi-yin* because she killed Jesus." Behind the three large images of Buddha you sometimes see the thousand-handed *Kwan-yin*, or the *Sung-ts neang-neang* mentioned above, and sometimes one of a variety of other idols. In the back part of this main building it is not uncommon to find a separate shrine erected to the God of War, and to other favorite objects of worship.

In the larger temples a third building is generally found, about the size of the second. This is used as a "Worship

Hall" for the priests. Less space is occupied by the images, and more is reserved for worshipers.

Besides the buildings mentioned above, in many temples others are added. The idols which they contain are very numerous, and in the disposition of them no regular order is observed. Most of them represent persons who are supposed to have been absorbed into Buddha, of which class there are in all more than five hundred. Some are taken from the popular deities of the people, and some even from the gods of Tauism. All these gods have their fabulous legends, which, though they might interest the curious, it would be as impossible as useless to give here. Sometimes lower side buildings are erected and divided into apartments, which are occupied by smaller images of all sorts and appearances, from one to two, three, or more feet in height. Several hundred of these images may be found in the same building. It is not uncommon to see in these side apartments several rooms representing the different divisions and tortures of hell. The god *Ti tsang hwang*, "Earth-concealed King," is supposed to preside over these regions. It is said that he was unwilling to become Buddha until he had rescued all the spirits in hell.

A DEPARTMENT OF THE BUDDHISTIC HELL.

Side buildings are also erected for the accommodation of the priests, generally with an upper story. The dining-room is often large enough to seat several hundred persons, and the kitchen is supplied with kettles, some of which will hold two or three barrels.

Some of the temples have pagodas connected with them.

PAGODA.

These are towers or monuments, substantially built of stone or brick, varying in height from eighty to two hundred feet or more. They form a very characteristic and beautiful feature in Chinese landscapes. Many of them show evidences of great antiquity. They were probably built originally to be the repositories of some revered relics, or to commemorate some noted person. Occasionally, though not generally, they contain idols.

In small towns and places without the means for building a large temple the principal Buddhist idols are, by being made of a smaller size, grouped together in one building, and made to answer the purposes of those who may not have the time or money requisite for going far from home to worship in a larger temple.

The idols are manufactured of the different metals, or of stone, or wood, or clay. The largest are made of a framework of wood covered with mortar, and are generally gilded on the outside with gold-leaf, though in some cases they are painted with different colors. It is considered essential that each one, large or small, should be supplied with artificial entrails, which are lodged in the body through a hole in the back. These represent the living spirit, without which the god would be regarded as worthless. They consist generally of representations in silver of the heart and other internal parts of the body. Sometimes pearls and precious stones, or live snakes or reptiles, are either substituted or added. This fact furnished a weighty reason for the iconoclastic practices of the Tai-ping insurgents of China, in addition to their professed hatred and contempt for idolatry. These images are generally well-executed as to their forms and postures. It is worthy of notice, as indicative of the character of the people and the art with which Satan suits the forms of idolatry to the minds of his deluded victims, that there is nothing horrid or indecent in the appearance of any of the idols of China, and none are represented as influenced by debasing passions; all are supposed to be virtuous men, or heroes of the past. They have also less of sameness in their appearance than might be expected, as they present in different degrees and combinations the expressions of love, pity, mirth, thoughtfulness, fierceness, and anger.

The general appearance of a large Buddhist temple or monastery is grand and imposing, calculated to inspire in the minds of the vulgar feelings of reverence and awe. The structure of the buildings indicates also not a little architectural taste and skill. They are well-proportioned, and in each one the plan of the interior is suited to the size and number of the idols which it is to contain. The large roof is generally made of the best tiling materials, and will last more than half a century without repair. It is covered with fretted-work, and grotesque figures of elephants, lions, horses, men, etc. The interior is ornamented with elaborate carvings in wood and stone; and a great variety of inscriptions on the walls and pillars, and over the heads of the idols, written in large gilt letters, serve at the same time the purposes of decoration and of setting forth the names, characters, and powers of the different divinities.

A short description of Buddhist temples and worship in Hang-chow, one of the great centres of Buddhist influence in China, may serve to give a livelier and more satisfactory view of the character of Buddhism and its practical workings. This is one of the provincial capitals, and contained before it was taken by the rebels about one million of inhabitants. It is a place deservedly renowned among the Chinese for its great natural beauty, which is often alluded to in the couplet, *Shang yiu tien tang, hia yiu Su Hang*—"Above is heaven, below are Su-chow and Hang-chow." This city and its suburbs are full of Buddhist temples, but the most noted of them are among the hills and mountains bounding the city on the south and west. They are to be found in the most romantic nooks of the valleys, perched half-way up the mountain-sides, or crowning a hill-top a few hundred or a thousand feet high.

Passing out from the south-western gate of the city in the direction of the mountains, a short distance from the wall you meet with a noted temple, called the *Tsing-z.* The buildings described in the previous part of this chapter are unusually large. This monastery was principally noted, however, for a side building containing the five hundred disciples of Buddha complete. These are all as large as a full-grown man, finely executed, and covered with gold-leaf. Each one occupied a platform about six or eight feet square. The size of the whole building affording this area for each image, and passages or aisles between them, may be imagined, and this was but an inferior and subsidiary part of the temple. I saw a similar temple, containing these five hundred images in one hall, in the city of Canton.

About three miles from the city, in one of the valleys, is the *Tien-coh-z*—"The Temple of India." This is very beautiful in its architecture and location, but its principal attraction is a curious subterranean passage, forming part of the path to the temple. It is said and believed that the hill covering this passage was transported from India in the night, and deposited here. Hence the name, "The Temple of India."

About ten miles from the city is a temple, which contained when I visited it about five hundred priests. It is reached by a beautiful avenue nearly two miles long, winding through a deep valley by the side of a clear mountain stream, and overarched by groves of pine and bamboo. The temple was composed of a large number of different buildings, connected with each other by such various and intricate passages that a stranger without a guide was in danger of being lost in them. This was a kind of fashionable watering-place, a favorite resort for wealthy families in the summer. Several of the buildings were occupied with apartments for the entertainment of these visitors. Here wealthy families would spend weeks, enjoying the quiet repose of the country and the delightful mountain scenery, hiring a hall of worship and a company of priests to chant prayers for the repose of the spirit of a deceased parent, or for the prolongation of the life of a parent living, or for some other desired blessing. It was not unusual for such families when leaving the temple, after paying roundly and perhaps ostentatiously for their other expenses, to provide for the illumination, by means of a large number of lamps, of the whole or part of the avenue leading to the temple.

There are more than a score of temples in this one locality, some of which are hardly less noted than those I have described. During the six months which I spent at this place in 1859, I had an opportunity to witness the crowds of pilgrims who come here to worship in the spring. The canals leading to the city were filled for miles in some directions with the boats of worshipers, many of whom had come long distances to pay their homage at these sacred shrines. The numerous paved roads or paths winding through the valleys in every direction were occupied by an almost continuous stream of visitors, the rich in sedans and the poor on foot. The air was loaded with the fragrance of the spring azalias, flowering shrubs, and the evergreens of different kinds which shaded the graves of the previous inhabitants of that vast city, millions of whom have found their last resting-place on these lovely hill-sides. Old women, tottering on their small feet and supported by their staffs, were making their last visits to these renowned temples, their last effort to prepare for a future state, and were then going home to die, ignorant, alas! both of the character of that state and the preparation for it.

As we approached some of these temples we found the roadside lined with beggars of a peculiar character. They were all diseased, and seemed to be gathered from every part of the country, to take advantage of this great concourse of religiously-disposed people to appeal to their sympathies. The tremulous and withered hand of age was extended with the prayer—"Do good deeds." Sightless balls, uplifted, appealed for charity, while the lips pronounced the blessing—"May you live a hundred years." Swollen limbs, frightful sores of every description, and the stumps of legs literally rotted off, were obtruded upon the gaze of the traveller, harrowing up the feelings, and making the heart sick.

Entering the temples, the sight was hardly less distressing. The people mad upon their idols; the priests rapidly gathering in their ill-gotten gains; old and young, with earnest and anxious countenances, pouring out the burdens of their hearts before idol gods, and bowing down and striking their foreheads on the paved floor so as to make a sound audible at some little distance. The impression produced upon my mind by that visit, and the conflicting emotions excited, I shall never forget. These retired solitudes, thronged with the living and peopled with the dead; the bright sky, the balmy air, luxuriant nature, and a beautiful landscape, and this scene of beauty overspread with a pall of moral darkness which might be felt; sin, sorrow, disease, death; man, the noblest work of God, blinded, debased, perverted, without one ray of light, without any knowledge of the only living and true God and Jesus Christ, the only name "under heaven given among men whereby we must be saved."

The priests of Buddhism generally become such at an early age, either because they have lost their parents, or because their parents are unable to support them, or because they are born under an unlucky star, and fortune-tellers predict that they will be delicate and short-lived. Of those who become priests in after-life some are led to this step by the loss of their parents, or of their wives and children; some by domestic difficulties, some by idleness, and some take advantage of the retirement and disguise of the priesthood to escape the punishment of their crimes. The number of those who really understand and believe the doctrines of Buddhism, and enter the priesthood to obtain any advantage except that of having rice to eat, is very small. Accordingly, they show little attachment to their order, and generally apologize for becoming priests by saying they had brothers to take care of their parents; and for continuing such by saying that they have now no other way to obtain a living. When a child enters a monastery as a priest he is placed under the charge of an older priest as his preceptor, whose duty it is to teach his pupil letters. In rare instances priests attend to this duty themselves; sometimes they send their pupils to study for a time with other children in the schools of the country. The most of priests, however, grow up unacquainted with letters, and exceedingly ignorant. They generally assent to every thing we say, and only defend their own religion by saying that it is, after all, identical with ours. They take vows of celibacy, profess to live on a vegetable diet, and wear no clothes made of wool or the skins of animals, as they consider it a crime to take away animal life. They also shave the whole head, and wear garments peculiar to their order. Many of them have marks burned upon their heads or arms, as the means and evidence of merit. Not a few have one of their fingers burned off for the same reason. There are unimportant distinctions in different schools of priests, with slight differences in dress and forms of worship, which it is not worth while to mention here particularly.

BUDDHIST PRIEST.

Each large monastery has its superior and overseer, which stations are filled by priests distinguished for their influence and intelligence. They are chosen by persons outside of the priesthood, who act as a board of managers. Some of the younger priests are engaged to a certain extent in servile employments about the monastery or in tilling the soil, but these duties are for the most part performed by hired laborers, while the priests lead a life of ease and indolence. Some spend the most of their lives in the same monastery, but not a few have a roving propensity, and have travelled over the most or all of the eighteen provinces. They easily beg their way as they go, and find convenient lodgings in the monasteries of their own order. They generally carry with them a passport or recommendation from a superior with whom they are acquainted. Without this, however, the laws of their order give them the privilege of stopping at any place for rest and refreshment. When they choose to remain for a time at any monastery, they can do so if there is a vacant place for them, and they are sufficiently well recommended to obtain it.

The best recommendation consists in qualifications for earning money. Each monastery is regarded as a large household. The wants of all are provided for by the superior, and, when priests earn money, part of it goes to the establishment, and part is kept by themselves. In consequence of the travelling propensities of these priests, large monasteries present striking instances of the confusion of tongues, and oftentimes priests can not understand each other without a third person to act as interpreter. The number of priests in these establishments varies from one to several hundreds, and is regulated by the size and resources of each particular monastery.

The incomes of the monasteries are derived from the voluntary contributions of the people, money paid to the priests in remuneration for their services at funerals, etc., the proceeds of public worship in the monastery, and the proceeds of the lands with which many of them have been endowed. The specific duties of the priesthood are chanting and performing different ceremonies in the temples, performing idolatrous ceremonies among the people, and begging.

The chanting of regular formal services is performed morning and evening, partly in the native and partly in the Sanscrit tongue, and is learned from books and by imitation. It is carried on in connection with the burning of incense and candles, prostrations, the beating of drums and bells and balls of wood, etc., and pacing backward and forward in front of the idols. The whole exercise lasts about an hour. In case a monastery is out of repair, or money is needed for any other purpose, priests are often sent to raise subscriptions from door to door. Wealthy individuals, and sometimes officers, give large sums for repairing temples, influenced partly by a desire to be seen and praised of men, and partly by the hope of securing happiness in a future state.

Connected with most of the large Buddhist establishments there are some priests, distinguished from their class by living in rude huts or caves among the hills in the greatest retirement and austerity. Their time is spent in keeping the taper lighted before their gods, reciting their chants, cooking their simple meals, and idleness. While professing to seek this retirement for the sake of meditation, they seem almost to lose their power of thinking, and spend their time in listless indifference to every thing around them. They are supported by the contributions of friends and temple-worshipers, and supplies from the monastery with which they are connected. It is commonly reported and believed that those who live thus attain to great longevity, and require very little sustenance to support life.

There are other priests who spend their time in closed rooms or cells. These are found principally in the larger monasteries. They commence their secluded life with considerable formality. On an appointed day they enter the room or rooms which are to be their future abode, and all the doors are sealed by numerous strips of paper, on which are written large characters, stating the day when the confinement commenced and how long it is to continue. Only one small hole is left in the wall, through which articles are handed in and out.

Here the blind devotee immures himself for years, and perhaps for life. Priests sometimes take refuge in these cloistered cells to escape punishment after having broken their vows by the commission of crimes. Rich men, believing it important to lay up a store of merit, and at the same time being too much engaged in laying up other treasures to do it for themselves, sometimes make an arrangement with a priest as follows: The man of wealth agrees to give him a certain amount of money for living in a state of confinement for a stipulated time, providing him at the same time with his food: the priest on his part promises to perform numberless prayers and prostrations, and at the expiration of the prescribed period part of the merit is made over to his employer, and part of it is retained by himself. Priests of this class are favored with many visits from curious people, who visit the temple and carry on no small amount of gossip with them through the hole of their prison.

There is a class of persons who escape the vows and austerities of the priesthood by the following compromise. Numbers are devoted by the fortune-teller to the life of a recluse, whose parents are too superstitious to disregard the decree, and have too much parental affection to give up their child. In such cases the parents choose a priest who is willing to sustain the relation of master to the child: the child as pupil pays his respects and worship to his chosen teacher; presents are exchanged; and the boy is henceforth regarded as nominally the disciple of the priest. He is permitted, however, to stay at home, and live in all respects as ordinary men, except that he is often called, by way of pleasantry or ridicule, "the young priest," and occasionally exchanges presents with his master.

BUDDHIST NUN WITH CAP AND ROSARY.

Connected with Buddhism there is a large number of nuns and nunneries. With regard to the worship performed in these institutions, the manner in which they are supported and their affairs conducted, they differ very little from the monasteries. As regards the character and practices of their inmates, it must be said that, with few exceptions, their reputation is far from being above suspicion.

CHAPTER VIII.

BUDDHISM—CONTINUED.

Worshipers in Buddhist Temples principally Women, and why.—Objects sought in Worship.—Mode of seeking a Response.—Making of Vows.—Procuring Drafts on Hades.—Forms of Worship.—Candles.—Incense.—Rosaries.—Social Intercourse and Gossip in the Temples.—Practice of worshiping Books.—Passport for Hades.—Self-righteous Character of those who frequent Temples.—Striking Parallelism between Buddhism and Romanism.

THE worshipers in Buddhist temples are for the most part women, and these are generally advanced in age. The young women are confined to their houses by the multiplicity of their domestic duties and the customs of the country, which forbid their appearing in public. The older women having comparatively little to do, and reminded by their age of the necessity of preparing for a future state, spend much of their time in the temples, and thus give a kind of variety to their otherwise unoccupied and monotonous hours.

In addition to the acknowledged superior religious susceptibility of women in every age and country, the very large number of female worshipers is thus accounted for. In accordance with the doctrine of the transmigration of souls, so prominent in the Buddhist system, the great end in the worship of Buddha is to secure a favorable position in the future state, in which it is supposed that individuals will ascend or descend in the scale of existence according to the preponderance of their merits or demerits in this life. In consequence of the inferior station of women in China and their peculiar trials, being a woman is regarded as a great misfortune; and in the "bitterness" incident to their present lives they console themselves with the hope that their earnest devotions at the shrine of Buddha will gain for them the position of "a man in good circumstances" in the future state. They suppose that the neglect of worshiping Buddha would result in being born again in one of the lower orders of animals. Men are sometimes seen making their prostrations before Buddhist idols, but generally with the design of gaining some present favor without reference to a future life.

In performing idol-worship the people do not choose lucky days, as they do so commonly in attending to other matters. Unusually large numbers of people may be seen at the Buddhist and other temples on the first and fifteenth of each month, and also on the birthdays of different gods. Special visits are made for special purposes at all times. Some go to pray for children; some to ask an omen or advice in cases of exigency or perplexity; some to ask medicine for sick persons, and some to make vows.

CASTING LOTS.

Advice in times of exigency is obtained in the following manner: The worshiper takes in his hand a cylindrical box, opened at the top, and containing a number of small labelled wooden sticks, and shakes the box in front of the idol until one of them falls out. The number written on this stick points out the corresponding slip of paper, or paragraph of a book, where the desired omen or response may be found. This is written in a very indefinite style, indicating whether the matter in question will terminate favorably or unfavorably, whether a plan proposed should be followed or not. The same device is used in asking for medicine, though the god interrogated is different, and the slips of paper contain medical prescriptions only. As a general rule, the Chinese call a physician, but the above expedient is resorted to both in trivial and alarming cases, when the aid of a physician is either unnecessary or unavailing, or when the disease is of a hidden or mysterious character. Seeking omens and medicines, though practiced in Buddhist temples, is more common in some others.

Vows are made in cases of distress and uncertainty. The person assuming a vow, in order to secure the assistance and protection of some deity, promises to provide a theatrical exhibition for the god to look at, or to feed hungry ghosts, or to furnish new clothes for some idol in the temple, as some of them, which are not painted or covered with gold-leaf, wear a variety of clothes, which are changed with the changing seasons. Vows of other kinds are made which need not be mentioned.

Persons visiting the temples under circumstances of peculiar urgency, as above described, often worship along the way for the distance of half a mile or more, stopping every few steps to make their prostrations.

Worship on ordinary occasions consists in simply burning candles and incense, making prostrations before the gods, and giving a few cash to the priests.

The following is a description of some peculiarities of the worship in Ningpo and its vicinity: The temples are generally visited on particular days appointed by the priests, and the great object of these visits is to obtain bills for the payment of money in Hades, which are called *tieh*. When the women apply to the priests for instruction and assistance they are answered much as follows:—"When you die your soul will pass into the land of spirits, where it may remain ages or hundreds of years before it is allowed to return to earth and inhabit another body. In your journeyings there, when you cross bridges you will have to pay toll; when you cross a ferry you must fee the ferry-man; if you wish good accommodations and attentions in the inns you must be able to pay well for them. It will be very desirable also for you to fee the inferior officers of Hades, so as to bring your case speedily before the courts for adjudication, and facilitate your release and advancement. In a word, money answers all things, in the land of spirits as well as in this present world." The women are further informed that the priests have opened communication with the land of spirits, and that their drafts are honored there. In one corner of the temple a priest sells these drafts, called *tieh*. When the paper has been bought it receives the great seal or stamp of the temple; and after the name *Na mi o mi ta fuh* has been chanted over it from three thousand to ten thousand times, it is regarded as veritable money, and is laid aside for future use in a safe provided for the purpose. It is supposed that each one will entitle the possessor to a number of cash equal to the number of times the name *Na mi o mi ta fuh* has been repeated over it. The priests have contrived to realize an abundant harvest from the sale of this paper-money. Only one *tieh* can be issued in one day, and the days for obtaining them are made as numerous as the credulity of the ignorant women will admit of. They are distributed and arranged as follows: The *Shih wang hwei*, or gathering for the worship of the "Ten Kings" of the departments of hell, requires ten days; one for the birthday of each one of these kings—the first day occurring in the first month, and the last closing with the thirtieth day of the seventh month.

The *Hiueh hu hwei*, or "Blood Lake Gathering," also requires ten days; one for each month, closing with the tenth month. It is supposed that women, on account of the pollution of child-bearing, will all be immersed after death in this blood lake if this punishment is not prevented by procuring these *tieh*.

The *Ta tsih hwei* continues during the first seven days of the second month. At this gathering the women bring presents to the priests.

Pah fuh hwei, or the gathering of the eighth month, is observed during the first ten days of that month.

Jun fuh hwei occupies the first ten days of the intercalary month in the years in which it occurs.

Whenever a temple is erected, a bridge completed, a temple repaired, or a bell cast, additional days are appointed for procuring *tieh*, represented as more valuable than those mentioned above. These are respectively called "Complete Temple *Tieh*," "Complete Bridge *Tieh*," "Open Light *Tieh*," etc.; and the days for procuring them are made known by placards posted at every corner.

The "Open Light *Tieh*" is so called because, while a temple is being repaired, a paper is pasted over the eyes of the idols. This is a polite invitation for the gods to withdraw, in order to avoid being offended by the noise and dirt of the workmen, and they are regarded as being absent until the work is completed and the eye-covering removed, or "light opened."

As there are fifty or sixty days in the year on which these *tieh* can be obtained, the women generally get about this number yearly; but with this the priests are not satisfied, as many women, from sickness or other causes, are not able to come to the temple on the regular days. Accordingly, for the consideration of a few hundred cash, the priests allow them to enter or be connected with a *hwei*, and their names being enrolled, though some individuals may not be present on the appointed days, a *tieh* is laid aside for each one, and they are allowed to come or send for it any time and to chant over it at home.

But the priests are not content even with this. In order to increase their gains they declare that of the *Wang hwei tieh*, mentioned above, no smaller number will suffice than one hundred and sixty, to obtain which would require sixteen years. She who dies with this number incomplete is doomed to be chained for a long period of time in one of the apartments of hell. As the poor women have many fears that they will not live to complete the full number of this *tieh*, the priests gladly relieve them of their difficulty, offering to perform a ceremony which will do away with the evil consequences of this deficiency for a certain remuneration. With this description of the *tieh*, let us now direct our attention to the temples.

On worship days a great number of women may be seen slowly making their way to their chosen place for worship. They generally go in small companies, having with them a little basket containing candles and incense-sticks. They are always dressed in their best clothes, or clothes hired for the purpose, as it would be considered disrespectful to the gods to appear before them in their every-day apparel; and they hope also, by their dress and behavior, to produce the impression upon the gods that they are persons of better circumstances than they really are.

Arrived at the temple, the worship is conducted in the following manner: A few candles are lighted and placed before the gods, either by the worshiper or a servant or priest in attendance at the temple. Incense-sticks are also lighted and inserted in the large bowl of ashes before each idol, or at least those to which the individual expects to pay homage. The design of the worshiper in doing this is to apprise the gods of her presence and intentions. These incense-sticks are about a foot long, and an eighth of an inch in diameter. They are made of fragrant wood, and one end is rolled in a composition of sawdust, so that when ignited it will burn a considerable time, emitting a good deal of smoke.

When the incense-sticks have been properly disposed, the worshiper returns to the place of starting, and makes her prostrations before each of the idols in succession. This is done by first bending the body and simultaneously making a vertical motion with the hands, the palms of which are placed together, and then kneeling down on a soft mat or cushion and striking her head against it. These acts are performed a number of times successively in each place.

The ceremony just mentioned is regarded as preparatory to the more important one which follows, and forms the chief object of the visit, namely, that of obtaining the *tieh*. This, which is bought at what resembles very much a ticket-office, may now be more minutely described. Each one consists of a printed paper, enclosed in an envelope, with blanks to be filled out after it is purchased. On one side of the envelope is written the name of the temple and the class or kind of the *tieh*, on the other side the religious name of the purchaser. Within is an engraving of Buddha and the name of the purchaser, with the year, month, day and hour of her birth, and the local temple with which she is connected, after which follows a few words promising happiness in a future state. The poor women, having purchased this paper, select a convenient place in the temple for spending the greater part of the day in the vain repetition of *Na mi o mi ta fuh*, having a rosary to assist in counting. Rosaries are made of different materials, and have generally one hundred and eight beads. Persons of wealth have them ornamented with pendants of gold and silver, such as representations of Buddha; a small tablet containing the religious name of the possessor; miniature representations of drums and other instruments used in temple worship, to indicate the religious character of those who use them; and a little lantern to represent the light which they hope will shine upon their paths in the land of spirits. These papers gradually accumulate, and after the death of the worshiper are, with other paper-money of different kinds, supposed to be transferred to the regions of the dead by being burned.

It might be inferred from the above description that these visits to the temple are dull and monotonous, but the very opposite is the case. The scene is full of lively interest, and affords abundant matter for the gossip of many days to come.

The rich are present to see and to be seen, dressed in costly attire, objects at once of admiration and envy. A few young girls, gayly dressed, have perhaps come out for the first time to see the busy world and get their first impressions of temples and temple worship. Old acquaintances meet and mutually entertain each other with news of neighbors, family difficulties, the virtues of their own children and faults of their daughters-in-law, and superstitious tales. With the chattering of voluble tongues is mixed the continually-interrupted chant of *Na mi o mi ta fuh*, which, when they are in their turn listening to the stories of others, their tongues seem to repeat almost spontaneously.

While all women engage more or less in temple worship, as above described, there is a class regarded as particularly religious, who are most assiduous and persevering in the practice of additional idolatrous worship of an entirely different kind. This class of women is by no means small, and is made up of some who have a real desire to prepare for a future state, of others who love the variety and excitement which this kind of life affords, and those who stupidly follow the example of others without knowing the reason why. These seek advantages in the future world by a ceremony called *Pai king*, or "worshiping books."

For this purpose they generally choose nunneries in preference to monasteries, on account of the advantages they afford of meeting only with their own sex. This exercise consists in worshiping every character of certain books successively, making prostrations as before to the idols. Proceeding in this manner, a person is able to worship a little more than a page of a book in a day. The first book used is the *Shwai chan*, the worship of which is supposed to take away moral uncleanness. The ideas they have respecting this ceremony are not unlike those of the Jews respecting ceremonial purification. The next book in order is the *Shau sang king*, the worship of which is made necessary by the following superstition.

It is taught that every individual, during the former existence, incurred more or less expense just before entering upon the present life, on account of which a debt remains in Hades unpaid, satisfaction for which will be exacted from the debtor in a future state if it is not cancelled in this. The debt is supposed to be paid by the worship of this book. Persons go over it from ten to ninety-six times, according to the amount of the debt, which is determined by the horoscope of each individual. The book must also be worshiped over several times in addition, to pay off the interest which has accumulated.

After these books are finished, others less important and indispensable may be added. Some perform a greater amount of this worship than is regarded really necessary, in order, by these works of supererogation, to make their future well-being more secure. Those who have purified themselves by the worship of the *Shwaì chan* are very careful to keep from being again polluted, and scrupulously avoid coming in contact with objects regarded as unclean. They are particularly careful not to enter a room occupied by women in child-bed. If they are obliged by the duties they owe to their own relations to enter such rooms, or if they do it by accident, they worship the *Shwaì chan* over again.

This class of women live on a vegetable diet, to avoid the sin of taking away animal life.

When the worship of any particular book is completed, a ceremony is performed in the nunnery, or monastery, called *Wan king*, or "complete book." This ceremony marks a period of rejoicing on the part of the worshiper, and of unusual earnings on the part of the money-loving priests.

Another ceremony, which may be mentioned in connection with the book-worship, is that of procuring a *Lu-yin*, or passport. This is a large sheet of paper, having in the middle an engraving of *Kwan-yin Poo-sah*, with several lines of characters and other embellishments. Individuals, having bought this sheet, go to the monastery and worship the engraving, continually chanting *Na mi o mi ta fuh*. The repetition of this name a certain number of times (generally one thousand) is marked by an impression on the paper with a round stamp. When the borders of this sheet are filled with these impressions the ceremony is finished, and the paper is laid aside until the death of the possessor, when it is burned, and it is thus supposed to pass to the departed spirit, and secure her uninterrupted entrance to any department of the regions of the dead.

The different kinds of worship in Buddhist temples, above described, may be performed by proxy, and many persons gain a livelihood by engaging their services in this way to the sick.

Of all classes of individuals to be met with in China none seem more hopeless and inaccessible to the truth than these self-righteous, inveterate paper-worshipers. It must be said of them, however, that they generally lead comparatively honest and blameless lives, and are much respected by their own people. The character of their employment is such as to keep them constantly on their guard, as others look to them as examples, and they thus become habitually careful to avoid open sins and improprieties.

Without dwelling longer on the details of Buddhist worship, it may be well to refer to a general resemblance between Buddhism and Romanism, so marked that it is recognized and acknowledged by the Romanists themselves, who account for this fact by the supposition that Satan has counterfeited the true religion so as to preoccupy and satisfy the minds of the people with the counterfeit, to the exclusion of what is true and genuine. This correspondence holds in minute particulars. Both have a supreme and infallible head; the celibacy of the priesthood; monasteries and nunneries; prayers in an unknown tongue; prayers to saints and intercessors, and especially and principally to a virgin with a child; also prayers for the dead; repetition of prayers with the use of a rosary; works of merit and supererogation; self-imposed austerities and bodily inflictions; a formal daily service, consisting of chants, burning of candles, sprinkling of holy-water, bowings, prostrations, marchings and counter-marchings. Both have also fast days and feast days; religious processions; images and pictures, and fabulous legends; and revere and worship relics, real and pretended. These two systems, wonderfully adapted to different circumstances of race, civilization, and religious intelligence, hold in spiritual bondage nearly four-fifths of the human race, gratifying, at the same time, the religious longings and the sinful perversions of our nature, providing objects of worship, but in fact leading the soul away from God.

CHAPTER IX.

TAUISM.

Lao-ts, the Founder of the Tauist Sect.—Origin of the word Tauism.—Lao-ts and Confucius contemporaneous.—Change and Deterioration in Tauism.—Its character Materialistic.—Its theory of the Universe.—The Five Elements.—Personification of Stars, and their Identity with some of the Gods.—Alchemy.—Elixir of Life.—Astrology.—Popular Belief respecting Lao-ts, and the origin of Tauism.—Legend of *Lu-tsu.*—Gods of Thunder and Lightning.—The Goddess *Tau-mu.*—The "Three Rulers."—The Dragon King.—His Likeness, how obtained.—Inferior Dragons and the "Dragon Examinations."—Worship of the Dragon.—Description of the *Tu-ti Poo-sah*, or "God of the Earth.—Connection between Tauism and State Worship. — Tauist Temples, Idols, and Priests.—Object or Aim of the Tauist Devotee.—Means and bodily Exercises made use of.—Animals may attain to the Condition of the Genii.—Worship of Women in Tauist Temples.—Sending Dispatches to the Spirit World.—Charms, and Spells, and Magic.—Moral Essays connected with Tauism.—The reason why Tauism is less popular than Buddhism.

The Tauist sect originated with Lao-ts, a Chinese philosopher, who was born B.C. 604. He is generally called *Tai Shang Lao Kiun*—"The Great Supreme Venerable Ruler." His remarkable work, *Tau teh king*—"Treatise on Truth and Virtue," occupies a prominent place in Chinese literature. The name Tauism is derived from the first character in the title of this book, *Tau*, which means truth or doctrine, and is the subject principally discoursed on in it. The writings of Chwang-ts, a disciple of Lao-ts, are more sententious and attractive than those of his master, and more read by scholars. These works, however, have never been popular, being too abstruse and transcendental for ordinary readers. Lao-ts was contemporaneous with Confucius, who, as we learn from the Confucian Analects, visited him and conversed with him respecting his system. He seems, however, not to have comprehended him, and to have been but little impressed and influenced by him. On the other hand, the early Tauist writers looked with contempt on the simple, unphilosophical, and practical doctrines of Confucius. But Confucianism has been adopted by the Chinese in its original form, while Tauism has been obliged to change its form in order to secure its perpetuation. It has passed from philosophy to superstition, and from inquiries after truth to pandering to the desire of our nature for the marvellous. It has busied itself with seeking after the elixir of life and the philosopher's stone, and at last degenerated into a gross form of idolatry. It gives evidence of being acted upon and influenced in a great degree by Buddhism.

The special characteristic of this system is *materialism*, and in its development it includes a theory of the universe and a professed science of alchemy and astrology. Matter is regarded as eternal. The grosser forms of different substances tend downward, and constitute the solid material of the earth; the more refined essences tend upward, and wander through space, possessed of individuality and life, and constituting, when they assume visible forms, the stars which look down from their spheres upon the lower world. While the earth is composed of the grosser and the heavens of the refined forms of matter, so also the body and the soul of man are similarly constituted.

The five special substances or elements of which the universe is composed are metal, wood, water, fire, and earth. The sublimated essences of these elements form five of the planets, respectively called metal star, wood star, etc. These stars sustain mysterious and important relations to the world and its inhabitants, and exercise a powerful influence on the harmony of the universe and the destinies of men. They may, and often do, descend to earth and become gods in order to enter into nearer relations with men, and undertake some special work of benevolence for them. In this way many of the gods of Tauism are identified with certain stars, or are stars personified.

In connection with this system, alchemy attempts the investigation of the essences of matter, and especially the discovery of some method of modifying and changing the outward forms of matter. Ages have been spent in endeavoring to obtain an elixir of life, by which to secure perpetual youth and vigor, and also some secret or art by which other substances may be turned into gold. Astrology endeavors to find out the peculiar characters of different stars, and determine their relations to the birth of individuals, and the events and changes in the histories of individuals and nations.

The popular belief respecting the origin of Tauism is embodied in the account given of it in the *Sau shin ki*. Lao-ts is represented as having existed as a living principle, pervading empty space, anterior to the creation, when the heavens were as yet without light and the earth without form. After the evolutions and transformations of thousands of years, this principle was personified in a deity called *Miau wu shing kiun*, the "Holy Ruler of Wonderful Nonentity." This deity, after innumerable ages and catastrophes, again appeared as the *Miau yu shing kiun*, or "Holy Ruler of Wonderful Entity." The next form which this deity, or principle, is said to have assumed, was that of *Hwan tun shing kiun*, the "Holy Ruler of Chaotic Confusion." We have here presented in this pantheistic form, a singular analogy to the scriptural view of the creation of existing matter out of nothing; and also the idea of a divine Trinity, which in more or less obscure intimations is found in Brahmanism and Buddhism as well as Tauism.

After the creation of men, Lao-ts is supposed to have appeared on the earth at different times in the form of kings of different dynasties, and as teacher or adviser of kings, though the world was not aware of his presence. When he appeared as the philosopher Lao-ts he is represented as having descended from heaven on a sunbeam, in the form of a round ball of variegated colors, which fell into the mouth of a sleeping virgin.

Conception having thus taken place, Lao-ts was born in a miraculous manner, after a period of eighty-one years' gestation. At his birth his hair was already white from age, and he was accordingly called, as his name Lao-ts implies, "*The Old Boy.*" The arrogant prerogatives claimed for this personage by his devotees may be learned from the following rhapsody, addressed to him by one of the kings of the *Sung* dynasty, nearly one thousand years ago:

> "Great and most excellent Tau,
> Not created, self-existent;
> From eternity to eternities,
> Antecedent to the earth and heaven.
> Like all-pervading light,
> Continuing through eternity:
> Who gave instruction to Confucius in the East,
> And called into existence Buddha in the West.
> Director of all kings;
> Parent of all sages;
> Originator of all religions;
> Mystery of mysteries."

This god is not a favorite object of worship, and generally occupies some small and unimportant, though *elevated*, situation in Tauist temples. Idolatrous worship is principally paid to the inferior deities, who are not so much elevated in character and dignity as not to concern themselves in the affairs of men. *Yuh hwang shang ti*, the chief of all the gods, generally occupies the most prominent position, though his place in the great hall is not unfrequently filled by *Chin-wu-ta-ti* or some other idol, no regular order being observed.

Among the most important idols of Tauism is *Lu-tsu*, corresponding somewhat in character to *Kwan-yin*, the Buddhist Goddess of Mercy; and like her, though an inferior deity, he is a great favorite with the people, because he is supposed most to pity them in their distresses, and often to have come from heaven for their relief. This is the great medicine-god of China, from whom the people beg prescriptions. He not only occupies a prominent place in Tauist temples, but has temples erected to him exclusively, and occupies also a place in the Pantheon of Buddhism. The history of this idol may be given as a sample of the whole.

Lu-tsu was formerly a scholar of the second degree, who lived in the *Sung* dynasty not far from a thousand years ago. On his way to the imperial capital to attend the literary examinations, with a mind eagerly aspiring after success and promotion, he was met at an inn near the end of his journey by one of the genii, called *Chung-li-kiuen*, who appeared in the form of a servant at the inn. The wearied scholar, receiving from the disguised *genius* a pillow to rest upon while his food was being prepared, soon fell asleep, and in his dreams imagined himself successful in the examination, and advanced from one office of dignity and power to another till he had arrived at the station of prime minister in the imaginary kingdom of *Hwa-su*. Supposing himself possessed of all that heart could wish, he was dreaming of being surrounded by friends and children of the second generation, on the joyous anniversary of his birthday, when he awoke and saw the supposed servant boiling his rice beside him, who addressed him in these words:—"Before the yellow rice is cooked, you have already visited in your dreams the kingdom of *Hwa-su*." The astonished scholar exclaimed—"I perceive that you are one of the genii." *Chung-li-kiuen* replied—"Do not be disappointed to find that what you have witnessed is only a dream; the reality is nothing more. Suppose yourself really possessed of all that you have imagined, when it is over what is it but a dream?" The scholar acknowledged the vanity of all worldly pursuits, and determined immediately to renounce the world for the cultivation of virtue. *Chung-li-kiuen* offered to assist him in gaining the condition and blessedness of the genii, saying—"That you may the sooner obtain the three thousand degrees of merit requisite, I will teach you a secret by which you may convert every thing which you point to into gold, and in performing good deeds, and relieving the wants of the distressed, the merit will be quickly and easily obtained." The scholar inquired—"Will the gold ever revert to its original properties?" His instructor replied—"Yes, after a period of years." "Then," answered Lu-tsu, "I decline the proffered boon, for I would not confer a temporary advantage to be followed by disappointment and sorrow." The genius replied—"This act of magnanimity is already equivalent to the three thousand degrees of merit; as a reward for it, you may become one of the genii at once."

Of the other idols of Tauism, the following may be mentioned as the most prominent:

Lue-kung and *Lue-po* are known as the Thunder God and his wife. The former is generally represented with a beak and claws, and sometimes with wings, agreeably to the superstition that electricity exists among the mountains in the form of birds. He holds in his hands a hammer and a drum, with which he is supposed to produce thunder. *Lue-po* is represented with mirrors attached to her hands and feet, whose reflections, when turned in different directions, are supposed to produce lightning.

LUE-KUNG, GOD OF THUNDER.

The goddess *Tau-mu* is represented with eight hands, and is identified with a constellation in the northern heavens. She is supposed to have the power of shortening and prolonging life.

Prominent among the idols seen in Tauist temples are representations of the *San Tsing*, or "Three Pure Ones," one of which is generally regarded as a personification of Lao-ts. It is supposed to be their special office to communicate instruction to mankind.

The *San-Kwan*, or "Three Rulers," generally called *Tien-Kwan*, *Ti-Kwan*, and *Shwuy-Kwan*, that is, "Rulers of Heaven, Earth, and Sea," are indispensable gods of Tauism. They are represented as three brothers, who, on account of their remarkable gifts during life, were after death advanced to these stations of dignity and importance. They are also described by Tauist writers as a trinity in unity.

THE THREE PURE ONES.

The Dragon, which is a universal and prominent object of worship among the Chinese, may properly be classed among the gods of Tauism. The wide domain of the dragon embraces all seas, lakes, rivers, and ponds, and over these he reigns supreme. All the living creatures of the waters are his subjects, and peculiar phenomena of clouds, celestial appearances, and water-spouts are ascribed to his presence and agency.

The exalted conceptions which the Chinese have of the dragon have made this word a favorite one to symbolize and represent the dignity and supremacy of the Chinese Emperor. He is spoken of as seated on the Dragon Throne; to see him is to see the Dragon Face, and his coat of arms is a dragon.

This monster is not regarded by the Chinese as a fabulous animal, but as a real existence which many profess to have frequently seen. Notwithstanding the vague ideas respecting his form and character, paintings and representations of the dragon are often seen, presenting the same uniform appearance. The obtaining a correct likeness is, in the history of the gods, accounted for as follows: A king of the *Tsin* dynasty, wishing to build a bridge over the surface of the sea, in order to enjoy the recreation and fresh air which excursions on such a bridge would afford, the dragon, out of respect for the king and because the work was to be performed within his own dominions, offered to take the superintendence of it. While engaged in this work, the king requested him to display his original form or appearance. This the dragon consented to do, on condition that the king would not cause his portrait to be taken. This condition being complied with, the dragon appeared in his peculiar shape and form, and the king, contrary to his promise, had his portrait taken by a skillful artist. The dragon, resenting the insult, immediately withdrew himself, and the king, to atone for his fault, erected to him a temple.

Besides the *Hai Lung Hwang*, or "Sea-dragon King," there are supposed to be inferior dragons almost innumerable. According to the general theory of correspondence, not only between the celestial and terrestrial, but between the terrestrial and watery worlds, it is supposed that the relative stations and degrees of dignity of the smaller dragons are determined by a series of competitive examinations similar to those described in the fourth chapter. This, by the way, illustrates the strong hold which the system of competitive examinations has on the minds of the people. They hardly think any government complete, or even possible, without it. The great examination of the dragons, which coincides in time with the corresponding literary examination of the people, occurs once in three years, and is held at the crystal palace of the Dragon King, supposed to be situated in some remote region of the sea. The competitors at this examination consists of fish, crabs, turtles, lobsters, snakes, and all kinds of water-reptiles, which have attained to the lower degrees of dragons by successful examinations in the several localities with which they have been connected. When the time arrives for this examination, according to a general command of the Great Dragon, the water in the small streams and canals is elevated, in order to

F

facilitate the egress of the aspirants to dragonship to the sea. An alleged fact that the water of streams and canals sometimes rises very perceptibly in seasons of drought, is often referred to as an evidence of the existence of this examination. It is also believed that there is a certain animal, living in subterranean caverns of the hills, which is assisted in its journey to the sea by a spontaneous flood of water passing from the place of its concealment to the nearest stream, and often carrying away and destroying houses and crops in its progress. It is very common to hear of such floods having occurred in different places, and it would be almost useless to attempt to convince any class of the people that they are not attributable to this cause. This superstition is not local, but general; and it is sufficiently evident that it is not confined to the ignorant and vulgar from the fact that proclamations are sometimes issued by the officers in different places, calling upon the people to hunt and destroy these animals in order to avoid the injury to life and property which they occasion.

The competitors having reached the palace of the Dragon King, the examinations consist in attempts to leap over a high wall, or dragon-gate, as it is called. Success in this attempt secures promotion to the higher degree of dragons, while failures in scaling the wall generally result in concussion against it and consequent death. Crabs, turtles, etc., not being remarkable for their powers of leaping, are supposed to secure the services of an active kind of fish, and to scale the wall by clinging to his tail. This superstition is made use of, and not inaptly, to represent the manner in which many scholars attain degrees by depending upon the assistance of others.

The inferior dragons, like the Dragon King, are supposed not to have material forms (except as they assume them). They are believed to exist in great numbers in the deeper places of rivers, ponds, and streams. Many such spots in different localities are specified as the dwelling-places of dragons. In times of drought the people resort to these places to pray for rain, and sometimes the civil officers go in person. Any reptile which may be found on the borders of the dragon pool, whether it be a frog, or worm, or snake, is regarded as the assumed body of the dragon, and is carried with great pomp and reverence to the office of the civil magistrate, who is required to worship it and pray for rain. In times of drought, persons have been known to sacrifice their lives, by drowning themselves in a dragon pool, in order by their earnestness to compel the dragon to send rain, and with a view to being deified on account of their merit. Temples are erected for the worship of the dragon throughout the empire, and, strange to say, he is in these temples represented in the form of a man.

Another object of worship, which is invested with great importance in the eyes of the people, is that of the *Tu-ti Poo-sah*, or "Earth God." To a passing traveller no object of idolatrous worship would be more observable than the idols of this class, as they are everywhere seen by the roadside. They are lowest in dignity of the gods of China, and on that account the worship of them is regarded as most important and indispensable, for the same reason that a citizen has more to do, practically, with the petty officers of his village than with his sovereign.

The size of the images corresponds to the inferiority of the god. They are generally made of stone, and are found in unfrequented as well as populous places. They are seen in little shrines a few feet high in the open country, or in resting-houses or pavilions by the roadside. In the lists of the gods they correspond to the country constables, who have the charge of small neighborhoods. Not only different neighborhoods but hills and bridges have their *Tu-ti Poo-sah*. Like other gods, those of this class are also supposed to be good men of former times, but they are so numerous and insignificant that they are not designated by particular names, but only by the general name *Tu-ti*, coupled with the names of the places over which they preside.

But the insignificant image of the *Tu-ti* fails to satisfy the people in paying their homage to the earth, and they also worship the divinity of the earth without an image. Respecting this worship the Chinese have very confused and conflicting views. They speak of this divinity as a divine emanation from the earth, or an all-pervading, life-giving influence, connected with and everywhere existing in earthly matter. They have the greatest dread of offending this deity, and hardly dare to move a clod of earth for fear of incurring his displeasure. Accordingly, when earth is to be removed for any purpose, a ceremony is performed, called *Kao tu*, or informing the earth. This ceremony consists in offering idolatrous worship, and sacrifices of food, in the usual manner, with the design of acquainting the divinity with the intention of the offerer, and of securing his favor and assistance. These ceremonies are always performed preparatory to laying the foundation of a house or a wall, or constructing kitchen ranges, tombs, etc. It is currently reported and believed that if any of the works are undertaken by an individual neglecting these ceremonies he will be punished by violent pains, if not protracted disease or death.

It is useless to refer to other gods of less note, descriptions of which might be added indefinitely. Many of the national gods, or deified heroes of China, might properly be regarded as belonging to Tauism, and many of the superstitious practices of the people, which will be described in subsequent chapters, seem to have been suggested by and naturally to belong to this system.

Tauism, on account of its native origin, or more pretentious character, or for both reasons combined, is preferred to Buddhism by the Chinese rulers, and Tauist priests and Tauist forms are constantly made use of in the State worship, which will be described in the next chapter.

Idols in Tauist temples are generally of a smaller size than those of Buddhism, and, unlike the latter, many of them are found in a second or upper story. In the general appearance of Buddhist and Tauist idols there is nothing to distinguish them; and the temples belonging to these different systems both externally and internally present very nearly the same appearance.

The priests of Tauism are comparatively few. Their ranks are filled in the same way as those of the Buddhist priesthood, and their employments in the temples are very much the same. They have a dress which distinguishes them from the common people as well as from Buddhist priests, and are not absolutely required to live on a vegetable diet. They do not shave the whole head like Buddhists, but the hair, which is left to grow like that of the common people, is, instead of being braided in a cue, tied in a knot on the top of the head.

While the object of the Buddhist devotee is to be absorbed into the unconscious being of his favorite idol, that of the Tauist is to become a *Sien-jin*, that is, one of the genii. It is difficult to give a clear idea of the Chinese conception of *Sien-jin*. They are beings who, by certain precautions, escape death, and with ethereal bodies, capable of assuming different forms and shapes, enjoy an uninterrupted existence of dreamy happiness, either separated from or mingling with the race of mortals at pleasure. The principal and favorite places of their abode are four sacred mountains, situated far in the unknown ocean, and separated from the abodes of men by a sea filled with a subtile fluid called *Joh-shwuy*—" weak water," which is not even capable of supporting a feather.

To the attainment of this state of blessedness three things are requisite: the cultivation of the heart, a peculiar discipline for the body, and the elixir of life, or a potion with an inherent virtue to insure immortality. The cultivation of the heart consists in leading a life of retirement, austerity, and meditation. The peculiar regimen to which the body is subjected is designed to husband and retain the natural energies of the physical system, and promote and increase its vitality. It consists in the unmeaning acts of sitting cross-legged, swallowing the saliva, rubbing the flesh (particularly the ears, the hands, and the crown of the head), rolling the eyes, and striking together the teeth. The work of preparing the elixir of life, which is called *Lien-tan*, must be performed by each devotee for himself. Having collected the proper ingredients, they are put in a large kettle and boiled over a fire, neither too hot nor too cold, for a period of eighty-one days. It is said that if the devotee has been laborious and conscientious in his previous preparation of mind and body, the attempt will prove successful; if not, all his efforts will be unavailing. Few at the present day have any idea of becoming *Sien-jin*, or regard the priesthood in any other light than as a means of obtaining a livelihood.

The *Shin Sien Tung Kien*, a "Complete Mirror of Gods and Genii," which is a work of four large volumes, gives an account of the history and character of more than three hundred *Sien-jin*, together with curious statements respecting the origin of the world and mankind.

While the above mode of becoming *Sien-jin* is regarded as the proper and authorized one, it is supposed that the same end may be attained in a shorter and easier manner by the use of magic, the invocation of evil spirits, and by obtaining in different ways the principle of vitality from other human bodies. This class of *Sien-jin*, though possessed of equal powers with others, are regarded as unauthorized intruders, doomed to a violent and untimely end.

It is remarkable that many kinds of animals are supposed to have the power of attaining to the same condition of spirits or demons, and that in doing so there are also for them authorized and unauthorized methods. It is said that a fox, according to the authorized mode, can attain to this state in one thousand years. Animals are, however, supposed generally to use other irregular means to expedite their progress. Cats are particularly liable to the suspicion of wishing to better their condition in the scale of existence, and are said to accomplish this end in two ways. The first and most effective is that of drawing the vital principle from the bodies of men, which desire is supposed to account for their fondness of proximity to the human species; another method is that of drawing a revivifying principle from the rays of the moon when full-orbed. It is said and believed that cats are often seen on moonlight nights drinking in with open mouth the virtues of these rays, and that they sometimes worship, after the manner of men, the bright-faced luminary. It is generally believed that a host of demons and evil spirits, which afflict and bring misery upon men, have their origin in this manner, and that after avoiding for a time the vengeance of the gods they are destined sooner or later to be destroyed by lightning, as no less subtle agent can affect them.

The people are accustomed from infancy to hear stories of ghosts and spirits and genii; and the natural desire for the marvellous, without the guidance and restraints of revelation, grows by what it feeds upon, and prepares the mind for the reception of monstrous absurdities, and for being swayed by groundless fears.

Comparatively speaking, there is little to attract women to Tauist temples as worshipers. There is, however, a system of fast days which is the source of some small gain to the priests. As it is regarded meritorious to fast, there are fast days connected with the worship of several idols, and the observance of these days is supposed to secure the favor and protection of these different idols. Some women observe the fast days of one idol, some of another, and some of several at the same time, and when the prescribed days are completed they resort to the temples to celebrate the event with thanksgiving, and are expected to leave more or less money with the priests. It is common, when an individual is sick, for different members of his family to assume vows to perform each one a different fast for his benefit. Children also, as a mark of filial piety, sometimes undertake fasts for the benefit of their parents. On the birthdays of different gods the temples are also visited by considerable numbers of women. The money derived from this ordinary worship, from occasional services at funerals, etc., and from the proceeds of the lands connected with different establishments, serves to keep the buildings in repair, and supports the few priests connected with them.

The following are prominent among the religious practices or ceremonies of Tauism:

Fah hih—"Sending a Dispatch," is performed in cases of sickness. A statement of the idolatrous worship which has been performed is written on a piece of paper, together with a petition to some deity for assistance. This paper is burned by the officiating priest, who professes to determine by observing the process of burning whether the god returns a favorable or unfavorable answer.

Shang-tien-piau—"Sending a Message to Heaven," also consists in burning a paper on which the message is written. The performer of the ceremony, in this case, feigns sleep when the paper is being burned, and it is believed that his soul leaves the body, conveys the message to heaven, and brings back an answer in return.

Another ceremony, called *Hwa-fu*—"Writing a Charm," consists in writing a few unintelligible characters, or delineating a rude representation of a god on a small piece of paper, which is regarded as representing or securing the presence of some divinity. Such pieces of paper are sometimes hung over the bed of a sick person as a spell.

A few of the more expert of the Tauist priests are supposed to be possessed of a knowledge of enchantments and incantations, which they generally profess to have derived from some of the *Sien-jin*, or genii. By the repeating of these incantations, they are believed to have the power of inflicting evil upon men, and calling spirits to their aid, and subjecting them to their commands. A book of six volumes, called *Wan fah kwei tsung*, a "Collection of a Thousand Magic Arts," contains a description in detail of different kinds of magic, sorcery, and juggling.

There is connected with Tauism a class of books which are designed to promote the cultivation of virtue, and are gratuitously distributed by those who wish to acquire merit by so doing. One of these is the *Yuh lih chau chwen*, which gives the different punishments of hell consequent on the commission of different crimes, with a view to deter men from the commission of these crimes.

The *Kung kwo keh*, or "Graduated Scale of Merit," gives the comparative amount of merit or demerit belonging to different actions. Other works of the same character, and moral tracts on the cultivation of different virtues, are frequently circulated by the rich, but it is done rather from the desire to secure merit and the praise of men than the hope of really benefiting others.

As compared with Buddhism, the number of Tauist temples, and the number of worshipers in them, and the amount of money expended in this worship, are insignificant. The reason why Tauist temples are comparatively so few, and so much neglected, is because this religion does not treat of sin, and escape from its consequences, and has for its object a prolongation of this life rather than preparation for the life to come.

CHAPTER X.

NATIONAL RELIGIOUS RITES AND BELIEFS.

These Rites originated in various Periods, and from various Sources.—They are regarded as possessed of a superior and orthodox Character.—Ancestral Worship.—Worship of the Kitchen God.—State Worship, or that performed by Officers in the Capital and in the Provinces.—Worship of Confucius and of the God of War, and the God of Literature.—Sacrifices to neglected Ghosts.—Welcoming of the Spring.—Worship of Deified Heroes.

I PROPOSE in this chapter to speak of various religious beliefs and forms of idolatrous worship which have originated at different times and from different sources, and have received a more or less formal recognition and sanction, not only from the people generally, but from the government. Some of these forms of worship present the idolatrous side of Confucianism, in distinction from the preceptive or moral features of it which were given in the third chapter. Other idolatrous rites seem to have resulted from the teachings of Buddhism and Tauism. The whole constitutes the natural outgrowth of the Chinese mind, under the various influences to which it has been subjected, and presents to their view a kind of superior, refined, authorized, and orthodox system of worship.

First and foremost among the national idolatrous rites of China stands Ancestral Worship, which properly belongs to Confucianism, having been practiced long before the time of Confucius, and sanctioned by his teachings and example. It is one of the oldest forms of idolatry now known in China; it has the strongest hold on the minds of the people, and is one of the principal obstacles in the way of the introduction of Christianity. Its observances are regarded as a necessary part of the duties belonging to filial piety, and they are engaged in with great preciseness and ostentation. Besides the motives arising from a grateful recollection of past favors, children are prompted to engage in acts of religious homage to their parents by the hope of being protected by them, and the fear of incurring their displeasure.

ANCESTRAL TABLET REPRESENTING ONE PERSON.

The visible objects of worship are ancestral tablets and painted portraits of the deceased. The tablets or paintings of both parents are invariably worshiped together if both are dead. The ancestral tablets are made of wood, and are about a foot high. The characters written upon them record the name and title of the deceased, with the precise hour of their birth and death, and the names of their sons. It is supposed that a man has three spirits, one of which, after death, resides in this tablet, and another in the tomb, while the third goes to Hades, and in process of time reappears in a new state of existence.

The paintings or effigies, which are also objects of worship, are taken after death. Though they may to some degree resemble the individual whom they represent, they are very unlike the portrait of a living person. They have also their peculiar name, which serves still further to mark the distinction between them and portraits of the living. These effigies are generally brought out and worshiped only at the beginning of the new year, on the birthdays of the deceased, and when they are honored with theatrical exhibitions.

The worship of ancestors differs very little in its character from that of idols, and consists in prostrations, offerings of cooked food, and the burning of incense, candles, and paper-money, and sometimes theatrical plays. It is performed at the dwelling-house, the family temple, or the tomb.

Family temples are large and costly edifices, resembling, in their external appearance, temples for the worship of idols. Like them, the high wall on the outside encloses a large open court, in one end of which is a stage for theatricals. In the building on the side of the court opposite the stage you see, instead of the idols found in temples dedicated to them, a large collection of ancestral tablets deposited on shelves, about four or five inches wide, extending all the way across the temple, and rising one above another from the front like the seats of a gallery. These tablets sometimes date back a thousand years, and are very numerous. In connection with ancestral temples are often found genealogical tables, but many temples with small incomes are unable to procure them, on account of the trouble and expense which they necessitate.

These temples are constructed by the wealthy in honor of their immediate ancestors, and at first contain only the tablets of a few generations. As the family increases from age to age, though it may contain many poor members, it generally includes enough wealth to keep the temple in repair and provide for its expenses. It is very common for persons of property at their death to leave a piece of ground for the use of the family temple, the yearly proceeds of which are added to a common fund for repairs and providing sacrifices and theatricals.

The tablets of deceased females are seldom found in the temples, though they sometimes occupy separate side apartments. The tablets of unmarried males are not generally admitted. In cases of the death of unmarried young men of particular promise and prominence, the following expedient is adopted to rescue their names from oblivion. An arrangement is made with another family which has lost a member of about the same age of the opposite sex, by which ceremonies representing the betrothal and marriage of the deceased parties are performed. After this, a child of some other member of the family may be reckoned to them, as a son, and so the line of the deceased be transmitted, and his tablet, with those of his reputed wife and descendants, placed in the family temple. Abandoned characters are also denied the privilege of participating in the ceremonies of the family temple while living, or having their tablets deposited in it when dead. Such persons are said to be "expelled from the family."

Ancestral temples are perhaps more numerous than any others in China. Almost every small village contains at least one, most of these villages being composed principally of inhabitants of the same name or family.

The ancestral temple is the most sacred spot on earth to a Chinaman. Here repose the spirits of his ancestors; this is the place for family meetings on sacrificial days; here he expects that his spirit will find its last resting-place, and share in the homage and offerings of future generations. These facts relating to ancestral worship explain the anxiety of the Chinese who visit our Western coast to have their bodies carried back to their homes in case of death. They wish their dust to mingle with that of their ancestors, and their spirits to be restored to their ancestral temples, else they would be unhoused, unfed, uncared for; wandering, starving, homeless ghosts in a foreign land—a condition than which nothing imaginable is more to be dreaded.

As regards the sacrifices in ancestral temples, we sometimes say to the people offering them, "Nothing is eaten; when you take it away to eat it yourselves, it remains the same in substance, weight, and taste. "True," they are apt to reply, "spirits do not partake of material food; they appropriate the spiritual or impalpable essence or exhalations, and when they have satisfied themselves, we make use of what remains." Others, more intelligent and thoughtful, reply, "We know that nothing is eaten; but we can not rest satisfied without giving some outward expression of our grateful feelings; we wish to indicate how fondly we cherish the memory of our ancestors, how happy we should be to have them sit down with us at our board, and to have the privilege of ministering to their wants."

GOD OF THE KITCHEN.

The worship of the *Kitchen God* occupies also an important place in the national religious rites. This form of idolatry is about as ancient as the one just described, and as universal, being practiced in every family. The Kitchen God has no temple, and no image. It is worshiped under the representation of a paper engraving, generally about a foot square, which is pasted on the kitchen range. This may be regarded as the household divinity of China. It is supposed that it takes cognizance of every thing which transpires in the family, and makes a report at the close of the year, in the presence of the chief of the gods, *Yuh-hwang-ta-ti.* The night when he is supposed to take his departure is regarded as a very important occasion. All the members of the family are present, and a feast is given for and in honor of the god, intended to propitiate him, and induce him to make as favorable a report at head-quarters as possible. At the close of the feast the paper god is removed from the kitchen range and burned; and thus in imagination is transported on the wings of flame to the spirit land, and the kitchen is for a few days without a god. On the first day of the new year a new paper is procured, and the Kitchen God is invoked to resume his place in the family. There can be little doubt that the belief of the constant presence of this god has the tendency to restrain from evil, and to bring the words and actions of the family into closer accord with what they deem to be right and proper.

The *State Worship* forms a prominent part of the national religious observances of the Chinese. By the term State worship as here used is meant, not forms of worship recommended by the State to the people, but those practiced exclusively by the rulers, in which the people have no part. It consists in the use of idolatrous rites and ceremonies, made binding by the Constitution of the empire on all its officers, including the Emperor and the imperial clan in the capital. These services being involuntary and constrained, are, of all the varieties of Chinese worship, the most formal and heartless. They are chiefly a perpetuation of ancient usages, and are conducted and regulated, for the most part, by rules prescribed in the ancient classics, particularly the Book of Rites.

In the capital, the Emperor and members of the imperial clan, and high officers of state connected with the Board of Rites, worship and sacrifice to objects which are divided into three classes or grades. First and highest are* "heaven, earth, spirits of deceased monarchs of the present dynasty, and gods of the land and grain, and the special patrons of the dynasty. Under the second grade are eight objects, viz: the sun, the moon, the *manes* of the emperors and kings of former dynas-

* Williams's "Middle Kingdom."

ties, Confucius, the ancient patrons of agriculture and silk weaving, the gods of heaven and of earth, and of the passing year." The inferior objects are "the ancient patrons of the healing art, and the innumerable spirits of deceased philanthropists, eminent statesmen, martyrs to virtue, etc., clouds, rain, wind, and thunder, the five celebrated mountains, four seas and four rivers, famous hills, and great water-courses, etc." The worship of these objects is performed in different temples, and with different ceremonies, which it is impossible to describe in detail.

Of the rites belonging to the State worship performed by officers in the provinces, among the most prominent are those connected with the temples called *Cheng-hwang-miao*. An edifice of this kind may be found in each city in the empire. Literally translated, these characters represent the "Temple of the Wall and Moat." These buildings contain the tutelar divinities of each city, whose offices and duties are supposed to correspond to those of the actual living officers. These two classes of rulers, spiritual and corporeal, are thus associated together, and administer the affairs of the city conjointly. This superstition is in accordance with a general notion very prevalent in China, that an exact correspondence exists between the visible and invisible worlds.

These *Cheng-hwang-miao* are among the largest and finest specimens of Chinese architecture, and in the eyes of the people form one of the chief attractions of every city. They are regarded much in the same light as the *Yia muns*, or residences of the city officers. Accordingly, in addition to the *Cheng-hwang*, or ruler of the city, the temple is filled with images of inferior officers and servants. In the back part are private apartments, containing images of the *Cheng-hwang's* wives, and a room completely furnished with a bed (which is made every day) and clothes-racks, clothes-presses, etc. Shoes and different articles of wearing apparel are frequently presented to the *Cheng-hwang* and his wives, whose clothes are continually changed with the changing seasons. On the first and fifteenth of each month, the officers visit this temple early in the morning, with a large retinue and great parade, to pay their respects, the ceremony consisting in making prostrations and burning incense. In times of exigency and doubt the officers also apply to the *Cheng-hwang* for assistance, as both the visible and invisible rulers are regarded as jointly responsible for the prosperity of the city and the execution of the laws. In times of drought or sickness the officers repair to the *Cheng-hwang* to pray him to intercede with *Yuh-hwang Shang-ti*, who is chief of all the gods, in their behalf. When difficulties arise among the people, or it is impossible to bring offenders to justice, the same expedient is sometimes resorted to.

As the business of the *Cheng-hwang* is supposed to call him occasionally away from the temple, a smaller image is made about the size of a man, which is borne through the streets as officers are, while the larger one always remains in its place in the temple.

It being customary in China for officers to be continually removed from one place to another by the will of the Emperor, so it is supposed that the divinities of each city are continually changing. Accordingly, the gods of this temple do not, like others, have permanent names. The same images answer from year to year, but the individual spirits are supposed to change. It is believed that a man in the province of Kiang-si, called *Chang-tien-sz*, who has an office which is transmitted in his family from one generation to another, is possessed of means of communicating with spirits, and he is continually consulted with reference to what individual of the past is exercising jurisdiction over particular cities.

But the people are also interested in the *Cheng-hwang-miao*, and it may be well to mention in this connection some of the ceremonies which they perform in it, though they are not a part of the State worship, being entirely voluntary. They look up to the idols which it contains as their protectors, and often appeal to them when they are wronged by their fellow-citizens, or fail to obtain justice from their rulers. The names of ten large idols found in the temple of a *Fu* city will indicate their characters and the use which is made of them. The first is *Hia-ti-sz*, who is supposed to take charge of the garments with which the dead are buried. After the death of an individual an accurate list is made of his clothes, which list is supposed, by being burned, to be transmitted to this god, whose business it is to see that the possessor is not robbed of them on his way to Hades. After this idol are seen in regular order *Fuh-luh-sz*, who presides over happiness and wages; *Chau-tsu-sz*, who presides over cursing and railing, keeping an accurate account of all sins of this kind which are committed; *Li-yih-sz*, who presides over boundaries; *Sang-chan-sz*, who presides over child-birth; *Tsai-sang-sz*, who presides over the slaying of animals; *Kiai-ngeh-sz*, who presides over persons in distress; *Wan-yih-sz*, who presides over the pestilence; *Suh-pu-sz*, the quick avenger, and *Yiu-shau-sz*, who adds length of days.

The *Suh-pu-sz*, or quick avenger, is worshiped more than all the other gods together.

Many are the wonderful tales which are told in proof of his vigilance and power. He is applied to for revenge by those who have been falsely accused; those who have had property stolen; those who, though in the right, have been overcome in lawsuits by persons possessed of wealth and influence; those who have difficulties in settling accounts, and by others under similar circumstances. His assistance is generally sought in the following manner: The suppliant goes to the temple in company with a priest, or master of ceremonies, who writes a *fu*, or charm, and nails it with a chicken's head before the god. This is done with the design of arousing him, and bringing the importance of the case distinctly before him. A paper is also burned, stating the character of the offense; and when this ceremony is performed the matter is left in the hands of the god.

Persons bitterly enraged against each other sometimes meet before this god to ask him to be the arbiter of their difficulties, and go away from his presence satisfied that the matter will be properly disposed of, and that the offending party will sooner or later meet with condign punishment. Some present their grievances before the god in a clandestine manner for fear of irritating the opposite party by a knowledge of the course that they are pursuing; some are frightened into the performance of duty by the threat of having their case brought before *Suh-pu-sz.* It is commonly reported that guilty persons who have been accused before this god are often seized with extreme mental and bodily anguish, and die uttering incoherent expressions respecting their crimes, and the punishment they are suffering for them from the hands of this avenger.

Each city in China contains also a temple erected to the honor of Confucius, in which officers are required to present worship and offerings on the occasions of the vernal and autumnal equinoxes. These temples, which are generally large and costly, contain no images, as the Chinese have too much respect for Confucius to worship him through an image. This would be degrading him to the level of ordinary gods. He is represented in the most prominent place in the building by a tablet, upon which is inscribed, in large gold characters, "The Great and Holy Sage." Tablets representing his principal disciples, to the number of several hundreds, occupy subordinate places. The services in this temple are performed by the officers and their attendants at the fifth watch, which is before day-break. Whole oxen, hogs, and sheep are

TRADITIONAL LIKENESS OF CONFUCIUS.

included among the offerings. The plates and dishes, as well as the instruments of music which are used, are of an antique style, and every thing connected with the worship is calculated to designate it as peculiarly important and sacred.

KWAN-TI, CHINESE GOD OF WAR.

The officers are also required to worship regularly in the temples of the God of War and the God of Literature, one of each of which may be found in every Chinese city. These gods, as well as the gods of the *Cheng-hwang-miao*, and other popular divinities, are all deified men of previous generations. The object of the government in prescribing worship in these temples seems to be, not so much to propitiate these deities as to secure the efficiency and loyalty of the worshipers, by keeping continually before them the most noted of the great and good of the past as examples, and perhaps holding out to them the hope of being hereafter gods themselves, as their reward.

An idolatrous ceremony is also required of the officers, for the benefit of neglected ghosts, which will be best understood by reference to its origin. The first Emperor of the *Ming* dynasty was in his childhood a herds-boy. He lost his parents when very young, and had no knowledge of the place of their interment. When he reached the throne, being unable to sacrifice at the graves of his ancestors, he commanded his officers throughout the empire to sacrifice three times a year to the shades of those whose graves are neglected. This ceremony is still observed, and is called *Siùh-ku*—"Pitying the Unfortunate." On the appointed days the officers, together with the *Cheng-hwang*, are borne in sedans outside the city wall,

PART OF A PROCESSION IN HONOR OF SPRING, IN WHICH A MOCK BUFFALO IS CARRIED THROUGH THE STREETS.

where the prescribed offerings are made, and ceremonies performed.

Another ceremony, called *Ying-chun*—"The Welcoming of Spring," is observed every year on the first day of spring. The officers go out through the east gate of the city, and find clay images of a ploughman and his ox, which have been previously made for the occasion. After witnessing a theatrical play in the temple of the God of Agriculture, which is designed to exhort the people to be industrious in agricultural pursuits, the two clay images are brought back into the city, when idolatrous worship is paid to them. On the following day they are broken in pieces in the hall devoted to the god of the passing year, which is found in Tauist temples. The fragments of these images are highly prized, and eagerly sought by the people, who carry them to their homes as a pledge of good luck for the season. The design of this ceremony seems to be to inculcate veneration for the ox and respect for husbandry.

Homage paid to *Deified Heroes* may properly be regarded as belonging to the national idolatry of China, as all these deities are prominent men in Chinese history, and have been deified by the express authority of the Emperor. The most of these gods are of comparatively recent origin. The births of but few date back farther than the *Sung* dynasty, which assumed the government of the empire A.D. 976. The title or office of a god is derived from the reigning sovereign. The conferring of these titles sometimes originates in the wish of the Emperor to hold up as an example one who has distinguished himself by his loyalty or efficiency in the civil or military service, and sometimes in the gratitude of the people, who introduce to the Emperor those who have won their hearts by favors, and purchase for them divine titles. When a community can not afford sufficient money to secure the public appointment and recognition of their favorite idol, they sometimes erect their temple and enshrine their god without this recognition. The different offices or degrees of divine honor conferred by the Emperor are no less than seven, exclusive of official titles of the living, which are sometimes retained after death as divine titles by those who are deified. The two lowest titles have now fallen into disuse, as it would be considered disrespectful to place a god at the foot of the list. Sometimes persons are deified by the Emperor while still living. The honors of the dead are also often increased, on account of some imagined interference or protection, and they are advanced to a higher grade in the scale of deified dignitaries. The most of those deified by the Emperor of his own accord are persons who have lost their lives in his service, and are thus held up as examples for imitation. It is a striking fact that, of all the gods, only the deities of the highest class attain to the title of *ti*, which belongs to the Emperor, who seems to regard it as an act of condescension to share this title with them, and adds to his own title the character *hwang*, meaning greatest.

Books which give the names and histories of the gods only present the most prominent of them, while by far the greater portion is not noticed. In the *Shin Sien Tung Kien*, or "Complete Mirror of Gods and Genii," compiled about two hundred years ago, an account of Jesus our Saviour, as a god of the West, is given, in connection with the histories of many of the gods of the Chinese Empire. It presents a succinct and truthful narrative of his birth, life, sufferings, and death, followed by statements respecting the deification and worship of the Virgin Mary; thus giving clear evidence of its Roman Catholic origin. Our indignation at seeing the name of our Saviour in such a connection is only abated by the consideration that it was done in ignorance; indeed, most Chinese would consider it a singular privilege and honor that a foreign name should be thus associated.

Of the gods which are known and worshiped throughout the whole empire there are comparatively very few. The highest rank and honors are awarded to Confucius. He was formerly enrolled among the deities of the empire with the title *hwang*, or king; but an Emperor of the *Ming* dynasty, thinking it an indignity that Confucius should only rank as equal in divine honors to other gods and to himself, determined that none of the ordinary titles should be applied to him, but that the whole nation should express their special veneration and indebtedness to him by calling him *Ta Ching Che Shing Sien S*—"The Great, Perfect, Most Holy Teacher."

Yuh Hwang Ta Ti, chief of all the gods, has temples erected to him exclusively, and his image occupies a prominent place in the Tauist temples. The people seldom pay homage to him, however, and when they do, it is rather in the form of adoration than petition, as he is regarded as too far removed in dignity from mortals to take any immediate cognizance of individual wants.

The God of War is everywhere worshiped, and has temples erected to him throughout the empire. During the present civil war in China the Emperor has heaped new honors upon him, professedly, on account of alleged deliverances, but no doubt principally to inspire confidence in the fortunes of his dynasty.

The God of Wealth, though inferior to many of the other gods in rank, is no doubt the one most regarded. He has not only large temples erected solely in honor of him, but every shop contains a small image of him in a little shrine, before which incense is continually burned. Other gods of general notoriety might be mentioned, but the above may be considered as the most noted, and most extensively worshiped. The histories of the gods great and small which are made up of frivolous and often incredible statements, would fill volumes. A condensed account of one of these histories may be of interest, as a specimen of the whole.

The popular story respecting *Tsai-shin Pu-sah*—"The God of Wealth," is as follows: He was originally a tax-gatherer, and once called upon a family who professed their inability to pay their tax, and determined to stay with them till he obtained it. Before retiring to rest, he was surprised to hear under his window the following address of an old hen to her young brood: "My master has a guest in his house, and has determined to kill me to-morrow to furnish his table. What will become of you, my dear little nestlings, weak in body, and inexperienced in the ways of the world? I must certainly give you my parting advice, as you will soon be left without any one to watch over you. Above, you must be careful that the hawk does not pounce upon you; below, that men do not tread upon you. You must not eat too much—you thus will avoid disease; born in the same nest, you must not quarrel."

The tax-gatherer, struck with this address, discoursed to himself upon it thus: "If a short-lived and insignificant fowl exhibits so much understanding, and makes such plans for the future, what is the dignity of man, and how should he provide for his future wants?" Influenced by such thoughts, he determined immediately to renounce the world, and set out at once to find a place of retirement, in order to lead the life of a recluse and cultivate virtue. With this resolution he proceeded on his way, and was met by a tiger, but so far from being terrified, he rushed forward, laid his hand upon his mane, leaped upon his back, and rode him away to his retreat. After attaining to the perfection of virtue he became a god. Such is the common popular tradition respecting the god most worshiped in China.

The less noted gods, which have only a local fame, are almost innumerable. They are officers who, by their impartial administration of justice and by acts of benevolence, have endeared themselves to the hearts of the people, or private citizens who are revered on account of their virtues. Some are known in but one place, and worshiped in but one temple; others are known and worshiped in several temples in the same vicinity. Some, though their fame may be confined to one place, receive there honors hardly second to those of any other god. Every section and country has its local god and local temple, with which the people of each place are identified, and in which they feel a peculiar interest. These temples furnish places for the inhabitants of each neighborhood to meet for deliberation and consultation on topics of general interest.

In cities men of each class or occupation have their own peculiar deities, to which, in addition to the gods which they worship in common with the people generally, they pay especial homage. Scholars worship the God of Letters; business men the God of Wealth; dealers in medicine the god who discovered medicines; carpenters the god who invented the measuring rule; sailors the goddess of the seas, lakes, and rivers over which they pass, and so on indefinitely. The temples of the patrons of different arts and employments are also used as resorts for general consultation by the craftsmen to whom they severally belong.

Sometimes the people, impatient to show their gratitude to their benefactors, erect temples to them while living. Two large buildings of this class in Ningpo were erected to officers who succeeded in draining unhealthy parts of the city.

CHAPTER XI.

MUTUAL RELATIONS AND INFLUENCES OF THE RELIGIOUS SYSTEMS OF CHINA.

Partial and imperfect Character of the Knowledge derived from Natural Religion.—Moral more clearly apprehended than Religious or Spiritual Truth.—Buddhism and Tauism attempt to supply the Defects of Confucianism.—Special Characteristics and Relations of these Systems.—Religious Views of the People vague and chaotic.—The three Systems generally regarded as Supplementary to each other.—A proximate Estimate of the Number of Idol Temples in China.—Description of different kinds of Sacrifices and Offerings.—The Doctrines and Practices of Idolatry perversions of great Truths.—Answer to the question, "Have the Chinese any Idea of one Supreme Deity?"—General Character of Chinese Idolatry as compared with that of other Countries.—Evidences of Discontent with Idolatry.—Encouraging Facts, and the Duty of the Church.

The history of religious opinions in China illustrates at once the glory and the shame of our fallen nature. We see evidenced in the very earliest period of Chinese history a desire to search out the principles of absolute and eternal truth, and an ability to a certain extent to do so. The main doctrines of the Confucian ethics are identical with those which have originated in other countries, and which we find in the Christian revelation. These doctrines are recognized and received by the people as necessary and self-evident truths of supreme authority. They are the revelation of God's will, and of his character in our common nature.

For some reason, however, the sphere of truth illuminated by the light of nature is partial and incomplete. Only the duties of man to man, in the relations of the present life, are clearly brought to view. The character of God, our relations to him, the nature of the soul, and our future destiny are subjects which the Chinese seem to have very imperfectly apprehended, or been entirely ignorant of.

This may have been because these subjects are more mysterious in their very nature; or because man, from his aversion to God, shuts his eyes to the truth, and will not see when he might; or because of judicial blindness, inflicted on account of disobedience and idolatry. It may be that the moral wreck of the fall would have been greater had not God in mercy, by a special intervention, abated the natural results of it so far as to leave enough of truth and enough of moral principle and impulses to form the basis of society and government, rendering man's condition in the world comparatively tolerable and happy.

However this may be, the fact is that more than 3000 years ago the Chinese were possessed of a great deal of moral truth, and a very little religious; and that from that time to this they have made no advance, but have rather been going backward.

But though Confucianism gives to the Chinese no religion, and discourages inquiries with reference to gods and things mysterious, as unnecessary and useless, still the religious instinct is so strong, and the desire to have objects of religious worship so imperative, that the people would have some religion, true or false. Buddhism came in to satisfy the religious want which Confucianism left unsupplied.

But Buddhism, while it treats largely of a future world and preparation for it, is very meagre in its teachings with reference to the present. The gods of Buddhism inhabited an ideal world or presided over the regions of Hades, and its votaries were directed to seek seclusion from the world and society. Tauism has held its influence over the people, because it appeals to instincts and wants which Buddhism has neglected or ignored. It has filled the earth and sea and skies with deities; endeavored to unravel the mysteries of nature; and furnished gods who cared for the wants of man's present state.

These two systems have their elements of attraction and

repulsion. While they recommended themselves to the Chinese on account of their supplying some religious wants, they were repugnant and unsatisfactory on account of their extravagant pretensions and want of evidence, and because they were antagonistic to the spirit and teachings of Confucianism. They were alternately persecuted and fostered, proscribed and patronized by different Chinese emperors. By degrees they impressed themselves upon the Chinese mind, and their ideas became incorporated with the language, literature, and social customs of the country. They are now neither persecuted nor fostered, but tolerated, as an integral and necessary part of the institutions of the country.

In the mean time, not only the people but the government of China was gradually influenced by these systems, and sanctioned many of their ideas and ceremonies, and adopted them in its State ritual. Those forms of religious worship growing out of Buddhism and Tauism, and either directly or by implication sanctioned by the government, I have associated with the ancient forms of worship practiced before the time of Confucius, under the general term National Worship, which embraces a variety of religious observances, originating in different periods, and of entirely different characters. As regards origin, they are not more national than Tauism, and, as regards general prevalence, hardly more so than either Buddhism or Tauism. I have called them national, because they are regarded by intelligent natives as more in harmony with the genius of the Chinese government, and receive an open and decided sanction and acknowledgment from the government which Buddhism and Tauism do not.

In their original and fundamental characteristics, Confucianism is moral, Buddhism metaphysical, and Tauism materialistic.* While the first of these systems has retained its original character the other two have been popularized, retaining, however, the original idea in a modified form. They

* See Edkins's "Religious Condition of the Chinese."

have conformed to the tastes and requirements of the people, or, rather, been modified by priests, so as better to please the people and attract them to the temples. At present, Confucianism may still be designated as a system of morality, the National Worship as formalism, Buddhism as religious fanaticism, and Tauism as superstition. The National Worship is nearly allied to Tauism, as both relate principally to this life rather than the life to come.

While these different religions or forms of worship are adapted to different classes, and to the tastes and religious proclivities of different individuals, they have not divided the Chinese into sects, and few of the people adopt any system exclusively. The religious notions of the masses are vague and chaotic. By a strange perversity of intellect, they have a kind of belief in all these systems, though diverse and inconsistent, while they can hardly be said to believe truly in any of them. Most of their worship is a matter of custom, rather than of serious conviction. They feel that they must worship something, and, to satisfy their consciences and avoid being singular, they pay their homage to the only objects of religious worship with which they are acquainted. Confused with the multiplicity of gods, some try to worship them all, for fear that the true one, or rather the most important one, may be neglected.

A few of the priests and a few among the people are sincere and earnest in their devotions at idol shrines, and seem to make religion the great end and aim of their lives. While the general government formally and ostensibly denounces the popular idolatry, as it is the stereotyped custom to do, the Emperor and officials of every rank contribute immense sums of money to build, repair, or beautify the temples. Officers, after attending to the formal and heartless rites of the State religion, worship with the common people in Buddhist or Tauist temples, or both.

Literary men are generally atheists or pantheists. Still they will say that it is very desirable for the common people, and women whose moral perceptions are obtuse, and who can not think, to have idols set before them to awe and restrain them; and out of regard to the general custom, or from force of habit, they will perhaps worship with them.

A few literary men, however, are earnest and outspoken in their opposition to idolatry in every form. I saw a masterly tract written by a man of this class, denouncing idolatry as essentially corrupt and debasing, inconsistent with reason and with the teachings of Confucius, and the fruitful source of moral, social, and political evil in every age. We can not help sympathizing with such reformers, but alas, they can only hand over their readers to the morality of Confucianism, which they represent as all-sufficient; it is all they have to offer. These representations and appeals, however forcible, have but little effect.

It is very common to represent these three systems as supplementary to each other, forming together one complete religion. There is now perfect toleration of them all on the part of Government.

The only forms of worship which are universally adopted are Ancestral Worship, the worship of the Kitchen God, and the worship of Heaven and Earth at the beginning of the year.

With respect to the full extent of idolatry, and the number of temples in the empire, there are no data for forming an accurate estimate. Though the numbers of the different kinds of temples are given in the several histories of the provinces, departments, and districts respectively, these estimates fall far short of the real number of temples which are known to exist, as these histories present only the more noted ones, and many have been built since they were compiled. An approximation to the real number may be made by taking the temples of any one place as a standard of comparison. With the help of an intelligent native, I endeavored to make such an approximation when in Ningpo. The temples within the walls of that city erected for the worship of deified heroes alone number more than eighty. Those of the same kind in the eastern part of the district are known to exceed one hundred. Reckoning the northern, southern, and western temples at only one hundred more, we have about three hundred temples of this one kind for the whole district, which is regarded by those familiar with it as a low estimate. If we assign the same number to each of the six districts of this department, we have for the whole eighteen hundred. By the same ratio of computation, the eleven departments of this province would contain nineteen thousand eight hundred, and the empire, reckoning only fifteen out of the eighteen provinces, would contain, in round numbers, three hundred thousand. The whole number of idols in these temples for hero worship, reckoning ten to each, would be three millions. The number of different and distinct idols, reckoning one to ten temples, would be about thirty thousand.

This estimate only includes the *Miau*, or temples disconnected from Buddhism and Tauism, devoted to the particular kind of worship which I have specified. The *Sz-yun* and *Tao kwan*, temples of Buddhism and Tauism, respectively, together, are about as numerous as the *Miau*. The *Ts-tang*, or ancestral temples, are much more numerous than the *Miau*. Accordingly, three times the number of the *Miau* will probably not be far from giving the whole number of different temples in China, which may be regarded, in round numbers, one million. These temples cost from five hundred to one hundred thousand dollars each. Regarding the average as only one thousand, we have 1,000,000,000 of dollars as the approximate value of idol temples in China, which is, I think, altogether too low an estimate. To give an idea of the entire expense of idolatry, we must add to the money spent in the erection of these buildings that required for repairs, and the still greater amount consumed by the idolatrous ceremonies performed in the temples and at the private dwellings of the people.

The want and misery which are the natural result of such an enormous waste of treasure may be regarded as part of the punishment of idolatry. But we know that God punishes this sin, so prominently portrayed and denounced in the fore-front of the Decalogue, with spiritual and eternal, as well as temporal judgments; and fearful indeed will be the doom of this nation if God should visit it according to the number of its idols.

At the risk of being tedious, it may be well to give here a general account of the sacrifices and offerings connected with different kinds of worship. At present none of these sacrifices are expiatory; they are regarded as food for gods and spirits, and are presented with the view of securing the kind offices of good divinities, and buying exemption from the inflictions of evil ones. They are not burned, but offered as food. Offerings in Buddhist temples consist of cooked vegetables, as it is contrary to the tenets of Buddhism to take animal life. Offerings to other gods are of meat almost exclusively, of which there are generally three or five different kinds. This meat is presented on large plates, containing whole fowls or fish, or large pieces of pork. It is generally cooked, but on some occasions most of it is presented raw, with a few cooked dishes, this kind of sacrifice being regarded as of a higher and more reverential kind. Salt and wine are added in separate cups.

The occasions on which offerings are made are such as betrothal and wedding days, the birth of a child, or the birthday of a parent. Sometimes they are made in consequence of former vows in times of distress, and sometimes with a view to securing the reformation of a dissipated son or relative.

In every instance, a paper engraving of the principal god to be worshiped is bought at a shop where such articles are kept, and placed above the table of offerings. The spirit is supposed to be present in this paper. On some occasions, and particularly during the ceremonies of the New Year, sacrifices are made before a paper representing all the gods. Candles and incense-sticks are kept constantly burning on the table of offerings, and in closing the ceremony the paper representing the god or gods worshiped is burned, together with paper-money. An explosion of fire-crackers is generally the signal for the spirits to disperse after the repast is over; a few crumbs of meat and vegetables are also thrown upon the roof of the house, though no one knows why, except that it is the invariable custom. Some surmise that it is for a certain god who has no temple to dwell in, and spends much of his time on housetops; some that it is for the attendants of the spirits which have been worshiped; and some that it is simply an offering for the birds.

The sacrifices which occur most frequently are those which are offered to the shades of ancestors and evil spirits. They are called *kung-fan*, "hash and rice," to distinguish them from offerings made to gods, which are called *fuh-li*—"happiness offerings." They consist not of large pieces of meat, but of dishes of chopped meat and vegetables, together with bowls of rice, the whole being prepared and presented in the same manner as a feast for man. The *fuh-li* offered to gods is often cut up and cooked over for such feasts; but the inverted order of presenting before the gods what has once been offered to spirits is never practiced.

Among the most common, and perhaps the most earnest of all sacrifices, are those which are made to evil spirits in consequence of the sickness of a relative. The diviner informs the afflicted family what particular spirit has been offended, and gives a minute list of the offerings required. These offerings are presented in the night, on the ground, outside the door of the dwelling. They consist not only of food of a greater or less amount, together with candles and incense and paper-money, but a paper sedan or a paper boat is burned with the money, in order to provide a polite mode of conveyance for the spirit on taking his leave.

The paper-money is made of paper covered on one side by what very much resembles tin-foil. It is manufactured in large quantities for idolatrous purposes, and is used throughout the empire. A superior kind of it is made up in hollow squares two or three inches long, which are united by a string, and hung up everywhere in shops for sale. This kind of paper is called *yuen-pao*, that which is of first or greatest value. It represents large ingots of silver, and is used principally in sacrificing to the gods. An inferior kind of this paper and foil is bought in sheets about eight inches square, and made up in a rough form by women, whose lips continually chant the words *O mi ta fuh*, while their fingers are busy with the paper. This is called *sih-poh*, silver-sheet, and represents small pieces of silver. It is used in offerings to ancestors and spirits during the seventh and eighth months. When offerings are made to hungry ghosts, an immense pile of this paper-money may sometimes be seen burned at one temple. Since the introduction of silver dollars from the West, representations of dollars in paper have been used in the same manner. Pieces of wheat stalks, after chants have been repeated over them, are also presented and burned in some places, to represent bars of gold. It is believed that the gods or spirits, for whose benefit these articles are burned, receive for them real gold and silver in the spirit world.

On funeral occasions, in addition to the money for the use of the departed spirit, representations in paper of male and female attendants are burned, and also paper sedans, horses, wagons, etc. In case of the death of opium-smokers, a paper opium pipe and lamp, etc., are burned, for fear of adding to the torments, or increasing the displeasure of the deceased, by neglecting to make these provisions.

The expense of these idolatrous sacrifices would be almost intolerable, were it not that the food offered supplies also the necessary wants of the family. Indeed, about as much is offered to the gods on any occasion as will suffice for feasting the guests during the festivities of that occasion. Another cause which helps to uphold this system of superstition is the Buddhistic notion respecting the sin of taking animal life, which is excused by the ostensible object of offering the animals slain to the gods.

It is evident that the people have a secret persuasion of the emptiness of these practices, while they at the same time so tenaciously adhere to them. In Ningpo they sometimes ridicule themselves for performing these ceremonies by repeating the couplet, *Pa pa lang zi hao gang*—"Spread it out till it is cold, and then stuff *yourselves* with it." Notwithstanding the evident absurdity of these debasing practices, all classes and conditions of men engage alike in them, and determining the matter of duty with reference to eating meats offered to idols is often a serious difficulty with the native converts.

The different forms of idolatrous worship described in the preceding chapters have been received and trusted in, because the ideas or doctrines which underlie them are perversions of great truths. We have in the multiplication of deities of different kinds, and presiding over different places, especially in the Tu-ti Poo-sah, a corruption of the great doctrine of the omnipresence and universal providence of God. The worship of the household deity, generally called God of the Kitchen, is an outward expression of the universal conviction of the omniscience of God. Different gods are clothed with different attributes, as love, mercy, justice, and vengeance, and perform different offices, such as protecting, instructing, and saving from temporal and future evils. The doctrines of sin, desert of punishment, a continued state of existence, rewards and punishments after death, and the necessity of repentance, reform, and propitiation, are most prominent. The worship of ancestors is a perversion of one of the highest duties and noblest instincts of our nature. These forms of idolatry, while they evidence God's revelation of himself in the human soul, are, with the most consummate art, so devised as to lead the soul farther and farther from God, and to turn the truth of God into a lie.

The long history of the Chinese race forms the most striking illustration of the statement that "the world by wisdom knew not God," and that the tendency of human nature is inevitably and universally toward idolatry. This tendency is strikingly described in the words of inspiration—"Because that, when they knew God, they glorified him not as God, neither were thankful, but became vain in their imaginations, and their foolish heart was darkened. Professing themselves to be wise, they became fools, and changed the glory of the incorruptible God into an image made like to corruptible man, and to birds, and four-footed beasts, and creeping things. Who changed the truth of God into a lie, and worshiped and served the creature more than the Creator, who is blessed forever. Amen."

Strange as it seems to have before us in this nineteenth century a whole nation of idolaters, it is really almost a greater wonder that we are not idolaters ourselves, and we may thank God who has made us to differ.

It is an interesting inquiry whether any trace is left in China of the knowledge or idea of one supreme overruling deity. If we examine the language and literature of this people, and interrogate native scholars and dictionaries, we will not find a word in the language which, according to present usage, conveys that idea; and it is almost impossible to find it at all well defined in the minds of any of the people. Still this conception, covered up and almost hidden by the superincumbent mass of idolatry and superstition, may be detected more or less clearly, particularly in the minds of the common people. It is generally associated with the term *heaven*. This word in the Chinese classics evidently has a meaning nearly akin to that of God, as in the saying of Confucius, "Life and death are determined; riches and poverty are from heaven." Scholars in their *wisdom* have given these and similar passages a pantheistic sense, explaining heaven to mean an all-pervading principle. I am satisfied, however, that the true idea is still retained, though it is difficult to find a clear expression of it. The following phrases are often used: "*Tien yin kin*—"The eye of Heaven is near;" also *Teo shang san tseh yiu shen*—"Just over our heads are deities," or "is God," the word "*shen*" being either singular or plural.

Notwithstanding the worship of heaven is reserved for the

Chinese Emperor, who, as the "Son of Heaven," is regarded as the only person of sufficient dignity to perform this service, the adoration of heaven by the people is by no means uncommon. Persons in the habit of practicing it sometimes have a little incense-vase fastened to the outside of their doors. In this they place a lighted incense-stick, and then, with uplifted eyes and hands, they stand and worship. This seems to be regarded as a higher and more spiritual homage than that which is offered to idols in temples, and is practiced sometimes ostentatiously, reminding one of the praying of the Pharisees in the corners of the streets. If you ask the worshiper what he is doing, he will say "I am worshiping heaven." If interrogated more particularly as to the real object of worship, he will probably repeat, in nearly the same language, "Oh, it is the great heaven above me." If pushed still further, and asked whether he means the vast expanse above, or the clouds, or the heavenly bodies, he will answer "No;" and, forced to give some explanation, he will probably fall into the misguiding formulas which the wisdom of the world has provided for him, and say, "Heaven is our father and earth is our mother; and heaven and earth produce all things; and so I worship heaven and earth." Beyond this the deluded votaries of idolatry are unable to go. If we speak to them of the God of heaven, his attributes and his works, and our relations to him, they are deeply impressed, but the glory of the uncreated God seems too bright and dazzling for eyes long accustomed to the darkness of heathenism, and they close them again, and relapse to the wonted current of their idolatrous thoughts.

Another evidence that the people have some faint glimmerings of the idea of the true God in connection with the worship which has been described is found in the fact that, after listening to and gaining a little knowledge of the Gospel as preached by missionaries, they are very apt to express their assent and approbation, declaring that it is identical with the worship of heaven and earth.

This half-smothered and dormant instinct is stimulated to greater activity, and finds a clearer expression in times of special emergency and trial. The insufficiency of idolatry is never so keenly felt as when the soul is overwhelmed with affliction. It is not uncommon for individuals who have lost their property, or who are afflicted with disobedient and vicious children, or who, in cases of oppression, have failed to obtain justice and redress from their officers and the worship of different gods, in the bitterness of their spirits to turn from the worship of idols, perhaps even curse their gods, and cry earnestly to heaven for help. Hence the common adage *Kih tseh hu tien*—"In your extremity you cry to heaven." It is as strange as it is sad, that these innate promptings and testimonies for God have been so repressed and chained down by prevailing errors, that they have never found a clear expression, or been construed into a consistent religious system.

Dark as the picture which has been given of Chinese idolatry is, it is not without gleams of light and hope. The very character of the idolatry itself contrasts favorably with that of almost any other nation of history. There is in China no deification of vice as in the systems of idolatry of Greece and Rome; no lascivious rites such as are practiced at present in India; and there are very few of those hideous and repulsive images which are met with in most heathen nations. It is a fact well worthy of notice also that the temples of China contain no nude images or figures except that of the infant held in the arms of the Goddess of Mercy.

Evidences have not been wanting in every age of the history of China that the people have not been satisfied with idol worship. New sects have sprung up in different parts of the empire, some of them formally renouncing idolatry. They have been, however, like the blind leading the blind. Unable to devise any thing better than Buddhism and Tauism, they have acknowledged the power and influence of these systems by recurring to their old ideas, and adopting them in grosser forms. These sects have died out, or been absorbed by the prevailing religions, or been proscribed and exterminated by imperial authority as corrupt and demoralizing, and dangerous to the State. So powerless is poor human nature to extricate itself from the ruin into which it has voluntarily plunged. Nothing can accomplish this work but the Gospel of Christ.

CHAPTER XII.

SUPERSTITIOUS NOTIONS RESPECTING SPIRITS, AND THE SCIENCE OF FUNG-SHWUY, OR GEOMANCY.

Sources of Superstitions relating to Spirits.—Character and Operations of Spirits called *Yau-kwei*.—Notions Respecting the Disembodied Spirits of Men.—Familiar Spirits, and Communications with the Spirit World through a Medium.—Written Communications from Spirits, Spirit-rappings, etc.—Character, Importance, and Uses of the mysterious Science called *Fung-shwuy*.—It has its own Literature, and its Doctors, or Expounders.—General Prevalence and Influence of this Superstition.—Difficulties and Family Quarrels growing out of it.—An Incident illustrating the Existence and Importance of *Fung-shwuy*.—*Fung-shwuy*, as applied to House-building.—Rearrangement of Houses sometimes made necessary.—Complaints against Foreigners for disregarding *Fung-shwuy*, and a Case in Illustration.—Means of attracting Good Luck.—Means of warding off Evil Influences.—*Fung-shwuy* as connected with the Construction of Canals and Bridges.

IDEAS respecting spirits occupy a prominent place among Chinese superstitions, and have an important practical bearing upon domestic and social life. The unsuspecting credulity with which the great variety of diverse and conflicting views on this subject are received, and the tenacity with which they are held, are only to be accounted for by the agency of Satan, the fears of a guilty and unenlightened conscience, and the acts of designing men, who encourage these superstitions for the sake of accomplishing private ends. Some of them may be traced to Buddhism, some to Tauism, and some have originated in works which were at first understood as principally or entirely fictitious, but afterward came to be regarded as authentic treatises.

Among the most prominent of the orders of spirits are the *Yau-kwei*, or genii, mentioned in a former chapter on Tauism.

They are supposed to be beings who, by different means, have escaped death, and exchanged corporeal for ethereal natures. They exist in various degrees of development or grades of attainment, and it is their continual aim and effort to rise higher in the scale and acquire greater power. They are supposed to be able to assume different forms, animate and inanimate, or to carry out their purposes as invisible spirits to suit circumstances.

That class of *Yau-kwei* which afflict men acquire their power, not by the authorized method of subjecting the body and mind to certain disciplinary rules, but by clandestinely stealing the vital principle from man. Nightmare and starting in sleep are attributed to attempts of this kind. Dreams incident to some states of bodily ailment and weakness are also attributed to these spirits. Persons thus affected endeavor to rid themselves of their nocturnal visitors in different ways. The first expedient resorted to is that of the individual rousing himself from sleep to utter curses and imprecations on the offending spirit. If this means fails, one or more persons in robust health are called to occupy the same room with the invalid, as it is supposed that an influence emanates from the bodies of strong and robust persons which spirits can not withstand, and that they principally attack those who are weak and delicate. Should the spirit refuse to yield to such means, a sword which has been wet with human blood is brandished over the bed of the sufferer, or the services of a person who professes to shoot spirits is obtained. Mirrors are suspended in different parts of the room, in order to frighten the spirit, and to detect his presence and position by reflection, though he should endeavor to avoid a direct view. The last resort when all other means have failed is that of making a formal complaint at the office of *Chang-tien-sz,* a man who resides in Kiang-si, and is supposed to possess authority over spirits throughout the empire, and to have not only them, but gods at his beck and call. This power he exercises by means of charms and enchantments, and a seal of acknowledged authority among spirits which has been transmitted to him from his ancestors.

A paper stamped with this seal, and containing a statement of the name, place, and circumstances of the afflicted person, is, by being burned, supposed to be transmitted to some god, who is instructed to see that the offending spirit is caught, punished, and restrained from committing further offenses. It is stated that these steps will not only certainly prove successful, but that before the messenger arrives with his complaint, his approach, with all the circumstances of his mission, are minutely placarded on a bulletin outside of the palace gate of the spirit king. It is also said that many spirits of this class are held in durance by this personage in sealed bottles, and that their querulous twitterings are often heard by visitors.

A singular fact may be noticed in this connection, that a missionary lady in Ningpo accustomed to the use of smelling-salts fell under the suspicion of using the bottle to confine spirits over which she had gained a controlling power. As she was seen frequently to have recourse to the smelling-bottle in certain neighborhoods, different diseases and maladies in those localities were directly traced to her agency.

The largest class of spirits is supposed to be that of the spirits of the dead, called *Kwei*. As it is generally believed that the soul is after death required to atone for its sins by confinement in Hades until it is permitted to reappear in another state, the Chinese find some difficulty in accounting for so many *Kwei* upon earth. The most consistent theory is that which supposes that they are spirits whose crimes are not sufficient to keep them in hell, and whose time for reappearing has not yet arrived. To the agency of these spirits almost every variety of disease is attributed. Their object in these inflictions is to obtain food, or rather the scent or exhalations from food. Accordingly, when a person is sick, a diviner is called to determine whether the sickness is due to the agency of spirits or not, and if it is, to tell what kind of

Kwei it is, and what its demands of food are. At funerals a feast is generally prepared for the spirits which are supposed to be the associates of the deceased, in order to secure a good understanding between him and his new acquaintances.

During the months of August and September, when diseases are unusually prevalent, the people suppose that the gates of hell are opened, and the spirits are turned out for a kind of holiday. At this time they are honored with ceremonies performed throughout the country, called *Fang-yin-kau*, or *Shi-shih*. The object of these ceremonies is to secure health and peace to the family or neighborhood which provides them, by satisfying and propitiating the spirits. Quantities of viands are prepared, which are set on tables in an open place or court; representations in paper of clothes of different sizes, styles, and colors are suspended near the table; and a company of priests and singers is employed to add variety and noise to the entertainment. After dark, lanterns are suspended from high poles to call the spirits from the distance, and indicate to them where food may be found. This food is of a very inferior quality, and is often given to beggars after the ceremony is over; but it is supposed that the incantations of the priests have the power to convert both the food and the paper into just what is required to satisfy the wants of those for whom they are intended. The amount of money spent in these childish ceremonies is immense.

In the province of Che-kiang it is generally believed that there is a place called Sang-chau, where a great part of the inhabitants are *kwei*, who come out in the afternoon and mingle with the people. It is said that they may be distinguished by their using paper instead of copper money, and by their not casting a shadow in the moonlight. It is also believed that in the *hien* city Fung-tu, in the province of Sz-chwen, there is a street called *Yin-yiang-kiai*—"Street of the Dead and Living," one side of which is inhabited by men, and the other by spirits. Volumes might be filled with current tales respecting ghosts and spirits and genii, which the narrow limits of a chapter do not admit of introducing. The Chinese have a large number of books on this subject, among the most noted of which is the *Liau-chai-che-i*, a large work of sixteen volumes.

It is believed that there is another class of ghosts, called *Kiang-shi*, which differ from those above mentioned in the fact that their bodies do not decompose at death, and the united soul and body are permitted during the night to range about at pleasure. Some bodies change their form so as to resemble beasts of prey, but some retain their original form and appearance. It is believed that the latter class, if they eat any material food, are immediately transformed into living men, only differing from other mortals in their being unable to behold the light of day. It is said that, if they allow the sun to shine upon them they die instantly.

Of all the superstitions relating to spirits, those respecting a class of them called *Tu-sien* have perhaps the greatest influence upon the minds of the people. *Tu-sien*, signifying a spirit in the body, designates a familiar spirit, by the assistance of which it is believed that persons are able to tell fortunes and converse with the dead. They are supposed to be the spirits of those who are not permitted to reassume a body on account of obligations incurred in a former state, from which they have not yet been absolved. They repay their debts of money or gratitude by serving their benefactors, who have preceded them in coming again into the world, in enabling them to acquire wealth by fortune-telling. They do this by dwelling in their bodies as familiar spirits, and being their medium of communication with the unseen world. Persons supposed to be possessed of these spirits are visited by multitudes, particularly those who have recently lost relatives by death, and wish to converse with them through a "medium." The fortune-teller, after a conversation with the applicant, invokes the aid of his or her spirit (many of these fortune-tellers are women), whose attention and active co-operation are signalized by sundry contortions of the body and a spasmodic jerk of the neck. The spirit is then directed either to gain the desired information respecting the future, or to find and bring reports from some deceased friend whose name, age, place of burial, etc., are given. As is the case in other lands, the spirit deigns or refuses a response according to circumstances.

Some of these fortune-tellers who have no indebted spirit to offer his services are obliged to devise means to secure the assistance of one. With this end in view, they first procure a little image made of the wood of the willow, for which they obtain a spirit in one of the following ways: Some go to a grave-yard, and after feasting the ghosts of the dead, make an arrangement with one to reside in the image. The image is then worshiped for several weeks continuously, and left out of doors during the night, to be wet with the dews of heaven, and drink in virtue from moonbeams; after which it is regarded as an oracle, from which the spirit speaks infallibly.

Another method of obtaining a spirit consists in writing on the little image the characters representing the horoscope of some clever living person whose spirit is desired, and then worshiping the image, and leaving it out-doors until this person dies, and his spirit enters the image, which it is said will surely take place in a very short time. In consequence of this superstition, those who are found possessed of these images sometimes fall under the suspicion of having produced the death and obtained the spirit of some lately deceased person of the neighborhood, and may be accused, tried, and condemned to death, being regarded as guilty of murder.

Written communications from spirits are not unfrequently sought for in the following manner: After the presence and desired offices of some spirit are invoked, two or more persons support with their hands some object to which a pencil is attached in a vertical position, and extending to a table below, covered with sand. It is said that the movements of the pencil, involuntary as far as the persons holding it are concerned, but governed by the influences of spirits, describe certain

WRITING WITH A FORKED PEN AN ORACLE ON SAND.

characters which are easily deciphered, and which often bring to light remarkable disclosures and revelations. Many who regard themselves persons of superior intelligence are firm believers in this mode of consulting spirits.

There is still another spirit, called the *Wu-tung*, principally noted for its propensity to steal and to frighten people. It is said to have its favorites among dwellers in the flesh, and also its objects of dislike; and that it secretly transfers money and articles of value from the latter to the former. It is also supposed to produce spirit-rappings in and about houses, and to cause burning flames to be seen; thus frightening the unoffending inhabitants, so that they not unfrequently fly from their houses to find safety and quiet elsewhere. As in the case of the common *Kwei* these enemies can be bought off by an idolatrous feast. It is probable that this superstition takes its rise from appearances of the "*ignis fatuus*," and the apparent ground on which it rests accounts for the strong hold it has on the minds of the people.

It is difficult to conceive of the fear, anxiety, and dread which these various superstitions occasion. They should lead us better to appreciate that gospel which delivers us from bondage to fear, by teaching us to recognize in every event and circumstance the hand of an unseen and Almighty Father, who controls all beings and events, and makes all things work together for good to them that fear him.

For want of a better term, the word *luck* is used to represent a something which is as important in the estimation of the Chinese as it is difficult of explanation. The term used by natives is *fung-shwuy*, composed of the two characters which mean wind and water. These however give but little assistance in determining the meaning of the compound word. This term designates an ethereal principle or influence which is supposed to pervade the earth and air, and to exist to a greater or less extent in different localities. Those which are supposed to have an unusual measure of it are valued above all price, and the most noted spots in the empire are those which have the best *fung-shwuy*. According to a general theory of correspondences of very wide application, the earth is supposed to bear a resemblance, in its organization, to living beings, having its veins and arteries, and a principle of life and vitality pervading the whole, which principle is *fung-shwuy*. As some parts of the body are more vital than others, so it is believed that *fung-shwuy* exists in some places in a greatly concentrated and intensified state.

The advantages expected from the vitalizing influences of such places are vigor of body, family prosperity, and success in business, to be enjoyed by those living in close proximity to them; but the blessings which are most prized and sought for are those which result to children in consequence of the bodies of parents being buried in these auspicious spots.

Securing a lucky place for the tomb of a parent is regarded as the great event of first importance in determining the fortunes of his family. The influence of the *fung-shwuy*, is supposed to be communicated to the body of the deceased, and through it to his descendants, wherever they may be scattered.

The reasons given by natives to show that their ideas on this subject are more than imaginary, are such as the following: It is said that tombs selected and prepared previous to the death of future occupants, present when opened very different appearances, indicating the nature of the ground, and the degree of the vitalizing principle which it contains. Some emit a vapor or gas, the presence of which is regarded as a very auspicious circumstance. In some are found fresh leaves of trees and flowers, and in some living creatures, such as snakes and reptiles, which are supposed to be the spontaneous production of the life-giving earth. It is said that the superior character of some tombs is proved by the fact, that lamps have been lighted in them when they were made, and found burning years afterward. The evidence for these reputed facts is generally nothing more than that "the people say so." The fact that bodies have been found in some places unchanged by decomposition, gives a show of reason to this universal superstition.

This imaginary science is of almost universal belief, and, with a few exceptions, has, if possible, a stronger hold on the minds of the educated classes than the common people. It has an extensive literature, embracing different systems and theories, and a class of men, called *fung-shwuy sin-sang*, or "luck-doctors," whose special business it is to investigate and apply its principles. These may or may not belong to the Buddhist or Tauist priesthood. They are generally men of great pretensions as to science and erudition, use in their conversation many technical terms which other people are not expected to understand, and are looked up to with great respect and deference. Some of them acquire such a reputation, that they are sent for from great distances, and receive high fees to secure their services. They are shown the general locality within which a grave is desired, and urged to exhaust all the knowledge of their art in finding *the* lucky spot. They write down the date of birth and death of the deceased, and other members of the family, spend a day or two, perhaps, in examining minutely the contour of the country, the hills, canals, and water-courses, and dragon veins and pagodas, their relative distances and directions, and then go home to consult their books and diagrams and work out the grand result. The spot selected may be in a neighbor's field, but it is bought, if possible, at almost any price. After burial, if a son of the deceased is successful in business or in the literary examinations, or a son and heir is born into the family, these evidences of good fortune are sure to be attributed to the fact that the right luck-doctor was employed, and the right spot secured.

The doctrine of the change of luck from one place to another is necessary to the *fung-shwuy* theory, in order to account for failures in the predictions of luck-doctors, and for the varied fortunes of the same family in different generations. If one individual of the family meets with exceptional bad fortune, it is easily accounted for by the simple explanation that, while the spot is a good one, he must have been guilty of sins unatoned for in a previous state.

That these superstitions pervade every rank of society from the highest to the lowest, may be seen in the fact that, in times of war and struggles between contending dynasties, it is the object of each party to destroy the ancestral tomb of its antagonist; regarding this as the most effectual way to check him in his road to fortune. In endeavoring to put down the Tai-ping insurgents, this expedient was adopted. An official announcement, made by the governor of Kwang-si in 1855, stated that the ancestral tomb of *Yang-siu-tsing*, then the leading spirit of the insurgents, had been destroyed, and that there was found in it a tortoise with green hair, which was killed. The affirmed existence and destruction of this prodigy readily accounted for the former success of the aspiring Eastern prince, and the speedy and terrible overthrow which followed.

Not unfrequently a family seeks satisfaction or revenge from another family with which it is at enmity by breaking or injuring its *fung-shwuy*. This consists in defacing a noted tomb, or cutting trees connected with it. Prosecutions before the officers on the charge of breaking *fung-shwuy* are entertained by them as offenses of the gravest character, and are treated with great severity.

The arch-deceiver has not only succeeded in making the whole nation slaves to this puerile and unfounded superstition, but has connected such features with it as to introduce endless difficulties and discords in families. The position on the left side of the tomb is the place of honor, and belongs to the first son; the nearest place on the right belongs to the second son, and thus the relative positions of the different members of the family with reference to the tomb are fixed. Now the position of one individual being in the direction of a hill or water-course may be propitious; while that of another, being in the direction of a hill or another tomb, may be unpropitious. Thus supposed interests are made to clash; one is as earnest to secure a certain place as the other is opposed to it, and quarrels and litigation ensue respecting the place of the burial of a parent which may last for life. Other notions respecting *fung-shwuy* add still further to the difficulties of burial, and sometimes postpone it for years, while the body of the deceased is kept in the house in a hermetically sealed coffin. One person may insist on having the burial postponed for a longer or shorter period of time, because the year of the Chinese sexagenary cycle clashes with his particular horoscope. Sometimes a family agrees to defer a burial, because the year in which it would otherwise take place happens to be one in which it is not lucky to build a tomb fronting in the particular direction designated by the nature of the place chosen.

A story well known in Ningpo, and often referred to as a conclusive proof of the existence and importance of *fung-shwuy*, will further illustrate the ideas of the people on this subject. In the late dynasty, a poor man of the name of Du died in time of pestilence, having no friends to superintend his burial. The authorities provided a coffin for the body, and engaged some beggars to take it across the river and leave it anywhere on the opposite side. While the body was being borne through the fields, the rope by which it was suspended broke, and it was determined to leave it where it fell. The question arose as to the direction in which the head should be turned; and it was decided by the position of the bamboo pole used in carrying the coffin, which had been thrown down at random. A luck-hunting priest, who had had his attention directed to this locality as one remarkable for auspicious influences, was vainly endeavoring to find the exact culminating point of the *fung-shwuy* when these occurrences took place. Proceeding to the spot, and taking the bearings of different important points, he exclaimed, "Why, this is the very spot I have been seeking; and, now it is discovered and occupied by accident, only one thing is wanting; the direction of the coffin is out of the proper line just a point!" While the priest was thus soliloquizing and musing over the mysterious designs of heaven in conferring happiness on such a poor man, one of the bearers came running back for a rope which had been left under the coffin, where it had fallen, and in pulling this out the coffin was brought exactly into the favored position. The consequence was, that the priest gave up his profession in disgust, and the fortunate son of him who had only beggars at his funeral rose to the third station of dignity and power in the empire. This story probably originated in the fact that many members of the Du family held offices under the *Ming* dynasty.

The methods by which the principles of *fung-shwuy* are applied to house-building are different from those which regulate the position and construction of tombs, and are generally attended to by a different class of men. Six stars are supposed to preside over the different parts of Chinese houses, which are composed of buildings more or less distinct, and separated from each other by courts. The building on the left side is under the auspices of the star Green Dragon, that on the right under those of the White Tiger, and so on. The dragon dislikes filth, and the tiger is afraid of heat; so, refuse must not be thrown in front of the left side, that is, under the Dragon's nose; and the kitchen must not be built near the head or the tail of the Tiger. The back part of the right side must not be built high, as the elevation of the Tiger's tail indicates that he is about to pounce upon his prey. It would be expected that the disregard of such obvious improprieties would be atoned for by frequent deaths in the family. These are the general and important principles of house-building which are level to the understanding of the people; the minutiæ of the science in its minor details is left to professional house-planners, who are governed to a great extent by their peculiar fancies. If a principal door is opened under one star, the family will be subject to the depredations of thieves; if under another, they will be liable to some other misfortune. A door may be opened in a given direction during one year of the cycle where it would not be prudent to do it in the following year. When necessity requires that a front door should be opened on a street in an inauspicious direction, the evil effects of the consequent bad luck are in a measure obviated by making the passage from the door tortuous and irregular. When a family is afflicted with sickness, or is unsuccessful in business, or mourns over what is regarded the greatest of misfortunes, that of having no son to perpetuate their name, and to sacrifice to the spirits of departed ancestors, the fact is discovered that they must have employed the wrong luck-doctor, and another one is called. After examining the premises carefully, he sagely remarks that the other man left out some important factor in his computation, or made some mistake, and he is glad to inform them that he understands the whole matter, and can make every thing right without much trouble. His recommendations are likely to be such as the following: You must close up *this* door, and open another *there.* The kitchen and cooking range must be readjusted; you should change your rooms for sleeping and eating; or if you *must* occupy the same rooms as sleeping apartments, at least change the position of the beds. When these directions are complied with, the hearts of the inmates of the family are quieted, and if the next year proves a propitious one, the same luck-doctor is sure to be called whenever the services of such a person are again required.

Scholars aspiring after literary honors are told that they will succeed at the examinations if they study by a certain window; and if the fronting of the window is hardly what might be desired, the difficulty may be remedied by an outside screen, or a lantern hung up at night to give the luck a slight change of direction.

A man is supposed to gain a great advantage by having his house higher than his neighbors. In consequence of this superstition, foreigners have found it very difficult to erect houses, and especially churches, in Chinese cities. Not a few of the complaints entered by natives against foreigners in their consulates relate to their utter disregard of the principles of *fung-shwuy*, and the injuries accruing therefrom to native interests. Many illustrations might be given of the jealousy of the Chinese in this particular, and the different calamities which they attribute to the houses of foreigners.

Some years since the inhabitants of Ningpo were much alarmed by the building of a Roman Catholic cathedral in the city. As it rose higher and higher, overtopping all other structures, the alarm increased, and became intense when the top of the steeple was crowned with a weather-cock. One part of the city, called Centipede Street, was in special danger. Its name was due to the small streets or alleys branching off from both sides like the legs of a centipede; and near the end of it was the city bell-tower, the highest building within the walls, which was regarded as the centipede's uplifted head. The steeple portended evil to the whole city, and particularly to the bell-tower, from which it had usurped the pre-eminence of height; and the weather-cock portended special evil to the Centipede Street, *because* cocks eat insects and worms of various kinds, including, of course, centipedes! The luck-doctor sounded the alarm, but the foreigners paid no attention. Unfortunately for the city, but fortunately for the reputation of the luck-doctors, the Centipede Street took fire, and part of it, together with the Chinese bell-tower, was reduced to ashes. Complaints in the foreign consulates now became more urgent, but the Chinamen were no doubt laughed at, and probably returned home complaining that "the stupid foreigners would not and could not understand any thing about it." They were obliged to have recourse again to the luck-doctors, and it is said that one of them very happily suggested that, "While cocks may be supposed to eat centipedes, wild-cats certainly eat cocks;" and a hideous wild-cat was depicted by an eminent artist on a high wall confronting the dreaded foreign edifice. Strange to say, in a short time the cathedral crumbled and fell. The Chinese bell-tower was, as if in defiance, built two or three stories higher than before, and again peace and tranquillity reigned in the city. Some have accounted for the falling of the cathedral by its having been built of brick not sufficiently burned; but the natives say that this is a characteristic explanation of the uninformed foreigners, who know nothing of the principles and effects of *fung-shwuy*. Notwithstanding all that may be said to the natives in opposition to this system, they will refer to the above well-authenticated facts, and similar ones with which their books are full, and facts are stubborn things—in China as well as elsewhere.

It is the unvarying custom in many places in China, whenever a new house is built, to suspend lanterns on high poles for several nights in succession after the erection of the frame-work, in order to attract luck to the new edifice. A great noise is also kept up during the night by gongs. The neighbors are obliged, in self-defense, to resort to the same means to avoid their luck being drawn away from them, each family striving to have its lanterns the highest. On such occasions, the appearance of a neighborhood, with its noise and illumination, resembles the celebration of a festival.

A house is considered unlucky, not only when it is surrounded by higher ones, but when the corners of other houses point toward it. The adverse influences to which a place under such circumstances is exposed are counteracted by figures of warriors with drawn swords, and lions and tigers with open mouths, and other similar devices, which are placed on the tiling of the house in such a position as to confront the object from which danger is apprehended. Mirrors are also sometimes used to reflect the evil influences back. The idea, in these cases, is not simply that of a negative evil, consisting of the abstraction of the luck which the house would otherwise be possessed of, but that of a positive influence the very reverse of *fung-shwuy*. A house standing at the terminus of a street or alley where the road branches off on each side, is supposed to be subjected to the same evil influence, from the stream of bad luck flowing along the street and beating against it. A stone slab is generally seen erected at such places bearing the inscription *Tai shan shih kan tang*—"I am, or I represent, the *Ta shan* rock, and am not afraid to withstand you." *Ta shan* is the name of one of the largest and most celebrated mountains in the empire; and as a solid mountain not only withstands all evil influences, but is the source of those which are auspicious, this name is used as a charm to frighten back the adverse tide of evil. No one ever supposes that these stones came from Ta shan, and it is amusing to see the inscription sometimes on a brick.

In the opening of canals and construction of bridges, one of the first considerations is, what will be the effect on the *fung-shwuy?* Some places which might be easily connected by a canal are obliged to be without the convenience of this means of communication, because a celebrated luck-prognosticator has said that such a canal would destroy the *fung-shwuy* of the neighborhood. In constructing bridges in a particular place, it may be imagined that the luck will be favorable for one family, and unfavorable for another; and difficulties and law-suits ensue, which are generally settled by an amount of money paid by the party supposed to have the advantage to his less fortunate neighbors.

In some sections the bridges are very low, and in time of high water it is necessary to have the covers of boats taken off, in order to pass under them. The people are subject to this great inconvenience, not because of the necessary expense of building the bridges a little higher, which would be comparatively a small matter, but because of the influence of a wealthy family, or several wealthy families in the neighborhood, which have had the good fortune to become rich, and are afraid their luck will be broken by any important change in the face of the country.

Natives who are not intimately acquainted with foreigners naturally suppose that we have no less regard for *fung-shwuy* than they, and that, from our superior knowledge of the principles of "heaven and earth," we are enabled to secure the most lucky place. Our fondness for visiting hills and watercourses, and collecting minerals, plants, etc., is attributed to the desire of finding precious metals and precious influences. When we stop to admire a beautiful view or landscape, a Chinese by-stander is almost sure to remark, "He is looking for *fung-shwuy*." On visiting a beautiful spot on a mountain-side, I once found a young man preparing a tomb for his father, whose interest and anxiety about the matter in which he was engaged so far overcame his surprise and curiosity on seeing a stranger and a foreigner in such an unfrequented place, that his first question was, "Have I really chosen a good location?"

A few of the people of the more intelligent class, who have been long connected with us, and know our utter disregard of these childish superstitions, will sometimes decry some of the most glaringly absurd of them; but, while they profess their contempt for the credulity of their countrymen in some points, they are sure to betray their own weakness in others.

CHAPTER XIII.

DIFFERENT MODES OF DIVINATION.

Importance of the Eight Diagrams.—Translation of part of a Preface of the Chinese Work, "Source of True Divination."—Mode of divining by Diagrams, Mode of divining by Means of the "Eight Characters." —An individual Case in Illustration.—Divination by Astrology.—Illustrative official Document.—Fortune-telling by the Use of Birds, Snakes, and Turtles.—Telling the Fortunes of past and future States of Existence.—Manner in which Failures are accounted for.—Physiognomy and Palmistry.—Choosing of "Lucky Days."—Effects of being born under certain Stars.—Divination by Dreams.

IN an unevangelized and superstitious nation like the Chinese, possessed of an ancient and voluminous literature, the existence of many theories and arts for unlocking the secrets of futurity might naturally be expected. The abstruse character of some of these mystic arts, which are not understood even by those who practice them, and which owe much of their influence to the prestige of antiquity, may be in a manner described, but can not be satisfactorily explained.

In the practice of divination, great use is made of the "Eight Diagrams," invented by the Emperor *Fuh-hi*, probably nearly three thousand years before Christ. About eleven centuries before Christ, *Wen-wang*, the Literary Prince, and his son, *Chow-kung*, developed these eight diagrams into sixty-four, attaching to them additional ideas and explanations. Confucius, about five hundred years before Christ, collected and perpetuated these relics of the past in the *Yih-king*, or "Book of Changes," which is still one of the most venerated of the ancient Chinese classics. These diagrams are nothing but arbitrary signs, the original meaning of which can not be satisfactorily determined. They are supposed to embody the principles by which the universe was evolved out of chaotic matter, and which, by necessary and unchanging laws, determine all the changes which take place in nature. Those who profess to be able to disclose future events generally rest their claims upon public credulity, on some new views gained of this book of mysteries, or on their familiarity with books written by others in explanation of it. They suppose that the mines of wisdom hid in these diagrams have never been fully explored, and that great advantages will accrue to those who have the penetration to find the key to their contents. It is a common remark among the Chinese, "If foreigners, with all their skill and ingenuity, possess themselves of the *Yih-king*, all the world will become subject to them." It is also said that Heaven will not permit the *Yih-king* to be taken out of the empire, and that, when the attempt to export it has been made, vessels bearing it across the sea have encountered storms and tempests until it has been thrown overboard.

In the latter part of the *Chau* dynasty, which continued to 249 B.C., *Kwei kuh sien sz* applied the *Yih-king* to the use of soothsaying, and is regarded as the father of augurs, though no book has come down to the present from him. During the present and preceding dynasties, many books have been written on this subject, among the most noted of which is the *Poh shi ching tsung*—"Source of True Divination," written in the forty-eighth year of the Emperor *Kang-hi*. This work consists of six volumes, and contains a minute and detailed system of elaborated nonsense, such as it would be difficult to find a parallel to in any language. The preface will perhaps give as clear an idea of its contents as could be otherwise obtained, and forcibly reminds one of the manner in which quacks in other lands decry the nostrums of others, while they extol their own. It contains, also, a true and lively picture of the evils which the system it advocates entails upon the people. The following is a translation of the greater part of it:

"The secret of augury consists in communication with the gods. Its object is to determine good and evil fortune, to settle doubt and anxiety, to discriminate between *yin* and *yang* in the different forms of the diagrams. The interpretation of the transformations is deep and mysterious. The theory of this science is most intricate, the practice of it most important. The sacred classic says, 'That which is true gives indications of the future;' therefore, if a person seeking a response is not sincere, he can not move the gods; if the interpreter of the response is careless and inconsiderate in his divinations, they will not be fulfilled. These two remarks are emphatically true and important. It is common to see persons seek a response when occasion requires, while sincerity is entirely forgotten. When, from intoxication and feasting, or licentious pleasures, they proceed to invoke the assistance of the gods, what infatuation to suppose that their prayers will move them! Besides, the wealthy or honorable affecting a contempt for the art of soothsaying, either look to a friend, or send a servant to ask a response in their stead, without showing their zeal and earnestness by presenting themselves in person. Hence, when no response is given, or the interpretation is not verified, they lay the blame at the door of the augur, forgetting that the failure is due to their want of sincerity. This is the fault of the one seeking the response. It is the great fault of augurs that, from a desire of gain, they use the art of divination as a trap to ensnare the people. For instance, in case of sickness (than which nothing can be more important), some, regardless of the principles of rectitude, have a private understanding with Buddhist priests, and nuns, and Tauists, by which they are to share in their gains, thus forgetting augury in their lust after money.* They determine whether to exact a greater or less amount from the applicant by observing his wealth or pover-

* The augur, as a return for directing the applicant to worship in a particular temple, is permitted to share the money paid to the priests of that temple.

ty; they recklessly prescribe that a certain number of chapters of prayer shall be repeated at some Buddhist or Tauist temple, or that a certain number of days shall be spent in chanting over a sacred book in a nunnery. The applicant, overcome by anxiety, readily assents to any thing. If the individual be wealthy, it matters little; if he be poor, he may be led to pawn his clothes, contract debts, and squander his property, and may be thus reduced to the severest straits and necessities, while he indulges in the hope that the sick person will be restored. But, in fact, before the prayers are finished, the sick person dies; while the sacred book is being read, the sufferer is no more. These injuries result from alliances with Buddhists and Tauists. Again, inexperienced physicians, unskilled in their profession, apply for assistance in gaining practice, and the augur, in his prayers and incantations, indicates clearly where this physician is to be found —thus furnishing him with employment. They do not consider that, while the augur secures in a year a little gain, the sick man, in an unsuspecting moment, meets death by the hand of his attendant. This is the sin of forming an alliance with physicians. These two evils exist everywhere, and are the plague of every city. I have suspended my sign in front of the office of the military magistrate. If the above classes of men come to tempt me, I take an oath to reject all their proffers, and will, in every case, carefully divine according to the diagrams, and no doubt my prognostications will prove true."

In every place of any considerable size fortune-tellers of this class are numerous. They are not unfrequently blind, and, when so, have an assistant. The manner of their divination is as follows: When a person wishing a response presents himself, a small box, containing three copper cash, is handed to him, which he takes very reverently in both hands, and with which he describes a circle around incense-sticks burning before paintings of the patrons of the art of divination. After having made his prostrations before these paintings, he proceeds in the same reverent manner to the door, and then invokes the aid of heaven, in a form somewhat like the following: "To day, I ——, residing near the temple —— on account of sickness in my family (or for some other cause, as the case may be), present myself to obtain a true response respecting this matter. Let me know the event, whether it be favorable, or the contrary." This ceremony being performed, the applicant places the box with cash in the hands of the diviner, who also, after asking a few questions, waves it with even greater solemnity over the table of incense. He then repeats a form of prayer, generally addressed to the patrons of the mystic art. The form prescribed in the book before referred to is the following: "Though Heaven has no voice, when addressed, there is a response; the gods are living, and, when invoked, are near. A man is now present who is harassed with anxieties, and is unable to solve his doubts and perplexities. We can only look to the gods to instruct us as to what is or is not to take place." This done, the box is shaken, and the cash are cast upon the table three times in succession. The upper surfaces of the coins are observed each time, and will indicate, according to the plan adopted by the augur, one of the eight diagrams. After another prayer, the cash are again cast three times, and the different combinations, together with the previous results, will point out one of the sixty-four diagrams. One of these having been in this way determined, the next question is how to interpret it. Three distinct considerations combine to fix this interpretation, and to give an endless variety to the meanings of each diagram. These are, the particular objects sought in the divination—the meaning, or power, of the two characters designating the current month, and the meaning of the two characters designating the day. The greater part of the book above referred to is occupied with minute instructions to aid in the right interpretation of the diagrams in all supposable cases and circumstances. The diviner being a close observer of human nature, is influenced, in a great measure, in his interpretations by what he has been able to learn through shrewd and indirect interrogations respecting the character and circumstances of the applicant. The diagram, with its explanation, is written out and handed to the inquirer, who sometimes has it interpreted a second time in another place. A larger or smaller sum is paid to these fortune-tellers, according to the circumstances of the applicant, and the importance of the matter in hand. As has been before intimated, no small part of the gains of those who engage in this occupation is obtained by making business for priests and physicians, for doing which they receive a consideration from them.

In the practice of divination above described, called *ki-ko*, the object is to determine the issue of any present difficulty or emergency. In less urgent cases, when a person is in doubt with reference to his business affairs, or has a curiosity to know the general fortunes of his future life, another method of anticipating the future is resorted to, called *swan-ming*, "reckon the life." In *ki-ko* the correctness of the divination is supposed to be due, not only to the right interpretation of the mysterious and unchanging principles of the diagrams, but to the indications of the gods, whose assistance is regarded most important. In *swan-ming* a knowledge of the future is supposed to be obtained by the use of hidden arts alone, the special assistance of the gods not being sought. The most common mode of *swan-ming* is that of "examining the eight characters," or, as it is sometimes called, *pi ming tsz*, "examining the paper of life." In describing this mode of divination, it will be necessary first to refer to the Chinese mode of reckoning time. This is done by the use of a sexagenary cycle, which gives names to years, months, days, and hours. It consists of sixty dissyllabic words, which are formed by a combination of two sets of characters, numbering ten and twelve respectively; the former being regarded as connected with heaven, or the *Yang* principle, and the latter with earth, or the *Yin* principle. Each of the twelve characters is used five times, and each of the ten six times. These combinations of two characters each are applied to designate sixty successive years, sixty successive months, sixty successive days, and sixty successive hours; these sixty names revolving in perpetual cycles, in the greater and lesser divisions of time. Each one of these two sets of characters is supposed to have a certain mysterious connection with one or other of what are regarded as "the five elements," viz., metal, wood, water, fire, and earth.

With these preliminary observations, we may get some idea of the manner in which *pi ming tsz* is practiced. A person presents himself before the diviner to ask the general question, whether the present period of his life is auspicious or otherwise, with special reference to the prosecution of business, change of residence, attending the examinations, etc. The applicant is first required to state the year, month, day, and hour of his birth. The couplets of characters representing each of these four divisions of time present together the "eight characters," which form the basis of the calculation.

The eight characters of the Chinaman, through whom much of the information in this chapter was derived, may serve as an example. The most important, or leading character, is always the former of the two representing the day of birth. This character happens to be, in the present instance, connected with the element *wood*, or *tree*, therefore the life of the individual in question has a mystical connection with a tree. The day of birth occurs in one of the autumn months, a time unfavorable to the growth and luxuriance of vegetation; hence, without some special reason to the contrary, the general fact is arrived at, that the individual will be weak and delicate. In addition to this, one of the characters representing the month, and one of those representing the hour, are connected with metal; metal cuts wood, therefore the condition of the individual is still more precarious! Two of the other characters are connected with earth, which produces metal, and this makes the case of the individual even more deplora ble! But, on the other hand, one of the characters is connected with water, which contributes to the growth of wood. This happy circumstance, together with others less easy of explanation, serves to counteract to some extent adverse influences. In every case, the divination consists in striking a balance between good and evil influences, in doing which there is a wide scope for the play of individual fancies. Those who practice this art are astute observers of character; and the circumstances and appearance of the applicant, together with information derived by subtle questions, have much to do in each case in determining the nature of the response. The eight characters not only form the basis for deciding the fortunes of an individual at the time when the divination is sought, but for any number of years in the future. The fortunes of any subsequent year are supposed to be decided by the question whether the characters representing that year have a propitious or unpropitious connection with the leading character of a man's life. Thus it is often remarked that such and such years will be difficult to pass. The minute details of this kind of soothsaying are presented in a work of four volumes, entitled "*Tsz ping yuen hai.*"

Divination is also practiced, by means of astrology, in a manner still more intricate. The events of men's lives are supposed to be under the influences of twenty-eight stars, each of which is an object of worship. In telling fortunes by this method, a representation on paper of a man's horoscope is prepared for each individual applicant. It has, first, a circular map or table, on the periphery of which are arranged the twenty-eight stars, in longer or shorter segments, to which they are severally assigned. The eight characters above described determine under the influences of what particular star an individual's life begins. Starting from this point, the life is supposed to revolve in this fixed circle, passing, in regular successiop, under different and varying stellar influences. The length of time during which one's life is under the influence of any particular star, is ascertained by a computation based upon the Chinese festivals. It would be as useless as it is difficult to attempt to give a minute account of this kind of divination. It commands the confidence of the people more, perhaps, than any other, either because it is more mysterious, or because of the natural disposition of mankind to connect their destinies with the influences of the heavenly bodies. It is supposed by some, and not without reason, that the sciences of astrology and alchemy originated in China, and were afterward introduced into the West from China by the Arabs. But to return to our subject. By referring to different tables, and going through long computations, the circular table is completed, and a greater or less amount of vague and wordy explanations is appended. The divination may be for one, or for a number of years. It may give a general representation of the fortunes of a year, or particular accounts of each month, or even of each day. When the period is long, and the divination minute, the written document becomes voluminous, and can sometimes only be obtained at a cost of several dollars.

The superstitions of the people respecting the influences of the stars may be further illustrated by a communication from the chief magistrate in Ningpo, dated April 11th, 1850, addressed to the British Consul, and having reference to the purchase of a building site in the city by foreigners. The spot of ground in question is occupied by a heap of ruins, said to be the remains of houses which were burned, with their occupants, about four hundred years ago; since which time no one has dared to build on it, for fear of the spirits which are supposed to secrete themselves in its heaps of rubbish. The Chinese officer, after having painted in fearful colors the inconveniences resulting from living in a place haunted by spectres, and made dismal by horrid sounds of shrieks and groans, often heard in the silence of the night, proceeds as follows: "On the other hand, an examination of the astronomical tables shows that the baneful star, directing its noxious influences to places and things, points out for this year the two astronomical characters *mow* and *ki*, meaning centre, or middle; thereby denoting that all places centrically situated will be unlucky this year. This spot being almost in the centre of the city, it is apprehended that any important changes made on it, or any removal of earth from it during the present year, would give rise to all sorts of objections on the part of the people."

A class of blind fortune-tellers may be continually seen in the streets of Ningpo, led by an attendant, and giving notice of their approach by playing lively airs on a kind of guitar of three strings. They gain from oral instructions a superficial knowledge of the general principles described above, and practice some of the most simple methods prescribed in works on fortune-telling. They are great gossips, become familiarly acquainted by mutual consultations with the neighborhoods in which they carry on their business, and are particularly skilled in eliciting facts by indirect questions, and delivering their responses in ambiguous language. They make their disclosures in a chanting tone, with a musical accompaniment on their instruments. They find the women their most successful dupes. Their services may be secured for eighteen or twenty cash—less than two cents.

Closely connected with the above methods of fortune-telling, there is the universal practice of "comparing the six characters," with reference to marriage contracts. This is a simple process, and may be attended to by any of the classes of fortune-tellers above described. The six characters are those which represent the year, month, and day of one's birth. Before a marriage contract is entered into, these characters of the female in question must be handed to the friends of the male party. They are carefully examined, to see whether they are propitious, in themselves considered, and particularly whether they agree or clash with the characters of the other party. Deception is often practiced in these cases, and false or substituted characters are perhaps more frequently sent than the true.

In addition to the modes of fortune-telling which have been noticed, and which are regarded as the most respectable and successful, a variety of others might be mentioned, which, though common, are regarded as of little importance. One method is carried on by means of birds, which are trained to select strips of paper containing a few words of good or evil import. Snakes and turtles are used much in the same way, the direction of their heads indicating which piece of paper is to be selected.

FORTUNE-TELLING BY MEANS OF A BIRD AND SLIPS OF PAPER.

A class of men gain a livelihood by gratifying the curiosity of those who wish to know who and what they were in a previous state of existence, and what they are to be in a succeeding one. This is done by means of the map or table of the three lives. The applicant is required to state his name and the time of his birth, and, the leading facts of his present life being known, he is informed what were his name, occupation, and place of residence in the past life, and what they are to be in the next. It seems to afford a kind of satisfaction to persons who are miserable in this life to be told that they have been persons of wealth and high position in a previous state, or are to be in a future one. This mode of revealing past and future events has the advantage that its statements can not be disproved. It may be said, however, with reference to the other modes of divination above mentioned, that when the event does not correspond to the prediction, it is still insisted upon, that what was foretold is what *would* have occurred in the natural course of things; and that the seeming failure is due to an unusual amount of guilt bringing its necessary reward of evil, on the one hand, or a fund of merit producing unexpected fortune, on the other. The guilt or merit may be in consequence of actions performed either in the present or previous life.

The manner of deriving responses from the gods, and of obtaining a knowledge of the unseen world by means of necromancy, have been described in the previous chapter.

Physiognomy presents another and distinct mode of arriving at a knowledge of a person's character and future history, and several extensive treatises have been written on this subject by the Chinese. This art, as it is now practiced in China, bears no slight resemblance to Western phrenology. Regard is had to the general contour of the head, the different bumps or developments, and the complexion. Various plates represent, with great minuteness, the divisions of the head, with their inherent qualities. With this art is also connected the kindred art of palmistry. Men have the left hand examined, women the right. Different parts of the head are also supposed to have a certain connection with the "eight diagrams," and one part, or diagram, is regarded as having a controlling influence over an individual's life at one period, and another at another. Closely connected with the practice of physiognomy is that of feeling of the bones of the body, by doing which it is supposed that the character and future destinies of an individual may be determined. Not only are the outward features of men believed to be indicative of their future destiny, but also the forms and features of idols and graven images. Before they have been taken from the shop of the artisan, persons professing a knowledge of this art predict which will acquire the greatest celebrity, and draw the greatest number of worshipers to its shrine.

Another practice designed to insure success and good fortune is that of choosing lucky days. This is sometimes done by consulting the almanac, in which the character of each day is marked. In more important matters, however, a more particular examination is necessary; and a person wishing to commence any work, or enterprise, under favorable auspices, repairs to the shop of a professional day-chooser. These shops are numerous, and, in passing through the street, you may always see the grave day-prophet, with pen in hand, surrounded by his numerous city and country customers. The characters of days are determined by the stars which are supposed to preside over them. Sometimes a day is under the combined influences of different stars, prosperous and adverse. It is necessary, in such cases, to determine what influences predominate, and to examine the relation of particular stars to particular objects and enterprises. In commencing business, opening a school, building a house, fixing a wedding-day, or in engaging in any thing of great importance, the choosing of a lucky day is regarded a matter by no means to be neglected. If a school is opened under an unfavorable star, it is believed that sickness will prevail in it, endangering the lives of pupils and teacher. If a person undertakes a journey under a particular star, he is in danger of not being permitted to return home again. Nothing strikes the attention of an observer so much on lucky days as the large number of bridal chairs, with their accompanying retinue and music, which on these days may be seen passing in every direction through the streets, and through the country.

The fact of a person's being born on an unlucky day is regarded as having an unfavorable influence on his whole life, and is taken into account in divination by the different methods. A girl born under the star denominated in colloquial the "Broom Star" is looked upon with suspicion: and it is generally supposed that the family which receives her as a bride will have their house swept clean of its luck. A woman born under the star *Hien-chi* is supposed to be in particular danger of dying in child-bed. The manner in which the danger is averted is singular. Mistaking the first character of the name for another of the same sound, meaning *salt*, they make it to mean Salt Lake, and have some vague suspicion of evil connected with it. Some time before the confinement of the unfortunate individual, a quantity of salt is secretly thrown by one of her friends into a jar of water used by the family; and if a person, not knowing what has happened, tastes of the water, and remarks upon its saltness, the spell of the Salt Lake is broken. This may serve as a specimen of a large number of tricks, or charms, which are resorted to under different circumstances to avert anticipated evil.

The particular year in which a person is born has also much to do in directing his steps during future life. Each of the twelve characters used in reckoning time is associated with some animal. Hence a person, according to the character which occurs in the year when he was born, is said to have been born under the rat, ox, tiger, rabbit, etc. A person born under a particular character, or animal, must not engage in any important work or public ceremony on days the names of which contain a character clashing with the character occurring in his birth-year. Exceptions are made allowing persons to attend the funerals of their relatives, when they would otherwise be excluded by this rule. On days of public meetings, placards are often posted by officers, in conspicuous places, designating the class of persons whose horoscope renders it inauspicious for them to be present, and requesting them to stay at home.

Passing over other superstitions of a similar kind, that of seeking directions and revelations in dreams is worthy of special notice. The deities of some few temples have acquired great celebrity by giving important intimations to their worshipers in visions of the night. On certain days, generally the last great festival of the year, these temples are visited by a large concourse of people, of whom some come from a great distance. Their object is, for the most part, to seek direction with reference to improving their condition in life by a change of occupation at the beginning of the coming year. They arrive at the temple before night, burn incense, make prostrations, and present their prayers before the gods, and then lie down in some part of the temple, generally on the cold floor, to wait for a dream. Those who are so fortunate as to have one, put such an interpretation upon it as to suit their own fancies and inclinations; some receive as a dream the vagaries of their own imaginations, which are sure to be busy about the absorbing matter which engages their attention; and some, less credulous and imaginative, are obliged to go home dreamless and disappointed. To avoid the inconveniences of going to a remote temple, a person sometimes makes his bed in the kitchen, to beg a dream of the Kitchen God.

The above superstitions appear in themselves too frivolous and unreasonable to engage our serious attention. They acquire their interest and importance from the fact that they are not curious antiquities, but present realities; they are not theoretical speculations confined to the few, but practical beliefs of universal prevalence, swaying the minds of millions, and presenting a most serious obstacle to the reception of the truth. These beliefs are nicely adapted to the hopes and fears of man's nature, and are clung to with great tenacity by those whose reason has been moulded and enslaved by them. Fate and a thousand inferior deities take the place of an infinite and omnipresent God, and render it difficult for the mind even to conceive of his universal sovereignty and overruling providence.

CHAPTER XIV.

THE LANGUAGES OF CHINA.

The Want of Analogy between the Chinese and other Languages.—Each Word represented by a separate Character.—The Language not Hieroglyphic.—The whole Number of Characters.—The Language Monosyllabic.—The written Language unintelligible to the Ear, and not capable of being used as a spoken Language.—An Explanation of this Fact.—Tones and Aspirates.—Explanation of apparent Inconsistencies.—The spoken Languages of China, and their Relations to the written.—The Number of the spoken Languages or Dialects, and the Extent to which they differ.—In what these Differences consist.—More numerous in the South than in the North.—Description of the Mandarin, or Court Dialect.—Chinese Mode of printing.—"How much Time does it require to learn the Chinese Language?"—"What Proportion of the Population can read?"—Excellences and Defects of the Language.

I APPROACH the task of writing on the languages of China with no small degree of reluctance and embarrassment, on account of the great difficulty of making the subject intelligible to those who have not made it a special study. This difficulty arises from an utter want of correspondence or analogy between this language and others with which we are familiar—a fact which furnishes a striking evidence of the extreme isolation of the Chinese race from the other nations of the world.

The written language contains no alphabet, but each word has its own independent representation or character, so that there are as many characters as words. In the first formation of the written language, which must have been at a very early period, these characters seem to have been ideographic, and must have been very few: for instance, ⊙ stood for the sun, ☽ for the moon, etc. The present forms of these characters are 日 and 月.

The impossibility of inventing forms which would naturally suggest every object in nature and every idea of the mind, necessitated the use of characters more or less arbitrary: for instance, 人 *jin*, man; 不 *puh*, not; 大 *ta*, great; 女 *nyu*, woman. Some of the characters are simple like the preceding, but by far the greater part are compounded of simple characters: as 洗 *si*, to wash; 指 *che*, to point. *Si* is compounded of *shwuy*, water, on the left, and *sin*, before, on the right; *che* is compounded of *sheo*, hand, on the left, and *che*, meaning or intention, on the right. In both these characters, as may be readily seen, the left part suggests the meaning, and the right the sound, and many combinations are similarly formed. The simple character *heart*, for instance, is a component part of many others representing faculties and affections of the mind. The character *man* is connected with others representing the different dispositions and relations of man, and so on indefinitely, the different component parts giving some hint or clew to the discovery of the meaning, and perhaps also of the sound. This is not always nor generally the case, however; for many of the combinations seem entirely arbitrary, as 答 *tah*, to answer or respond; being made up of *chuh*, bamboo, and *hoh*, to unite; also 儀 *yi*, righteousness or uprightness, which is composed of *jin*, man, on the left-hand side, and on the right-hand *yang*, sheep, on the top, and *wo*, I, on the bottom.

I have referred thus particularly to the formation of characters, so as to correct two very common mistakes, both tending to produce the impression that the written language is much easier of acquisition than it really is. The first is, that the language, as now written, may be properly called ideographic. The fact is, on the contrary, that even the few characters which seem to have been such at first do not, in their present forms, indicate with any certainty the object represented. Most of the simple characters are, or seem to be, entirely arbitrary; and the compound characters, which give some intimation of their meaning, do it very vaguely and indefinitely. The other mistake is that of supposing, that though the language has no alphabet, the elementary characters unite together, according to a system governed by fixed rules, and affording advantages tantamount or, at least, similar to those of an alphabet, which is by no means the case. The mistake, however, has a slight foundation in fact, and is an error only in degree.

The whole number of characters in the Imperial Dictionary of the Emperor Kang-hi, which is complete in six large volumes, is about 40,000; most of these, however, as is the case with the larger proportion of words in our own large dictionaries, are obsolete forms, or characters very seldom used. From five to seven thousand comprise all those in ordinary use. These characters are unvarying in their forms, and admit of no inflections of any kind whatever. Distinctions of number, tense, etc., are made by the use of additional characters.

The languages of China, whether written or spoken, are strictly monosyllabic; that is, every syllable is a distinct word by itself. Occasionally two or more characters are used together as a compound word; but they are still seen to be distinct monosyllables as, in our language, *farm-house*, *foot-stool*, etc.

It is a striking peculiarity of the written or classical language, that it is not understood as spoken. By this it is not meant that it has fallen into disuse as a spoken language, but that it is not capable of being used as a medium of oral communication even by the learned who are familiar with it. It speaks to the eye, and not to the ear. The Scriptures, or any other book, or a letter, accurately read to a person unacquainted with its contents, though perfectly familiar with the language in which it is written, would be almost, if not entirely, unintelligible. This fact may be best explained by referring to the monosyllabic character of this language. The number of monosyllables which it is possible to form with the vocal organs or spell with an alphabet is necessarily limited. In

China the number used in any given place is about five hundred, while the number of characters in ordinary use is not far from five thousand. We have then only one-tenth as many monosyllabic sounds as characters, and, on an average, about ten different characters must be called by the same name or sound. There are then so many characters which have the same name, that hearing one pronounced does not indicate definitely what particular character is meant. Suppose a person hearing read the first chapter of the Gospel of John, the first sentence of which is "*Yun s yiu tao*," the question arises in the mind of the listener, which *yun* of many is it. And so with reference to the other characters; and as they are rapidly pronounced one after another, the mind is lost in a maze of uncertainty. We have analogies in our own language of the same sound, belonging to entirely different words: for instance, *write*, *rite*, *right*, *wright*; also, *sound*, a noise; *sound*, a body of water, and *sound*, to fathom. In the former illustration, the different words, though pronounced the same, are written differently, which is always the case in Chinese; in the latter illustration, the words are both written and pronounced alike. In our language, these monophonous words are so few that the other words in the sentence clearly fix the meaning; but what is exceptional with us is general with the Chinese.

The indefiniteness in distinguishing monosyllabic words is diminished much, though by no means fully obviated, by the introduction of *tones* and *aspirates*. Thus, four words spelled precisely alike, for instance, *chang*, *chang*, *chang*, *chang*, may, by being uttered with the different tones which belong to them respectively, be made as distinct and intelligible to a Chinaman's ear as if they were differently spelled and pronounced. To illustrate the aspirates: *tien*, with an aspirate (a slight *h* between the *t* and *i*), means heaven; without it, a dot; *ting*, with an aspirate, means to hear; without it, a nail. These important distinctions belong both to the written and the spoken languages, but, as stated before, they are not sufficient to make the written language intelligible to the ear.

By a singular contrariety (as the Chinese seem to be our antipodes in almost every thing), while we, in reading to ourselves, seldom read aloud, they almost always do, notwithstanding the sounds convey no meaning to the ear. This custom may be followed partly from force of habit, having studied in this way in school, or in order to fix the attention more closely by using the voice; but is due principally, I think, to a desire to heighten the pleasure of reading by catching the rhythm of the sentences with the ear while the sense is conveyed to the eye.

But a reader may object, "Are not the Confucian Classics composed in the written language of China?" "Certainly." "And do we not hear that the Chinese quote these classics orally in conversation?" "Yes." "Are they intelligible as thus quoted?" "Most certainly." "Then is not this inconsistent with what has just been stated, that the language can not be understood as heard?" This would seem contradictory in *English*, but is not in Chinese. A new or unfamiliar composition heard for the first time is unintelligible; but a familiar one, and especially one which has been committed to memory, is recognized at once, and each word or sound becomes definite, and brings up to the mind's eye the character which it represents. The sounds would not be recognized separately, or in new combinations, but they are in old or familiar connections and associations. The first sentence of the first chapter of John, which has been quoted, would be recognized by the ear of every Chinese Christian who reads his Bible, because he has become acquainted with them as thus associated, while he has probably never heard them pronounced together, and in the same order, in any other composition. Illiterate Chinese who can not read at all will also quote the classics intelligibly, just as one may use an occasional word or sentence of French without having ever studied that language.

It may be objected again, "If, as is frequently said, the language speaks to the eye, how is it that it is not ideographic?" The answer to this question will perhaps serve to add clearness to the answer to the previous one. For want of a better, I will make use of the following homely illustration: "I wish you to imitate the examples of Smith, Jones, and Brown." Now the hearing of this sentence would not bring before the mind the particular individuals of those numerous families designated, nor, as a matter of consequence, the traits of character to be imitated, any more than three monosyllabic Chinese sounds would designate the particular characters which they represent. Suppose these individuals were brought before you; if they were perfect strangers, you could not, by merely looking at them, tell with any certainty either their individual names or peculiarities. Their faces would probably be just about as ideographic as the Chinese characters. You might think that, from some fancied family resemblance, you were able to guess the name of one or more of them, and, from the general appearance of another, you might learn something of his probable character and peculiarities, but you would be very apt to make mistakes. If, however, you were familiarly acquainted with these men, a sight of them would bring up to the mind, by association, all that you knew of them. So of Chinese characters: to one who has studied and become acquainted with them individually, they convey to the eye a great deal; to those who have not, little or nothing.

The *spoken* languages of China are various, and they all differ widely from the written, as might be necessarily inferred, from what has been said above. They resemble the written language, inasmuch as the great proportion of words, and also many of the idioms, or constructions, are the same in both. They differ principally in this, that the spoken languages are less compact, using very often two words for one in the written. It is in a great measure, by this means, that the indefinite words of the written language become clear and specific in the spoken. The character 民 *ming*, meaning people, would be unintelligible, as heard pronounced, but the colloquial for people, viz., *pah-sing*, could hardly be mistaken. It could not be determined by the ear whether the monosyllable *kung* represented the character 公 *kung*, fair or just, 工 *kung*, a laborer, 攻 *kung*, to attack, 功 *kung*, merit, 恭 *kung*, respectful, 供 *kung*, to provide, or some one of several other characters, all of which have precisely the same *pronunciation* and *tone*. But the colloquial words *kung-tao*, just, *kung-tsiang*, laborer, *kung-kieh*, to attack, *kung-lao*, merit, *kung-kin*, respectful, *kung-yin*, to provide for, etc., are recognized by the ear at once. The former illustration is an example of substituting a different compound word in the vernacular for the single one in the written language, *pah-sing* for *ming;* the latter illustration presents the same words in the two different forms, a simple monosyllable in the written language, and the same in combination with another one in the vernacular.

The other points of difference between the written and spoken languages are different pronouns and particles (which, though comparatively few in number, are in constant use), and variations in constructions, idioms, and pronunciations.

The relations subsisting between the written and spoken languages are similar, in many respects, to those between the Latin and the spoken languages of Europe a few hundred years ago. The Latin had many points of resemblance with these spoken languages, and was made use of to enrich them all. The Latin was understood by scholars only. It was the common medium of communication between the learned, who spoke different vernacular languages, while the illiterate had no common medium of communication. The analogy referred to holds in all these points.

The written language of China is understood by the learned, not only of the whole Chinese Empire, but also of Japan, Loo-Choo, Corea, Manchuria, and Cochin China; and through it a far larger proportion of the human race can be reached and influenced than through any other language of the world. When illiterate men wish to communicate by letter with friends in other provinces, they go to a literary acquaintance or to the village school-teacher, and communicate their wishes to him in their vernacular. The scholar, recasting the ideas in a new form, composes the letter in the written language. When it reaches its destination, the person who receives it, if he is not a scholar, engages some one else who is able to do it to translate the letter into *his* vernacular. In this way persons communicate with each other who can not write at all, and who could not converse intelligibly, were they together.

With reference to the variations of the spoken languages and their relations to each other, somewhat different representations have been made. They are often spoken of as different dialects or variations of the same language. This is true in a degree, but, without explanation and limitation, is calculated to mislead most readers, as they may, with equal propriety, be spoken of as different languages. In the province of Shantung, a good scholar of that region, after listening some time, and intently, to a conversation between myself and a Ningpo man in the Ningpo dialect, asked me if we were speaking English, not recognizing a single familiar syllable or sound. Natives from the Northern and Southern provinces are as unable to communicate with each other in their vernaculars as an Englishman would be to communicate with a German or a Spaniard. Visiting the southern part of China, familiarly acquainted with the Ningpo dialect and the Court dialect, in listening to long conversations and to sermons in the Amoy dialect, I was not able to detect at first a single idea or word. In Canton I could catch the general drift of sermons, though I could distinguish but a very few words.

An estimation of the number of different spoken languages or dialects in China will depend, of course, upon the degree of divergence or unintelligibility which shall be regarded sufficient to constitute a different language. In most cases, the vernaculars shade off into each other by almost imperceptible gradations. In travelling twenty or thirty miles in the south of China, you may notice slight changes in the speech of the common people. In travelling eighty or one hundred miles, the changes are more marked, and oral communication becomes difficult. In many directions, a journey of one hundred and fifty or two hundred miles will bring you into a region where your vernacular is almost useless, except as you may happen to find a person who has lived in the locality where it is spoken, and will act as your interpreter.

The variations of these dialects consist in the use of different pronouns and particles, and differences of words and expressions, pronunciations and tones. Though at first a new dialect, when heard spoken rapidly, seems entirely different, a little attention and study will bring to light familiar words and expressions in new forms, and the transition from one dialect to another is easy, compared to the first acquisition of any of them. It is often noticed that persons always speak the first dialect which they learn with greater accuracy and purity than any acquired afterward, as one is apt to carry peculiarities of the first into all others which are based upon it.

Variations of dialects take place much more rapidly and widely in some parts of the country than in others. A marked distinction in this respect is seen between the Northern and Southern provinces, the degree of variation being very great in the South, as compared to the North. South of the River Yiang-tz a great number of dialects is spoken; north of the river, but one general language, or dialect, with comparatively unimportant variations. Different dialects, having common affinities, may be grouped into classes or families. Those which are more generally spoken have been reduced to writing, and have their own separate literatures. Of these, the Canton, Fu-chau, and the Northern or Court dialect, may be particularly mentioned. The most of the dialects are not written, have no literature, and it is difficult to write them purely by means of the characters used in the written language, because many words occur in the vernaculars which do not occur in the written language, and, consequently, have no character in it to represent them.

The Court dialect is worthy of particular notice, since, as before stated, it is spoken with variations over nearly the whole of Northern China. It has been fixed upon by the government as a common spoken language, to be learned by all its officials, and used in all the yamuns throughout the empire. Hence the term Court dialect. It is also often called by foreigners Mandarin, which is, I believe, a Portuguese word, from the Latin "*mando*," "to command." The Chinese word is *Kwan-hwa*, the "language of officers." Many of the fictitious works of China are written in this dialect. On account of its prominence and importance as a written language, and perhaps because Mandarin books present precisely the same appearance as books in the literary language, some suppose that the Mandarin and the written language are identical; this is altogether a mistake. The Mandarin is simply one of the many spoken languages of China, and bears the same relation to the classical language, or language of books, that the other spoken dialects do. It owes its prominence to the three facts stated above, viz., that it is spoken over a wider region of country, it is the common medium of communication between officials throughout the empire, and is reduced to writing and has an extensive literature.

Many persons in the United States and England have also received the impression that the Mandarin dialect is a kind of superior or more refined spoken language, used by the higher classes and scholars in contradistinction to the common people. This is also a mistake. Scholars and the higher class in every part of the empire speak the vernacular of their own locality in common with the masses, and generally know no other. When they go to the capital to attend the examinations, they naturally become more or less acquainted with it by hearing it constantly spoken; and when they succeed in the examinations, and obtain official positions, they are obliged to learn it as the universal and exclusive medium for transacting official business. Many of the officers of the empire speak it very imperfectly it being corrupted and vitiated by their original dialects or mother-tongues. Scholars, men of leisure, and business men and travellers, often learn this dialect as an accomplishment or a convenience. A person acquainted with it will find a few in almost every part of the empire with whom he can communicate; if nowhere else, certainly in the yamuns.

A very singular-spoken language, called Pigeon-English, has sprung up on the coast of China during the last thirty years, which merits a special notice, not on account of its character or general prevalence, but because it is the almost exclusive medium of communication between natives and foreigners at the open ports. This language has grown out of the necessities of the condition in which the two races are placed, and certainly nothing but extreme necessity could justify the use of such an uncouth and ridiculous jargon. Neither party, natives or foreigners, has the time or opportunity to learn the language of the other, but they must communicate ideas at once. A compromise has been effected in forming a language made up mostly of English words in a modified or corrupted form, with an admixture of Portuguese and Chinese, wrought into Chinese idioms. The manner in which many English words are changed or corrupted may be illustrated by the *pigeon* of "Pigeon-English." This new and peculiar language is used principally in carrying on business, and business is a very important word in it. In asking the Chinaman to pronounce this word, he is found utterly unable to do it, and produces a sound which it is difficult to catch or spell with any precision, but which somewhat resembles the word *pigeon.* So the accommodating foreigner, finding that the Chinaman can pronounce pigeon with tolerable ease and accuracy, takes the liberty of giving the word business the *modified form* of pigeon, so that the Pigeon-English is simply the Business-English. Our arbitrary and artificial language is further simplified, I believe (for I can not speak authoritatively on this subject), by making the word *my* stand for the different cases and numbers of the first personal pronoun, *you* for the second, and *he* for the third. Various other liberties which foreigners take with their mother-tongue need not be mentioned. The whole language, or dialect, is exceedingly meagre, containing, perhaps, only a few hundred words. Foreigners learn to speak it intelligibly (?) in a few weeks, and *fluently* in a few months, and make it answer all practical purposes. Natives seeking foreign employ sometimes take lessons for a few days of a native professor, who advertises to teach "Red-haired Talk," which many of them think is pure English. Others take a position in a foreign establishment, in which they only have to do with their own people, and pick up the language by degrees as they have opportunity. I saw, before leaving China, a translation into this dialect by an Englishman of the address familiar to most school-boys, "My name is Norval; on the Grampian Hills, my father feeds his flock," etc.; a few sentences of the beginning of which may be given, by way of illustration, as follows: "My name b'long Norval. Top side Keh-lam-pian hill; my fader chow-chow he sheep." Hardly a word of the next sentence, "A frugal swain, whose constant care is to increase his store," has any equivalent in this poverty-stricken tongue, so a free translation is made: "My fader very small heartee man—too much likee dat piecie dolla."

A few words on the Chinese art of printing may be of interest to some readers. Every page and character of every book is engraved on wooden blocks expressly for that book. In other words, the Chinese do not use movable metallic types. The matter to be printed is beautifully written on a sheet of the usual Chinese transparent paper the same in size as a leaf of the book to be published. This sheet is pasted, with the written side down, on the block or board to be engraved. The engraver cuts out all the blank spots in and around the written letters, leaving them in relief upon the board. An impression taken from the block will give, of course, an exact counterpart of the written sheet. A block is engraved for each page, and the impressions are taken by hand, without any press or machinery. It would seem that the introduction of our art of printing in China would save a great deal of time and expense. The difficulty, however, is that we are obliged to prepare a font of four or five thousand types in the Chinese instead of less than thirty, as in our language. Several excellent fonts and printing-presses have been introduced, but, as yet, we can hardly say, on the whole, that we have made much advance upon the Chinese art of printing either in cheapness or elegance.

Chinese books are read from the right side of the book or page toward the left, and from the top to the bottom of a page, in vertical instead of horizontal columns.

The accompanying representation in parallel columns of the different styles made use of in writing and printing Chinese characters, is taken from Williams's "Middle Kingdom." The sentence expressed in each column, character for character, is, "Writing has six forms, called *chuen*, called *li*, called *kiai*, called *hing*, called *tsau*, called *sung*." I avail myself of the explanations or descriptions of these various forms taken from the same work.

"The Chinese have six different styles of writing characters, which correspond to black-letter, script, italic, Roman, etc., in English, but are much more unlike than these. The first is called *chuen shu*, from the name of the person who invented it, but foreigners usually call it the *seal character*, from its most common use in seals and ornamental inscriptions. It is the most ancient style of writing, next to the picture hieroglyphics, and has undergone many changes in the course of ages. It is studied by those who cut seals in inscriptions, but no books are ever printed in it.

"The second is the *li shu*, or style of official attendants, which was introduced about the Christian era, as an elegant style to be employed in engrossing documents. It is now seen in prefaces and formal inscriptions, though to a small extent,

書有六體曰篆曰隸曰楷曰行曰艸曰宋

書有六骵曰篆曰隸曰楷曰行曰艸曰宋

書有六體曰篆曰隸曰楷曰行曰草曰宋

書有六體曰篆曰隸曰楷曰行曰草曰宋

書有六體曰篆曰隸曰楷曰行曰草曰宋

書有六體曰篆曰隸曰楷曰行曰草曰宋

and requires little or no special study to read it, as it differs but slightly from the following.

"The third is the *kiai shu*, or pattern style, and has been gradually formed by the improvements in good writing. It is the usual form of Chinese characters, and no one can claim a literary name among his countrymen if he can not write neatly and correctly in this style. Books are sometimes printed in it.

"The fourth, *hing shu*, or running hand, is the common hand of a neat writer. It is frequently used in prefaces and inscriptions, scrolls and tablets; and there are books, prepared in parallel columns, having this and the pattern style arranged for school-boys to learn to write both at the same time. The two differ so much that the running hand can not be read without a special study; and although this labor is not very serious when the language of books is familiar, still, to become well acquainted with both of them, withdraws many days and months of the pupil from progress in acquiring knowledge to learning two modes of writing the same word. Shopmen use the running hand, and are sometimes better acquainted with its abridged forms than they are with the fuller one of books.

"The fifth style is called *tsao tsz*, or plant character, and is a freer description of running hand than the preceding, being full of abbreviations, and the pencil runs from character to character without taking it from the paper almost at the writer's fancy. It is more difficult to read than the preceding, but, as the abbreviations are somewhat optional, the *tsao tsz* varies considerably, and more or less resembles the running hand according to the will of the writer. The fancy of the Chinese for a "flowing pencil," and a mode of writing where the elegance and freedom of the caligraphy can be admired as much or more than the style or sentiment of the writing, as well as a desire to contract their multangular characters as much as possible, has contributed to introduce and perpetuate these two styles of writing. How much all these varieties of form superadd to the difficulty of learning the mere apparatus of knowledge, need hardly be stated.

"The sixth style is called *sung shu*, and was introduced under the *Sung* dynasty, in the tenth century, soon after printing on wooden blocks was invented, and still continues to be used more than any other in well printed-books. It differs from the *kiai shu*, or pattern style, merely in a certain squareness of shape and angularity of stroke, which transcribers for the press only are obliged to learn. Of these six forms of writing, the pattern style and running hand are the only two which the people learn to any great extent, although many acquire the knowledge of some words in the seal character; and the running hand of every person, especially those engaged in business, approaches more or less to the plant character."

In writing, the Chinese use a fine soft camel's-hair pencil or brush, holding it in a vertical position with the thumb nearly upright, and the fingers nearly vertical, the lower part of the pen passing between the two middle fingers. Their ink is the common India ink, which is ground on a stone.

It is a question often asked, "How much time does it require to learn the Chinese language?" A person of ordinary ability, with close application and perseverance, will be able to acquire one of the *spoken* languages, so as to speak it accurately and intelligibly, in about a year, though with a small vocabulary. In the course of two or three years, he ought to possess a good vocabulary, and fluency in using it. To become familiar with the written language of China is almost the work of a lifetime.

Another important question is frequently asked, "What proportion of the population of China can read?" Some English writers have made the estimate very large, and some very small. The answer which we will adopt as the true one will depend upon what we regard as *reading* in China. Many persons who have attended school a few years, and learned the names of a considerable number of the most common characters without having learned their meanings, may be able to read a page of a book, or most of the characters in it, very much as a person may read a page of Latin, without knowing any thing, or but very little, about the language. If we include these persons among the readers of China, their number will be large; but it is evident that this is not reading in any proper sense. Again, a person in a drug-store may become familiarly acquainted with the characters designating every article in the store, and also with terms and expressions used in keeping books and writing business letters. Within this little sphere, he may be said to read and write intelligibly and accurately, while he may know little or nothing of the language as a whole. The same is true in other occupations. If we exclude this class as well as the former from those who can understand literature generally, the proportion of readers is very small.

Learning to read Chinese is very different from learning to read English. We have an alphabetical system, by which we read *our own spoken language;* the Chinese must learn a new and difficult language, and also learn to read every word separately and individually. Hardly any of the women in China are taught letters at all; very few of the farmers and artisans, who form the large proportion of the males, can read intelligibly; and few of the shop-keepers can read the language as a whole. The fact is, there are not many who understand general literature, as the masses of our country do, except professed literary men or scholars. It is my opinion that the whole number of those who can read in this sense is not more than three per cent. of the whole population. But we must remember that this three per cent. forms an aggregate of twelve millions, and that they are scattered uniformly over the whole country, and influence all the rest.

The principal excellences or advantages of the Chinese written language are its remarkable compactness, and its power of expression. It is justly admired for the beauty and variety of its characters, its copiousness, and the delicate shades of meaning which it expresses. To show its fullness in some points, take the following illustrations: In the place of our one word to carry, the Chinese use *kih*, to take or carry in the hand; *pao*, to carry in the arms; *kyih*, to carry under the arm; *pung*, to carry extended in both arms; *ting*, to carry on the head; *pe*, to carry on the back; *tiao*, to carry suspended from the ends of a stick resting on the shoulder; *tai*, to carry suspended from the middle of a pole, or poles, resting on two men's shoulders.

The Chinese language, on account of its monosyllabic form, and its being without changes or inflections, has been represented by some modern writers as the most primitive and simple of all languages. Though this may be true, in a certain sense, it is certainly, in its present form, one of the most, if not the most, artificial and elaborate. The difficulties of composing in it may be compared to those of composing in a high style of classical Greek. While many missionaries are able to compose fluently and accurately in the spoken language in the course of two or three years, and prepare vernacular books for the press with very little assistance or revision from native scholars, there are very few of those who have been studying the written language ten, fifteen, or twenty years, who feel competent to write a book in it unaided by a native literary man.

The great difficulties connected with the thorough acquisition of the written language will necessitate some change or modification of it when the Chinese introduce Western arts and sciences. When matters of more importance claim their attention, their devotion to the study of language simply must be abated. Probably one of the first effects will be that of lowering or simplifying the style of the written language, and bringing it into nearer accordance with the spoken.

CHAPTER XV.

BENEVOLENT INSTITUTIONS OF CHINA.

The Origin of these Institutions, and the Distinctions between them and those in Christian Lands.—Orphan Asylums.—Asylums for Old Men.—Asylums for Animals.—Institutions for the Relief of Widows.—Free Schools.—Chinese Dispensaries.—Institutions for collecting old Paper, etc.—Society for the Suppression of immoral Books.—Beggars.—A benevolent Society embracing a Variety of Objects.—Various Benefactions and Modes of acquiring Merit.

THAT benevolent societies are found in a heathen land, may appear strange to Western readers; but it is a fact that they exist in China in numbers and variety hardly exceeded in Christian lands. In comparing these institutions with those of the West, one is also struck with the similarity which exists in their nature and objects. We have here Orphan Asylums, Institutions for the Relief of Widows, as well as for the Aged and Infirm, Public Hospitals, and Free Schools, together with other kindred institutions more peculiarly Chinese in their character. Moral tracts are also distributed to a great extent.

Roman Catholics have claimed the honor of introducing these societies into China, but there is evidence that they existed anterior to the introduction of Christianity; and there is no necessity for seeking for them a foreign origin, as they grow naturally out of the customs and institutions of the people. These associations, whether in China or in Christian lands, have their common origin in the instinctive sentiment of pity which mankind everywhere feel for the unfortunate and distressed, and the natural promptings of the heart to afford the necessary relief. But in projecting and executing extensive plans of benevolence, a stronger motive is required than a temporary emotion or impulse. It is in the character of this permanent motive that the distinction between these institutions in Christian and heathen lands is found. Among Christians, the strength of this motive is due mainly to high moral principle, and a sense of duty and responsibility. In China, the principal ingredient in it, though it is strengthened, no doubt, by the higher and nobler impulses of our nature, is selfishness. The characteristic feature of the false religions of China is the performance of meritorious actions with a view to the attainment of selfish ends. In doing an act which the conscience pronounces good and right, a Chinaman imagines that he is justly entitled to some personal advantage or reward corresponding to the character of the act performed. Each donor, in conferring his bounty, has one or more objects in view more or less specific. The most common objects sought for are success in business, the prosperity and happiness of one's family, fame, and civil promotion, and the atonement of sin and consequent blessedness in a future state. With these introductory remarks, I propose to present a succinct view of the character and operations of some of the principal benevolent societies which now exist in China.

Orphan Asylums are found in almost every city, and frequently in country villages. They are established by a wealthy individual, or several individuals associated together, and are sometimes supported by a permanent fund, or the proceeds of lands given for that purpose. Most children brought to these establishments are infants whose parents are too poor to support them. The great majority of them are girls. They are put in the charge of foster-mothers, who generally live at their own homes, and are required to present them for inspection at the asylum every half-month, when they receive their regular stipend. When the children are about two years old, they are brought back to the establishment, and several are put under the care of one nurse. When they have arrived at a suitable age, boys are put out as apprentices to learn trades, or sent to free schools; girls are sold to the poorer classes, according to the custom of the country, as wives. Children of both sexes are, however, not unfrequently adopted, and treated by their benefactors as their own. While the benevolent design of these institutions is generally at first thoroughly carried out, and the children are well taken care of, the conduct of them afterward too often falls into the hands of those who are only interested in securing their own advantage, and use the funds intrusted to them for their own purposes. The large proportion of children who die in these asylums is sufficient proof that they are not cared for as they should be.

In Hang-chow, the provincial capital of Che-kiang, I found, in connection with a variety of benevolent institutions, an Asylum for Old Men, in which I became particularly interested, and which I frequently visited. It contained, in 1859, about five hundred inmates. The building was large, the beneficiaries were made very comfortable, and every thing connected with the establishment was carried on with as much order and system as in a similar institution in our own country. In addition to an immense dining-room, kitchen, and sleeping apartments, conveniences were afforded in separate buildings for making different articles of handicraft, and the inmates were at liberty to spend as much time as they chose working at some trade, and to make such use as they pleased of whatever they might earn in this way.

Not far from the same city, and forming a part of the large and celebrated Buddhist temple *Yuing-si*, is, or rather was, an institution such as I have not met with or heard of elsewhere, which illustrates at the same time the desire of the Chinese to acquire merit, and the practical influence of the doctrine of the transmigration of souls. The institution referred to is an Asylum for Animals. It was a large building a short distance from the temple, and almost every department of the animal kingdom was represented in it, and some in large numbers. It was supposed that these animals, placed under the fostering influences of this celebrated temple, were almost sure to rise in the scale of being, and that they would probably become men in the next state of existence. Some were family pets which had received this greatest of evidences of affection, that of being made occupants for life of this institution. Many had been bought in the market, and rescued from the butcher's knife, by persons coming to the temple to worship, who had thus obtained the double merit of saving life, and aiding in the securing of a higher existence in the life to come.

Societies for affording pecuniary aid to widows are very common, and exist either independently or in connection with societies embracing several distinct objects conjointly. Immediately after the death of her husband, a widow receives a larger stipend than at any subsequent time, in order to assist her in providing for her young children. This allowance is gradually diminished; and as old age approaches, women of this class, if they have no children able to support them, are sometimes transferred to another establishment which provides for the wants of the aged and infirm. When a respectable and worthy widow is in want, and the limited number of beneficiaries in the public asylums is complete, private individuals frequently make contributions to afford relief in these particular cases. The peculiar interest felt in this class of women is due to the views of the Chinese respecting the disreputableness of the second marriages of widows. Among the poor, and in case of widows who have no children to depend upon in after-life, a second marriage is allowable, though the opposite course is spoken of in terms of the highest commendation as honorable and meritorious. The ground for this feeling seems to be respect for the memory of the deceased husband. Not only are widows assisted in remaining in the single state as above mentioned, but they are still further encouraged to do so by the hope of having stone tablets erected to their memory by the special order, and partly at the expense of the Emperor. These tablets are in shape like a large gateway, and are everywhere seen forming one of the principal objects in Chinese scenery. They are generally in a conspicuous place by the roadside, near the residence of the family with which the person commemorated was connected. They are built about twenty feet high, of the finest hewn stone, with sundry ornaments and inscriptions elaborately carved. It happens occasionally that a daughter devotes

HONORARY STONE PORTAL TO THE MEMORY OF VIRTUOUS AND FILIAL WIDOWS.

her life to taking care of her parents, refusing ever to marry; in which case she is regarded with still greater respect, and is honored with a still finer monumental arch. It is part of the business of these societies to be at the trouble and expense of bringing these cases before the notice of the Emperor, and securing for those who are incapacitated for attending to this business themselves that public consideration and respect which it is supposed they deserve. In the present condition of the empire, it is difficult to obtain money from the imperial treasury for such objects, and a modification of the old practice has been adopted, which consists in inscribing several names on the same tablet.

Free Day Schools are everywhere to be met with, and some of the larger cities contain several of them. Each one is usually instituted and supported by the benefactions of a rich individual or family. It is not considered very respectable to attend these charity schools, and the pupils in them are, for the most part, the children of the poor. As a general thing, they are also not so well taught as other schools. It need hardly be remarked, that while it is not considered very respectable to attend a native free school, it is still less so to attend a foreign one. This is owing not only to the invidiousness of depending upon foreigners for education, but to the fact that foreign as well as native books are taught in them. Pupils are obtained for foreign day schools, either by procuring a superior teacher, or by presents to the boys, or by locating the school where there is no native school to compete with it. An effort to start a Christian day school some years since in the city of Chinhai induced the natives to add to the number of their own schools, so that another pupil could not be obtained in the city.

In some parts of China schools for girls exist, taught by female teachers. In most places, however, females are seldom taught letters, and schools for their benefit are not known. Foreigners, in establishing them, invariably give a little sum of money or some rice for each day's attendance, and it is thought that these schools could not be kept together in any other way.

The gratuitous distribution of medicine is quite common in China. In the summer especially, certain remedies much prized by the people may be obtained free of charge from societies which include this among other objects for which they are instituted. There is a very common mode of practicing the healing art, professedly from benevolent motives, in which a selfish object is too apparent. Notices may continually be seen placarded in public places calling the attention of the public to some distinguished personage of the Esculapian school who has learned his art at the capital, or from some foreigner, or from some distinguished native practitioner, or by communication with the genii, who is desirous of relieving those who are in a condition of suffering and distress, and will give them an opportunity to avail themselves of his knowledge and skill without charge, *except for the cost of medicine.*

Perhaps the most popular of all the methods of obtaining merit in China is that of collecting old scraps of printed paper. This is practiced extensively by individuals and families, as well as by societies. Persons are hired to go about the streets, and in shops and houses, to gather every thing of the kind which can be seen. The merit of the practice is supposed to consist in keeping the Chinese written character, so much and so extravagantly revered, from being trampled upon, thrown away with other kinds of refuse, or otherwise treated with disrespect. No distinction is made between the written and printed character; between an old leaf from one of the classics, and one from a vulgar song-book; between a proclamation of an officer, and the copy-book of a school-boy. In school-rooms, shops, private residences, and sometimes by the roadside, baskets or boxes designed for the reception of these revered scraps are placed in conspicuous situations bearing the inscription, "Respect printed paper." When a large quantity of this paper has been collected, it is burned,

MAN WITH BASKETS GATHERING LETTERED PAPER.

and the ashes are generally carried by junks to the sea, where they are thrown overboard.

In this custom of the Chinese we have one of the principal reasons why the Christian books which we distribute among them are respectfully used and carefully preserved. It is also worthy of remark, that few things excite the feelings and prejudices of the Chinese, or produce a more unfavorable impression with regard to foreigners, than the manner in which we are accustomed to treat useless printed paper. It is often referred to as an evidence of our want of right views and principles. Christian Chinese are hardly less under the influence of these feelings than the rest of their countrymen, and, in the different parts of China, they have frequently and earnestly expostulated with their foreign teachers with reference to the course pursued by them in this particular. Some missionaries purposely disregard these prejudices, on the ground that they have their origin in a veneration for the God of Letters, and a fear of offending him. Others are of the opinion that this superstition is of a more innocent character, and is chiefly owing, even in the minds of the heathen Chinese, to an overweening regard for the characters themselves, on account of their antiquity, their beauty, the associations connected with them, and the advantages derived from their use. The fact that native Christians, who are thoroughly freed from idolatrous superstitions, still sympathize with their countrymen in this particular, adds to the probability of the latter opinion. It is a question whether regard to the weak consciences of our native brethren, and a care lest the Gospel should be evil spoken of, should not induce us to treat with more forbearance and consideration what may be but an innocent and harmless prejudice.

These singular notions respecting the character have, within the past few years, been carried to a still greater extreme, causing no little trouble and annoyance. The people have noticed the inconsistency of gathering up fragments of printed paper, while they have paid no regard to broken crockery bearing inscriptions. Accordingly, these societies, which easily gain the concurrence, and the sanction and co-operation of the authorities in carrying out their plans, have succeeded in prohibiting, to a great extent, the practice of ornamenting china with their universally admired chirography. Arrangements have also been made in some places for buying up at cost all this kind of ware in the shops. Through the influence of these societies, the authorities have also forbidden the working of Chinese letters in embroidery. Not only common symbols now in ordinary use, but other figures and designs bearing no resemblance to any character whatever, are declared to be modifications of ancient characters, and are included under the common interdict.

A new enterprise originated a few years since in the city of Suchow, and has since been introduced into other places, which can not but be regarded with peculiar interest. Its express object is "the suppression of immoral books." This enterprise has also gained the sanction and concurrence of the authorities, and has already done much toward checking the influence of this source of demoralization. The people are not only requested, but required to bring such books as have been prohibited to the head-quarters of this society, where they receive nearly an equivalent for them in money. Not only books, but the stereotyped blocks from which they are printed, are thus collected at a great expense, and all are together at stated times committed to the flames. Several of the celebrated standard novels of China, which, in a moral point of view, will bear favorable comparison with some of the current popular literature of our own country, have fallen under the ban of this society, and can not now be obtained without great trouble and expense. Instances have occurred in which booksellers who have continued to sell immoral works in the face of these regulations have become obnoxious to public authority, and incurred a great sacrifice of reputation and property.

Not a small portion of the benefactions of the Chinese is given to beggars—a class which is very numerous. It is not only regarded as meritorious to give to them, but very unpropitious to send them away empty. Accordingly, the people are much afraid of beggars, and meekly put up with all sorts of impertinence and insolence from them. They are scarcely ever turned away from a shop without at least a worn-out cash (in value less than one-tenth of a cent), though they sometimes wait a long time to get it. Those who are most boisterous, and give the shop-keeper most trouble, get their allowance soonest, and leave to beset some one else. They are clothed, when clothed at all, in the most disgusting manner possible, in order that the people may be anxious the sooner to get rid of them. Some introduce themselves with a boisterous, grating song; some attract attention by an annoying rattle; some carry a snake trained to dart out its tongue, to operate upon the fears of those whose sympathies are not so easily reached. Sometimes a company of clamorous women with children may be seen together besetting a shop-keeper. If the unfortunate man is unwilling to comply with their demands, or undertakes to drive them from his door, they pour upon him a torrent of abuse, and not unfrequently beat upon his counter in defiance. There is no help for the poor victim; though provoked to the last degree, he looks the very picture of despair, afraid to give vent to his anger for fear of calling together an additional number of these harpies, and thus adding to the confusion. Beggars are, in many respects, the most independent men in the empire, and it is surprising to see how passively the people submit to their inflictions. The class referred to, however, are the worst kind, and may be called professional beggars. They demand their cash as their right, and return no thanks for it. They usually have a leader, who is distinguished from the common herd by his superior insolence and daring, and woe betide the man who has fallen under the displeasure of this beggar-king, and is visited by him and his motley crew to seek revenge. These gangs are mostly to be feared on wedding and similar occasions. Disturbances may be avoided at such times by giving an amount of money to one of these leaders, who then guards the door for the day, and either buys or beats off all other comers.

A more worthy class of mendicants may sometimes be distinguished from these, who are really objects of charity. They usually beg by the roadside, in an imploring tone of voice, and repay their benefactors with the wish that they may live a hundred years. The expression used in begging is, "Perform a good act," intimating that the person conferring a favor, not only relieves the one receiving it, but acquires merit for himself. In some cities and towns arrangements are made for buying off these beggars. Each shop or family pays a yearly beggar's fee; the fund thus obtained is given to the fraternity of beggars, and they are expected to appeal for nothing more, and leave the people unmolested—at least, those streets which have paid their contributions.

There are in Chinese cities public asylums, sustained at the expense of government, containing a limited number of diseased and disabled poor, who receive a daily allowance, insufficient for their support, and eke out the remainder of their living by begging. They are more successful than others, as they carry the evidences of their misfortunes in their physical infirmities, and some of them amass considerable property. These also have their heads or leaders, some of whom are brokers and bill-shavers. They sometimes buy bad bills at a discount, and collect them by attacking the house of the delinquent debtor with an army of beggars, until he is glad to get rid of them by paying it.

The most popular of the benevolent institutions in Ningpo, and the one having by far the largest income, includes a variety of objects. It has a fund for providing coffins for the poor, a fund for carrying coffins which have been thrown carelessly aside to some suitable place for interment, and one for collecting and burying again human bones which are found exposed to view; also a fund for providing medicine in summer, and warm clothes in winter; a fund for the relief of widows; one for gathering old printed paper, and the only one in Ningpo for suppressing immoral books. This society has a large building, with as many secretaries and superintendents as are necessary for the orderly and efficient carrying on of its extensive operations.

It is also worthy of remark, that most of the roads and fine arch bridges, as well as the public buildings of China, are constructed by voluntary donations. In connection with these public works it is very common to see stone tablets erected, containing the names of the donors and the amounts of their subscriptions.

Tea is in many places provided for travellers, and offered gratuitously in resting-houses by the roadside. Poor scholars are furnished with money for travelling expenses in attending the literary examinations.

A family in Ningpo is quite celebrated for hiring a company of masons during a part of the year to go about the country repairing graves so old that it is not known to whom they belong. Though not a remnant of a coffin or of bones can be found in them, new bricks are made to enclose the place which once contained the coffin, and these are covered with flag-stones, on which earth is piled in the form of a new tomb. Though nothing can be seen in them, it is said "the ashes still repose there." A young member of this family has lately been successful in the provincial examination, and his good fortune is supposed to be due to the merit resulting from this enterprise. It is currently reported that his compositions were rejected by one of the public examiners at first, but were afterward forced upon his attention in dreams on successive nights by crowds of interested earnest persons, believed to be the grateful spirits belonging to the graves which have been repaired.

To attempt to enumerate all the modes of acquiring merit in China would be as tedious as it would be useless. The institutions referred to above have been cited as the principal and most important, the practice of tract distribution being reserved for a separate chapter. The names and objects of these societies differ in different sections of the empire.

It is a remark often heard in China from those who are urged to seek for happiness in a future state, that they are poor, and can not perform deeds of merit. How little do we who are possessed of it appreciate the blessings of that Gospel which is preached to the poor, and makes those who are rich in faith alone heirs of a heavenly and unfading inheritance.

CHAPTER XVI.

THE MORAL TRACT LITERATURE OF CHINA.

The Literature of China, various and extensive.—The Relation of moral Tracts to the Chinese religious Systems.— Different Kinds of Tracts.—Table of Contents of "Light in the Dark Dwelling."—Motives to which the distributing of Tracts is due.--The Work is done by Individuals, and not Societies.—These Works evidence the Teachings of natural Religion, and the Necessity of a superior Revelation.—Translation of "Ode on Emptiness."—"Ode on Discontent."—Treatise on "Rewards and Punishments."—Tracts presented to Gods.—Their Influence on the People.—Our Encouragements and Discouragements in distributing Christian Tracts.

THE literature of China is very extensive, and embraces a great variety of works: classical, historical, metaphysical, controversial, poetical, fictitious, medical, biographical, and dramatic; and also works connected with Buddhism and Tauism, and those relating to the different arts, sciences, occupations, etc.

Passing over these departments of literature with the simple reference to them, I propose in this chapter to speak of books on practical morality, having for their special and professed object the inculcation of virtue, the reforming of the age, and the elevating of the standard of morals.

The fact that the gratuitious distribution of tracts has long been practiced in China, is hardly less remarkable than the moral tone and character of the tracts themselves. This literature is different from books distinctively belonging to the three religions, the latter treating of their respective systems in detail, and containing little of interest to the general reader, on account of their prolixity and abstruseness. Moral tracts are, for the most part, written by Confucianists whose minds are strongly tinctured with Buddhist and Tauist views. The training which scholars obtain in the school of Confucius gives to their books a richness of diction and a high literary finish, while the other two systems, particularly Buddhism, supply those ideas respecting superior and inferior deities, departed spirits, and a future state, which so naturally and strongly impress the human mind.

These tracts, though differing in size and form, have for their common object the inculcation of one or more of the esteemed virtues. Some are large, and comprehend the whole circle of virtues as held by the Chinese; some are small, and relate only to one. Some, on account of their superior excellences in matter or style, are regarded as standard works, and are known throughout the eighteen provinces; others have only a temporary and local fame. The former generally have, as their basis, reputed revelations from different deities relating to the performance of various duties, to the strict superintendence of the gods over the actions of men, and the rewards and punishments of a future state.

Prominent among this class of works may be mentioned "The Sacred Edict;" "Traditions for Reforming Manners;" "A Book to be Revered and Believed;" "A Book to be read by Every Body;" "Guide to Prosperity;" "A Book on Rewards and Punishments;" "A Book on Daily Self-examination," and "Light in a Dark Dwelling." The authors of these works are, for the most part, men high in station and influence, and the first one named was written by one of the most renowned Emperors of the present dynasty.

Perhaps a correct idea of the character of these books, and the matter which they contain, could not be better conveyed to a person not conversant with the Chinese than by translating the table of contents of the last one in the above list. The first volume is principally occupied with the most important of the revelations of the gods, to most of which are appended explanations and remarkable events, for the purpose of showing their genuineness, and the good they have been the means of conferring on the people. These professed revelations are obtained in the manner described in Chapter XII. The first volume also contains "An Ode on the Acquisition of Happiness;" "An Ode on Contentment;" "An Ode on Discontent;" "An Ode on the Emptiness of all Human Things;" "An Essay to dissuade from drowning Female Children;" and, lastly, "Resolutions of Doubts which might be suggested to the Mind of the Reader in perusing the foregoing Sections." The second volume contains, first, "A general Dissertation on Mirrors" (i. e., facts of history, reflecting lessons of the past); then follow "The Mirror of reverencing Heaven;" "The Mirror of Filial Duty;" "An Ode to exhort to Filial Duty;" "An Ode of Eight Opposites or Contrasts;" "The Mirror of the Fraternal Relation;" "The Mirror of the Conjugal Relation;" "The Mirror of Loyalty;" "The Mirror of Friendship;" "The Mirror of Kindness," etc. Other chapters follow on the subjects of licentiousness, geomancy, litigation, deceit, selfishness, the bringing to light of secret things, virtue, lowly-mindedness, forbearance, evil-speaking, the duties of teacher and pupil, and the duty to refrain from taking animal life. To these are appended a chapter on maxims to be kept continually before the mind, and one containing exhortations to abstain from the use of opium, with eight reasons.

The injunctions of these books, relating almost exclusively to the duties of the Five Relations, and being deduced from the knowledge of right and wrong which God has made a part of the intuitions of man's moral nature, are, for the most part, just and admirable; and many of the arguments by which they are enforced are clear and striking. Some of these books are almost entirely taken up with statements of moral duties, and collections of excellent precepts and maxims, with a very little admixture of superstition and idolatry. In the great majority of them, most of the motives by which these duties are inculcated are superstitious and frivolous in the extreme; forming a strange and pitiable commingling of light and darkness, truth and error, the inconsistency and incongruity of which the people seem utterly unable to perceive. In order to urge man to the performance of duty, the greater part of some tracts is taken up with accounts of wonderful interpositions of the gods in behalf of men who have performed meritorious actions, evidences of men being changed into animals on account of sins in a previous life, and sundry revelations of gods and spirits relating to the unseen world. According to Chinese morality, this deception and falsehood are regarded as excusable when they are practiced in order to frighten either children or men into the performance of duty. Hence the many incredible stories with which these books are filled, which, with their precise dates and names of persons and places, are now regarded as authentic, probably owed their origin in the first instance to the (in the Chinese view) laudable endeavor to deceive, coax, or frighten people for their good.

The motive which leads to the distribution of these books is, with few, if any, exceptions, a selfish one. This work is regarded as one of merit, in consequence of which great advantages will accrue to those engaged in it. The end sought is to secure the favor and interposition of the gods in times of special emergency and danger, or to avert some anticipated calamity, or to obtain some other object earnestly desired. The circumstances under which tracts are most frequently distributed are the following: the severe and dangerous illness of one's self, parent, or near relative, the being without a son and heir, delicate health, and the apprehension of premature death, and a desire to obtain wealth or success at the literary examinations—these objects relating, in most cases, to the present life.

As might be inferred from the above, there is in China nothing to correspond to the publishing societies of Western countries. Individuals, in printing the first edition of a book, generally intimate on the title-page at what place the blocks may be found, so that any other persons may afterward strike off any number of additional impressions by incurring only the expense of paper and printing. These books are disposed of gratuitously, or at a price barely sufficient to cover the cost of publishing. They are distributed sometimes by a person employed to carry them from house to house, sometimes by being placed in book-stores, to be taken by those who wish them, and sometimes at the public literary examinations. The last method has the two great advantages of giving books a wider circulation by means of persons collected from different sections of the country, and also putting them in the hands of those who are most able and disposed to read them. Missionaries at the different ports have taken advantage of this mode of circulating books with much encouragement.

The tract literature of China is invested with peculiar interest and importance, not only on account of its presenting a correct portraiture of the religious and superstitious views of the people, but as giving a practical illustration of the amount of knowledge which can be derived from the light of nature, and of the necessity of a superior revelation.

Among the most prominent facts which the tracts of the Chinese disclose is a consciousness of sin and personal responsibility which is the basis and originating cause of all their idolatrous systems. Connected with this consciousness of sin and fear of future punishment is a restlessness and longing for some way of escape from sin and its consequences. Different modes devised all recognize the essential idea of *merit* as an atonement for ill-desert. The idea of rewards and punishments is not only held in its general form, but it is universally taught, and usually believed, that an accurate account is kept of all men's actions with reference to a strict and just examination and award in the future. Men are so impressed with this belief, that near the close of life they sometimes effect a thorough reform, and are earnest and persevering in the use of such means as their systems prescribe for the atonement of past misdeeds. A noted Chinese scholar who lived in the city of Chinhai, who had spent much of his life in writing and printing verses of an immoral tendency, was led by remorse and fear to endeavor to undo the evil influences of his past conduct, and devoted his talents during the remaining part of his life to writing books of an entirely opposite character.

A prominent idea in most of these books, and one which forms the key-note of some, is that of the vanity and unsatisfactory nature of all earthly things. A literal translation of a Chinese ode on "The Emptiness of all Things," taken from the tract whose contents are given above, may be of interest in showing the universality of the sentiment, "Vanity of vanities, all is vanity." Versification of this and the following ode is not attempted, and it is but just to add that these translations only approximate to the terseness and force of the originals.

"ODE ON EMPTINESS.

"Observe the floating multitudes of living beings coming from the south and going to the north, walking hither and thither: all is vanity.

"Heaven is emptiness, earth is emptiness; so also is insignificant man, dwelling between them.

"The sun is emptiness; the moon is emptiness; they rise in the east and set in the west, and what is the advantage of it?

"Fields are emptiness, land is emptiness; how many different proprietors are they continually exchanging!

"Wives are vanity, children are vanity; in the winding roads of yellow-streamed Tartarus they are seldom permitted to meet.

"Gold is emptiness, silver is emptiness; after death, how can we retain them in our grasp?

"Houses are emptiness, mansions are emptiness; in the twinkling of an eye, they are exchanged for the lonely mound outside the city wall.

"Station is vanity, office is vanity; when the tide of fortune is spent, the retributions of justice begin, and remorse is without bounds.

"Chariots are vanity, horses are vanity; the thing remains, the man departs; a shadow leaves no trace behind.

"It may be said of every thing in earth which affords happiness, after a little time the gratification passes away, and it is, after all, but emptiness.

"The conclusion of all is, that only one thing is real, and that is the effect of virtuous deeds leaving their lasting impress on our individual being."

An ode on discontent, from the same work, is as follows:

"ODE ON DISCONTENT.

"A man busily employed all day becomes hungry;
When hunger is satisfied, he thinks of clothing.
Abundantly supplied with both food and clothing,
He mourns that he has in his house no fair-eyed wife.
Possessed of a charming wife and beautiful concubine,
He finds that he is without suitable vehicles for appearing in public.
With numerous vehicles, and droves of horses and mules,
His land is found insufficient to supply his wants.
He purchases thousands and tens of thousands of fertile acres,
But, without official station, men treat him with disrespect.
He regards the seventh and fifth rank with dissatisfaction,
And the fourth and third are also too low for him.
Advanced to the first position of prime minister at court,
He conceives the wish of being Emperor a short time.
His desires gratified, he becomes the Son of Heaven,
And again wishes for ten thousand ages to escape death.
His numerous and foolish longings know no stopping-place;
At last a coffin forever hides him,
And he passes away, still hugging his discontent."

We learn from these books that the idea of the necessity of a revelation from heaven is natural, and that it is a conclusion to which the tendency of the human mind invariably leads. Man feels that no light but that of heaven can dispel the darkness and doubt in which he is involved; and refusing to be satisfied without it, readily accepts the spurious revelations which are offered him. These are but the transcript of the popular superstitions, framed by designing men to satisfy a felt want, which in process of time come to be regarded as authentic documents; thus giving to vague surmises the dignity of revealed truth, and the higher sanction of divine authority. One or more of these pretended revelations usually forms the basis of the larger and more noted tracts. Some of them, on account of the beauty of their style, and the importance of the truths which they present, have acquired a universal celebrity, and may almost be ranked among the Chinese classics. The one perhaps most frequently met with is a professed revelation from the founder and principal god of the Tauist sect. The whole is worthy of perusal; but the limits of a chapter will only allow of a few extracts from different parts of it, which may serve as a fair sample of the whole.

"TREATISE ON REWARDS AND PUNISHMENTS.

"Ta-shang said, Misery and Happiness have of themselves no door of access to man, but man invites them; Virtue and Vice are connected with their appropriate rewards as the shadow follows the substance. Heaven and earth have divinities which preside over the sins of men, and, according to the degree of their aggravation, subtract from each individual's merit. This lessened, misfortunes follow; the offending man meets with innumerable troubles and distresses; his fellow-men hate him; punishment and sorrow follow him; auspicious influences flee from him; baleful stars pursue him; when the allotments of fate are fulfilled, he dies. Over the heads of men there are also the three divinities of the Northern Constellation, who make a record of all their offenses, and snatch from them the original allotments of fate. * * * * * * *

"When you see the way of truth, enter it. What is not truth, avoid it. Watch not in false ways. Do not deceive yourself in committing sins in secret. Add to the store of your virtues, and thus increase your merits. Let your compassion extend to every object. Be loyal, dutiful, and affectionate. Reform yourself, that you may reform others. Pity the desolate, compassionate the distressed. Honor the aged, be kind to the young. Have a care not to harm either reptiles or plants. Sympathize with the unfortunate, rejoice over the virtuous. Help those who are in difficulty, save those who are in distress. Regard the good fortune and losses of others as if they were your own. Do not make a display either of the faults of others or of your own excellences. Suppress what is evil, give currency to what is good. Decline the greater advantage, and be content with the less. Receive abuse without resentment; receive favors, as it were, with trembling. Dispense favors without asking a return. Give to others without after regrets.

"As regards the virtuous man, all men honor him; heaven protects him; happiness and fortune follow him; evil influences flee far from him; divine spirits attend him; whatever he does will prove successful; and he may aspire to being one of the genii of heaven. If you wish to become one of the genii of heaven, it is necessary to perform 1300 meritorious deeds; if to be one of earth, to perform 300. * * * * * *

"Avoid stepping over a well or over a fire-place; leaping over food or men; destroying children before or after birth; doing things in a secret and underhanded manner; singing or dancing on the 12th or 30th of the month; getting in a passion on the first day of the month; shedding tears, spitting, etc., with the face toward the North Star; reciting or chanting verses or wailing in the presence of the Kitchen God; lighting incense-sticks with fire from the kitchen; using filthy fuel in cooking food; rising and going out in the night undressed; punishing criminals on either of the eight festivals; spitting at a shooting-star; pointing at the rainbow, or the sun, moon, and stars; gazing for a long time at the sun or moon; hunting in the spring; cursing with the face toward the North Star; killing turtles and beating snakes without a cause; for such sins as these, according as they are trivial or aggravated, the gods who preside over destiny subtract a smaller or larger number of years from the allotments of fate. If punishments still remain, they are visited upon one's descendants. Moreover, if riches are acquired by unlawful means, the retribution falls upon one's wife, children, and family, until they die; or, if their lives are spared, the work of retribution is done by floods, conflagrations, and robbers, destroying property, and introducing want, disease, dissensions, and domestic evils, until the full price of ill-gotten wealth is exacted. To kill another from revenge is but providing a sword for one's own destruction. To appropriate to one's self ill-gotten gain, is, as it were, to allay hunger by poisoned food, or to quench thirst by poisoned wine; not that it does not afford temporary relief, but death quickly follows. If a desire to do right arises in the mind, though that desire has not been acted upon, propitious divinities are present to aid and bless. On the other hand, if the mind harbors evil purposes, though they have not yet been carried out, divinities are also present to inflict evil. If a person has been guilty of wicked deeds, and afterward repents, rejects every thing which is evil, and follows after every thing which is good, he will in due time certainly be rewarded. This is what is meant by misery being changed into happiness."

The estimation in which this production is held, and the benefits which are supposed to result from the use of it, may be gathered from the following paragraph, which is appended to it in a noted Chinese tract: "The chanting of it once a day will destroy sin and cancel guilt. If you strictly observe its precepts for a month, your happiness and good fortune will be secure. If you follow its injunctions for two years, even your remote ancestors will immediately ascend to heaven. If you persevere in willing and permanent obedience to it, your days will be indefinitely prolonged; the gods of heaven will respect and reverence you, and you will be enrolled among the chief of the genii."

It is a singular fact in connection with this subject, that

books of this class are offered as presents, not only to men, but also to the gods, and still more singular, that it is supposed that they are conveyed to the deity for whom they are designed by being burned up! This shows the low estimation in which gods are held, inasmuch as they are supposed to be instructed by the productions of men, while they are dependent upon men for putting them in possession of these productions. Numerous instances are given of dangerous diseases being instantly cured, and extraordinary benefits conferred in consequence of offering these books to certain of the gods.

With reference to the influence of Chinese tracts, it can not be doubted that, in the absence of any thing better, they have the effect of checking and restraining the vices of the people by means of presenting prominently the doctrine of future rewards and punishments. The exhortations to perform most of the duties enjoined find a hearty response in the hearts of those to whom they are addressed, while the sanction of deities which are both reverenced and feared gives to them additional force. At the same time, many of the considerations which are, in reality, empty and frivolous, are peculiarly adapted to work upon the superstitious notions of the Chinese.

From a consideration of this subject, we are better able to understand the light in which Christian books are regarded and received by the people.

The distribution of moral and religious tracts is a practice with which they are already familiar, and one which immediately begets a high degree of respect and confidence for those engaged in it. There is, however, a vast amount of error and prejudice to be overcome before our doctrines and our object can be appreciated. We are regarded as good but, perhaps, misguided men, who are endeavoring to introduce a new god, Jesus. In examining our books and comparing them with their own, they are disappointed in finding so little prominence given to "the five relations." The ideas presented are foreign, and many of them do not strike them with as much force as the views presented in their own works. The literary style of most Christian tracts is also comparatively inferior — a matter of great importance in their estimation. When reference is made to one supreme God, his spiritual nature, his sovereignty, and his providence, these ideas are strange, and hard to be understood. Most of the evidences of Christianity will be readily admitted; but to their minds no miracles are more wonderful, and no fulfillment of prophecies more extraordinary than the spurious ones with which they are already familiar. No ideas of future happiness or misery are so striking and so readily received as those the human mind has framed to please itself; no way of salvation from future punishment is so willingly accepted as that based on self-righteousness.

Another difficulty in writing Christian tracts exists in the Chinese language itself. Having been originally employed as a vehicle for conveying heathen and idolatrous ideas, it is difficult to use it without bringing up those old associations which are everywhere connected with it. The language is rich in religious terms, and has some word approximating to almost every idea we wish to present, though, in nearly every case, with a different meaning, a different use, and different associations. The question is, whether we shall coin new words, or use old ones; whether we shall encounter obscurity on the one hand, or misconception on the other. We find, then, even here, where we naturally hope to gain easy access to the hearts of the people, and to obtain a great advantage by the use of a most efficient agency prepared to our hand, that this door of access is, in a measure, barred, and this means of doing good rendered nugatory.

CHAPTER XVII.

SOCIAL CUSTOMS, ETC.

The Family Tie strong in China.—Minute Distinctions of Relationships.—The Position of Women in China.—Chinese Politeness.—Hospitality.—Costumes.—The Queue.—Small Feet of the Women.—Chinese Houses.—Food and Mode of Eating.—The Use of Tea.—Chinese Wine.—The Use of Tobacco.—General Want of Cleanliness.—Betrothals and Marriages.—Polygamy.—Infanticide.—Slavery.—Funerals.—Coffins.—Graves and Grave-yards.—The extravagant and burdensome Expenses of Chinese Weddings and Funerals.

THE family tie in China is strong, and the people are clannish. They seldom change their place of residence, and most of them live where their ancestors have lived for many generations. You will frequently find the larger proportion of a small village bearing the same name, in which case the village often takes its name from the family, as *Chang Kia*, the the Chang Family; *Sie Kia*, the Sie Family.

Books on filial piety and the domestic relations recommend sons not to leave their parents when married, but to live together lovingly and harmoniously as one family. This theory is carried out in practice in many, and perhaps to some extent, in most instances, though there as elsewhere it is very often found more satisfactory for each married couple to have a home of their own.

In the division of property, some regard is had to primogeniture; but different sons share nearly equally. The eldest simply has a somewhat larger portion, and certain household relics and valuables.

Nice distinctions are made between different degrees of consanguinity, and the names of the varied relationships are almost endless. Not only do they call the wife's parents by different titles from those given to their own, but also the children of brothers by a name denoting a very different and much nearer relationship than that sustained to the children of sisters, and so on.

The position of woman is intermediate between that which she occupies in Christian and in Mohammedan and other heathen countries. The manner in which they regard their lot may be inferred from the fact, related in a previous chapter, that their most earnest desire and prayer in worshiping in Buddhist temples is, generally, that they may be men in the next state of existence. In many families girls have no individual names, but are simply called No. Two, Three, Four, etc. When married, they are Mr. So-and-so's wife, and when they have sons, they are such-and-such a boy's mother. They live in a great measure secluded, take no part in general society, and are expected to retire when a stranger or an acquaintance out of the family of the opposite sex enters the house. Among the poor, whose dwellings are small, and who are obliged to depend upon the females of the family to do the work, it is impossible to carry out fully these rules of seclusion, and the separation of the sexes is less marked. In some localities the people are more strict in this regard than in others. I heard in the province of Shantung of a stranger being driven out of a village by a mob on account of taking the liberty of asking a woman in the street the road to an adjoining town.

The claim of one's parents and brothers upon his affections and love is considered to be paramount to that of his wife. A reason given for this doctrine in a celebrated Chinese work which treats of the domestic relations and duties is, that the loss of a brother is irreparable, but that of a wife is not! Women are treated with more respect and consideration as they advance in years; mothers are regarded with great affection and tenderness, and grandmothers are sometimes almost worshiped.

It is but just to say that a strong attachment often springs up between husband and wife, though they have had nothing to do in making choice of each other, and have never seen each other before marriage. It should be further stated, that the Chinese have found the theory of the inferiority of woman a very difficult one to carry out in practice. Perhaps one reason why they deny education to the "weaker" sex is because they find it sufficiently difficult to keep her in her proper place without it. While customs and theories vary, human nature and woman's nature are the same the world over. Women in China have also their ideas of "Woman's Rights." There are many families in which the superiority of her will and authority is sufficiently manifest, though not cheerfully acknowledged; and the most that we can say is, that "henpecked husbands" are perhaps not so numerous as in America and Europe.

The rules and conventionalities which regulate social life are exceedingly minute and formal. Politeness is a science, and gracefulness of manners a study and discipline. Many peculiarities of Chinese manners seem to be almost excessive. The persistent, graceful, and successful effort of a retiring visitor to pass from the reception-room through, perhaps, two or three courts, without turning his back upon his host, backing, bowing, and going sideways by turns; and his earnest and oft-repeated wish that the host should not take the trouble to accompany him to the outer door, and the as oft-repeated asseveration of the host that his feelings of gratitude and respect oblige him to do so, are calculated at first sight to provoke a smile. The bowings, compliments, and congratulations which are required in the meeting of two officials are so numerous and difficult to be gone through with properly, that when such persons come upon each other by accident in the street, they pass sometimes without apparent recognition, as there is no proper medium or compromise between the formal courtesies required and ignoring each other altogether. When a number of individuals are walking together, you may generally infer their age or rank or position by the order in which they naturally and almost unconsciously range themselves. Literary men and gentlemen are expected to walk the streets with a dignified, measured, and superior bearing.

The excessive politeness of the Chinese is noticed in the language as well as the manners of the people. In asking a friend his place of residence, though you know him to be poor, and that he probably occupies an inferior house, you must use the expression "Where is your mansion" or "honorable mansion?" and he replies, "My hut" or "hovel" is in such a place. This last expression is equally used by wealthy persons living in fine and costly houses. The following, and a great variety of similar expressions, are constantly heard: "What is your honorable age?" "My empty" or "worthless number is forty-five." "Is your honorable wife living?" "The mean person of the inner apartment is still in life." "Is your noble son doing well at school?" "The contemptible little dog has learned a few characters." "Indeed, you are too polite and deferential." "I dare not presume to claim such a reputation." The language used in the epistolary correspondence of literary men abounds in words and phrases containing graceful and delicate compliments, and expressions of respect for the person addressed, together with corresponding ones of self-depreciation. These forms of expression are used with about as much regard to their literal meaning as in our own language, "Your most obedient servant," etc.

The people are hospitable and generous to a fault—their desire to appear well in these respects often leading them into expenditures entirely disproportionate to their means.

When, under the influence of passion excited by injustice or insult, quarrels arise in the family or on the street, the women resort to cursing and abuse, which are violent and extreme in proportion to the length of time during which the feelings which prompted them have been restrained. Men bluster and threaten in a manner quite frightful to those unaccustomed to it, but seldom come to blows. In cases of deep resentment, the injured party often adopts a mode of revenge which is very characteristic. Instead of killing the object of his hate, he determines rather to kill himself. In this way he would fix the stigma of murder upon his adversary, whom the people generally regard as the cause of this catastrophe, and responsible for it. A person under these circumstances sometimes commits suicide by hanging himself in his own house; but the most common mode is to swallow opium, and then hire coolies to carry him to die at the door of his enemy. An additional motive leading to self-destruction is probably the hope of having greater advantages for inflicting injury and gaining revenge as a disembodied spirit than while living in the flesh. The suicide, at least, enjoys the anticipation of the terrible fright which he will give to his adversary.

The Chinese costume of both sexes is loose and flowing, and changes in fashion are slow, and slight in degree, as compared with ours. The masses of the population wear homespun cotton. The wealthier classes wear silks, satins, gauzes, furs, and other more costly materials. Summer clothing is very thin and light, while the number of garments and amount of clothing worn in the winter is quite remarkable, and does away with the necessity of using fire-places and stoves.

The official rank and position of the Chinese are indicated by the color and peculiarities of buttons, feathers, caps, and embroidered insignia on their garments. These official distinctions are much regarded. In meeting with a company of foreigners, they are very apt to notice us carefully, to discover by what outward badge or mark our rank is indicated, and are apt to conclude that it is by the variety of caps or hats we wear, or, perhaps, by our using or not using walking-sticks, or using those of a particular kind.

The men shave the front part of their heads, reserving a small portion on the top and back part, which is left to grow, and is braided into a queue. This was not a Chinese custom originally, but belongs properly to the Tartars, and was imposed upon the Chinese as a token of subjection to the present dynasty. It has now become a necessary part of one's dress, and is attended to with a great deal of care. Fops and exquisites add false hair to make it longer and larger, and also braid black silk thread to the end of it, increasing its length so that it almost sweeps the ground. The women comb their hair back straight from the forehead and sides of the head, arranging it in a style very elaborate and artistic, adding oftentimes a profusion of gold and silver ornaments, and natural and artificial flowers. With a general resemblance, the styles in which the women dress their hair vary considerably in different parts of the empire, and indeed of the same province.

The practice of binding girl's feet is almost universal. There is a class of women in Canton, and also in Fuchow, who have natural feet; but these are the rare exceptions. In all other parts of the empire which I have visited, women of all classes conform indiscriminately to this objectionable custom, and large-footed women are almost unknown, except those who have come from Canton of the class already referred to, and women in the Tartar cities, who do not adopt this Chinese practice. There is, however, a marked difference in the *degree* in which feet are compressed. Country women and the poorer classes have feet about half the natural size, while those of the genteel or fashionable class are only about three inches long.

LARGE OR NATURAL-FOOTED WOMAN AT FU-CHOW.

The process of compressing is commenced after girls have

thoroughly learned to walk, and have developed the muscles for locomotion — generally at the age of five years. A cotton bandage two or three inches wide is wound tightly about the foot in different directions, and, in the case of the higher classes, the foot can hardly be said to grow from this time. It assumes the shape of an acute triangle, the big toe forming the acute angle, and the other toes being bent under the foot, and almost lost or absorbed. A strong resemblance to the gait of these women may be produced by an attempt to walk on one's heels without allowing the toes to touch the floor. Strange as it may seem, women having small feet, less than the average size, walk ten, fifteen, and more miles a day, to worship at Buddhist temples. Though the effect of this custom is to produce real deformity, and a miserable, tottering gait, even foreigners naturally come to associate it with gentility and good-breeding, and to estimate the character and standing of women much as the Chinese do, by the size of their feet.

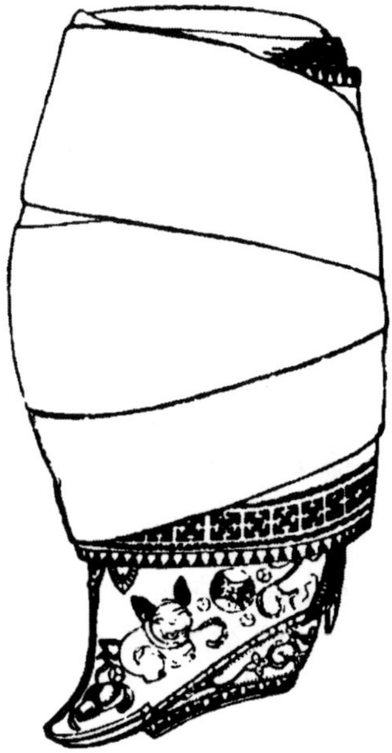

APPEARANCE OF A SMALL SHOE ON THE FOOT.

This custom has existed for a long time, and the Chinese can not account satisfactorily for its origin. It probably arose from a strife among women for the pre-eminence of having the smallest feet, fond mothers commencing to bind their daughters' feet before they were grown, and the time for beginning the process being gradually changed to an earlier period. The Chinese insist upon it that the custom of compressing women's feet is neither in as bad taste, nor so injurious to the health, as that of foreign ladies compressing the waist.

There, as here, not to follow the prevailing fashion is almost to make one's self an outcast from society.

Chinese houses are ordinarily furnished with chairs, tables, stands, or tea-poys, and bedsteads. Tables are nearly uniform in size, furnishing a seat for one person on each of its four sides. When large companies are entertained, separate tables are added indefinitely, so that the size of a company invited to a feast is described by the number of tables required. The two sexes eat separately in different rooms. A great deal of urging and declining is gone through with in determining who shall take the first place at each table, and in giving proper places to other guests. In ordinary meals, different members of the family of both sexes sit down together with much less formality.

On the tables of the rich and the poor, morning, noon, and night, you see, with few exceptions, the same unvarying bucket of plain boiled rice, or, in the Northern provinces, millet, which takes the place of it. The difference in the quality and expense of the food of the rich, as compared with that of the poor, consists principally in the kinds of "relish" eaten with the rice or millet. The poor have simply a dish of salt vegetables, or of fresh or salt fish, or two or three of these, or other similar dishes combined, which cost comparatively little, in addition to what they depend upon as the main article of subsistence. The rich have pork, fowls, eggs, fish, and game, prepared in various ways. Before each chair is placed an empty bowl and two chop-sticks, while the dishes containing meat, vegetables, fish, etc., occupy the centre of the table, the food which they contain being cut up in small pieces. The chop-sticks are about eight inches long, and resemble somewhat a common pen-holder. They are made of bamboo, wood, or ivory. When seats are taken at the table, a servant, or one of the women of the family, fills the bowls with hot rice. Following the lead of the person at the head of the table, each individual takes up his or her chop-sticks in the right hand, and holding them between the thumb and fingers in such a manner that the lower ends approach each other like a pair of pincers or tongs, selects one or more mouthfuls from the dishes in the centre of the table. Then the bowl of rice is raised to the lips by the left hand, and the rice is pushed into the mouth by the chop-sticks in the right. The eating of a Chinese meal consists in a constant alternation between picking up mouthfuls from the plates in the middle of the table and taking rice from the bowl in the manner described. When a feast is made, a great variety of dishes is served in numerous courses, and rice is not brought on till toward the close.

The Chinese find as much difficulty, and make as awkward work in using knives and forks as we do in using chop-sticks. The latter they regard as much the more suitable and convenient, and, in using them, will take up and hold firmly objects so small that they would slip between the tines of a fork. To their view, the use of chop-sticks is an evidence of a superior culture; and the use of such barbarous instruments as knives and forks, and cutting or tearing the meat from the bones on the table, instead of having the food properly prepared in the kitchen, evidences a lower type of civilization.

The wide and almost universal prevalence of the impression that "rats, cats, and puppies" are articles of food in common use among the people, is a notable example of a local and exceptional custom being taken for a national and universal one, and producing false ideas of a people in the minds of whole nations. I have never seen or heard of a rat, cat, or puppy being eaten in China, though I presume they may be occasionally by paupers. I have been told that dogs are sometimes eaten in Canton. It was here, no doubt, that this rumor originated. Some early visitor in China, seeking for sensational news, has sent home this item of information. In our ignorance of that country this interesting fact was eagerly made use of, and illustrated by a special engraving in that part of the geography which treated of China. The ideas suggested by this engraving of the geographers of twenty or thirty years ago constitute a large proportion of what many of our people know, or think they know of China.

Beef is never exposed for sale in the Chinese markets. The meat of the few cattle which are used for ploughing is, when they are killed, disposed of privately, almost clandestinely. There is a strong and almost universal prejudice against eating beef, and the practice of doing so is declaimed against in some of the moral tracts. The reason generally given for this prejudice is that we are so much indebted to the patient labors of the ox and cow for ploughing our fields. Milk is hardly used at all in the eighteen provinces; and in many places our practice of drinking it and using it in cooking is regarded with the utmost disgust. In all the open ports beef and milk are supplied for the use of foreigners.

Tea is a universal beverage in the South, and is much prized in the North; though in the provinces where it is not produced—and is for that reason more expensive—the poorer people can hardly afford it. It is generally taken rather weak. It is common to steep it in a tea-pot, but the most polite way to serve guests (and no visitor or caller enters a house without having it offered him) is to have the servant put a few leaves in each cup, then fill the cups with boiling water from the tea-kettle, and place over them the covers which always belong to them.

There is a beverage very common in China which is called by them *lao-tsiu*, and by foreigners Chinese wine, though it bears very little resemblance to any article in Western lands called by that name. It is manufactured from certain kinds of rice and millet, though I am unable to say by what process. It is always drunk warm, and its stimulating or intoxicating properties are about equal to, if they do not exceed, those of light grape wine. Many people drink this wine with their meals habitually. It is always freely used at weddings, and on other festal occasions. Old men especially are recommended to make use of it as a stimulant to promote digestion. A spirit, called *Siao-tsiu* or *Sam-shu*, is distilled from this wine,

PART OF A BRIDAL PROCESSION EN ROUTE TO THE HOUSE OF THE BRIDEGROOM ON THE WEDDING-DAY.

which is very strong and intoxicating. Drunkenness in China is rare, as compared with Western countries.

Nearly all the men and many of the women smoke tobacco, but generally with moderation. They have not yet reached the point of chewing it, and show no disposition to imitate the example of foreigners in this respect. The proportion of opium-smokers is not large, as compared to the whole population.

The want of cleanly habits presents one of the most disagreeable features of Chinese life and character. Houses, even those of the rich, have generally a dusty and untidy appearance. Under-clothes are not often changed. Clean bed-linen is unknown. Parasitic vermin are too common to be a disgrace, and offensive sights and smells are so familiar to the people from infancy that they do not seem to be affected by them as we are.

Weddings in China are celebrated with a great deal of formality and expense. Betrothals are generally contracted at a very early age. Persons are never betrothed of the same family name, however distant the relationship. The initiative is almost always taken by a class of women called "go-betweens," or match-makers. They are a class employed at weddings and funerals in superintending the toilet, and affording assistance as servants generally. As they go about constantly from family to family, they are familiarly acquainted with every one in the neighborhood, and suggest to parents where they may find girls who would make a desirable match for their sons. They form the medium for carrying on communications between the two families. It would be regarded as improper and indelicate for the parents of either party to ask to see the other, or for parents to arrange the matter themselves, without the intervention of these conventional "go-betweens" or others who perform the same offices. As for the boys or young men, they are supposed to be entirely indifferent as to the whole matter; and the idea of courtship, love-letters, etc., would, according to Chinese views of propriety, be quite shocking to all right-minded persons. The betrothal is consummated by the exchange of presents, and the making over to the parents of the groom a formal document or agreement. The relation of husband and wife is thus constituted, and the engagement is regarded as almost as sacred and binding as if the marriage had been performed. Chinese women sometimes live as widows for life, whose husbands

BRIDE AND BRIDEGROOM WORSHIPING THE TABLETS OF HIS DECEASED ANCESTORS.

died when very young boys. In many instances these widows who have never been married spend their lives with the parents of their deceased husbands, and devote themselves to ministering to and nursing them.

The preliminaries, formalities, ceremonies, and superstitions connected with marriage, would, if given in full, almost fill a volume. Previous to the wedding-day the bride has her eyebrows pulled out, so that she is recognized ever afterward as a married woman. On the morning of the "lucky day" chosen for the marriage, she is carried from her own home to that of her future husband in a beautiful and highly ornamented bridal chair. The religious part of the ceremony consists in the bride and groom's worshiping together the spirit-tablets of the ancestors of the groom. The parties first see each other's faces when, seated by the bridal bed, the bride's veil is removed, and the two parties drink wine out of the same cup. The day is spent in feasting, congratulations, complimenting the bride, and general hilarity.

In the province of Shantung, in the north of China, weddings are celebrated in the night, and remind one very forcibly of the Jewish marriage customs referred to in the parable of the virgins, in the twenty-fifth chapter of Matthew. I once attended one of these weddings. The house was full of guests, the bridal chamber was beautifully furnished and ornamented, and every thing was in readiness for the reception of the bride when the bridegroom should make his appearance with her. We waited a long time till all were impatient, and some drowsy, and persons would frequently go out with a lantern to see if there were any signs of his coming; and it was not till near midnight that the cry was heard, "The bridegroom cometh: go ye out to meet him."

Polygamy is not common, and is only considered allowable, or, rather, respectable, under special circumstances. The saying occurs in the writings of the philosopher Mencius: "There are three kinds of filial impiety, the greatest of which is to be without male descendants." It is regarded as of the greatest importance that every family should have a son, not only to perpetuate the family name, but, more especially, to make sacrificial offerings, or feed the spirits of deceased ancestors. Hence, if a person has no children at the age of forty, it is expected that he will take another wife. The first wife retains her original position in the family; and, if children are born of the second, they regard the first also as their mother, and she has the principal care and oversight of them.

Infanticide prevails to a greater or less extent in certain parts of the empire, and is confined almost exclusively to female children. The existence of moral tracts denouncing this practice and warning the people to avoid it, is sufficient evidence both of the prevalence of the custom, and of the acknowledged wrong or immorality of it. In some places, as about Fuchow, infanticide is common; in other parts of the empire it is very rarely that you find well-authenticated instances of it. In poor families which have a large number of children, infants frequently die for want of sufficient care and nursing, and perhaps without many regrets on the part of the parents; but these cases could hardly be properly included in what is generally called infanticide.

The large number of castaway bodies of dead infants seen in many parts of China is often regarded, though unjustly, as evidence of the prevalence of this crime. Their bodies are wrapped up in a mat and thrown in the river, or by the side of the city wall, or hung from the branches of trees to keep them from the dogs, or, which is very often the case, thrown into structures called "baby-houses"—little buildings, with a small hole in one side, erected by benevolent persons for this very purpose.

This denial of burial to infants is due, at least in many places, to the following superstition: When they die, it is supposed that their bodies were inhabited by the spirit of a deceased creditor of a previous state of existence. The child during its sickness may be cared for with the greatest tenderness, and no expense spared in employing a physician and procuring medicine; but if it dies, parental love is turned to hate and resentment, and it is called *Twan-ming Kwei*—"short-lived spirit" or "devil." It is regarded as an enemy and intruder in the family, which has been exacting satisfaction for the old, unpaid debt; and having occasioned a great deal of anxiety, trouble, and expense, has left nothing to show for it but disappointment. The uncared-for and uncoffined little body is cast away anywhere; and as it is carried out of the door the house is swept, crackers are fired, and gongs beaten to frighten the spirit, so that it may never dare enter the house again. Thus do heathen superstitions dry up the fountains of natural affection.

In cases where infanticide is common, males predominate to such an extent that it is difficult for parents to obtain wives for their sons, and they often make arrangements with a family which has an infant daughter to spare her life and betroth her to their son. In these cases, the girl at a very early age becomes the inmate of the family of her betrothed husband. Parents of the lower and middle classes, whose daughters live with them till they are married, feel that they are entitled to some remuneration from the parents of the husband for all their expense and trouble in bringing her up. For this reason, when a girl is betrothed with the expectation of her remaining in her own family, her parents expect a considerable amount of money; so that the transaction has very much the appearance of a matter of buying and selling. Many men are doomed to a life of celibacy because they are too poor to buy and support a wife.

A mild form of slavery is found in China, but in no place do slaves form more than an insignificant fraction of the laborers. The absolute right of husbands to their wives, and of parents to their children and their control over them, are such, that they may sell them if they choose to do so. I have known an instance of an opium-smoker, who, after having sold his wife to provide means to satisfy the cravings of his insatiable appetite, sold his only son to obtain money for travelling expenses in coming to Ningpo to be cured of this terrible habit.

The funerals of grown persons, and especially of parents, are as remarkable for burdensome ceremonies, extravagant manifestations of grief, and lavish expense, as those of children are for their coldness and neglect. When an individual dies, the house is often filled with weeping and wailing, and importunate cries to the spirit to come back again. Candles, incense, and offerings of food are placed before the corpse. A company of priests is engaged to chant prayers for the departed spirit. An abundance of clothing is deposited with the body in the coffin. Various services and ceremonies are performed during several days immediately after death, and on every subsequent *seventh* day, closing with the *seventh seven*. This use of the number seven presents almost the only marked analogy between Chinese and Jewish or Western usages with which I am acquainted.

When the coffin is carried out for burial, men and sometimes women follow in the procession, clothed in coarse white garments, white being used for mourning. The men have white braided into the end of their queues, which they continue to wear as a badge of mourning for several months. In most places which I have visited, the mourning and weeping in funeral processions is left principally to the women. I saw, however, in the city of Hwang-hien, in the province of Shantung, a funeral procession composed only of men, who, as they walked solemnly through the street, gave at each tread a deep sigh or groan, producing a strange and somewhat impressive effect.

Coffins are prepared with a great deal of care. They are generally purchased at the undertakers, where they are constantly kept on hand, but are often made at the house under the immediate inspection of the person for whom the coffin is intended. Very excellent and well-seasoned timber is selected, the planks are sawed very thick, and nailed together in a kind of cement with large spikes, and the whole is covered with numerous coatings of a very hard and durable varnish. The coffin is so heavy that it requires an effort for a strong man to lift one end of it. When it is taken out with the body for interment, from twelve to twenty men are employed to carry it. The Chinese are quite shocked with our custom of burying dear friends in light coffins whose boards are not much more than an inch in thickness.

They have not the aversion to coffins and their associations that we have. These last resting-places of the body are often ostentatiously exposed near the entrance of the house, or in some other place, to be examined and remarked upon by guests and visitors. Sometimes a coffin containing a body is kept in the house for a considerable length of time while arrangements are being made for a burying-place and other preliminaries are attended to. The lids being nailed down in cement, a well-constructed coffin is perfectly air-tight. In travelling in China, and being entertained by natives, my wife and I have occupied sleeping apartments containing several coffins; whether empty or not, we did not inquire.

The Chinese generally bury near the surface, and heap up a conical tumulus over the grave. The coffin is often placed on a cement floor, and covered over with an arch of brick laid in cement. They are sometimes exhumed scores of years after burial in an almost perfect state of preservation.

I am not aware that the Chinese ever procure and lay out a spot of ground for a public cemetery, but some places become large burying-grounds in process of time. Those portions of the country which are comparatively unproductive, and consequently cheap, especially hill-sides which have a general reputation for being lucky, are filled with the graves of the poorer classes. In the vicinity of cities some of these burying-grounds are of great extent. I noticed one near the city Han-yiang (or Hankao, as the foreign settlement is called), which is said to be about ten miles long, and on an average one mile wide. This area seemed so fully and closely occupied that a vacant spot could hardly be found in it. In this vast congregation of the dead, probably not far from 20,000,000 of human beings have found their last resting-place. And this is but one of the burial-places in connection with one of the cities of China. What a solemn thought, that all these myriads have gone down to fill idolatrous graves, without any knowledge of the God who made them, and of Jesus Christ whom He has sent!

The amount of expense rendered unavoidable by the customs of the country in attending to the ceremonies of weddings and funerals, and providing coffins and graves for the dead, is almost intolerable. As a natural result of these often useless expenditures, very many families are burdened with debt from one generation to another. In order to furnish for a few days an ostentatious and empty display in honor of the dead, the surviving descendants are embarrassed and distressed for a lifetime.

CHAPTER XVIII.

NATIONAL FESTIVALS, CUSTOMS, AND AMUSEMENTS.

The Chinese Divisions of Time.—Number and Variety of Festivals and Anniversaries.—Welcoming of Spring.—The Customs and Festivities connected with the New Year.—The "Feast of Lanterns."—"Festival of the Tombs."—The Season of flying Kites.—Idolatrous Processions.—Chinese Theatres.—Their Connection with Idolatry.—How conducted.—Character of the Plays and Actors.—Puppet Shows.—Gambling. — Public Fasts enjoined by official Proclamations. — Common Practice of using obscene Language.

THE Chinese attach a great deal of importance to the division of time, and are careful to make these divisions in accordance with fixed principles inherent in nature. The year is composed of lunar months, which begin with the new moon; and its appearance being the same on corresponding days of each month, the number of the day suggests the phase of the moon, and *vice versa*. The same word is used in Chinese both for moon and month. The new year commences with the first new moon after the sun enters Aquarius, which is some time between the 21st of January and the 19th of February.* This period seems to have been fixed upon because it marks the time of the first indication of reviving spring. The four seasons of the year correspond to ours. The months being lunar, twelve are not sufficient to complete the year, and an intercalary one is added, when necessary, causing the ensuing year to commence about twenty days later than the preceding. This added month is placed after the sixth, and called the sixth intercalary month. Months contain either twenty-nine or thirty days, and are designated accordingly

* Williams's "Middle Kingdom."

small or large months. The day is divided into twelve hours, each being twice the length of ours.

In addition to the four seasons, the year is divided into eight parts, called *Tsih*, "joints" or divisions, and these are again subdivided into sixteen more, called *Kyi*, "breaths," or sources of life. These twenty-four divisions, most of which are more or less imaginary, are associated with different changes in nature, and the germination, growth, and maturing of grains and plants. They may be regarded as festivals, and each has its appropriate ceremonies and observances.

Besides these, which might be called natural anniversaries, but which, in the arrangement of lunar months, do not fall on the same day of the month in successive years, there are numerous other anniversaries, commemorative of the birthdays of distinguished individuals, great historical events, etc.

A scholar from Nankin, whom I employed several years ago to write out a description of the festivals of China, gives an account of the character and observances of those which are most important and are generally observed, numbering, in all, forty. They do not occur at regular intervals, and there is no periodical return of a day of rest and recreation corresponding at all to our Sabbath. The origin and ceremonies of many of these festivals may be accounted for and explained, while others perpetuate ancient usages, of which no one can tell where or when they originated, or what they are intended to commemorate.

Those who are curious to learn more respecting the national and social customs of the Chinese will find much interesting information on these subjects in Doolittle's "Social Life of the Chinese" and Williams's "Middle Kingdom." I will only refer in this chapter to a few of the most prominent festivals.

The ceremony of Welcoming Spring has been spoken of in connection with the National Worship of China. It takes place on the day called in the calendar *Kai chwen*, the "Beginning of Spring," which occurs a short time before or after the new year.

PREPARATIONS FOR THE NEW YEAR.

The festivities of the new year exceed all others in their prominence and continuance, and in the universality and enthusiasm with which they are observed. These ceremonies are looked forward to with interest during the whole year, and great preparations are made for them. They are familiarly designated by the terms *Kwo-nien*—"Pass-year," or Passing from one year to another," "Thank the year," "Bid adieu to the year," "Worship the year," etc. They relate to the old and to the new year, both of which are almost personified and made objects of idolatrous worship.

As the day approaches, quantities of provisions are purchased for the anticipated sacrifices and feastings; and a few fowls which have been reared about the doors of the poorer families, who seldom taste of animal food at other times, are now killed. According to a universal and authoritative custom, all accounts must now be settled. On the last day of the year the streets of Chinese towns and cities present a very busy and animated appearance. A great deal of money changes hands in a short time. Provisions, clothing, and presents are bought in large quantities, not only because they are needed to commence the new year, but because all shops are shut for several days of the first month. Some families who are unable to satisfy their creditors in any other way, part with old family relics, or curious and valuable ornaments; and these coming into the market at low prices, persons who have the capital and wish such articles are on the lookout for them.

It is a mistake to suppose, as is often asserted, that all debts are paid at this time, for a great proportion of the Chinese continue in debt from year to year; but an arrangement satisfactory to the creditor must be made. It is especially necessary to attend to shop-keepers' debts, as articles must be bought of them during the coming year. Debts incurred in borrowing money of relatives and friends for funeral or wedding expenses, or in time of sickness, are very apt to go over the year, and are often never paid. This is the harvest-time for pawnbrokers, who are very numerous, and many of whom amass great wealth. Sometimes a debtor tries to avoid and defraud his creditor, in which case the creditor feels authorized, and is allowed by the customs of the country to adopt summary measures—proceeding to the house of the delinquent, seizing any thing he can lay his hands upon, perhaps breaking and destroying things generally, and frightening and intimidating the inmates, especially the female portion of them. Nothing is more dreaded than such a procedure on account of the disgrace of it to the debtor, and the superstitious fear of such an inauspicious beginning of the new year. A man is sometimes seen seeking a creditor on New Year's morning. This he is permitted to do if he carries a lantern with him, indicating in this way that he is still engaged in last night's business, and that practically it is yet night with him. The apparition of such a visitor when the person he is thus seeking is engaged in entertaining and feasting his New Year's callers, is calculated to excite feelings of shame and mortification which can be better imagined than described.

As the midnight hour approaches, the members of the family come together for a formal service. Sacrifices are offered to the Kitchen God, to deceased ancestors, to other gods which may be objects of worship in the family, and also to the old dying year. As a part of this last ceremony, the head of the family, representing all the other members of it, kneels down and worships, and thanks the departing year. After this, wine is sometimes drunk, called "dividing the year wine." Thus the old year passes away, and a new year takes its place, with thanksgivings and rejoicings, a grand illumination of candles, and the uninterrupted sound of fire-crackers.

Early New Year's morning idolatrous worship is performed similar to that described above, but having a prospective instead of a retrospective reference. A continuance of the favor and blessing of the Kitchen God, of deceased ancestors, and heaven and earth, is invoked. After religious homage and offerings rendered to these objects of worship, the living ancestors take their seats, and the children worship them—the same words, and nearly the same forms, being used as those which are connected with the worship of gods. The members of the family now offer to each other their congratulations. The servants come and pay their respects to their employers, and receive the expected New Year's gift.

Many of the people, after paying their respects to their household gods, visit some of the temples. The *Cheng-hwang-miao*, described in Chapter X., is a favorite place of resort at this time. Early in the forenoon it is almost filled with worshipers, nearly all of whom are men. As they can find a vacant place in front of the principal image, they kneel and strike their heads against the floor, and, rising, cast their incense-sticks in a large vase in front of the idol, from which a constant volume of smoke rises and fills the temple.

After worshiping the gods, the people pay their respects and congratulations to their near relatives and friends. As you pass through the streets, a striking contrast is presented to what was witnessed the day before. Every shop is closed. All is quiet except the shouting of boys and the explosion of firecrackers. There are many persons seen passing to and fro in the streets, but every one seems a gentleman in dress and manners. All are clothed either in silks, satins, or furs, and wear a cap of ceremony. Those who have not fine clothes of their own hire them by the day or the hour, and have the privilege of appearing as gentlemen at least once a year. The streets present a new and improved appearance. During the night the large paper engravings pasted on the doors, representing the "Door Gods," or "Keepers of the Doors," have been changed, the old paper being replaced by a bright new

HAPPINESS.

one. New inscriptions in large red characters are also seen over the doors, presenting some sentence of joyous or propitious import. Many families make use of the single character *fuh*, "happiness," presenting the great end and object after which man is longing and striving everywhere, and which, alas, in this sinful world it is so difficult to obtain.

Guests, in passing from house to house, are, after the formal salutations, always treated with tea and refreshments, and perhaps urged to stay and take lunch or dinner, which invitations are generally declined. These New Year calls are con-

MANŒUVRING THE DRAGON.

tinued till the 15th, but become less numerous every day. Shops begin to be opened on the third or fourth day, and by degrees the people of every class resume their usual occupations.

During the festivities of the New Year it is very common to see a company of boys bearing aloft a representation of a huge dragon, made of a frame-work of split bamboo covered with cloth. With this they visit house after house, asking of the inmates the privilege of taking the dragon inside their dwelling to frighten away evil spirits, and insure good luck for the coming year. While the boys enjoy the sport greatly, they also fill their pockets with cash presented to them by the families whom they visit.

On the 15th of the first month occurs the "Feast of Lanterns." For several days previous, a great number and variety of lanterns are exposed for sale in the shops. They are made with a light frame of bamboo covered with transparent paper, and represent birds and animals, and other objects of interest. Some of them are made to run on wheels. Others are so contrived that the motion of the air produced by the burning of the candle sets wheels and machinery at work, and makes the object appear like a thing of life. A great deal of ingenuity is manifested in these toys which please the old as well as the young. Large quantities of them are sold. Each family contributes to the general illumination, an unusual number of people is seen in the streets, and they retire to their homes at a late hour.

One of the most interesting of the Chinese festivals is the *Tsing-ming*—"Clear and Bright." It occurs in the spring, and is the time when the people visit the graves, on which account it is often called the "Festival of the Tombs." At this lovely season, all nature bursting into life, and the air loaded with the fragrance of spring flowers and blossoms, the hills are filled with visitors, each group seeking out the well-known grave. Offerings of food and paper-money are made to the departed spirit; worship is performed; the place is swept; a few clods of earth are added perhaps to the top of the mound; and a stick is inserted in it, with a small piece of paper attached, to show to the passing observer that this spot has not been forgotten by surviving relatives. These visits to the hills are not always made on the same day, but about this time, sooner or later.

The ninth day of the ninth month is a great time for flying kites. Mr. Doolittle, in the "Social Life of the Chinese," states, in speaking of a hill in the vicinity of Fuchow, that "Probably thirty or forty thousand people visit that hill to

M

fly their kites, especially if the weather is fine on that day." He thus describes the kites: "The air is full of them. Some are in the shape of spectacles; others represent a kind of fish; others are like an eel or some similar-looking animal, being from ten to thirty feet long, and of proportionate size; others are like various kinds of birds, or bugs, or butterflies, or quadrupeds. Some resemble men sailing through the air." "A foreign resident or transient visitor passing along the street about this period often sees at a distance in the air what seems to be an immense bird, and he is filled with surprise and joy at having so near a view of the unusual phenomenon, until he is reminded by its nearly stationary position and mechanical movements that it is nothing but a paper kite."

Idolatrous processions are conspicuous among the national customs of China, and are a principal means of popular amusement and recreation. They are made in honor of different gods, occur frequently during the year, and are accompanied with a great display of pomp and finery, and an immense outlay of money. An image of some god or gods is always borne at the head of the procession, followed by crowds of men and boys bearing aloft any object which will strike the gaze of the beholder, and add to the interest and novelty of the scene. Families or mercantile establishments contribute some article which serves to bring them prominently before the people, and gives evidence of their generosity and public spirit.

Boats or other objects, curiously and fantastically constructed, are borne on the shoulders of men, decked off with costly trappings and ornaments, or filled with musicians. Here and there may sometimes be seen an exceedingly natural representation of an elephant, or a camel, or giraffe, walking in the procession. These are frames of light split bamboo, covered with paper, which is painted so as to resemble the animal represented, while two men, with the upper part of their bodies concealed in the hollow body, furnish, one the fore-

BOAT CARRIED IN PROCESSION ON MEN'S SHOULDERS.

legs, and the other the hind-legs, having been trained to keep step and imitate the proper gait or motion.

In and about Ningpo variety and interest are added to these processions by a still more curious exhibition. On a platform borne on men's shoulders is seen a beautiful and finely-dressed female (it is hardly necessary to say that these are not of a very respectable class), and another one, standing tiptoe on the uplifted hand of the first, is elevated high in air, a very conspicuous object, and much admired and commented upon. The manner in which these figures are supported seems to the uninitiated stranger very mysterious. The mystery is explained by the existence of strong iron frames, which are nicely adjusted so as to give support to the body, and are concealed under the clothing. Beautifully-dressed children riding on horses led by grooms follow in the train.

Flags, banners, and streamers are interspersed, some of them representing and distinguishing the neighborhood from which the persons and articles in a particular part of the procession have come.

A man is occasionally seen personating a criminal, wearing hand-cuffs or a chain, or a *cangue* (a wooden frame which is sometimes fastened on the necks of criminals, and contains an inscription stating the offense of which they have been con-

WEARING THE CANGUE AS A TOKEN OF GRATITUDE.

victed). These men are recognized at a glance to be persons who have made a vow in times of distress or danger to the god in whose honor this public demonstration is given, promising, in order to secure his favor and interposition, to walk all day with this dress, and in this assumed character.

Some of these processions are from a quarter to half a mile long. They pass from street to street, according to a prearranged plan, and the inhabitants, in anticipation of their approach, are ready, in their holiday dresses, to welcome and admire them, thronging the streets, filling up all the vacant areas, and occupying the doors and second-story windows.

The motives which prompt to providing for the regular recurrence of these displays are a desire to adhere to old customs, a fondness for excitement and amusement, and the hope of propitiating and pleasing the gods and deriving benefits from them.

Theatres are very common in China, but the character and associations of the stage are very different from those of Western lands. The principal and professed object of theatres is to honor or propitiate some god or spirit, which is supposed to be present in an image, or tablet, or paper engraving, to which is assigned the most prominent and honored place. In front of the object of worship may always be seen a table spread with sacrifices or offerings, in order to satisfy the palate, as well as the eyes and ears of the unseen spirit.

There are no large permanent buildings erected specially for theatrical exhibitions. Plays are performed in temples, in private dwellings, in the street, and by the roadside. Temples of every kind have each a stage or platform in front of the idols, designed particularly for theatrical purposes. Wealthy families have a temporary stage erected in the large interior court. Sometimes a family, or several of them together, have a stage erected on a vacant plot of ground near their house. In business streets theatricals are frequently exhibited in front of a shop for the benefit of its trade, in which case a stage is erected across the street, the floors being sufficiently high to allow the people to pass under it.

The expense of these exhibitions is borne by the temple, shop, family, or families which contract for them. Friends receive special invitations, and have seats assigned to them, and a feast provided for them. Any one may be present who is willing to stand in the crowd as a common spectator, and the greater the number of these outside observers, the better pleased are those who give the entertainment.

The times or occasions of these performances are very numerous. On the birthday of a god, a theatre is given to that god in the temple belonging to it by the neighborhood or village connected with the temple. On many of the festivals plays are performed in the ancestral temples. The birthday of a parent, either living or deceased, may also be celebrated by these exhibitions. Theatres are often given in consequence of vows. In times of conflagrations persons frequently prostrate themselves on the ground and promise one in honor of the Fire God in case their dwelling is protected. This kind is called *Sie ho hi*—"Thank-fire Theatre." In times of peace and security, a person or neighborhood, in order to avert future calamities, often provides what is called *Pau ngan hi*—"Secure-tranquillity Theatre." The noisy ceremonies of feeding hungry ghosts, described in a former chapter, are generally terminated by a play called *En shin hi*—"Tranquilize-gods Theatre," which is intended as a kind of an apology to the local deities for making so much disturbance in the places which they preside over. The birthday of the reigning Emperor is celebrated by theatricals of several days' duration in the yamuns, or public offices. Other occasions for theatres might be mentioned, but the above are sufficient to give a general idea of the whole.

The plays performed present much which strikes a foreigner as whimsical and ridiculous. Still, making allowance for the difference of national tastes and literary attainments, they differ less from corresponding performances in the West than might be expected. Some are historical, presenting events and characters of former dynasties, and some are purely fictitious. Some are the productions of the past, and some of the present age. They are regarded by the people as aids to virtuous living, as the characters represented generally meet with their just deserts of rewards or punishments. The various kinds of costume employed differ widely from that used at the present day, and are oftentimes exceedingly grotesque and ludicrous. The performers recite their parts in a high, drawling, falsetto tone, which, though unnatural, and never used in common conversation, is required by Chinese taste in theatres. These exhibitions are characterized by an undue amount of action: the performers are continually advancing and retiring, bowing and gesturing, twisting and turning. They often engage in loud altercations, violent gesticulations, and mock conflicts, which, though we might suppose they would only excite laughter, seem to inspire awe in the minds of Chinese spectators. The termination, not only of each act or scene, but, in some cases, of each sentence or paragraph, is marked by a flourish of gongs and other musical (or rather, to our ears, unmusical) instruments. The plays being composed and recited, for the most part, in the terse written language of China or in the Mandarin dialect, are very imperfectly understood, even by literary men. The meaning is derived, not so much from what is heard as from what is seen. The auditors are also assisted by occasional sentences spokėn in the colloquial dialect, and by additional explanations from theatre-going people in the audience. It is but just to say, with reference to the morals of Chinese theatres, that their most objectionable feature is their connection with idolatry. Vulgar and immoral plays, though not unknown, are comparatively rare, and, being proscribed by law, are generally found in obscure villages in the country. Theatres, like almost every thing else in China, have evidently deteriorated, and the natives often remark of them, as of other things, "They are not what they were of old."

Play-actors, being employed to amuse and serve the people, are regarded as an inferior class. In Ningpo the occupation falls exclusively to a proscribed class, who are the descendants of a family which formerly fell under the displeasure of the Emperor. Females as a general thing do not appear upon the stage, but men act the parts of female characters with a remarkably accurate imitation of their voice and general appearance. Children designed to follow this mode of life from an early age are carefully taught to observe all the niceties of voice and gesture regarded as so essential in their profession, and are required to commit to memory an immense amount of matter with the greatest accuracy. Proficients in the art of play-acting become teachers and heads of companies. Children are indentured to these teachers with the express stipulation that, if the child is beaten to death, his life shall not be required at the teacher's hands. This provision is made, because it is supposed that excellency can not be attained in this branch of learning without constant and severe castigation. Poor children doomed to this life of servitude get very little sympathy, as their sufferings are regarded as a necessity of their condition, and they are expected to get used to them. They have also the satisfaction of knowing that they are only treated as their master was before them. A theatrical company generally sells its services for a year to some wealthy individual, who furnishes them with an outfit and employs a superintendent, whose business it is to keep them occupied, and to collect pay for their performances. These companies consist of from ten to sixty persons, and they may be engaged for from three to twenty dollars a play. Several plays may be performed by the same company in a day, and they are often continued for several days in succession in the same place. Sometimes a wealthy individual employs a theatrical company for a definite length of time for the special amusement of himself, his family and friends, and his gods. These actors being despised by their countrymen, have little respect for themselves, and find their place below mediocrity in the scale of morals.

BOY DRESSED LIKE A FEMALE IN ACTING A THEATRICAL PLAY.

While it may well be a matter of surprise and rejoicing that these theatres are not worse, in a moral point of view, than they are, we can not but notice the masterly art of Satan in infusing into this, and indeed into almost every other means of popular recreation and amusement, the subtile poison of idolatry.

So universal and frequent are these theatrical exhibitions, and so well suited to national tastes, that the people have little time or disposition to meet often for other entertainments. Gatherings for the purpose of listening to public addresses and harangues are almost unknown.

The puppet-shows of China are, on account of the very clever way in which they are performed, and their popularity among the people, worthy of special mention in this connection. Generally two men go together, one to exhibit the show, and the other as an assistant, to beat the gong, collect the contributions, etc. Sometimes one man goes alone, and carries his whole stock in trade on his back. He passes along the street beating his gong, to give notice of his readiness to amuse any who may wish to employ him, and is invited to play before a house, or chooses a convenient place where he can attract a crowd from the street. He stands on a chair, upon which rests also the stick or post which supports the box containing his show or mimic theatre. The upper part of his body is thrust inside the box, and the curtains descending from it conceal most of his person. The front of the box is open and contains a little stage, on which the puppets are paraded. The characters represented are generally a man and his wife engaged in a domestic quarrel. They scold and gesticulate and threaten, and, when these resources are exhausted, proceed to the use of fists and broom-sticks. The actor behind the screen, by means of wires and strings, manages the motions of the puppets with great ingenuity, and imitates the voices and language of the two sexes most perfectly. The husband, after a great assumption of dignity and authority, is generally driven off the stage ignominiously. The appreciation of the audience is often attested by loud shouts of applause. Having witnessed this show both in China and England, I was struck with the fact that it is in these two countries, almost identical, and that the Chinese seem rather to excel in performing it.

Gambling is very common in China, and is practiced in a variety of ways. Its immorality and evil effects are acknowledged, and there are laws prohibiting it; but they are a dead letter.

A very interesting custom prevails of observing public fasts on appropriate occasions. It is not uncommon for the chief officer of a city in time of drought, or to avert some dreaded public calamity, to forbid for several days the slaughter of animals and the sale of animal food in the market, in order to move the gods to pity, and to secure their kind offices in affording the desired relief.

In speaking of the national practices and peculiarities of the Chinese, I can hardly avoid referring to the very common habit among the middle and lower classes of using obscene language. This practice seems to take the place of profanity in Western countries, and is followed by the same class of persons to about the same extent, and apparently from about the same motives. These obscene expressions seem designed primarily for the purpose of reviling and abusing one who is the object of hatred and anger, but are often used carelessly, and almost unconsciously, without any regard to their original meaning.

Many other national traits and peculiarities might be mentioned, but the above are those which have appeared to me most prominent and characteristic of the race.

CHAPTER XIX.

GENERAL ESTIMATE OF THE CHINESE CHARACTER AND CIVILIZATION.

Opinions generally entertained of the Chinese.—The Impressions we have made upon them.—Difficulties in the Way of obtaining reliable Information in the foreign Communities at the open Ports.—National peculiarities of Chinese Temperament and Character.—Evidences of Intellectuality in the Chinese.—The Manner in which they are regarded by other Eastern Nations.—They have taken the Lead in many of the practical Arts.—Many of their Peculiarities due to Education rather than to Differences of Race.—Morality of the Chinese.—Opinions which we have mutually entertained of each other in this Respect, and the Reasons for them.—A Look at ourselves through Chinese Glasses.—Facts illustrating the better Side of Chinese Character.—The injurious Effects apprehended by some from speaking well of a heathen People.

I AM aware that, in many of the opinions which I shall advance in this chapter, I shall be obliged to go in opposition to generally received conclusions. "The Chinaman" has almost become a synonym for stupidity, and his habits and peculiarities afford abundant occasion for pleasantry and ridicule. This impression has become so fixed and so general, that correspondents and editors of newspapers who wish to make their articles on China and the Chinese readable and interesting, gladly seize upon and exaggerate any thing which can be made to appear grotesque and ridiculous. In speaking of this people, their pig-tails, shaven pates, thick-soled shoes, assumption of dignity and superiority, and great ignorance of many subjects with which we are familiar, make up the unfailing material upon which newspaper writers generally draw. Some of the religious papers even follow in the same strain. A comparatively moderate article in one of them a few weeks since characterizes the Chinese as the "largest, oddest, and most *absurd* of the social organizations now existing on the earth."

It would be but a poor answer to these views to say that they correspond remarkably with those which the Chinese entertain of us. They also enjoy a great deal of pleasantry at our expense, finding it almost impossible, with their associations and habits of thought, to regard otherwise than as ludicrous our short-cropped hair, tight fitting, ungraceful and uncomfortable-looking clothes, gentlemen's thin-soled leather boots, tall stiff hats, gloves in summer-time, the "wasp-like" appearance of Western ladies, with their small waists and large hoops, our ungraceful manners, our remarkable ignorance of the general rules of propriety, and the strange custom of a man and his wife walking together in public *arm in arm!* These views we can afford to laugh at as relating to comparatively trivial matters, but they think they have the evidence that we are also inferior to them in intellectuality, in refinement, in civilization, and especially in morals.

It is evident that one party or the other has made a serious mistake, and it would be but a natural and reasonable presumption that both may have erred in being influenced too much by the common tendency of our nature to "think of ourselves more highly than we ought to think."

We should look at this matter neither from a Chinese nor Western stand-point, and take into view not simply facts which are comparatively unimportant and exceptional, but those which are fundamental, and of wide-spread influence, and should construe these facts justly and generously.

It may be well to state here in advance some reasons why general views relating to the Chinese character and civilization, formed in foreign communities in China by those who are unacquainted with the Chinese language, should be received with a great deal of hesitation.

In the open ports, where a large foreign commerce has sprung up, an immense number of Chinese congregate from the interior. Many or most of them are adventurers, separated from the restraining influences of their families and of home society, who come to these places to engage in the general scramble for wealth. As it is but too common for foreigners, in their treatment of native servants and employés, to be haughty, harsh, and overbearing, Chinamen of independence and self-respect generally prefer to be employed by their own people, and are consequently not numerous in the open ports. Moreover, foreign ideas and customs prevail to a great extent in these foreign communities, and the natives, whatever they might have been originally, gradually become more or less denationalized, and present a modified type of their race. Foreigners and natives speak almost exclusively the meagre and contemptible "Pigeon-English" described in Chapter XIV., which is incapable of expressing dignified thought, and the very use of which gives an unpolished and ludicrous air to both parties. The Chinese being every day brought into contact with drunken sailors, swearing sea-captains, and unscrupulous traders from the West, new lessons are constantly learned from them in the school of duplicity and immorality. They conclude that, as the foreigner has come to their country to acquire wealth in dealing with them, it is but fair that they make as much money as they can out of the foreigner. Thus the associations and influences of the foreign community tend to deterioration and demoralization. The Chinese of this class are no fitting type of their race, and foreigners who have only associated with *them*, and that solely through the medium of the "Pigeon-English," are very imperfectly qualified to give an opinion from personal experience and observation of the character, morals, and ideas of the people generally. I have dwelt thus at length on this point, because many of the impressions obtained at home of the Chinese are derived from returned merchants and ship-captains, and transient travellers whose sphere of observation has been very limited, and whose information has been mostly obtained, either immediately or second-hand, in the imperfect manner just described.

The Chinese as a race are, as compared with European nations, of a phlegmatic and impassive temperament, and physically less active and energetic. Children are not fond of athletic and vigorous sports, but prefer marbles, kite-flying, and some quiet games of ball, spinning tops, etc. Men take an easy stroll for recreation, but never a rapid walk for exercise, and are seldom in a hurry or excited. They are also characteristically timid and docile. The oft-made assertion is probably true that an army of ten or twenty thousand Europeans could march without serious opposition from one end of the empire to the other. This remarkable disparity is, however, due principally to our knowledge of modern military science, and our possession of better warlike implements. Chinese well drilled, with confidence in their leaders and in each other, and equipped with modern fire-arms, would form an army which it would not be prudent to oppose with a force very much inferior in numbers; though I have no doubt that, with the same training and advantages, they would still be found inferior to Europeans as soldiers.

But while the Chinese are deficient in active courage and daring, they are not in passive resistance. They are comparatively apathetic as regards pain and death, and have great powers of physical endurance, as well as great persistency and obstinacy. On an average, a Chinese tailor will work on his bench, or a literary man over books or with his pen, more hours a day than persons of our race can.

Physical development and strength and longevity vary in different parts of the empire. In and about Canton, from which we have derived most of our impressions of China, as well as in most parts of the South, the people are small in stature; but in the province of Shantung, in the North, men varying in height from five feet eight inches to six feet are very common, while some of them are considerably taller, indeed, almost giants in stature. In this part of China I have known laborers over seventy years of age, working daily at their trades, and it is not unusual to hear of persons who have reached the age of ninety or more. Other local peculiarities, physical and mental, need not be specially dwelt upon.

The intellectuality of the Chinese is made evident, by so many obvious and weighty facts, that it seems strange that persons of ordinary intelligence and information should ever have questioned it. On this point it is better to state facts than individual opinions. We have before us a system of government and code of laws which will bear favorable comparison with those of European nations, and have elicited a generous tribute of admiration and praise from our most competent and reliable writers. The practical wisdom and foresight of those who constructed this system, are evinced by the fact that it has stood the test of time; enduring longer than any other which man has devised during the world's history; that it has bound together under one common rule a population to which the world affords no parallel, and given a degree of prosperity and of wealth which may well challenge our wonder. Notwithstanding the rebellions and political agitations which have marked the history of this people, such has been their character, and the vital and recuperative energy of the ideas into which they have been educated, that these disasters have been but temporary impediments in the continuous growth and development of the empire. It is intelligent thought which has given China such a prominence in the East, and also in the eyes of Christendom. She may well point with pride to her authentic history, reaching back through more than thirty centuries; to her extensive literature, containing many works of sterling and permanent value; to her thoroughly elaborated language, possessed of a remarkable power of expression; to her list of scholars, and her proficiency in belles-lettres. If these do not constitute evidences of intellectuality, it would be difficult to say where such evidence is to be found, or on what basis we ourselves will rest our claim to intellectual superiority.

China has been so arrogant and extravagant in her assumption of pre-eminence, that we have perhaps for this very reason been indisposed to accord to her the position to which she is fairly entitled. It should be remembered that ignorant, until recently, of Western nations, as they have been of her, she has compared herself simply with the nations around her; and a partial reason or excuse for her overweening self-conceit may be found in the fact that she has only regarded herself as the nations with which she is acquainted have regarded her. She *has* been for ages the great centre of light and civilization in Eastern Asia. She has given a literature and religion to the 30 or 40,000,000 of Japan, and also to the inhabitants of Corea and Manchuria, and is looked up to by these and other smaller nations as their acknowledged teacher. While many in our country regard the Japanese as superior to the Chinese, they do not entertain this view of themselves. The Japanese have produced no great teachers or sages which they would presume to compare with those of China; and it is the clearest evidence of their acknowledgment of the literary superiority of the Chinese that they use the Chinese classics as text-books in their schools, much as we do those of Greece and Rome. Japanese books of high literary pretensions are also written in the Chinese language and character, if the author is able to use them, rather than in the Japanese. The Japanese excel the Chinese in some of the mechanic arts, but certainly not in intellectuality or morality. Perhaps the principal difference between the two races is this: that the Japanese, having been accustomed for ages to learn from the Chinese and the Dutch, naturally take the position of pupils, and are, for this reason, outstripping the Chinese in learning from Western nations a knowledge of the modern arts and sciences; while the Chinese have been too proud to learn, have regarded the suggestion that there is any thing outside the "Middle Kingdom" worth learning as a reflection or aspersion on the wisdom of their ancestors and the sages of the past, and have preferred to remain in ignorance, rather than be indebted to others for information.

But it may be asked, "What have the Chinese ever done?

What do they know? Have they ever made any contributions to science? Are they not utterly ignorant of all the modern arts and sciences?" It is true that the Chinese know hardly any thing of the *modern* arts and sciences, and that there is no word in their language to designate some of them; but how much did our ancestors know two hundred years ago of chemistry, geology, philosophy, anatomy, and other kindred sciences? What did *we* know fifty years ago of the steam-boat, the rail-road, and the telegraph? And is our comparative want of knowledge a few years ago and that of our ancestors to be taken as evidence of inferiority of race and intellect? Perhaps this test which some are so ready to apply will, if we go back a few hundred years, establish the claims of the Chinese as the superior race. Printing, which is second in importance to none of the arts of civilization, originated with the Chinese, and was made use of by them hundreds of years before any thing was known of it in the West. They have taken the lead also in the use of the magnetic needle, the manufacture and use of gunpowder and of silk fabrics, and china-ware and porcelain.

Intellectual power manifests itself in a variety of ways, and glaring defects are often found associated in the same individual with remarkable powers and capabilities, as particular faculties, both of mind and body, are often cultivated and developed at the expense of others. Chinese education has very little regard to the improvement of the reasoning powers, and Chinese scholars are deficient in logical acumen, and very inferior to the Hindoos in this respect; but, in developing and storing the memory, they are without a rival. Again, their system of training effectually discourages and precludes freedom and originality of thought, while it has the compensating advantages of creating a love of method and order, habitual subjection to authority, and a remarkable uniformity in character and ideas. Perhaps the results which they have realized in fusing such a vast mass of beings into one homogeneous body could have been reached in no other way. I believe that the Chinese are not naturally deficient in ingenuity and originality, and that, when these qualities are encouraged, this race will show a fertility of brain the existence of which has hardly been suspected.

The Chinese have labored under another serious disadvantage, that of almost entire isolation from other races, and consequent ignorance of them and their ideas. We have been possessed of all the stores of knowledge of all the different nations of Europe and Western Asia for centuries; and it is impossible to imagine what our condition would be to-day, were it not for the advantages we have derived from the stimulus and teachings obtained from other countries, and more especially from Christianity.

There have been but few opportunities of comparing the intellectual capabilities of the Chinese with our own. Those who have visited our shores are not, with a few exceptions, fitting representatives even of the middle laboring classes in China. Only a very small number of the Mongolian race have been educated in our institutions of learning, but they have uniformly acquitted themselves not only creditably, but with honor. A few years since, a Chinaman in Yale College bore off the first prize in his class for English composition, and I have been told by several of his classmates that this award was not a matter of favoritism, but of stern merit. Wherever they have had an opportunity to compete with us on the same ground, and with equal advantages, they have shown that the difference between them and us in intellectuality is so slight, if it exists at all, that it does not become us to say much about it.

The *morality* of the Chinese presents another subject about which there is a wide difference of opinion. They are so generally spoken of as a "nation of thieves and liars," that a person who is not disposed to adopt or sanction these and similar stereotyped expressions, is in danger of being regarded as either ignorant or prejudiced. I was asked a short time since by a very worthy and intelligent gentleman who finds much to love and admire in the African race, whether I had ever found any traits of character in the Chinese calculated to inspire, in any degree, feelings of respect and affection. It is a question worth considering by persons who entertain such views, on what theory they will account for a great, prosperous, and stable government being composed of such utterly worthless materials.

It may be also a matter of interest and profit to turn for a moment to the views which the Chinese generally entertain of our morality, and their reasons for these views. They are all familiar with the fact that foreigners introduced opium into China in opposition to the earnest and persistent remonstrances of the Chinese government; that out of the opium trade grew the first war with China; and that when the representatives of Christian England urged the Chinese government to legalize the trade and make it a source of revenue, the Chinese Emperor replied that he would not use as a means of revenue that which brought suffering and misery upon his people.

A large proportion of the representatives of our race in China are sailors, many of whom, when on shore, are in a state of intoxication, and are addicted to all kinds of wickedness and violence, while their tongues are constantly employed in taking the name of God in vain in the most horrid, offensive, and heaven-daring oaths. For years foreigners of this class have commanded many of the piratical fleets on the coast of China, and foreign thieves and robbers have infested some of the inland canals and rivers. In business dealings with strangers from Western lands, the natives find that duplicity and dishonesty are not confined to their own people. Moreover, they observe a certain and numerous class of native women in the foreign communities, which are known to belong to the foreigners, and who appear in the streets with a boldness and effrontery which would be regarded as utterly indecent and intolerable in most Chinese cities. Stereoscopic views are imported from the West in large quantities, of the vilest and most obscene character imaginable, picturing before the eye vices and crimes of our race which we would blush to name. My indignation knew no bounds when, a few years since, I found these stereoscopic views exhibited in the streets of a city six hundred miles in the interior by a Chinaman who had invested a little capital in them, and was making a large income by showing them to hundreds of natives daily. Is it strange that, with such facts as these forced upon their attention, the Chinese should come to the conclusion that as a race, we are ambitious, unscrupulous, violent, covetous, and licentious?

I would be very sorry to be regarded as preferring wholesale charges of immorality against foreigners in China as a class. Such a course is certainly the farthest from my intentions. It is hardly necessary to state that there are not a few to be found there, in the civil and naval services as well as among merchants, ship-captains, and seamen, who are men of the highest moral and Christian character, and whose lives are above reproach. It is also sadly true that many sustain a very different character, and that it is in the power of even a few unprincipled and wicked men to bring reproach and shame upon their whole nation and race. The facts to which I have referred, and others of the same class and character, are familiar to every one who has been a few months in China.

But, it may be said, these ideas of us are derived from an acquaintance with a very few individuals who are away from home and its restraining influences, while our opinions of the Chinese are obtained from a view of Chinese society on Chinese soil. Let us suppose then, that a Chinaman has come to our country not prepossessed in our favor, to gain from facts on the ground a knowledge of the morality which prevails among us.

Going on shore, he is asked to pay to the carriage-driver a fee which seems to him most exorbitant. Being shown to his room in one of our first-class hotels, he discovers a printed notice informing him that "Valuables, in order to be safe, must be locked up in the iron chest; guests leave their overcoats in their rooms at their own risk; and the proprietor will not be held responsible for boots left outside the door." Taking up the daily papers, he finds a large portion of them occupied with accounts of robberies, burglaries, murders, cases of poisoning, suicide, forgery, defalcation, divorces, elopements, etc., etc. Turning from these daily items of news to the advertisement columns, he finds in many papers which are regarded as respectable, and are freely received into every family, that the attention of the public is called, in language carefully worded but well understood, to some new and approved method of destroying the incipient life of their offspring. In the political papers he sees wholesale charges of corruption, disloyalty, and selfish, private, and partisan schemes. What materials for illustrating American morals, gathered on the ground from competent witnesses the very first day!

When the Oriental traveller, in pursuit of the desired information, visits the drinking-saloons in almost every street and alley, and the gambling-houses, so numerous in our large cities, to say nothing of other haunts of profligacy, his preconceived opinions of the morality, or, rather, the immorality, of our people would not be much changed for the better.

Or we may imagine him landing on our Western shores and deriving his first information from his own people who have immigrated there. They state to him the facts that, from their first arrival in California, they are subjected to extortion and plunder; and that after paying for a license to work in our mines, other charges are exacted on false pretenses, either by officials or those who feign to be so. If any of them are so fortunate as to obtain a spot in the mines which yields a rich return, they are summarily driven from it. If it be known that a Chinaman has accumulated gold, he is in great danger of having it taken from him, and is fortunate if his life is not taken with it, for well-known murders of this kind have not been infrequent. With all these oppressive grievances, this inoffensive, industrious, and misused people have no means of defense. They are not permitted to bear testimony in our courts, and they seldom find an American who will be a witness for them. The undeniable result is soon reached by the inquiring visitor that, in this boasted land of liberty and law, there is for them no justice and no redress.

The Chinese traveller would find the statements of his countrymen in California confirmed by the independent testimony of our own people such as the following from a prominent preacher in Brooklyn: "We pretend to be an asylum for the oppressed, a school-house for the ignorant of the earth, and yet grant no means of advancement beyond manual labor, and no adequate means, even of legal protection, to the industrious but unknowing Chinaman. This is too true a picture. There can be but little doubt but that one of the first things to be attended to by the newly-arrived Chinese Embassy will present itself in the civil disabilities and outrageous treatment of the patient Mongolians in California. And it should be; their position here is scandalous to a Christian nation, still more so to one claiming the peculiarly Christian principles of self-government, and mutual equality before the laws.

"Last winter a bill came up in the California Legislature to allow Chinamen to testify in certain cases in the civil and criminal courts; but the Assembly rejected the bill, and virtually gave free license to all ruffians and robbers, provided they are white men, to inflict such outrages as they choose upon the poor Mongolian without fear of legal penalty.

"The fifty thousand Chinese in California are, taken all in all, if not the most intelligent, highly educated, and wealthy, certainly the most patient, quiet, law-abiding, industrious, peaceable, and honest set that California can show. The proportion of criminals and law-breakers among them is wonderfully small, as compared with all other classes; and as they evidently have in them the elements of good citizens, the State ought to protect them in every way, encourage their industry, foster their good disposition, and prepare them at some future time to become full members of the community."

And now, what do all these evidences which a Chinaman might collect to prove the immorality and injustice of Europeans and Americans show? They show how easy it is to confirm preconceived judgments by an array of partial facts, and also that we are far from being faultless in matters whereof we accuse others.

There are many other facts which tend to give a more favorable opinion of the Chinese than is generally entertained of them. It is the testimony of foreigners generally that the laboring classes make excellent servants. There are exceptions to this statement, some persons representing them as very inefficient and unreliable. The probability may be inferred in these cases that the employers have been unfortunate, either in the selection or management of those in their service. During our residence of ten years in China, we hardly ever had occasion to dismiss a servant; in nearly every case a strong attachment sprang up between them and us; and, in more instances than one, I have felt personally grateful for services and attentions which I could not reasonably have required, and which were all the more gratifying, because rendered spontaneously and heartily. The only thing which I recollect to have had stolen was an old clock, which was taken by an opium-smoker, and found a few days afterward. We had so little fear of theft that our doors and drawers were often left unlocked, and servants and numerous visitors had free access to every part of our house. I am aware that others, both missionaries and merchants, have had a different experience, and that, especially in the foreign communities, it is as dangerous to leave coats and umbrellas near the hall-door when unlocked as it would be in New York or Philadelphia. I have travelled hundreds of miles in the interior, at different times and in different parts of the country, sometimes entirely alone, and have been completely in the power of perfect strangers, who knew that I had about my person money and other articles of value;

but have always felt nearly as great a sense of security as at home, and have hardly ever been treated with rudeness or violence, though I have been often annoyed beyond measure by exorbitant charges and useless detentions. I have heard the testimony of prominent merchants who have had large business transactions with the Chinese, both in China and California, who have represented Chinese business men as very prompt and reliable in meeting their business engagements. The confidence often placed in Chinese agents is seen in the fact that they are sent into the interior with large sums of money to purchase silks and tea, the persons employing them having no guarantee or dependence but that of their personal honesty. I have known genuine "one-priced stores" in China where you are sure to obtain a good article at a reasonable price. There are also false "one-priced stores," and it is not safe to trust them from simply looking at the sign.

I may say further, that I have met with some of the most beautiful instances of affection, attachment, and gratitude in China which I have ever known; and that it has been my privilege to form the acquaintance of not a few Chinese, whom I regard with more than ordinary affection and respect, on account of the natural amiability of their dispositions, their sterling integrity, and thorough Christian principle and devotion.

On the general subject of Chinese morality, and especially of the Chinese moral teachings, I am happy to be able to quote the opinions of two prominent English writers, who, from long residence in China as civil officers of the English government, and a familiar acquaintance with the people and their literature, may certainly be regarded as competent witnesses. The following passage is quoted with approbation by Thomas Taylor Meadows, from the writings of Sir John Davis: "The most commendable feature of their (the Chinese) system is the general diffusion of elementary moral education among the lower orders. It is in the preference of moral to physical instruction that even we might perhaps wisely take a leaf out of the Chinese book, and do something to reform this most mechanical age of ours." The opinion of Mr. Meadows on this subject is thus expressed: "No people, whether of ancient or modern times, has possessed a sacred literature so completely exempt as the Chinese from licentious descriptions, and from every offensive expression. There is not a single sentence in the whole of their sacred books and their annotations that may not, when translated word for word, be read aloud in any family in England."

It must be acknowledged that the Chinese give many evidences, not only in their literature, but also in their paintings and sculpture, of a scrupulous care to avoid all indecent and immoral associations and suggestions. I have already remarked, in a former chapter, that a nude representation of the human form is hardly to be found among the innumerable idols and images of the Chinese Empire. I can easily imagine the members of the Chinese Embassy, when visiting the United States, much shocked by some of the representations in painting and sculpture which they see in our art galleries. We have borrowed this custom of the public exhibition of nude figures from the idolatrous nations of Greece and Rome, the morality of whose people and gods was below that of the Chinese. A professed admiration of the beauty of "the human form divine" is but a poor excuse for this custom, while in our fashions and mode of dress we adopt models which are any thing but natural, and, by following which, an artist would meet with universal and merited reprobation and disgrace.

In referring to the above peculiarity of Chinese views and customs, I am not, of course, speaking of the private lives and practices of this people, but of their standard of propriety, and of what the public taste requires in objects which are openly represented, to be seen and admired by the young and old of both sexes. It may be said of the Chinese as truly as of others: "It is a shame even to speak of the things which are done of them in secret."

What, then, is the conclusion of this whole matter? Simply this, that it is not difficult to find every species of vice and

N

immorality both in China and at home, and that, on the other hand, we may find exhibitions of the better principles of our nature in both countries if we are disposed to seek them. The standard and the practice of virtue are almost necessarily, and, as might be expected, lower in China than in Christian lands, but the wonder to my mind is, considering our superior advantages, that the difference is not greater. It is certainly not so striking as to form the basis of a very marked contrast, or to render it modest or prudent for us to designate any particular vice, or class of vices, as peculiar to, and especially characteristic of the Chinese. I believe that, taking into view our religious and spiritual privileges and training, we are more to be blamed as individuals and as a nation for not having reached a higher standard of morality than the Chinese are.

I am persuaded also that the effect of close and familiar acquaintance with the Chinese or any other nation is to produce and deepen the impression of a common origin and nature. At first we notice external peculiarities of complexion, dress, and manners, which are superficial, accidental, and unimportant; but by degrees we become almost unconscious of these outward differences, as we notice multiplied evidence of common instincts and longings, doubts and fears, joys and sorrows, virtues and vices. We see the same indications of a noble and godlike nature suffering under the effects of a terrible catastrophe or fall, swayed by conflicting tendencies and impulses, and utterly unable to find the ark of rest and peace. In the Eastern or Western hemisphere, "as in water face answereth to face, so the *heart* of man to man."

It is quite probable that the views which I have presented will be regarded by some as prejudicial to the interests of religion and missions. Indeed I have been expostulated with by some worthy and pious people, who have told me that if I represented the Chinese as, on the whole, "so well off," and in many respects "a very good sort of people," Christians would not care to do any thing for them. That a high degree of intellectual, social, and even moral culture, is consistent with the greatest spiritual ignorance and destitution, seems to many inconceivable or impossible, though the fact has been illustrated in every period of the world's history. Strange and inexplicable as it may appear, that a thinking and intelligent race like the Chinese should be so ignorant of God, and such gross idolaters, it is not more so than that the majority of those in nominally Christian lands who are possessed of an acknowledged revelation from God should live in almost utter disregard of it. A system of morality may be as effective a means of keeping the soul away from God as one of idolatry, and, in some cases, more so. Pride of intellect and false systems of philosophy have the same tendency. In China Satan has used all these instrumentalities combined.

Some persons are so accustomed to associate ignorance of God with the lowest moral degradation and lawlessness, that they expect to hear, in the representations of missionaries from whatever part of the heathen world they may come, only of scenes of barbarism and tales of horror. I have known of a profound impression having been produced by an address of a returned missionary from the East many years ago, who stated that such was the character of Chinese society and the condition of women, especially of daughters-in-law, in the husband's family, that he had known of "five sisters who, several years after their marriage, met for the first time at their own father's house. On recounting their experiences of tyranny and ill-treatment from mothers-in-law and husbands, they were so impressed with the utter worthlessness of lives such as theirs, and the miseries of their intolerable lot, that they resolved upon suicide, and all went hand in hand to a neighboring canal and buried themselves beneath its waters." This has been remembered for more than thirty years, and has gone far to fix, perhaps, in many minds the character and condition of the "wretched Chinese." It would be easy to collect enough of such incidents to fill up an evening lecture, giving to it a thrilling interest, and producing, perhaps, a profound impression; but the impression produced would be partial and incomplete to such an extent as to be absolutely false. Most conditions in life have a sunny as well as a shady side; I have endeavored to bring to view both, and to present the condition and character of the Chinese as it is, confident that no harm can result, either to religion or science, from the statement of facts. The inhabitants of Rome and of Athens at the beginning of the Christian era were very intelligent and respectable people, and their condition, as regards this life, was not such as to excite commiseration; but these facts do not seem to have dampened the missionary zeal of St. Paul, or caused him to relax in his efforts to preach to them the Gospel of Christ. It is but a weak, sickly, and imperfectly enlightened Christianity, which can only be roused to activity by tales of physical distress, while it is insensible to the spiritual condition of vast multitudes who are without a knowledge of God and of a way of salvation; treats with comparative indifference the solemn command of Jesus to evangelize the nations, and finds no powerful motive to exertion in the work of extending the spiritual triumphs of the Redeemer, and contributing to the establishment on earth of His universal kingdom and glory.

CHAPTER XX.

INTERCOURSE OF WESTERN NATIONS WITH CHINA.

Isolation. — Antiquity and Chronology. — Early Reference to China in Greek and Roman History.—A Jewish Colony in Kai-fung-foo.—The Nestorians and their Labors.—Marco Polo.—Early Romish Missions.—First War with England, and the Opening of the Five Treaty Ports in 1842.—Events which led to the last War with England and France, and to the Treaties which are now in Force.—Our present Relations.

One of the most remarkable facts in connection with China is its comparative isolation for thirty centuries from other nations of the globe—an isolation which at times has been so complete that the "Middle Kingdom" has been almost as unknown to the rest of the world as if it belonged to a different planet. Between Western nations and the nations of Central Asia, many evident connections may be traced in their histories, languages, traditions, and religions, but not so with China. It seems to have been a world by itself, uninfluenced by the ideas, and undisturbed by the convulsions of other countries, having a form of civilization and government peculiarly her own, and resembling other races only in this, that its people are possessed of the same common nature.

The isolation of the Chinese Empire has been due to its position in the extreme limits of Eastern Asia, and the great difficulties which for ages prevented reaching it by sea, and which still render it impracticable to reach it by an overland route across the Himalaya Mountains.

I do not propose to enter upon the vexed and difficult question of the antiquity of China, or to endeavor to fix the boundary between its mythological period and its authentic history, much less to note the long succession of its dynasties and the events connected with them. But as the subject of its antiquity is one of much interest, I will simply give the opinion and conclusions relating to it of some of our most trustworthy modern writers.

Among those who place the period of reliable Chinese records nearest to our time is Sir John Davis, whose views are expressed as follows: "The period of authentic history may be considered as dating from the race of Chow, in whose time Confucius himself lived; for although it might be going too far to condemn all that precedes that period as absolutely fabulous, it is still so mixed up with fable as hardly to deserve the name of history." The reign of the race of Chow begins about one thousand years before the Christian era. The principal evidence referred to by this writer to cast discredit upon antecedent records is found in the assertions that "Yu is described as nine cubits in height; and it is stated that the skies rained gold for three days." In answer to this objection, Williams justly remarks: "This height is but little more than that of Og of Bashan; and if *Kin*, here called gold, be translated metal (which it can just as well be), it may be a notice of a meteoric shower of extraordinary duration."

The following is Williams's opinion: "Chinese mythological history ends with the appearance of Fuh-hi, and their chronology should not be charged with the long period antecedent varying from forty-five to five hundred thousand years, for the people themselves do not believe this duration. These periods, however, are a mere twinkling, compared with the Kulpas of the Hindoos, whose highest era, called the "Unspeakably Inexpressible," requires 4,456,448, ciphers following a unit to represent it.

"The accession of Fuh-hi is placed in the Chinese annals B.C. 2852." This would be five hundred and eight years before the Deluge, according to the chronology of Usher; and three hundred and three years after, if we follow that of Hales.

In endeavoring to discover points of contact of the history of China with that of other countries, an attempt has been made to identify the Noachic Deluge with a notable flood recorded in the Chinese annals in connection with the Emperor Yu, which, if we credit Chinese history, took place B.C. 2293. This flood, according to Usher, synchronizes with the Deluge of Scripture, with the variation of only fifty-five years. It is the general opinion, however, that the Chinese record refers to an unusual inundation of the Yellow River, and that this supposed single coincidence between the sacred Scriptures and the early history of China is not established by sufficient evidence.

Thomas Taylor Meadows, in his work "The Chinese and their Rebellion," gives the following statement: "Authentic, though not full records, embodying ethical and political doctrines, extend back to B.C. 2357, or to about eighteen hundred years before Confucius, while the Chinese philosophy originated with Fuh-hi, who lived, according to the tradition, some twenty-three generations before the exact chronological era, which latter took place B.C. 2637, with the institution of the national cycle of sixty years. Allowing thirty years to one generation, this would place Fuh-hi about B.C. 3327."

It will be seen that, while writers who have investigated this subject, differ widely in their conclusions, none of them fix the period of the authentic history of China less distant from our time than about three thousand years.

References of a vague and uncircumstantial character to a country now generally believed to be China are found in the works of Greek and Roman historians, principally in the writings of Ptolemy and Arian, who lived in the second century. Ptolemy states that he derived his information from the agents of Macedonian traders. These agents, who probably belonged to some of the Tartar tribes of Central Asia, gave him an account of a journey of seven months from the principal city of Eastern Turkistan in a direction east, inclining a little south. They represented the most eastern nation of Asia under the name of Serica, and stated that on the borders of this kingdom they met, and traded with its inhabitants, the Seres.

Herodotus speaks of the Isadores, as a people in the extreme north-east of Asia. Ptolemy also mentions these tribes as a part of Serica, and under its sway.

Ammianus Marcellinus, a Roman historian of the fourth century, speaks of the land of the Seres as surrounded by a high and continuous wall. This was about six hundred years after the great wall of Northern China was built.

Virgil, Pliny, Tacitus, and Juvenal refer to the Seres in connection with the Seric garments, which seem to have been made of fine silk or gauze. This article of dress was much sought after in Rome by the wealthy and luxurious, and as late as the second century is said to have been worth its weight in gold.

Now, from the length and direction of the route of the traders just referred to, the description of the mountains and rivers which they passed, the character of the people with whom they traded, and the articles of traffic, the evidence seems almost conclusive that the nation which the Greeks and Romans designated by the name Serica is that now known to us as China.

The particular countries visited by the caravans which brought the silk to Europe were probably the dependencies or territories of China on the west, or possibly cities within the extreme north-west limits of China proper. The information conveyed by these traders, who were probably ignorant of the Chinese language, was necessarily imperfect and limited, and the communication carried on through them had little or no effect either on China or the West. Little was known of the Seres, except that such a people existed, and that one of their productions, silk fabrics, excelled in richness and beauty any article of dress in the known world. These fabrics were spoken of by the Romans as a product of barbarian luxury; and the traders from Macedonia and Rome were no doubt spoken of in China as barbarians from the West, who had been attracted to the "Central Flowery Land" by the benign influences of its superior civilization, and a desire to carry back to their own territories the evidences of its luxury and refinement.

The introduction of Judaism in China is evidenced by a Jewish synagogue which existed until quite recently in Kai-fung-foo, a city in the province of Honan. Connected with this synagogue were some Hebrew manuscripts and a few worshipers, who retained some of the forms of their religion, but very little knowledge of its real character and spirit. They are called in China the *Tiau-kin kiau*—"The Sect which plucks out the Sinew." There is a great deal of uncertainty as to when the Jews came to China, though they have, no doubt, resided there for many centuries. The remaining buildings and timbers of this synagogue have recently been sold, and this little remnant which has been preserved long enough to afford evidence that Jews and Judaism have reached the extreme limits of the East will probably soon be extinct.

Nestorian missionaries entered China some time before the seventh century. The principal record which they have left of the success of their missions is the celebrated Nestorian monument in Se-ngan foo. This monument contains a short history of this sect from the year 630 to 781, and also an abstract of the Christian religion. The missionaries of this sect have left but few records of their labors, or of their observations as travellers. The churches planted by them seem to have existed until a comparatively recent period. The Romish missionaries, who entered China in the beginning of the fourteenth century, found them possessed of considerable influence, not only among the people, but also at court, and met with no little opposition from them in their first attempts to introduce the doctrines of their Church. It is natural and reasonable to hope that, during the period of near eight hundred years in which Nestorian Christianity maintained its foothold in China, large numbers from that empire became savingly acquainted with the truth as it is in Jesus. There is evidence, however, that, in process of time, the Nestorian churches departed widely from the truth and simplicity of the Gospel. After the fall of the Mongolian Empire, they were cut off from connection with the West, and not having sufficient vitality to resist the adverse influences of heathenism, their people by degrees either relapsed into idolatry or adopted the Romish faith.

The first Western writer whose works are extant, who has given any thing like full and explicit information respecting China, is Marco Polo. He went to China in the year 1274 in company with his father and uncle, who were Venetian noblemen. At this time the independent nomad tribes of Central Asia being united in one government under the successors of Zinghis Khan, it became practicable to reach Eastern Asia by passing through the Mongolian Empire. Marco Polo spent twenty-four years in China, and seems to have been treated kindly and hospitably. The suspicion and distrust which the Chinese have manifested toward Western nations during the last few centuries are not so much the result of their natural dispositions, or the teachings of their sages, as of their unfortunate and prejudicing experience in their intercourse with foreigners.

After Marco Polo's return home, he was taken prisoner in a war with the Genoese, and during his confinement wrote an account of his travels. The description he gives of the vast territories of China, its teeming population and flourishing cities, the refinement and civilization of its people, and their curious customs, seemed to his countrymen more like a fiction of fairy-land than sober and authentic narrative. It is said that he was urged when on his death-bed to retract these statements and make confession of falsehood, which he refused to do. More recent discoveries and information have served to confirm the truth of his statements, and to establish his character as one of the most remarkable travellers of any age.

During the period of the Mongolian Empire, which comprehended under its sway the greater part of Asia from China on the east to the Mediterranean on the west, an intense desire was kindled in the Romish Church to convert this powerful nation to its faith. Among the first and the most noted of the missionaries sent to China at this time was John of Mount Corvin, who reached Pekin in 1293. He was afterward made archbishop. From time to time bishops and priests were sent out to re-enforce this mission, but they met with indifferent success; and when the Mongols were driven from China the enterprise was abandoned as a complete failure. After the fall of the Mongolian Empire, direct overland communication with Eastern Asia was interrupted, and for about two hundred years China was again almost completely isolated from the Western world.

The use of the magnetic needle and improvements in navigation introduced a new era in intercourse with the East. It is supposed that the first voyage from Europe to China was made by a Portuguese vessel in 1516. From this period commercial intercourse with that empire has been more and more frequent, and various embassies have been sent to the Chinese Court by different nations of Europe. Unfortunately, the growing familiarity of the Chinese with Western nations did not increase their respect for and confidence in them. This was due partly to the servility of most of the embassies to Pekin, but principally no doubt to the want of honesty, and the general lawlessness of the greater part of the traders from the West. The consequence was that the Chinese became desirous of restricting foreign intercourse, and exercising as strict surveillance over their troublesome visitors as possible.

Immediately after a connection was established between Europe and the far East by sea, another and a more successful effort was made by the Romish Church to propagate its faith in the Chinese Empire. Francis Xavier, in his attempt to gain an entrance into the country, died on one of the islands on the coast in 1552. Matteo Ricci, who may well be regarded as the Apostle of the Romish Church in China, established himself in Canton in the garb of a Buddhist priest in 1581.

He was a man of varied intellectual gifts and extensive learning, united with indomitable energy, zeal, and perseverance, and great prudence. In 1601 he reached Pekin in the dress of a literary gentleman. He was much admired, and acquired a great influence over the literary and ruling classes. His labors and those of his associates resulted in many conversions, and in the establishment of churches in different parts of the empire. His successors during the one hundred and fifty years following his arrival in China succeeded in establishing several bishoprics, and numbered their converts by hundreds of thousands. During this period, controversies and dissensions sprang up between the Jesuits and Dominicans, which, together with other causes, produced suspicions in the minds of the Chinese rulers, and in the year 1723 an edict was promulgated prohibiting the further propagation of this religion in the empire. From this time the Roman Catholics were subjected to frequent and sometimes violent persecutions, with alternate periods of comparative toleration. They have retained their position in the face of great difficulties and trials, and since the late treaties with China their converts have rapidly increased.

The most important events in the modern intercourse of Western nations with China are its wars with England and France, and the treaties to which they gave rise. The first war with England, sometimes called the Opium War, from its relation to and effects upon the opium trade, resulted in the treaty of 1842, which opened five Chinese ports to foreigners, and ceded to the English the small island of Hongkong. In a few years the United States and other governments availed themselves of the advantages secured by the English in this treaty. It does not fall within my plan to discuss the merits of this first war with China. Justifiable or not, it was made use of in God's providence to inaugurate a new era in our relations with this vast empire. Hitherto trade had been carried on by sufferance, and traders were subjected to many restrictions and annoyances. Foreigners were not allowed to take up a permanent residence on shore, and were regarded as an inferior race of barbarians and vassals.

A few Protestant missionaries had commenced their labors in some of the Chinese colonies along the coast, but the great Middle Kingdom was still sealed against them. Morrison had gained an entrance into Canton as an employé of the East India Company, and was engaged in labors indirectly bearing upon the missionary work, but did not deem it prudent to attempt the open proclamation of the Gospel.

After the treaty, the Chinese were obliged to regard and treat with foreigners more on terms of equality; a new impulse was given to trade, and Protestant missionaries, as well as Roman Catholic, under the protection of this treaty entered the five ports, built houses and chapels, established schools, and engaged in public preaching.

A great advance had been made, but the work of opening China was yet incomplete. The Chinese, in their intercourse with Europeans, still maintained as far as they were able the same tone of superiority and authority, and showed a disposition to reduce the privileges extorted from them in the treaty to a minimum. Foreigners were closely confined to the treaty ports, and, if found trespassing beyond assigned limits, were apprehended and brought back to their consuls. In Canton the spirit of opposition and prejudice was so strong that the people insisted on keeping foreigners outside the city wall, and succeeded in obliging them to take up their residence in and confine themselves to the suburbs.

It was impossible for such a state of things to continue long without producing another outbreak. In 1857 a serious difficulty originated between the Chinese and British authorities in Canton. Rev. W. A. P. Martin wrote in May, 1858, from the north of China, where he was engaged as interpreter for the American Embassy, as follows: "The quarrel originated in an occurrence of the most trivial character, and has grown to its present magnitude by a concatenation of events which no human power could have arranged, or human sagacity foreseen. It presents a striking instance of what is so often noticed in the course of history—God accomplishing his great and wise purposes by allowing man to pursue his petty, private, and even unjustifiable ends. In this case the Divine purpose appears to be the opening of China for the free promulgation of his blessed Gospel. The wedge which he employed to cleave the first fissure in this hitherto unyielding mass was the iniquitous traffic in opium; and the unjustifiable practice of granting the protection of the British flag to Chinese vessels has furnished the occasion for the demolition of the remaining barriers."

A native vessel making use of the British flag (without, as the Chinese assert, any right to do so) was called to account, and summarily dealt with by the Chinese authorities. The English, feeling that their flag had been treated with disrespect, demanded certain concessions and acknowledgments which the Chinese were unwilling to grant. In consequence of this refusal, hostilities were commenced by the English, who took some forts on the Canton River, and bombarded and took possession of the city of Canton on the 29th of December, 1857.

The demand was now made that imperial commissioners should be sent from the capital with authority to adjust the differences between China and England, and to form a new treaty. In this demand the French government, as an ally of England, joined, and Shanghai was the place designated by them for the meeting. The Chinese, in accordance with their traditional policy to keep foreigners as far from their capital as possible, insisted that the interview between its commissioners and the representatives of the foreign powers should be held in Canton as formerly.

The foreign ministers determined not to submit to this arbitrary and unreasonable requisition, and proceeded to the Peiho, the port of Pekin in the north, and insisted on an interview there. Here new difficulties arose. It was hardly to be expected that matters would progress harmoniously with two

CAPTURE OF THE PEIHO FORTS.

parties, each of which felt its superiority, and was determined to dictate terms to the other. The English and French expressed themselves as dissatisfied with the powers of the imperial commissioners, and refused to treat with them, and sent word to the Emperor that if an officer of higher authority were not sent from the capital, they would bombard and take the forts at the mouth of the Peiho River. The Emperor disregarded this message, and the forts were attacked and taken on the 20th of May, after two hours' fighting, and considerable loss on both sides. Possessing themselves of these forts, the allies moved on rapidly toward Tien-tsin, accompanied by the plenipotentiaries of the United States and Russia, "who had nearly completed the revision of the treaties, when the rupture with the English and French broke off their negotiations." The arrival of the foreign embassadors in Tien-tsin, accompanied by an armed force, occasioned great excitement and trepidation at the capital. Two commissioners of high rank and enlarged powers were dispatched to meet the foreigners, and, if possible, adjust the difficulties which had arisen. These men are thus described by Mr. Oliphant, private secretary of Lord Elgin:

"The senior commissioner, Kweiliang, was a venerable man, of placid and benevolent expression, with a countenance full of intelligence, though his eye was somewhat dimmed, and his hand palsied from extreme age. His manners were polished and dignified, and his whole bearing that of a perfect gentleman. He is a Tartar, and has risen to his present high position after a long course of services. His full titles, with which he signed the treaties, were as follows: 'Kweiliang, a Senior Chief Secretary of State, styled of the East Cabinet, Captain-General of the Satin White Banner of the Manchu Banner Force, and Superintendent-General of the Administration of Criminal Law.' His colleague, Hwashana, a Mandarin of the same grade, was a much younger man, with a square solid face and a large nose. In general appearance, he reminded me strongly of the pictures of Oliver Cromwell, and in the lines

KWEILIANG, FIRST IMPERIAL COMMISSIONER.

of the lower part of his countenance much firmness and decision of character were apparent. He styles himself one of his Imperial Majesty's Expositors of the Classics, Manchu President of the Office for the Regulation of the Civil Establishment, Captain-General of the Bordered Blue Banner of the Chinese Banner Force, and Visitor of the Office of Interpretation."

After sundry delays and ineffectual attempts on the part of the Chinese commissioners to avoid concessions demanded by the English, the treaty was at length agreed upon. Lord Elgin, during all the negotiations, preserved a very determined and authoritative bearing, and succeeded in gaining every point on which he insisted. It was said that "a mere hint of proceeding to Pekin was sufficient to take the most doubtful clauses through the perils of diplomacy."

Peace was now restored, a better understanding between China and Western powers established, and new and important advantages secured to traders and missionaries. All that remained to be done in closing up these negotiations was

HWASHANA, SECOND IMPERIAL COMMISSIONER.

to send the treaties to Europe and America to be sanctioned and ratified by Western governments; after which, they were to be formally ratified by the Emperor at Pekin.

Early in the summer of 1859 the representatives of "the four treaty powers," England, France, the United States, and

Russia, appeared at the mouth of the Peiho with the treaties, to obtain their final ratification. The speedy consummation of this event was confidently anticipated by foreigners and natives generally, though it had been rumored for months that the mouth of the Peiho had been filled with obstructions to prevent the entrance of foreign gun-boats, and that extensive warlike preparations had been made to resist and exclude the foreign embassadors. I believe the Chinese did not contemplate breaking faith with foreign nations, but they found it very difficult to accept the position in which they found themselves, and to submit with a *good grace* to the terms of a treaty which seemed to them so humiliating, and which had been exacted from them the previous year with such a dictatorial air and haughty assumption of superiority. They felt that they could not surrender to " barbarians " that pre-eminence which, from time immemorial, they had claimed and exercised. The Chinese commissioners, with earnest professions of cordiality, and a forced assumption of dignity and authority, informed the foreign plenipotentiaries that they were expected at Pekin, but that the channel of the Peiho was effectually closed, and that they must proceed to the capital by another route. They assured them that the Chinese government intended to treat the foreign ministers with all due consideration and respect, but that they regarded them as their guests, and would expect them to leave their gun-boats at the mouth of the river, and, with a limited escort, put themselves under the care and guidance of the servants of the Emperor, who would provide them with suitable conveyances and necessary supplies. This proposition no doubt seemed to the Chinese natural and reasonable, while the English saw in it a persistent determination to treat them as inferiors, and to subject them to petty annoyances, and some supposed that the Chinese wished to draw the foreign embassadors into a position where they would be entirely in their power, by separating them from their ships and their soldiers. Under these circumstances, the English and French expressed their fixed determination to go to Pekin by the usual and direct route, through the Peiho, and to take with them as large a company of foreign soldiers as they wished. Here was another antagonism as clearly defined as that of the previous year. Neither party would recede from its position, and an appeal was again made to arms.

The Chinese had made every possible preparation for this emergency in case it should arise, and succeeded in offering such a determined and effective resistance as was not expected from them. After several gun-boats were disabled by the fire from the forts, and a storming-party had utterly failed in effecting its object, the allied forces having suffered severe losses of men and vessels, were obliged to withdraw and give up the attack as a complete failure. While the English and French quietly retired, the Ministers of the United States and Russia, who had not taken part in this encounter, went to Pekin, as desired by the Chinese government, and exchanged their treaties.

Quiet was again restored, at least for a season. The "Great Middle Kingdom" had gained a decided victory, and the Chinese were jubilant—in some places almost insolent. But all felt that this quiet was delusive. The political sky was not cleared, and another more terrible storm was apprehended. The Empire was for a time freed from the presence of a foreign foe, but in the distance was heard the roar of the English Lion, and seen the glittering of French bayonets.

Early in the summer of 1860 the expected allied army made its appearance off the mouth of the Peiho. It was now determined to carry the war to the very gates of Pekin, and make the Chinese acknowledge the supremacy of Western nations. The invading army was composed of the best troops, both cavalry and infantry, which England and France could furnish, numbering in all about twenty thousand men. No expense had been spared. The expedition was too important to risk the chance of a failure. The Chinese government opposed the invading force by an immense army, led by their famous general Seng-ko-ling-sing. They gave unexpected evidence of resolution and courage; but as they had been two proud to learn the art of war from foreigners, all their efforts to guard the capital of the "Son of Heaven" from being desecrated by barbarians proved fruitless. As the conquerors approached Pekin, the Emperor fled in great haste into Tartary. The Western plenipotentiaries, with foreign guns trained upon the walls of the Chinese capital, exacted the ratification of their treaties, with additional clauses and conditions still more galling to the Chinese, every new act of resistance on their part being made the occasion of demanding new privileges and advantages.

These treaties opened for foreign residence and trade two new ports on the island of Formosa, Swatow on the south coast of China, Cheefoo and Tien-tsin in the north, one city in Manchuria, and three on the great river Yiang-ts. It conceded the right to travel with passports throughout the eighteen provinces, and contained also a special clause giving protection to foreigners and natives in the propagation and adoption of the Christian religion. The further condition was imposed that the Chinese should pay the expenses of the war.

The moral effect of this war was very great. The superiority of Western nations, at least in this one art, could no longer be questioned, and a much more favorable impression was made by the moderation, magnanimity, and clemency of the victors than by their military power.

As the invading army marched inland from the coast, the people, expecting nothing from them but wholesale slaughter and plunder, fled before them in consternation, and many committed suicide. It was soon found, however, that the English treated those not in arms with kindness, and paid a fair price for every thing they wished. The country people brought in all kinds of provisions, and I have been told by an English officer that he had never known a better market than that which followed them in all their course from the coast to Pekin. They even bought pack-mules and horses at a very

SIGNING OF THE TREATY OF TIEN-TSIN.

low price. The French, adopting a less kindly policy, were obliged, as a natural and merited result, to go to the English market to buy their provisions, and to be subject to the rules and regulations which they had imposed. It is but just to add, that the character of the French army was further tarnished by the unjustifiable act of burning a valuable library connected with the Emperor's summer palace.

Within the short time which has elapsed since the ratification of the last treaties in 1860, an important trade has sprung up in all these newly-opened ports. Ideas of progress and change are constantly being taught to millions of the interior provinces by more than a score of large steamers plying between the coast and the city of Han-Kow, six hundred miles in the interior—a place containing near 2,000,000 of inhabitants.

Shanghai, one of the five open ports, has grown from a small settlement to a place numbering five thousand foreign residents, and the shipping anchored here at one time often contains near five thousand traders and sailors. Protestant missionaries have entered nearly all the new ports, and in most of them may be found already a company of native Christians and organized native churches.

O

CHAPTER XXI.

MISSIONARY LIFE IN CHINA.

A Sea-voyage a good Preparation for Missionary Life.—First Impressions on Shore.—Novelty succeeded by Monotony.—Longing for Home.—Missionary Houses, Mode of Living, Salaries, Servants, etc.—Importance of Female Laborers.—Married and Unmarried Missionaries.—The Study of the Language with a Native Teacher.—A Missionary may be Useful from the very first.—House-keeping, and a Missionary's Home as an important Centre of Influence.—Chapels and Chapel-preaching.—Itinerations in the Interior.—The great Difficulty of communicating Christian Truth in a Heathen Language.—Distribution of Tracts, and the Manner in which they are received.—The natural Effect of a correct Apprehension of the true Character of the Gospel.

A SEA-VOYAGE is in many respects a good preparation for the life-work of a missionary. Separated both from his father-land and the one to which he is looking forward for a home, a wanderer on the wide waste of waters, it is a time for solemn thought, to examine one's motives, to estimate aright the character and value of life and its pursuits, and to gather strength and courage for future duty. Cut off from all intercourse with the busy world at large, he finds himself in a little world having a character peculiar to itself, where he is brought into the closest contact with his fellows, studies human nature in new aspects, and finds abundant occasion for the exercise and cultivation of patience, forbearance, sympathy, and self-control. Here the strongest attachments are formed, and the most decided antagonisms developed, not only between ship-masters and passengers, but between the passengers themselves. The voyage is looked back to by some as the most delightful episode of their lives, and by others as a most vexatious and unendurable imprisonment.

These experiences refer to the long voyages in sailing-ships, where passengers are necessarily brought into the closest relations with each other. In the shorter voyages of ocean steamers, which carry a large number of travellers, and have extensive accommodations, passengers can choose their own associates according to their natural affinities.

The monotony and privations of life on ship-board are to many persons almost compensated by the pleasure of going ashore in a foreign land. After being tossed for months on the restless ocean, it is a delight to tread *terra firma* anywhere, especially in places where every object is novel, or strange, or picturesque. To a missionary, the first introduction to the land of his choice has new elements of delight. He does not come on shore simply to enjoy the novelty of the scene, to satisfy his curiosity, or gather interesting or useful information. This is to be his future home. Hither his affections have flown, and clung by anticipation. The new race of men which he looks upon for the first time with a peculiar and absorbing interest, he has already learned to love. He has come to labor with and for them, and for Christ.

If his destination is a mission-station already established, he has the additional pleasure of being met and welcomed by his colaborers; and the happiness of this meeting is heightened by its being so thoroughly reciprocal. The arrival of new recruits is hailed by missionaries on the ground as an evidence of remembrance and sympathy at home, and as a direct answer to the oft-repeated prayer that God would send forth laborers into his harvest. The glow of health mantling their cheeks, and the fire of zeal beaming in their eyes, add new strength and hope to those who have been bearing the burden and heat of the day. The new-comers are perhaps entire strangers, and bring no news of individual homes and firesides; but they can speak of a common country, of revered instructors and halls of study, of the loved church of their choice, and of the work to which they have given their lives in obedience to the call of the Master.

But the novelty of the missionary's position soon passes away, and he settles down to the monotony, toil, and trials of every-day duties. He feels the want of home society and recreations, and the stimulus and excitement of coming into daily contact with the active busy world. He may discover that his associates are without those elements of congeniality which form the basis of warm and confiding intimacies and attachments. The language is perhaps found very difficult, and intercourse with the natives vexatious and annoying. Under these circumstances, nothing but a strong motive can keep the mind fixed to its purpose. Merchants may be willing to expatriate themselves for a few years, from the powerful motive of acquiring wealth; solacing themselves for a time by the excitement of their active employments, the society of those similarly situated with themselves, and the hope of soon returning to their native land to enjoy a life of ease and affluence. The only motives which can make a missionary contented and useful are earnest love for his work, and sympathy with those for whom he labors. Individuals may, and I believe some do, leave home to engage in this work without a just conception of its true character, and without counting the cost—influenced in part, though unconsciously, by a love of adventure, or romantic interest, or temporary enthusiasm. Such persons are apt very soon to become disappointed and disheartened, and to work simply from a sense of duty. Some have found that they had made a mistake before even the outward voyage was over. Whenever it comes to this, that a man performs his work as a drudgery, regards his having become a missionary with regret, labors with a kind of half-heartedness, makes very little progress in gaining a knowledge of the language or influence with the people, and pines for home, the sooner he goes home the better: the more pity he ever came away.

I am glad to say that, as far as my experience and observation go, such cases have been very few in China. Missionaries generally acquire a growing delight in the work, even in the most difficult, discouraging, and unhealthy fields; and are rather prone to stay too long, to the detriment of their health and permanent usefulness, requiring to be urged, and sometimes almost forced away by their brethren.

Missionaries generally live at first in native houses, altered and fitted up in some degree in accordance with our ideas of comfort and convenience—putting in a few glass windows in place of the paper ones, and substituting boards for the flooring of a few rooms in the place of cement or brick. As soon as practicable, permanent houses are built somewhat after our own style of architecture.

Our mode of living is similar to that at home. China furnishes nearly every article of food which we find in our own country. The native mode of preparing and cooking it is, however, very different from ours, and, in many respects, not suited to our tastes and habits. Most missionary families have an American cooking-stove, and servants are taught to prepare food according to our way, so that our tables and meals correspond very nearly to what we have been accustomed to at home.

A great deal is said in some quarters about the luxurious manner in which missionaries live in the East, occupying "palatial dwellings, employing a large number of servants, and riding on the shoulders of the men to whom they are sent to preach the Gospel."

Such remarks are so common that a reference to them needs no apology.

In China our usual allowance for buildings is from twelve hundred to two thousand dollars for a house. This will furnish us with a plain dwelling, inferior in style and accommodations to most country parsonages at home.

As for servants, there is no caste, as in India, almost necessitating the employment of from six to ten different persons in a family, but we generally think it desirable to employ about three, though some have but two, and some have managed to get along with one. It should be understood that our circumstances are very different from those of home. Instead of having water brought to the kitchen by pipes, or supplied by a well and pump conveniently situated, our servants are often required to bring water for washing and cooking, etc., a distance varying from several rods to a quarter of a mile or more. Instead of having the convenience of the market-wagon calling at the door every day, the cook is often obliged to walk one or two miles to buy his meat, vegetables, and groceries. In Chinese cities we have no arrangements for receiving our letters at every corner, and delivering them in any place where we may wish to send them; and if we have communications to send to other parts of the city or country, we must either waste our time in taking them ourselves, or send a special messenger. In going from place to place, we would be glad to make use of street cars if we had them, but we must forego this luxury. We would not feel that we could afford to hire a carriage, even if there were roads and carriages. We generally prefer to walk when we are not too tired or ill to do so; but when ladies or gentlemen are obliged to use a conveyance where boats are not to be had, they adopt the same mode of travelling that natives do, rich and poor, and engage a sedan at the rate of about twenty cents per hour, or a dollar a day; and the bearers are very glad to get the employment. Being accustomed to take a great deal of out-door exercise, and requiring it, I have made comparatively little use of sedans, but would regard it as exceedingly unwise and injurious for all missionaries to follow my example.

The salaries of the missionaries of the various societies of the United States generally range from eight to twelve hundred dollars a year. This sum is not fixed as pay, or as an equivalent for their services, but as a mere competency for their support, while they give their labors and themselves to the work which they have undertaken. This salary for a missionary and his wife is much lower than many, if not most, young unmarried clerks receive the first year of their coming out to China.

But it is asked, Could not the missionaries economize still further, and live on a considerably lower salary? This would no doubt be possible, but the question is, Would it be desirable? Would it promote the object for which we go to China? There are some missionaries who advocate living on reduced salaries, and we might barely subsist, for a time at least, on a still smaller sum than even they would adopt. Many artisans and day laborers at home live and thrive and support their families on two or three hundred dollars a year; and in China living is somewhat cheaper, and we might perhaps exist on even less. In doing so, however, we would hardly represent those from whom we are sent, and I fear that the result would prove that we had been exercising a very poor economy.

If Christians at home were really unable to furnish the present stipend, I trust that the men and women who are now laboring for Christ in China would, rather than abandon His cause, be willing to remain at their posts, receiving only the minimum necessary for a bare subsistence. But there is, in fact, no such necessity. Few will deny that the Church is giving but a small part of what she might easily give, and ought to give, and it would be a positive advantage for her to give.

Or further, if living with a stricter economy, and on a smaller salary, would increase our influence among the people and promote our ultimate usefulness, we certainly ought to do it. But I believe that, from such a course, no good results would follow, but rather harm. The Chinese are accustomed to associate poverty with inefficiency; to see persons who are not pinched with want live generously; and they intuitively judge of a man's character and social position, in a great measure, by his dress, manners, and style of living. So far are intelligent and earnest native Christians, even those who are themselves very poor, from wishing us to adopt their style of living, that I have known them to be so much exercised by the shabby appearance and ungenteel manners and mode of life of some foreign teachers, as to insist upon the importance of their dressing better, and in every way living more respectably, in order to increase their influence and usefulness.

A missionary might try to do his own marketing, and his wife might spend the most of her time in the kitchen, and thus save the expense of one servant, and perhaps two; but, after many years of expensive preparation for their great work, it seems but a miserable economy to spend their energies and a considerable portion of each day's time in doing that which a Chinaman can be employed to do for five dollars a month, neglecting the special work to which Christ has called them, to say nothing of producing dissatisfaction and complaints from servants, unpleasant remarks among neighbors, and acquiring the reputation, which is not at all enviable or desirable, of being penurious and narrow-minded. In China labor is cheap, and is divided among different kinds of servants. It is a very difficult matter to change the customs and views of as numerous and intelligent a people as the Chinese, and it is much the best way to conform to these customs in matters which are indifferent and unimportant.

I learned a short time since that a church in our connection was greatly shocked by the statement of a missionary from India, who had spent twenty-eight years in earnest and efficient labor, and literally worn himself out in the service of the Church, respecting the number of servants they employed there, and, in consequence, almost determined never to contribute any thing more to the cause of missions. I have little doubt that an effort on the part of this missionary to do with a less number of servants would have resulted in inconveniences, annoyances, and interruptions, which would have gone far toward neutralizing his influence and destroying his usefulness. I have noticed, as a matter of fact, which individuals may account for as they choose, that these objections and insinuations are generally made by those who do or give little or nothing for the cause of foreign missions themselves.

The same sensitiveness is manifested in the views and feelings which some professed Christians entertain with reference to missionaries returning home to recruit their health, thus "wasting so much time and so much money." I have also heard the return of missionaries deprecated on account of the "unfavorable effect it had on the Church at home." I have known of an individual's writing to a missionary friend abroad, who was in a very precarious state of health, that if he had given himself to the work of being a missionary he would die before he would come home. These individual opinions would not be worth noticing, were there not reason to believe that those who entertain them are representatives of a class. Now I trust the missionaries are willing to die, if need be, for the cause of Christ, and for the heathen; but they have no disposition to sacrifice life and the hope of future usefulness out of regard to views and theories of professing Christians, so impracticable, unreasonable, and romantic as these. It might be well for those who entertain such exalted ideas of the character of the missionary work, and the standard of Christian consecration, to consider whether, as the command to evangelize the nations is given to the whole Church, and rests equally upon every individual member of it, they ought not to become missionaries themselves, and to put in practice their own principles. Or if, for any reason, they choose to remain at home, they might even here have the fullest opportunity of practicing at least one species of the self-denial which they would recommend to missionaries, namely, that of economy; and might adopt at once the minimum necessary to keep soul and body together; vigorous health and ability to labor not being so absolutely indispensable here as for missionaries abroad.

With regard to this whole matter of salaries and mode of living, I do not hesitate to state it as my opinion, that in China American missionaries at least, have erred on the side of a false and injurious economy, which has interfered, in some cases, greatly with their health, influence, and usefulness. We have no reason to complain, because we ourselves generally fix the amount of our salaries. What I mean is, that it is the natural and general tendency of missionaries to stint themselves in order to have more funds to apply to other purposes.

In this connection it may be well to speak briefly of the opportunity for missionary labor of Christian ladies. It is a prevalent opinion that the wives of missionaries are necessarily so much taken up with domestic duties that it is not practicable for them to accomplish much in direct efforts for the evangelization of the heathen, even for those of their own sex. I believe that the fact that so little is expected of them has had the effect, in many cases, of discouraging them from attempting and accomplishing much that they might and would gladly have done. In instructing the women of China, there is an important sphere of labor which especially belongs to Christian ladies; and experience has shown that, even with a large family to care for, they may, without neglecting any domestic duties (making use of necessary assistance from servants), accomplish a great deal in visiting native women at their homes, superintending schools and female assistants, gathering women into industrial and Bible classes, and writing books for the use of schools, inquirers, and church members or others. While the missionary's wife should perhaps be left entirely free to attempt direct missionary work or not, and to follow her own tastes and inclinations, she should at least be heartily encouraged to share in the privileges of missionary labor whenever she has the ability and disposition to do so. Personal interest and employment, and bringing ignorant idolaters to Christ, is at once the best antidote to homesickness, and the purest source of happiness.

While there is an important work for Christian women to do in the East, it is an interesting and gratifying fact that a large number of unmarried ladies are offering their services to our Boards. May we not recognize in this fact a special providence, and the necessity of so arranging and adjusting our plan of operations as to avail ourselves of this important agency which God is raising up for the Church?

The practical question often arises as to the comparative advantages of married and unmarried missionaries. While it would be a great misfortune, as I conceive, for a mission to be composed wholly of unmarried men, I think it is a mistake hardly less serious to suppose that an unmarried man can not be a most useful missionary. Both classes of laborers are needed. Persons without family ties have advantages in itinerating and moving from place to place which are peculiar to their condition; at the same time, the influence of Christian women on the missionary body itself is too important to be foregone, to say nothing of the influence of Christian families upon the heathen, and the labors which ladies may perform among those of their own sex. It is sometimes stated by those who recommend young men to go out unmarried that wives are apt to lose their health, and to bring their husbands home with them. But it is equally true that they often keep them longer in the field, and add greatly to their efficiency while there.*

But to return to the employments of the newly-arrived missionary. Whatever special work he may choose for himself in a later period of his life, the preparation for all kinds of work is the thorough acquisition of the language. This task must be undertaken resolutely, systematically, laboriously, and persistently. When thus prosecuted, few persons of ordinary ability will fail to master, at least, the spoken language, so as to be able to communicate freely with the people and preach to them in their "own tongue the wonderful works of God." A Chinese literary man is employed at once as a personal teacher, generally called a *sien-sang*. He becomes the constant attendant and companion of the missionary; and out of this daily and intimate intercourse often grows a mutual attachment strong and lasting. After the knowledge of the

* For a more complete view of woman's work in China, and fuller information respecting missionary life in general, the reader is referred to a recent work, entitled "Our Life in China," written by Mrs. Nevius, and published by Carter and Brothers, New York.

spoken language is partially or fully acquired, the *sien-sang* is often still retained as a scribe, and an assistant in further literary studies and compositions.

The question is sometimes asked, How soon after his arrival in the field may a missionary be really useful? I answer, to a greater or less degree, from the very first. He may relieve his brethren of much secular work, and also assist in forming plans for the general interests of the mission. In the course of a few months he can begin to communicate with his teacher, who learns to catch his meaning before he can be understood by others; and who may be won to Christ, and become a brother beloved, and a true yoke-fellow in the work of bringing others to Christ.

Missionaries, on their first arrival in China, generally board for a few months with other families until they have acquired some knowledge of the language. In the course of six months or a year, they ordinarily commence housekeeping by themselves. From this time they not only have a teacher under their daily influence, but also servants, and Chinese visitors and guests, if such are cordially encouraged to come to the missionary's house. I regard one's own family, including, of course, all natives in any way connected with us, as one of the most interesting and hopeful spheres of missionary labor, and one which we are too apt to neglect. It may be said most truly, and adopted as a motto, that missionary work in China properly begins in the missionary's own home. It is natural, perhaps, to regard our servants *simply* as servants, while our chief interest is directed to work in the study, or to labors for the masses of heathenism outside our doors. There is often a disposition to undertake work on a large scale, rather than, in a small way, with those in humble stations and of comparatively little influence. These servants sent to us in the providence of God from different quarters are a powerful agency through whom to influence others. Brought within the inner sphere of our domestic life, they see us, and form an estimate of our real characters as others can not. It is but natural for them to observe us very closely; they are familiar with our hourly employments, and judge of our real objects, and aims, and motives. They are closely questioned with reference to us by neighbors, by the men on the street whom they meet with in making their purchases, and by their families and acquaintances in the neighborhood where they reside. It is but right for us to presume, or at least hope that Christ has sent them to us to be educated for Him, and prepared for usefulness in His vineyard.

The careful selection of servants, and organizing them into a well-regulated household, is a matter of much importance, though by no means so simple and easy as might at first be imagined. If we would keep them long with us and do them good, we must show a kindly interest in and sympathy with them and their families; and, while we require of them strict attention to their business, we must show a generous appreciation of their faithfulness. In seeking their spiritual welfare, we have the great advantage of being able to meet them every day in family worship, and give them regular and familiar instructions in the truths of God's word. In our own family a considerable portion of time was always given in the morning to this exercise. Those who could read were required to do so, and those who could not were taught. We not only read a small portion of Scripture, but conversed familiarly about it, sang a hymn when the servants were able to join in it, and had an examination every day on the lesson of the previous one. In looking back upon my missionary life, these morning exercises are among my most pleasant recollections. They were generally as interesting to my little audience as they were delightful to me. I remember one man, an excellent servant, and one who remained with us till we left China, who though he persistently declared his unwillingness ever to be a Christian himself, still seemed to take a special pleasure in answering difficult questions in family worship, and in giving the best synopsis of the lesson of the previous day. I have occasionally found him with his Bible before him while he was at work, though he would have preferred not to have me see his interest in it. The seed thus sown, and accompanied by affectionate exhortation and prayer, can hardly fail of producing its appropriate fruit. A considerable proportion of the first converts, and the first catechists and preachers, in most mission stations, are from the employés in mission families. I find, in going over the list of our domestics while in China from first to last, that about one-half of them were brought into the Church while connected with us. I regret to say, however, that some of these have not fulfilled our expectations of them, having subsequently renounced Christianity, or led lives inconsistent with it.

With a well-regulated household, and sympathizing and attached servants, some of them Christians who love to bear testimony for Christ, a missionary has a great advantage in receiving and interesting Chinese visitors, not being forgetful of the injuuction of Scripture to use hospitality in entertaining strangers. In my opinion, every missionary residence should have accommodations for receiving and entertaining Chinese guests, and making them feel at ease there. There are few places where the Gospel message can be brought home with so much point and power. However, the desirableness of giving prominence or not to this particular mode of reaching the people will depend much on the tastes, disposition, and habits of different missionaries. It is attended with many practical difficulties, but I believe that there are few modes of labor which will be found more encouraging or effective.

The first attempts at preaching outside of one's family are generally made by the roadside or in the chapel, and these efforts are often commenced satisfactorily and intelligibly in less than a year. Every mission in the open ports has one or more of these chapels. They are simply convenient places for meeting, conversing with and preaching to the people; situated generally on or near a public thoroughfare, and fitted up with seats or benches, and a platform and desk for the speaker. Sometimes a sign or placard at the door indicates the character of the building, and invites passers-by to come in. Persons in the street are often attracted by the sight of the foreigner, who is seen sitting or standing on the platform, through the open door. When a chapel is first opened, neighboring residents and shop-keepers enter in crowds, but their curiosity soon passes away, and those whom we meet are generally strangers from a neighboring village or from a distance. The motive which brings them to us in most cases is mere empty curiosity. They wish to see a foreigner with their own eyes, and observe his features, dress, and manners. Our audiences vary from one or two to a hundred or more, according to the place and other circumstances. A coolie, or burden-bearer, looking in at the door and seeing convenient seats for resting, deposits his burden in the corner, and perhaps lights his pipe and sits down for a smoke, and to see what is going on. A well-dressed gentleman enters and reluctantly takes his seat, hardly knowing whether or not he is compromising his dignity in stopping in such a place and with such company.

The mode of conducting the exercises in our chapels varies widely, according to the character of the audience, and the views and habits of the missionary. Some prefer a formal service, consisting of reading the Scriptures, preaching, and prayer. This is practicable in places where the missionary is well known, and a considerable proportion of the audience have had some lessons in the proprieties of Christian worship, and, by their influence and example, help to keep the rest quiet. In most places, however, with promiscuous, uninstructed, and ever-changing audiences, it is almost useless to attempt a continuous discourse or formal service. The people have never been accustomed to remain quiet in any public assemblages. At weddings and on funeral occasions, and in attending theatres, they walk around, converse with their friends, or make remarks about what is going on, without any restraint whatever. A formal discourse, lecture, or harangue is something almost unheard of in China, and which we seldom read of in their books. Their sages and public teachers have influenced the masses through individuals, and have communicated their instructions by adopting the conversational or catechetical method. The recorded teachings of Confucius are all in this form. At present, when the natives wish to instruct or influence others, they generally do it in long conversations with single persons. When a company meets together for conference, their business is conducted informally, politeness and deference for each other being the only parliamentary rules for deliberative assemblies with which they are acquainted.

I have known instances in which missionaries have attempted to hold a formal service, when, as soon as their eyes were closed in prayer, the people would engage in conversation, making remarks about the singular ways of the foreigners, etc. In some cases, after a short prayer the speaker opens his eyes, and finds that his audience has retired, leaving him alone.

Some missionaries adopt the method somewhat familiar to the Chinese, called *kiang shu*—"explain the book." This gives a kind of authority and dignity to his teachings, while the speaker may use great freedom in varying his exercise by introducing illustrations and indulging in digressions according to circumstances.

I have always preferred making a wide distinction between services for the uninstructed multitude, and for those who know and love God, and come together to engage in his worship, and to be instructed out of his word; and have generally adopted the practice of meeting and dealing with these promiscuous and fluctuating audiences which come into the chapel in the same free conversational manner as in my own home, allowing the character of the exercises to be governed very much by circumstances. In this way I have been able to get nearer to my audience, to interest them more, and hold them longer than I could do otherwise. When the interest of the audience is excited and their attention arrested, many excellent opportunities are afforded for introducing and explaining the truths and doctrines of the Gospel at some length. Our religious services with the native Christians correspond almost exactly to those in our churches at home.

The occasions when scholars assemble in the cities of China to engage in the literary examinations often afford unusual advantages for preaching. The streets are thronged with intelligent strangers, drawn from a large extent of territory; and many of them, not having seen foreigners before, are disposed to seek an interview with them. At such times the doors of the chapel are kept open as much of the time as possible. These audiences, like those of the less educated classes, are generally respectful, and little disposed to raise objections and discussions. Our experience in this respect is very different from that of missionaries in India. The Chinese generally assent to what you say, and will often answer with more politeness than sincerity, "That is in accordance with doctrine;" "It is true;" "That is so precisely," etc. This natural indisposition to controversy is due to different causes. Some are too proud to discuss such matters with foreigners; some are too polite; and most of them are afraid, being, as a race, of a timid disposition, comparatively uneducated, and unused to the logical exercise of their reasoning faculties, and having an intuitive consciousness that the truth is on the other side. When they are willing to discuss Christian topics, it is generally from a real interest and a desire for information, and their questions and objections are presented with a great deal of candor and politeness.

I was particularly pleased with the intelligent interest and frankness of the scholars of Shantung, who visited us in large numbers during the first year of our labors there, and with whom I had many interesting discussions. Some of the topics introduced by them were characteristically Chinese, such as the defense of idolatry in some of its forms, of Confucianism as a complete and all-sufficient system of truth, or as a system altogether in harmony with Christianity. Some objections were urged to show the inferiority of Christianity as compared to Confucianism, such as the following: "Why does Christianity constantly appeal to motives resting upon the doctrine of future rewards and punishments, instead of taking the higher ground of urging men to the practice of virtue simply because it is right, and obligatory?" Some objections were identical with those which have long been urged in Western lands, such as the following: "Is it consistent with the justice of God to punish the innocent and clear the guilty, as he does in visiting the penalty of death on the Saviour and letting the sinner go free?" "How can the doctrine of the unity of God be reconciled with the existence of three distinct persons in the Godhead?" "How was it possible for Christ to be born of a virgin, and for the human and divine natures to be united in the person of one man?"

After we have become familiar with the spoken language, and with Chinese modes of thought, and have acquired some experience in presenting to the people Christian truth, when the weather and our employments will permit, we undertake preaching excursions in the country. This is a very important and difficult part of missionary work. When we pass through districts which have never before been visited by foreigners, we are everywhere followed by immense crowds. On these excursions we generally go two by two, with one or more native assistants, if we can obtain them, in order to relieve and assist each other. It is easy to imagine the effect which would be produced in one of our quiet interior towns or villages in the United States by the announcement that two Chinamen, evidently literary gentlemen, and dressed in their native costume, were about to harangue the people in the public square. The same effect is produced in China when a boy in the outskirts of a town sees us coming in the distance, and after he has satisfied himself that he may credit his own senses, runs down the street, shouting at the top of his voice, "The red-haired men are coming!" or "The white devils are coming!" (these are the names by which they generally call us).

The whole town is thrown into a state of excitement. Women forget the proprieties of social life, and mingle in the jostling crowd to catch a sight of the strange apparition. Schools are emptied at once of pupils and teacher, and business is suspended for a time in the shops. A few of the more staid and respectable citizens look on and smile at the excited multitudes. We take our stand in some open area, or on the theatrical stage in the court of a temple, and are soon surrounded by an immense crowd; the boys shouting, and the men making more noise than the boys in their vain efforts to keep them still. Every thing connected with us is an object of curiosity; the color of our eyes and hair, the material of which our clothes are made; and those who can get near enough are examining with their eyes and fingers, boots, coats, buttons, shirt-bosoms, etc. After a few moments, by the uplifting of the hand and the utterance of a few familiar words, the audience is in a measure quieted, and all are intent on hearing what the unexpected visitor has to say.

But here we meet with difficulties which it is not easy for persons at home fully to appreciate. How shall we speak of God and the things of salvation in a language every religious word of which has only heathen and idolatrous ideas and associations? A language is the expression of the thoughts and ideas of the people who use it; and naturally conveys to them only the ideas which they have been accustomed to connect with it. Would we speak of God, we must either use the name of some particular heathen deity, or a general term applied to all their objects of worship; and the question arises in their minds, Is he speaking of this, that, or the other of the hundreds of gods which sit in our idol temples; or does he wish to introduce some strange god from foreign shores? Many of the religious terms which we use are, for want of better ones, borrowed from the idolatrous system of Buddhism; for instance, the word *heaven*, which presents to their minds the Buddhist heaven. So of hell, sin, merit, etc. We are thankful if we can, by circumlocution, explanation, and illustration, present clearly and forcibly one great truth, which would be conveyed to the mind of a child in Christian lands, by one word or sentence. We feel that we have accomplished much if we can leave behind us the thought of the unity, or the omnipresence, or the love of God, or of salvation by a redeemer; for these ideas, once lodged in the human mind, are vital germs, which will develop and grow, and, in process of time, bring forth their appropriate fruit.

Passing from town to town, the same scene is constantly repeated, and our voices grow weak and hoarse, and our whole frames weary. In the south of China, where we travel mostly in canals, we can take refuge for the purpose of eating and resting in our boats. But even there, when we have anchored our boat in the middle of the canal, men will sometimes wade out to it, and we will see a score of eyes peeping at us through the cracks and holes of the mat covers, while a dozen tongues are busy descanting on what we eat, and how we eat it; and an occasional burst of laughter indicates how much they are surprised and amused. Now this is all very annoying, but it is the better way to put up with it patiently. In the north of China, where there are no canals, and we travel on horseback, we must face the crowd almost from morning to night. It is worse than useless to claim the privilege of taking refuge in your inn. The Chinese are not accustomed to shut their doors on any one, nor to allow others to do so; and they claim that, if they receive you kindly and treat you politely, they have a right to expect corresponding treatment from you—at least, the privilege of seeing you; and see you they will. Using force and barring the door against the crowd, would very likely result in a mob, the breaking down of the doors, much injury and loss to the inn-keeper, and a very unfavorable impression with regard to the foreigner.

On an excursion from Ningpo in 1856, in a city about two hundred miles in the interior, an English missionary and myself were followed by an immense and excited crowd almost ready to accord to us divine honors, and really saying to us,

"Your visit is as if the gods had come down to our insignificant city." An officer sent us a polite invitation to visit his yamun. He met us at the door, and received us with great cordiality. We thanked him for his polite invitation, but told him we feared that the crowd which was following us would give him so much annoyance and trouble that it would be better for us on his account to deny ourselves the pleasure of the visit and leave him at once. He assured us that there was no danger, and urged us to enter, which we did. He no doubt knew more about his people in many respects than we did, but this was an experience which was new to him. He remained without a short time to disperse the crowd, and to charge his servant to keep them from entering. In a few moments, however, the people had broken through two doors, and we heard loud voices and altercations between them and the servant in the adjoining court. Seeing that his excellency was somewhat alarmed, I offered to go out to speak to the intruders. A few kind words and gentle reproofs, and a good opportunity to look at me satisfied them, and most of them dispersed in a good-humor.

The best and right way is always to attack a Chinaman on the side of kindness and politeness. No other course will answer here. It is useless, at least at first, to tell them that you have no time to talk to them, or that you are tired. In the north of China I have, after preaching from horseback in a score of villages during the day, spent an hour or an hour and a half in the evening satisfying the curiosity of the people before I could disperse the crowd, and go into the inn for food and rest.

The presence of these interested audiences affords the missionary a rare opportunity, seldom enjoyed in the same place afterward, to explain to the people his real character and object, to fix upon their minds some great Christian truth, and to produce as favorable an impression as possible; thus preparing the way for the more quiet labors of those who are to follow.

On these itinerations we are able to distribute as many

books as we can carry with us. The people are almost wild with excitement; and we are often in danger of being overborne by them, and having the books snatched from us. They have no idea, at least most of them, of the contents of the books, and many of those who seek them can not read intelligibly; but as books are being given away they must have one. It will be a memento of the foreigner and his visit; it may contain something very curious or valuable; at least, it may be sold for waste paper. Many of these books fall ultimately into the hands of readers, and much Christian knowledge is no doubt imparted by them.

Some of the experiences detailed above are calculated at first to excite sanguine hopes of great and perhaps speedy results. But there are darker shades necessary to complete this picture and make it a truthful representation of missionary life. I have described the first reception of the missionary in districts which have never before been visited. The same scenes are seldom if ever repeated in subsequent visits. When the missionary has left town, and the popular commotion has subsided, his character and employments are calmly discussed. Some shrewd scholar who knows something of us, and has perhaps read Christian books, expresses his views to the people in language like the following: "It is a pity that you should have been carried away by excitement, and treated this foreigner with so much respect, and spoken of his new and dangerous doctrines so flatteringly. The religion which he would introduce is exclusive, intolerant, revolutionary. It strikes at the root of all our cherished civil and social institutions. It would destroy every temple in the empire, however famous or costly, and abolish even the homage paid to the Emperor, to Confucius, and to deceased ancestors."

These conclusions are literally true, and it is not difficult for intelligent Chinese to reach them. Christianity is an exclusive religion, and it must supplant all others. There must be a conflict between truth and error before the former gains the ascendancy. Wherever the Gospel is introduced and apprehended the saying of Christ is verified, that he came not to send peace on earth, but a sword. When we visit a place the second time, we find that the former excitement and interest have been succeeded by suspicion, alarm, and an almost studied coldness of manner on the part of the people. No crowds follow us in the streets, and but few pay any attention to us. Some who have been impressed by the truth, and are desirous to learn more of it, may come to us privately, and under cover of darkness, like Nicodemus of old. The earnest and intelligent sympathy of these affords some compensation for the loss of the sympathy of the multitude. Alas! like Nicodemus, most of them are unwilling to confess Christ openly, for fear of the reproach and opposition of their people.

When the missionary has become familiar with the language, and the circumstances and wants of his particular field, and has learned his own personal adaptations, he is prepared to determine the question of duty as regards his special sphere of labor.

From the foregoing, the reader may gain a general idea of the manner in which the missionary's time is spent. His office is no sinecure; but he is cheered in his work by the consciousness that he is laboring for Christ, and the assurance that the cause with which he is identified shall ultimately triumph. In this heaven-appointed service, the lives of some of the noblest and most honored sons of the Church have already been spent; and not a few have fallen at their posts in China. On the populous plain of Ningpo; on the island of Kulangsu; in the grave-yards of Canton, Hong-kong, Fuchow, and Shanghai; and on the rocky promontory which looks from the northern boundary of China across the sea to Manchuria; beneath the waters of Hang-chow Bay and the Pechele Gulf; and in other spots known to loving survivors, and to the more loving Saviour, they rest from their labors.

CHAPTER XXII.

DIFFERENT METHODS AND AGENCIES EMPLOYED IN MISSIONARY WORK.

The great Mission of the Christian Church.—The Character of the Work the same now as in the Times of the Apostles.—Advantages and Disadvantages peculiar to different Times.—Auxiliary and preparatory Agencies.—The Work of the Medical Missionary.—The Scripture Idea of Preaching.—The Question of adopting the native Costume.—The Importance of Mission Schools.—Error of applying Principles drawn from one Field to another and different one.—Objections to English Schools as Missionary Agencies.—The Use of the Press.—Character and Use of Tracts.—The Sphere of the Bible in the Work of Missions.—The Importance of feeding the Flock.—The Necessity of training Native Christians to Habits of Activity and Independence.—The Importance of raising up and training a Native Ministry, and the Difficulties attending this Work in China.

THE great mission of the Christian Church imposed upon her by the express command of her glorified Head is that of making known the "Good News" of salvation to every creature under the whole heaven. It is not to teach mechanics and civil engineering, or foreign languages or sciences; not to Christianize heathen nations by civilizing them, as some plainly assert; but to Christianize them, and leave them to develop their own form of civilization. In understanding the nature of the duty imposed by the great commission, we can surely have no better guide than the practice of the Apostles. Wherever they went they knew nothing but Christ and Him crucified. Those who declaim against introducing among uninstructed heathen what they are pleased to represent as the difficult and incomprehensible doctrines of Christianity, and advocate the commencing with other simpler and more practical matters and educating them up to these things gradually, have evidently received "another Gospel," widely differing from that presented in the Bible.

The spiritual condition of the heathen world, and consequently the character of the missionary work, are essentially the same now that they were when the immediate disciples of Christ commenced their labors. The moral condition and spiritual wants of our common nature have not changed. The end and object sought, namely, the conversion and spiritual regeneration of the soul, are precisely the same; God's revealed truth is still the means to be employed; man is the feeble instrument, and God's Spirit the almighty agent.

The plans and methods made use of in bringing the truth to bear upon the minds of the heathen are various, and may and should be changed and modified according to different conditions and circumstances. While the apostolic history furnishes us with our true and only guides and models, we are not to suppose that we must in every respect do just as the Apostles did, for this would be impossible; nor that the Apostles would not have pursued a somewhat different course under other circumstances.

They had advantages in the prosecution of their work which were peculiar to their age; while, on the other hand, we have our advantages and compensations. They were not only possessed of the gift of tongues, and the power of working miracles, but they labored in regions comparatively near home, and having almost the same climate; and among people belonging to the same empire, acknowledging the same laws, speaking, for the most part, the same language, and having, in the main, the same customs and usages. Furthermore, the Jews and Jewish proselytes scattered throughout the Roman Empire had made the true idea of God and of spiritual worship more or less familiar to those among whom they dwelt, and the Jewish synagogue was a place where the first missionaries of the Gospel might always find intelligent and appreciating hearers. These circumstances gave them great facilities in commencing their work at once, and with the highest degree of efficiency, and also in constantly changing the sphere of their labors.

The advantages of the missionary of the present age are these: Christianity is not now the religion of a small, unacknowledged, and despised sect, but of the most enlightened and influential nations of the world; its doctrines are more clearly developed and defined than formerly; its evidences are the accumulations of the thinking minds, and of the experiences and providences of ages. Christian nations hold the controlling influence of the world; have opened new communication with every part of it; and have obtained almost everywhere a toleration and protection for Christianity which did not exist in the Roman Empire; while the press makes information general and easy of acquisition.

No feature of the labors of the first propagators of Christianity was more prominent than this, that the Gospel was proclaimed in connection with acts of kindness and humanity—healing the sick, raising the dead, and comforting the distressed. One striking sentence of the inspired Scriptures characterizes the whole life of our Saviour. "He went about doing good." Miraculous powers were given the Apostles, and constantly made use of by them in their ministry. One of the reasons for conferring this power was, no doubt, to give to the new religion a divine authority and sanction; but another very important one was that of attracting attention, removing prejudice, gaining the confidence and affection of the people, and stamping the religion of Jesus as one of love, of human sympathies, and of "good-will toward men."

This great principle and rule of action illustrated in the life of Christ and of the Apostles is as important and applicable now as ever. A missionary who has little regard for the temporal wants and sorrows of those with whom he comes in contact, and regards his duty discharged when he has taught the sin of idolatry, denounced the law against the transgressor, and pointed him to Christ as the only refuge, very imperfectly illustrates the spirit of Christ's Gospel, and is likely to have a comparatively fruitless ministry. It is true that we can not relieve a hundredth part of the misery which we are obliged to witness, but we may and ought to do what we can toward it. We may show a lively sympathy and good-will, if we have it, in a thousand ways. In order to convince and inform the understanding, we must first reach and influence the heart.

To secure this object, the co-operation of foreign Christian physicians is of great importance. It is impossible to tell how much of our success in gaining the confidence of the people is due to this agency. I remember that when I was endeavoring to establish a station in the interior city of Hang-chow, and the people were regarding me with considerable prejudice and suspicion, one day, while I was speaking to a crowd in the street, a soldier forced his way toward me, and, addressing me very cordially and respectfully, pointed to a deep scar on his cheek. He said he had once been severely wounded in battle, and that in the hospital in Shanghai Dr. Lockhart had dressed and healed his wounds and saved his life. Another man in the same company said that he had received similar kindness from Dr. M'Cartee in Ningpo; and both testified that in the hospital they were taught the same doctrine that I was then preaching. Hundreds and thousands such as these scattered along the coast, and in some of the interior provinces, are constantly bearing testimony in our favor.

Aside from relieving suffering, and having an influence to dispose the people kindly toward us, the practice of the healing art affords the most clear and decided evidence of our superiority in the knowledge of some branches, at least, of medical science. Native practitioners are so ignorant of physiology, anatomy, and surgery, that some of the surgical operations performed by Western physicians seem to them little less than miraculous. There is great need of medical missionaries in China, and a noble and important work for them to do, not only in practicing their profession, but also in preparing a medical literature and introducing medical science among the people. I may add here by the way that, notwithstanding the Chinese appreciate and acknowledge our superiority in surgery, most of them, and many even of the native Christians, prefer their own physicians in fevers and other familiar diseases of the country.

So much for agencies which are introductory and auxiliary to the primary and ultimate work of the missionary—that of preaching the Gospel.

It is a very important question, which meets us at the outset: what are we to understand by the preaching of the Gospel? There seems to be a tendency to interpret this duty according to our modern and specific idea of preaching, namely, the formal addressing of public audiences. I believe the scriptural idea is a much more general one, embracing every possible mode of presenting Christian truth. The great missionary commission is given in its fullest and most clearly defined form in the Gospel of St. Matthew: "Go ye therefore, and teach (literally make disciples of) all nations; baptizing them in the name of the Father, and of the Son, and of the Holy Ghost; teaching them to observe all things whatsoever I have commanded you." Our work, then, consists of three distinct parts: making or gathering disciples; baptizing and organizing them into churches; and teaching them and building them up in the faith. Disciples are gathered by bringing before them the truth as it is in Jesus. This the Apostles did in a variety of ways—by casual conversation, by visiting from house to house, by mingling socially with the people in their feasts and public gatherings, by teaching, by epistolary correspondence, and by formal public addresses. The fact that speaking or preaching to large audiences is almost unknown in China, and the importance of the social and individual presentation of the truth, have been spoken of in a former chapter.

To facilitate free and familiar intercourse with the people, some have recommended the adoption of the native costume. By making use of it in visiting places for the first time, a missionary in a great measure escapes notice, and is not followed by such large crowds. This renders his itinerations more quiet and less laborious; but for this reason, they would probably be less effective. As the natives soon learn to recognize the missionary as a foreigner whatever costume he adopts, his dress becomes a matter of comparatively little importance. The great and essential point is to cultivate and manifest a warm sympathy and interest, and a cordiality of manner. Without these, the adoption of the native costume would only make the missionary's deficiencies the more striking; with them, I believe the use of our own national costume will not at all detract from the esteem, familiarity, and respect with which we will be regarded.

The question respecting the practicability and desirableness of mission schools in China is one of much importance. Many missionary societies have discarded them, as an agency expensive, absorbing a great deal of the missionaries' time and strength, and comparatively fruitless in results; urging those whom they send out to devote themselves chiefly, if not exclusively, to preaching. I am decidedly of the opinion that this principle is a mistaken and an unfortunate one, as regards the Chinese Empire. It seems to have been adopted as a result, principally, of a discouraging experience with English schools in India. But it does not follow that because schools have not proved successful in India they therefore will not in China; much less that because a particular kind of schools has not answered our expectations in one place, the same result will follow the establishment of all other kinds of schools everywhere.

It is a serious error among Christians at home, though I believe a very common one, to apply rules and principles drawn from a limited experience in one missionary field to missionary operations generally. Some persons seem to regard the heathen as all belonging to the same class, and conforming to one type; while in fact they differ very widely, each nation having a marked individuality of its own. What a wide difference between the uncultivated tribes of Africa and the inhabitants of the Chinese Empire! and again, between either of these races and the Nestorians and Armenians, who can hardly be called, with strict propriety, heathen. And when we look at the Mohammedans, the inhabitants of India and Japan and Siam, and the islands of the Pacific and our Western Indians, we find that each race and nation has its own peculiarities, and requires, in the mode of introducing the Gospel special modifications and adaptations which can best be devised and applied by the missionaries on the ground.

But to return from this digression: the result of more than twenty years' experience with our boy's boarding-school and girl's boarding-school in Ningpo is to show that schools of this kind are among the cheapest and most efficient missionary agencies which can be employed in China. They have had devoted to them less than one-fourth of the time and labor of our missionary force, and during the early history of our Church in that place they furnished a large proportion of its members—I believe more than one-half; while the greatly-increased number of accessions during the last four or five years in our out-stations is due mostly to the efforts of native laborers, who have been brought into the Church through these institutions for educating and training the young. In a word, the growing success of the Ningpo Mission in bringing souls to Christ and establishing churches in our out-stations may be traced, in a great degree, to the two schools above referred to.

The same results have not followed the establishment of English boarding-schools. Indeed, it must be admitted, they have added very little to the membership of native churches, or to the efficient working force of the missions with which they have been connected. The Ningpo Mission, anticipating the results which have followed in other places, excluded English from its schools at an early period, aiming at the thorough acquaintance of the pupils with their own language and literature, and their familiarity with the Scriptures and Christian doctrines.

The facts and circumstances bearing upon the subject of teaching English are these: In China there is an urgent demand for interpreters who understand both the English and Chinese languages. The "Pigeon-English," described in Chapter XIV., is made to answer as a medium of communication for ordinary purposes of trade; but Chinamen who can speak English well are still much sought after, and command salaries from five to ten times as large as the same persons would receive if they were familiar with their own language only. Here is a strong temptation to draw boys acquainted with our language from mission schools even before the time of their indenture expires. Most of the pupils from those schools where English has been taught have yielded to these temptations, sought employment in the foreign communities, and been lost to the missions; and some of them have formed such habits and acquired such characters, as to bring reproach upon themselves and the cause of missions with which they have been in a measure connected. If a few are hopefully converted, and retain their connection with the church and the mission, their knowledge of English gives them little or no additional influence with their countrymen; while they have acquired it at the expense of a thorough Chinese education, and can hardly secure the respect of their own people as literary men or teachers. More than this, they are apt to think that it is very moderate and reasonable for them to expect one-half or one-third as large a salary as they can command in the foreign communities; and thus, while a knowledge of English does not add to their efficiency as agents of the mission, it adds much to their expensiveness.

Of course, there can be no objection to the establishment of English schools in China; and they are, indeed, much needed; but, under the circumstances, this matter should be attended to by the foreign communities, and not by Christians at home; and such schools should not be regarded as distinctively a missionary agency. Were they established by benevolent and enterprising merchants in the foreign communities, having for their express object the supplying of English and Chinese interpreters, and also a knowledge of Western science and literature, and placed in charge of efficient Christian teachers, they might accomplish great good in facilitating intercourse between China and Western nations; and at the same time prove an important auxiliary to the work of missions.

It appears to me that the teachings and example of the New Testament do not sanction or authorize any indirect methods of propagating the Gospel except in a manner incidental, subordinate, and auxiliary to the great end. Human science has no regenerating and sanctifying power in it. An acquaintance with Western languages not only introduces the student to the stores of religious and scientific knowledge, but to works which teach rationalism, infidelity, and "science falsely so called." As a result of introducing our language into India, English works on infidelity are now republished there, and are eagerly sought after by educated young men who have been taught in mission and government schools; and there is reason to fear that missionaries may find the educated talent which they have helped to create arrayed against them and Christianity, armed with weapons drawn from the deadliest enemies of our faith. It is true that the period of controversy must come, and that the truth need fear no opposition or attack; but it will come soon enough from the preaching of the simple Gospel in the language of the country; and in this way it will come in a form much more likely to insure the signal triumph of the truth. Christianity, on its introduction into heathen countries, does not generally affect first the learned minds of the country, and through them the masses, but it finds its first converts among the middle and lower classes; its leaven operates silently and almost unperceived among the masses; it becomes widely diffused; strikes its roots deep and firm into the native soil, and powerfully affects and controls the native mind. As the natural result of this process, a controversy would arise, not between the foreign missionary and a few semi-Christianized or science-Christianized natives, in which the people generally would have little or no interest, but one between native Christians and the representatives and defenders of the old forms of idolatry. This controversy would not be the reproduction of those originating in other ages and countries entirely foreign to native thought and circumstances, calculated only to place the whole subject of Christianity in a false and prejudicial light before the people, but one naturally growing out of, and belonging to, the present. It would be a controversy not in a foreign tongue, but in the language of the people, moulded and directed by native thought, taking a form suited to the native mind; forming a new epoch, and marking the period of the downfall of idolatry, and the establishment of the religion of Jesus.

While I believe the experience of missionaries in every field tends to emphasize the importance of the apostolic practice of the oral presentation of the truth, in methods adapted to varying circumstances, and to the degree of intelligence and information of different individuals; still, the powerful agency of the Press must not, in this age, be neglected. Christian tracts should be regarded as taking the place as far as they can of the oral teacher; having the one advantage of traversing wider fields, and perhaps reaching more individuals than the living preacher can. Like oral teachings, they should be specifically adapted to the native mind; looking at the truth from the native stand-point, and as logically connected with the prevailing religious systems, doctrines, and modes of thought. For this reason, reprints of our standard and most valuable tracts would be almost useless; and hardly a single one, as far as I am aware, has been translated for the purpose of general distribution. We have the "Pilgrim's Progress," "Henry and his Bearer," "Come to Jesus," and a few works of this class; but they are not adapted to the heathen population of China, and are appreciated and used principally by persons who have obtained more or less instruction in connection with our established missions, and occupy much the same position with regard to Christianity that unconverted persons do in our own country. Hundreds of tracts, some of them medium-sized books, and others containing but a few sheets, have been prepared by missionaries with special reference to those who have never heard of Christ. Very great use has been made of them, and many millions of pages have been scattered throughout the empire, especially along the coast. The results which they have produced will be noticed in the next chapter.

It is proper, and almost necessary, to refer in this connection to the distribution of the Bible in China, and its legitimate place and use among the different agencies for evangelizing heathen countries. I find that many at home regard the work of the missionary as made up in a great measure, if not principally, of efforts to distribute the Bible among the heathen. Immense sums of money have been contributed, especially by Christians in England, to be appropriated to this special object. Views and plans of this kind proceed, as I apprehend, upon a mistaken idea of the character and design of the Bible; which, if we carefully consider the subject, will be seen, I think, to be neither adapted to nor intended for the instruction of the heathen *as such.* Some have replied to such statements as this: "Is not the religion of the Bible a universal one, and adapted to the wants of man everywhere? and does not God know how to present His own truth to men infinitely better than we do?" On these questions all Christians can but be in perfect unity of sentiment and feeling. But the fact is, no part of the Bible was addressed primarily to a heathen people (if we except a few such portions of it as St. Paul's address at Lystra and on Mars' Hill). On the contrary, every part of it is addressed to persons in some degree instructed and informed, and presupposes a great amount of knowledge which is necessary to the correct apprehension of it, and of which heathen nations are in a great measure ignorant.

The difficulties in the way of the right understanding of the Bible by the heathen are of two kinds: the one growing out of the inability of their language to express Christian ideas; and the other relating to allusions to historical facts and personages, and national usages and religious rites, with which they are entirely unacquainted.

The former difficulties were spoken of in the previous chapter, in which it was remarked that nearly all the terms in the Chinese language have only idolatrous and heathen associations, and do not clearly express Christian truth to the native mind until new Christian ideas have been associated with them by oral teachings and explanations. The difficulties of the latter kind are sufficiently apparent from the general statement above, without further specifications.

It may be said that the Bible will explain its own language, and also its references to facts, customs, and usages, etc. If the intelligent reader will only study it carefully, this is true; but few persons have been found in any heathen land who have succeeded, unaided, in searching out its real meaning. Even to those who are interested, and desire to understand it, the difficulties it presents are great. If Philip had reason to address to the Ethiopian eunuch just returning from Jerusalem the question, "Understandest thou what thou readest?" and if there was reason in the reply of the eunuch, "How can I, except some man should guide me?" is it strange that the Bible should present almost insuperable difficulties to those who have hardly any idea even of the being and character of God?

But the difficulties to which I am referring may, perhaps, be best illustrated by a few practical examples. Some of the historical portions of the Old and New Testament are, of course, in their primary meaning and scope, perfectly intelligible. Take, for instance, the history of Joseph, which has been printed separately by our press and widely distributed; the book following in the main the text of the Scripture narrative without explanations or comment. The first page introduces the subject of the history by a reference to Abraham and Jacob, stating that Jacob had "two wives," and afterward "two concubines," of whom were born the twelve patriarchs, Joseph being one. This beautiful portion of the Bible is accurately and truthfully presented; but who would expect the Chinese reader to understand its relation to the whole Scripture history and Christian revelation? How could the distribution of this and similar parts of the Bible without note or comment be regarded as carrying out the command of our Saviour to evangelize the nations? It would be only natural for the Chinese reader, in the absence of any explanation, to suppose that the examples and customs presented in the book were at least sanctioned by those who distributed them; and it is difficult to conceive how, without special providential interposition, he could avoid the conclusion that polygamy and concubinage were sanctioned, if not recommended by our religion.

As an example from the simpler portions of the New Testament, take the commencement of the Gospel of St. Mark: "The beginning of the Gospel of Jesus Christ, the Son of God." This seems perfectly simple to us, and it may appear strange to some that any difficulty can be found in it; but almost every word in the sentence is an enigma to the heathen Chinaman. According to the Chinese idiom, the translation runs thus: "God's Son Jesus Christ Gospel beginning." The word God suggests a thousand deities supernal and infernal, but certainly not the God of the Bible, for alas! they know Him not. "God's Son" would certainly not convey to the reader any idea of the second person of the sacred Trinity, or help to form a just conception of the character of the God referred to. The names of our Saviour Jesus Christ are translated by Chinese characters resembling as nearly as possible the sounds of the original, and representing simply foreign names without meaning or associations. Gospel is translated by two characters meaning, respectively, "happiness" and "sound;" but the combination is a new and peculiar one, and it would be difficult for the uninstructed reader to tell with certainty its meaning. The next, and last, word "beginning," which is evidently connected with the two preceding it, forming the expression "happiness sound beginning," affords no assistance toward making it intelligible. Each of the following verses, looked at from the Chinese stand-point, presents similar difficulties, and is liable to some other misconception.

Thus we are brought back to the precept and practice plainly revealed in Scripture, that it is principally by the instrumentality of the living teacher that God will save them that are lost. When the heathen are brought to Christ, "As new-born babes they desire the sincere milk of the word," and turn to the Scriptures as to their natural food. Then their introductory instruction, and the influence of the Spirit by whose inspiration the sacred volume was written, furnish the keys for unlocking its mysteries. Different truths and historical facts are perceived in their true connection and relations; the whole volume assumes its symmetrical proportions as a perfect revelation of God's will to man; and in it are seen the infinite holiness and perfections of the Divine nature, and the true portraiture of sinful fallen man, who presents not one perfect example, and is only to be imitated in those peculiarities which accord with the perfect example of Christ.

Having endeavored to state these views fully and clearly, which I may say are, I believe, held in common by most missionaries of experience with whom I am acquainted, and also by intelligent native Christians generally, I would be careful to guard them against misapprehension. The Bible should accompany and follow the labors of the missionary, rather than precede them. Were we confined to oral teaching, without any translation of the Scriptures, we would feel very imperfectly equipped for our work. All missionaries distribute the Word of God among the heathen to a considerable extent, but not broadcast, without explanation, note, or comment. A few verbal explanations, or a short introduction to the Bible, relieve its general distribution of many of the objections which have been stated. Without such explanation or introduction, the natural and reasonable inference of the Chinaman when he receives a work written in his own language is, that the book was prepared and intended for educated men like himself; that it is supposed to be adapted to their circumstances, and makes use of no words, expressions, or references which he may not be naturally expected to understand. Finding that it is full of difficulties, he comes to the conclusion that we are ignorant of them and their language, and are not fit to write a book; and the idea has become very common among them that our Christian literature is unintelligible; and this fact is sometimes given as a reason for their not receiving tracts from us. If, however, we have an opportunity to tell them that the Bible did not originate with us, but in different countries from our own, and in remote ages; that it is the sacred book of our religion, containing a revelation from the only God of heaven to the whole world; that we give, as nearly as possible, a literal translation of it from the original languages, without daring to make any change; stating, at the same time, that they will meet with difficulties in understanding it, and urging them to study it carefully and seek for explanations of it in other works and from the missionaries, its character is appreciated at once, and it is regarded perhaps with more profound respect than if it were easily understood. We often give away the Bible, or parts of it, in connection with tracts; especially such as contain some account of its origin, character, and design, or put it in the hands of intelligent scholars who have visited us from motives of curiosity and interest, and with whom we have had the opportunity of communicating religious instruction orally.

The views which I have presented with reference to the general distribution of the Bible in China have no application whatever to mission fields in Roman Catholic and Mohammedan countries, or among the different corrupt Christian sects of Syria and the Turkish Empire. Among most of the inhabitants of these countries, ideas more or less correct of the character and offices of the three persons of the sacred Trinity are familiar as household words, and the Bible is received and acknowledged as a revelation from God, and the authoritative and ultimate standard to which all religious truth must be referred. The sphere of the Bible's influence in China is almost daily widening as a general knowledge of Christianity is extended, and we trust the time is not far distant when the utterance of the name of the Book of books will awaken the same associations and feelings in the minds of the Chinese people that it now does in ours.

My principal reason for dwelling on this subject so much at length is to establish the general and important principle that the Bible can not be used as a substitute for the missionary; nor can the Christian Church be absolved from its duty to give the Gospel to the heathen by contributing money to send to them any number of Bibles. The living messengers of the Church must go and introduce the truth of Christ among the natives first and principally by oral instruction in their mother-tongues; by acts of kindness and sympathy; by lives embodying and illustrating the Gospel which they preach.

In addition to the work of bringing the heathen to the knowledge of Christ, a very important part of the duty of the missionary which is brought prominently to view in the great commission is that of feeding the flock as under-shepherds; teaching those who are brought into the Church of Christ to observe all things whatsoever he has commanded. The missionary who gathers a little and feeble church, and leaves it comparatively uncared for, influenced by the idea that his principal work is to preach the Gospel to the heathen, will be in danger of finding that the converts he has made are more a trial to him than a comfort or help. Weak in the faith, imperfectly instructed, not wholly freed from heathen and idolatrous habits and associations, and surrounded by temptations, they need line upon line—here a little and there a little —a careful watch, a tender sympathy, to be cherished as a "nurse cherishes her children." The missionary, if he would build up for Christ living, earnest, active churches, must know how to reprove, rebuke, exhort with all long suffering and doctrine. His influence, even upon the people generally, is far greater when it is exerted indirectly through native Christians, than when he spends his whole time and energy in direct preaching to the heathen. He can preach to them most extensively and effectually by preparing and stimulating every one who has named the name of Christ to go everywhere preaching the word; to be living epistles, known and read of all men.

The first stage of a missionary's work in China is very different from the subsequent ones. Of course he must do all the preaching until natives are brought into the Church to help him. This period of waiting for the first-fruits is, in some places, a long and trying one. When a little church is gathered, he is still obliged to act for some time as its pastor until a suitable person can be found in the native church itself to assume the office. Such native Christians should be brought forward as soon as possible; the missionary ever remembering that it is not his appropriate work to assume the pastoral care of a single native church longer than such a course is absolutely necessary; and that, by doing so, he may be inflicting a positive injury upon it. His special business is to plant independent, self-supporting Christian institutions, and to raise up a native ministry. One of his most important duties is that of teaching and training native Christians to rely upon themselves and Christ rather than the foreign missionary, and of devolving work and responsibility upon them just as fast as they can bear them. The opposite course will cramp their intellectual and spiritual development, dwarf their manhood, and make them permanently dependent and inefficient. That kindness is a mistaken one which would do for them what they can do for themselves, though it may be with difficulty, and at first imperfectly, or would lighten the cross which Christ has laid upon them.

As the number of the native churches increases, and the missionary's work grows upon him, he finds himself wholly unequal to it, and he must have help; and this help must come principally from the native Christians. They should not only all of them bear witness for Christ from the first, but also, as soon as possible, furnish from their number elders and pastors, teachers and evangelists, both to look after their own spiritual interests, and to carry the Gospel into the regions beyond.

This important matter of raising up a native ministry claimed a large share of the attention of the Apostles; and it constitutes one of the most necessary and difficult parts of the work of the modern missionary. The two extremes equally dangerous should, as far as possible, be avoided, of introducing men into the sacred office who have not the necessary intellectual, biblical, and spiritual qualifications, and that of not making use of the material at hand from timidity or misjudged prudence. In the early stages of the missionary work, high literary and theological qualifications are not indispensable. The essential prerequisite is sincere and earnest piety. As native Christians increase in knowledge, the churches require pastors of more thorough preparation and training, and the higher the standard to which they can be brought the better.

Providing China with suitable teachers and evangelists is now a matter of immediate and pressing importance. In our most flourishing stations churches are increasing almost more rapidly than pastors can be found for them. It is a fact for which we should be thankful, that we are not without the material for native laborers; but the difficulty is in giving them the necessary preparation. As yet, there is no theological school in China, and the work of teaching candidates for the ministry is performed by the missionaries at the different stations, in connection with their other labors. Some who think that the advantages of theological instruction in a seminary or school hardly compensate, even in our own country, for its disadvantages, as compared with instruction under the superintendence of a pastor and in connection with daily pastoral work, would naturally conclude that on mission ground these institutions would certainly be superfluous, if not injurious. There are, however, some circumstances peculiar to the mission fields in China which constitute special reasons for the establishment of theological schools, which reasons may be briefly referred to.

Ministers are able to attend to the instruction of candidates at home because in our language we are supplied with a great variety of text-books, in the study of which the student's time is mostly spent. In China we have hardly the one-hundredth part of the helps to study which may be had at home, and therefore must depend principally on oral instruction, which requires so much time that missionaries, in addition to their other duties, find it difficult, if not impossible, to give to this work that attention which its importance requires. It must be remembered further, that while all pastors at home are supposed to be competent to superintend the studies of candidates for the ministry, this is by no means the case with all missionaries, as this undertaking in China requires an additional preparation which must be made on the ground, including, at least, a thorough acquaintance with the spoken language, while a familiarity with the literature and religious systems of China is very desirable. Such qualifications are the result of years of hard study, and are not to be expected in one who has only been on the ground a few years. It sometimes happens, even in a large mission, that owing to an imperfect knowledge of the written or the vernacular language, or both, or from pressure of other duties, there are few if any who are able to attend to the studies of the candidates for the ministry, at least as they would wish to, and students are obliged to be without instruction the greater part of the time simply from necessity; and, after spending two or three times the number of years which are generally considered to be sufficient for a course of theological study, they are obliged to give up in despair, or to enter the ministry imperfectly prepared.

Again, candidates at home are better able to forego the advantages of a course of instruction in a theological seminary, because they have usually spent years in a thorough course of intellectual and literary training in college and preparatory schools, while most of our theological students in China have been almost entirely without any corresponding advantages of this kind. To give them that attention which they require, some missionary or missionaries must devote themselves principally or exclusively to this department of labor. With our present small missionary force for each station, to attempt this work separately seems an unnecessary waste of time. Should it be assigned to a few persons specially qualified for it, and candidates from different quarters be gathered together in a general school, at least such as are in circumstances to leave home and to undertake a thorough course of study, other missionaries would be greatly relieved thereby, and would have more time to devote to other labors. The theological teachers would almost necessarily be obliged to prepare text-books which would be of use throughout the empire, and promising young men who should enjoy the advantages of a higher training-school would also become qualified to assist in teaching others.

It is impossible to treat this subject here in detail. It is my object simply to point out its great importance, and the practical difficulties which attend it.

The work of missionaries in China is fast becoming one of general superintendence of native laborers and churches; the preparation of a Christian and theological literature; and the training of a native ministry. As the work develops and assumes a different character, a great deal of practical wisdom is required in changing plans to suit changing circumstances.

CHAPTER XXIII.

RESULTS OF MISSIONARY WORK.

Unfavorable Reports respecting the Work of Missionaries, and their injurious Effects.—The Unreliableness of these Reports, and the Manner in which they originate.—The true Character of the Missionary Work, and the Difficulties attending it.—Detailed and Statistical Accounts of different Mission Stations not attempted.—Much has been accomplished in necessary Preparation for the direct Work of preaching the Gospel.—Effects produced by the general Diffusion of Christian Truth among the Masses.—Ripe Fruits.—The Classes from which the first Converts are usually drawn, and the Means by which they are brought into the Church.—Illustrative Experiences of Individuals and Families.—The Influence of Native Converts of both Sexes in building up Native Churches.—The Work of Native Preachers in the Out-stations.—General Statistics of the Results of Missions in China.—Special Reference to the Growth of Churches at Ningpo and in the Ports recently opened. —Remarkable Work in Lao-ling.

On the subject of this chapter very different opinions are entertained. It is often asserted by those who have spent years in China, and profess to speak intelligently and advisedly, that the missionary work there has been a failure. These reports have been so widely and persistently circulated, and have had such a decided and injurious influence upon many to whom we had naturally looked for confidence, sympathy, and co-operation, that it seems almost a necessity to give them a special consideration. It is but just to say that they are, in most instances, repeated frankly and openly, and that many honestly believe that they present the facts of the case. The derogatory testimony of others, however, is given with such an *animus* as ought to excite the suspicion of the most careless; presenting as it does the most conclusive evidence either of ignorance or malevolence.

In the published views of a Dr. Marron, a person connected with a Prussian scientific expedition which visited China, Japan, and Siam a few years since, the following sentences occur in connection with much else in the same strain: "There is—and when abroad I hear only one opinion—no institution more useless than these missionaries."* * * "I deny that there is a single Christian among the Chinese, that is, one who has comprehended the Christian doctrine, and whose Christian social views have become the mainspring of all his actions," etc.

Before leaving China, I copied the following from the *Hong-kong Daily Press*, written by an "occasional correspondent:" "Ask any man of mind and of experience in China, and he will tell you that it is childish to expect to convert them (the Chinese) by any means yet attempted to what we call in England, Ireland, and Scotland, Christianity. And this brings me to another subject; the farther I travel, the more I am convinced that from Exeter Hall, by way of Shetland and Connaught, to Pekin, practical philanthropy must be the pioneer to *bona fide* Christianity. Teach the Arab to construct and inhabit some more civilized dwelling than the low mud hovel you see along the railroad side from Alexandria to Suez. Show the Chinamen by precept and example that honesty is the best policy, and that cleanliness is health. I say try, if it be possible, to send out good and sensible men of the civil-engineer class to educate the ignorant in these matters, and you will do more for Christianity in fifty years than the old lady's string of tenets uttered from the mouths of maudlin missionaries could effect in fifty centuries." It is not difficult to infer the religious tenets and character of the writer of this article, or to determine how much weight should be given to his estimate of the Christian character of Chinese converts. I have not heard whether, since his return to England, he has succeeded in finding and sending out persons answering to his ideas of the model modern missionary.

I would not quote these extracts at such length, did they

not, as I believe, afford a good index of the real feelings and opinions of many, if not most of the foreign residents in China. I was told by a very respectable and intelligent American connected with one of our prominent mercantile firms in Shanghai that the above extract from the Hong-kong paper presented his views and those of nearly all of his acquaintances.

Even some Christian travellers have helped to circulate these reports which they find current in the foreign communities; and by their character, and supposed sympathy with the cause of Christ, have given to them an authority and plausibility which they would not otherwise obtain. I met in China an English chaplain who was collecting information with which to enlighten the Christian public at home. He had just come from Amoy, where there were at that time at least two self-supporting native churches in connection with one mission (that of the Reformed Dutch Church of the United States), and where converts were multiplying rapidly, and the missionary work was full of interest and encouragement. He informed me that he had made particular inquiries about the missionaries, and had learned that they had accomplished hardly any thing; that their attempt to Christianize the Chinese was a failure. It is unnecessary to state where he obtained his information; he certainly did not obtain it from missionaries, or from any one who knew any thing about the subject.

It could not be expected that these views, which are entertained by so many foreign residents and travellers in China, would not have a decided influence at home. Returned missionaries meet with them everywhere.

A few months since, after addressing a church in Brooklyn on the subject of missions in China, a lady was introduced to me who said that she was very glad to have heard my statements; for she had been told repeatedly by an acquaintance of hers that the missionary work in China had accomplished nothing, and that missionaries generally led idle, useless, and, in many instances, immoral lives. I replied that I was glad to be able to give her a more favorable opinion of our work; and that I would also be very happy to see the gentleman referred to, and, if possible, to correct or modify his impressions by the result of my own experience and observations. I was accordingly invited to meet him at tea the next evening at the house of a common friend. I was disappointed in not seeing him there, however, as he declined the invitation, saying at the same time that his views were based on hearsay, and that he had only heard of one instance of immorality among missionaries, and that occurred about twenty years ago, and he had forgotten the man's name! This is about what these reports generally amount to; and those who hear them, and are so often troubled by them, will find, by subjecting the persons by whom they are circulated to a short catechizing as to the sources of their information and the reliableness of their testimony, that "they understand neither what they say, nor whereof they affirm."

Not long since a course of popular and scientific lectures was delivered in different places in Western New York by an individual from one of our Eastern cities. The object of the lecturer appears to have been the glorification of the great Anglo-Saxon race. He had human skulls and portraitures, and historical facts and scientific deductions, to prove conclusively to his delighted and complacent auditors that they belonged to a race far superior to all others. Other peoples and tribes were the results of separate creations, and could never share with us either our form of civilization or of religion. To show clearly that his statement and facts were true as applied to China, he stated that efforts to introduce the Christian religion in the Chinese Empire had been so fruitless and discouraging that they had almost been given up as useless, and Christian societies were actually recalling their missionaries from that country! These statements, and the conclusions drawn from them, though rather startling, seem to have been accepted and believed by the great majority of those who heard them; for was not the speaker a popular lecturer, and an editor of a New York City paper, and (in his own estimation at least) a careful, learned, *scientific* man?

The effect produced upon some Christians at home by the testimony of merchants and others who have been in China is seen in a short paragraph in the *New York Observer* of June 25th, 1868. I have no doubt that the editor of that excellent paper feels a real and a deep interest in the cause of missions, and that he would be glad to believe that missionaries are faithful in the discharge of their trust; but he appears to be rather unsettled and doubtful on the subject. His remarks are as follows: "There is a lamentable want of sympathy in China between the commercial and religious interests of the Western nations. Seldom do we meet an Englishman or an American engaged in commerce in that portion of the East who seems to have a favorable regard for the labors of the missionaries. We do not intend to give reasons at present for this state of things, but merely express genuine regret at its existence, and the hope that new relations and interests may result in making all men of Christian nations alike active and earnest for the spread of Christian civilization and Gospel faith."

With reference to all these reports, I do not hesitate to say that they are based upon a misapprehension of the true character of Christianity, of the Chinese, and of the missionary work; and that they are as unfounded in fact, as they are ungenerous in spirit and injurious in effect. Missionaries will freely admit that they are not exempt from the weakness and imperfections that belong to other professions; that some of their number may perhaps have mistaken their calling; and that the labors of the whole body of missionaries have not been followed by the degree of success which might have been hoped for, and which a higher devotion might have secured. But we are far from admitting that missionaries as a class will not bear favorable comparison as respects intelligence, efficiency, and devotion to their calling, with the members of the ministerial or other learned professions at home or abroad, or that the missionary work has been in any proper sense "a failure."

If it be asked, "How, then, have the views referred to above become so prevalent?" the fact is easily explained. Most of the work of the missionary is of such a character as not to strike the attention of superficial observers. It is performed in the study, in the chapel, and in villages and cities in the interior. A large proportion of the converts are to be found in country out-stations, unvisited and unknown in the foreign communities; and it is not strange that merchants hardly ever see them or hear of them. Should they happen to meet a company of native Christians, they could not distinguish them from the rest of their countrymen; nor could they, being unacquainted with the language, hold any communication with them. Merchants usually obtain their information from their body-servant or "boy," who is generally quick and shrewd, and as *au fait* as his master in the use of the Pigeon-English; though not often of the educated or well-informed class, or at all acquainted with missionaries or native Christians. A few of the English-speaking young men who have been trained in mission schools, and have acquired a by no means enviable reputation in the foreign communities, are pointed to by those who are willing to take up an evil report as representative types of native Christians generally, though they may never have made any profession of religion whatever.

We would be most happy to communicate information on the ground respecting our work both to foreign residents and travellers, but it is a cause of regret that we have few opportunities to do so. Merchants are so absorbed in their business that they seldom have the time or disposition to visit us. Travellers and officers in our navy, whom we are always most happy to see and entertain, are generally more interested in going to a heathen temple, or gathering curiosities in the shops, or making an excursion into the country, than in visiting a native Christian family or an out-station, or in listening to detailed accounts of our work. These persons often come to us with opinions as to our work already formed and minds prejudiced. It is as difficult to remove these prejudices as to decide what course to pursue in entertaining them. Should we determine not to turn aside from our daily employments, and to make no special effort to render their visit agreeable, we would do violence to our own feelings, and be justly chargeable with being deficient in hospitality and ordinary politeness. On the other hand, if we give ourselves up for the time to social enjoyment and recreation, and endeavor to furnish our tables with somewhat such food as our guests are accustomed to, we are in danger of producing the impression that this is a sample of our daily life and occupations. This has, in fact, again and again been the result of our attempts to "use hospitality."

I should be very forgetful and ungrateful not to mention that there are a few from every class to be met with abroad who visit us when they can, who go with us to our work, and examine carefully into its details, and whose testimony with reference to us and to missions is almost more favorable than we deserve or wish. But this testimony, if published, is found in papers which those of opposite opinions and sympathies seldom read; and, if given in conversation, is received with prejudice and suspicion. It should be added further, that the ports where most foreigners are found are the ones where missionaries have accomplished least, and there are consequently fewer results to point to than in other places.

These discouraging representations of missionary work, while they are innocently circulated by many who suppose them to be true, originate, for the most part, with those who would fain believe that there are no consistent native Christians in China; as such would be a standing reproof to them, reminding them of their own inconsistency and neglect; perhaps of broken vows and a shipwrecked faith, and a life on account of which the name of God is blasphemed among the heathen.

In forming a just estimate of the kind and degree of results which might be reasonably expected, it is necessary to take into view the nature of the work, and the circumstances under which it is prosecuted. First, and principally, the greatest of all difficulties which we find in every land, and in our own individual consciousness, exists in China unrestrained and intensified. This difficulty is clearly expressed in Holy Writ: "The carnal mind is enmity against God; for it is not subject to the law of God, neither indeed can be." And again: "The natural man receiveth not the things of the Spirit of God, for they are foolishness unto him; neither can he know them, because they are spiritually discerned." To the opposition and blindness of our common nature, there are superadded in China many obstacles which are unknown in Christian lands, and which it is difficult for most persons fully to appreciate. The minds of the people are preoccupied by systems of error adapted to satisfy their religious longings and allay their fears; systems sanctioned and confirmed by the usage of their ancestors for thousands of years, and interwoven with all their social and civil institutions. Idolatry and superstition have entered into and corrupted their language, and the very constitution of their minds, so that it seems at first that every avenue through which they can be reached by the truth is closed.

It must be further remembered that those who have undertaken this work are very few. The whole number of Protestant missionaries now in China from Europe and America is about one hundred. Were England and the United States supplied with religious teachers at the same rate in proportion to the population, they would have about ten ministers of the Gospel each.

In view of these and other difficulties which might be mentioned, some of them originating with foreigners, such as the opium-trade, which is a standing objection to Christianity, and the notorious immorality and lawlessness of many who belong to nominally Christian nations, the Christianizing of

China by the preaching of Christ and Him crucified might well be considered (judged of by ordinary principles of cause and effect, aside from special divine interposition and aid) as visionary and impossible. Our ground of confidence is in the fact that the Christian religion is equally adapted to, and designed for all ages and peoples, and that God has declared that it shall prevail over the whole world.

Between the opposite and equally extreme and unreasonable views that the Christianization of heathen nations is impossible, and, on the other hand, that we have a right to be surprised and disappointed if they do not embrace Christianity in large numbers on the first presentation of it, we have the scriptural view that the success of the Gospel, wherever it is preached, is certain, and that it generally reaches its results from small and almost imperceptible beginnings. The kingdom of Heaven is compared by Him who is the head of that kingdom to the "least of all seeds" and to the "hidden leaven." Its progress and workings are silent, gradual, and unperceived; but certain, continuous, and irresistible, according to a fixed law of life and development.

War and commerce change the relations and conditions of nations rapidly, and sway and constrain the minds of vast populations in a body, producing those marked changes in the outward condition of nations which are seized upon by the historian as great national epochs. These changes are, however, often as superficial, evanescent, and disappointing in their results, as they are rapid and startling in their manifestations. The Gospel of Christ does not perform its work upon nations in the aggregate. Its sublime mission is that of conquering and subduing nations by subduing its individual members, bringing into captivity every thought to the obedience of Christ. It does not overpower and constrain for the time the will, but enlightens the mind, convinces the understanding, and regenerates the heart. It goes down to the very foundations of individual life, society, and government; and its greatest triumphs are realized before its outward effects are perceived. The leaven, though hidden, is constantly working, and pervading the whole mass. The mustard-seed, though unperceived and undiscoverable, is every moment developing its germ, and calling into action those vital forces by which it is to come forth to the light and spread wide its branches. It is unreasonable and useless to expect the harvest without waiting for the early and latter rain, or to gather ripe and abundant fruit from trees which have been but just transplanted, and are but beginning to send forth their roots into the soil. The order of nature and of grace is "First the blade, then the ear; after that, the full corn in the ear."

These preliminary remarks and explanations, which have been prolonged far beyond my first intention, I trust the reader will not regard as inappropriate or uncalled for, under the circumstances; and I now proceed to the main subject of this chapter.

The limits which I have prescribed for myself will not admit of special and detailed reference to individual missionaries or missions, or even to the history and operations of the particular stations with which I have been connected. It is rather my object to state facts and principles applicable to missions in general. But in giving a general view of our work and its results, it seems very desirable and almost necessary to make free use of illustrative facts taken from missionary life. In doing this, I shall draw principally upon my own experience; partly on account of the labor and time which would be necessary to collect the same materials from other sources, and partly because, in speaking of facts and occurrences with which I am familiar, I can with greater certainty avoid inaccuracy and misrepresentation. I hope that these statements in explanation will relieve me from the charge of egotism, or a want of interest in, or appreciation of the labors of others.

The actual results of missionary labor may conveniently be arranged under three general heads.

1st. *Advancement in the necessary preparation for the diffusion of Christian truth.*—It is evident, to any reasonable and thoughtful person, that years of preparation are required in China before entering effectively upon direct evangelistic work. A most difficult language must be acquired, and also more or less familiarity with the literature and religious systems of China and native modes of thought. At first it is not easy to determine upon the best plan for reaching the people, and the proper agencies to be employed. The amount of labor of this kind performed in China it is difficult to estimate, or for those who have not become familiar with it by personal experience fully to appreciate. It should ever be borne in mind that such occupations as these, though at first they have only a literary character, are in the strictest sense missionary work, and, when successfully prosecuted, result in a most important advantage to the cause. Most of the missionaries in China speak the language not only intelligibly, but accurately and fluently. Some of them who have been long in the field are now ripe Chinese scholars, having gone on increasing in their qualifications for usefulness during most of the period since the opening of the country. Dictionaries, grammars, and vocabularies have been prepared; careful translations of the Bible have been made, not only in the universal literary language, but in many of its local dialects. Schools have been established, and text-books prepared for those schools; tracts suited to the Chinese mind have been written; houses and chapels have been built; materials and appliances for extending our work have been gathered, and plans for future labor have been matured. These preliminaries are as indispensable in our work as it is for an army to provide itself with stores and equipments, to become acquainted with military tactics and drill, and with the position, character, and resources of the enemy, before entering upon a campaign. When this preparation is made, a stage of progress is reached, a positive result secured, and a real approximation made toward the great end in view.

2d. *The general diffusion of elementary Christian truth among the masses* is another result of great importance.

When a missionary has acquired the language, he may direct his attention to general labors among the masses, or concentrate his efforts upon a comparatively few individuals who are brought within the sphere of his daily influence. Most persons carry on both of these kinds of labor together. The natural effect of the former is to produce a partial and imperfect result on a large scale; while that of concentrated effort is to produce a complete and ultimate result on a small scale, and in a comparatively short period of time. In scattering the seed broadcast by the distribution of tracts, or in desultory preaching to transient hearers, the system of Christian truth as a complete whole is not clearly apprehended. Still, some simple doctrines are received into many hearts, and are gradually communicated from one to another. It is a fact full of encouragement that much Christian knowledge, though fragmentary and imperfect, has been treasured up in the minds of many who are not yet disenthralled from the slavery of idolatry; and though for the present overshadowed by the ranker growths of error, and chilled by the cold and blighting atmosphere of idolatry and superstition, these imperishable seeds of divine truth, though for a time dormant, will, under favoring circumstances in the good providence of God, spring up and produce an abundant harvest. These truths are talked of in ten thousand homes; they are allaying prejudice, undermining old systems, and daily becoming more widely diffused and more clearly understood. It is quite possible that those efforts which seemed in the beginning to be fruitless, will prove in the end to have been most blessed; and that many whose sorrowful complaint through life has been "Who hath believed our report? and to whom is the arm of the Lord revealed?" will have reason, when they see the wide-spread effects of their work of faith and patience, to thank God for the special labors to which he assigned them. Many instances might be cited in the experience of different missionaries in China in which persons who had received religious instruction, and had afterward been lost sight of and almost forgotten, have, after a period of years, reappeared, sought further instruction, and become earnest and useful Christians.

A very decided effect is often produced upon the masses before any converts have been received from them into the Church; an effect which for the time seems to repel rather than attract the people, though it marks a legitimate and important advancement in the progress of our work. In 1861 Baptist and Presbyterian missionaries from the United States commenced their labors in the city of Tung-chow, in the province of Shantung. The people received us with a great deal of cordiality and respect, and we had many visitors from the more influential and literary classes, and also from the officers. We were received and regarded simply as foreign scholars and teachers, and were the objects of much interest and curiosity. When the simple doctrines of the Gospel were first presented—the unity of God; His character as the one Father in Heaven; salvation from sin through Christ; the immortality of the soul, and eternal happiness in Heaven, these sublime truths were in the main received with interest and delight. In the course of the year, however, the whole aspect of the work and the feelings of the people were changed. As they learned more of Christianity, and discovered that it imposed a life of self-denial; was in irreconcilable conflict with all false systems of religion; and tolerated no object of worship beside the true God, their prejudices and opposition were aroused. The fact that several of our servants and teachers united with the church about this time, tended still more to draw the attention of the public toward us and our work. To the great majority of the people, the fact of a Chinaman's renouncing his own gods and the idolatrous practices of his countrymen, and worshiping the God of the foreigners, was inexplicable. That an extraordinary influence of some kind had been brought to bear upon the minds of native converts was evident; but the people had no idea of the power of Christian truth, much less of that of the Holy Spirit. It seemed most reasonable and satisfactory to them to account for our influence by the supposition of the use of magic and mysterious arts. It was generally believed that, in serving tea to our guests, we added to it some foreign medicine or drug, by which we gained a controlling influence over those who partook of it and made them our willing slaves. It was rumored also that the whole community was in danger, as we were insinuating, by means of paid agents, our foreign medicine into the flour used in the city, and flour cakes from the bakeries were at a discount for some weeks. We were at that time wishing to rent a house, and, in looking for one, visited a number of places in the city. Wherever we went we were carefully watched; and as we were noticed to go to the well in each place, and to spend some time about it, it was suggested that we were poisoning the water of the city; and well-cleaning became the order of the day. In many of the wells a little bag of red powder was found, supposed to be the dreaded medication. This no doubt originated with the well-cleaners, who were reaping a rich harvest, and were interested in confirming and continuing the suspicions of the inhabitants. The excitement increased; people looked angrily at us as we met them in the streets. Inflammatory placards were posted in different parts of the city maligning our character, and warning the people against being entrapped and deceived by us. Violence was threatened, and the city magistrates thought it necessary to issue a proclamation to restrain and quiet the people. The citizens were thoroughly frightened; and those most opposed to us were afraid that they too might catch the infection and become Christians in spite of themselves. If persons more intelligent and better informed than the rest expressed the opinion that these reports were foolish and groundless, they were suspected of being in league with us, or unconsciously influenced by us. This public commotion, which was occasioned by evident conversions to Christianity, and a growing knowledge of our real character and aims, tended greatly to bring missionaries and their work more prominently before the people. Our character and operations were universal topics of conversation; many matters were explained of which they were before in doubt; and, when the excitement subsided, it was generally understood that the only means made use of by us was the simple preaching of the Gospel, and that the only constraint by which natives were led to embrace it was that of a conviction of its truth. Since the period referred to, the people generally have not been as cordial and free in their intercourse with us as before, but the number of hopeful converts has constantly increased.

3d. We now come to the consideration of *ripe fruits* of missionary labor; of real conversions from heathenism, and the establishment of native Christian churches.

The great majority of the first native Christians of China, as I have before intimated, are persons who have been under the missionaries' daily influence; who have had line upon line, precept upon precept; who have thus become acquainted with the whole system of Scripture truth; and have not only learned of it from oral teaching, but also seen it illustrated in the life. They are literary men employed by us as scribes and to teach us the language; servants in our families, and pupils in our schools. With most of them we have daily opportunities for reading and explaining the Scriptures, pressing home upon their hearts and consciences the matter of personal religion, and uniting in social prayer and praise. They become as familiar with the Scriptures as most persons are in our own country; the truth is, by the influence of God's Spirit, made the wisdom of God and the power of God unto their salvation, and they are constrained to take up the cross and follow the Lord Jesus.

I can not better illustrate the manner in which individuals are brought into the Church in China, and made use of by Christ in carrying on His work, than by referring to an example from each of the classes above designated, taken from the converts belonging to our mission at Ningpo. They may be regarded as representative types of many of the native Christians to be found in connection with the different missions along the coast.

About twenty years ago, a Chinese scholar whose family name was Lu was employed by one of our missionaries as a teacher. After a time he was desirous of leaving home in the employ of a Chinese mandarin to spend several years in the interior as a scribe or attendant. He introduced to his employer his son Lu Kyiæ-dzing, a young man then about twenty years of age, and recommended him as a fit person to supply his place as teacher. The son was accepted, and the father left home, communicating privately to his wife this parting injunction: "Should Kyiæ-dzing wish at any future time to embrace the religion of the foreigners you must not oppose him; for their religion is true." In the course of a few years, Kyiæ-dzing, as his father had anticipated, was brought by his convictions of truth and duty to decide the great question whether he would accept or reject Christ and His salvation. He resolved to be a Christian, and made known to his mother his determination. This announcement awakened on her part violent opposition and abuse. She declared that she could not and would not survive the disgrace of her son's renouncing the religion and the customs of his ancestors and "following the foreigners;" and that if he should persist in being baptized, she would drown herself in the river—a very common mode of committing suicide in China. The trying position of Kyiæ-dzing in a country where filial piety and obedience are regarded as the first of all virtues may be easily imagined. In deciding the question of duty, he was made to feel the force of those striking words of our Saviour which seem designed to meet just such cases as this: "He that loveth father or mother more than me is not worthy of me." This trial affected his mind and body to such an extent that he became seriously ill and delirious, and his life for a time was almost despaired of. He recovered, however, and made a public profession of Christianity. Time would fail to describe the opposition, annoyances, and petty persecutions which he met with in his family; the attempts to prevent him from engaging in his religious duties and private devotions, and to draw him back to heathenism. A firm adherence to his own religious convictions in opposition to the wishes of family and friends proved in his case, as in many others which I could name, the greatest blessing to those he loved, and bound them to him by new and tender bonds of love and gratitude. It was a work of years, but one after another every member of the family, his wife, his mother, his grandmother, his sister, and a cousin were through his instrumentality brought to Christ; and they became a united family in the Lord, and one of the most interesting Christian households it has ever been my privilege to know at home or abroad. Kyiæ-dzing was one of the first of the native elders of the Ningpo church, and nearly every member of the family has filled some useful sphere of missionary labor. Thus the influence of the foreign missionary brought to bear upon one Chinaman twenty years ago was not only made the means of his conversion, but has brought a whole family into the Church, and is now operating through them upon scores of others who are brought within the sphere of their influence.

Nearly twenty years since a young man named Dzing Shih-nyiao was employed by Rev. W. A. P. Martin in Ningpo as servant and printer. While connected with him he became a Christian, and afterward a catechist. Through his faithful efforts an acquaintance of his was brought to Christ, who became the first native pastor of the Presbytery of Ningpo. He now has the charge of a church numbering nearly one hundred members, many of whom were converted through his instrumentality. Dzing Shih-nyiao is at present laboring at an out-station more than a hundred miles in the interior, where a native church is being gathered.

More than twenty years ago a little boy named King Ling-yiu was brought to the Boys' Boarding-school at Ningpo. At a comparatively early age he became a Christian, and had his attention directed to the Gospel ministry. He was an earnest student, acquired a familiar knowledge of the Scriptures, and the outlines of Christian doctrine; and, after years of study and employment as a catechist, he was in 1864 formally ordained as an evangelist. More than a year since he was called to his rest; but a church of eighty members, and grateful and cherished memories of his zeal, wisdom, love, and faithfulness, still bear testimony to the fact that he was an instrument chosen of God, a workman who needed not to be ashamed.

During the first stage of the history of a mission the greater proportion of the converts are generally males. This is accounted for by the fact of the seclusion of females in China, the comparatively small number of female missionaries, and the employment chiefly of males as servants and teachers. During the second stage of progress, when the work of making known the Gospel falls into the hands of natives, the state of things is reversed. In every age and country there has seemed to be in the nature of woman a peculiar susceptibility to religious impressions, and a readiness to respond to the call of a Saviour's love. In China converted husbands have often been the means of bringing their wives into the church, sons their mothers; and when a native preacher, with a Christian wife, commences his work at an out-station, female converts generally predominate greatly.

In out-stations conducted by natives, the most effective method of building up a church is still found to be that of laboring for and with individuals, rather than random preaching to crowds. When a native preacher first settles in a new station, he is usually regarded with much suspicion and dislike. His enterprise attracts some notice, and strangers, influenced by curiosity, make him a visit, manifesting, however, a distant reserve. Every movement is carefully watched and weighed. His boldness in standing up alone as the exponent of a foreign and despised religion, coupled with a conciliating spirit and deference to others, commands respect; his meekness and self-control under opposition and rebuke excite sympathy; the truth which he utters rivets the attention of some auditor, sinks deep into the mind, and perhaps awakens an earnest interest. By degrees, in answer to the oft-repeated invitation to come to the chapel, he has the pleasure of receiving a few visitors, almost always from the poorer and humbler classes. They are welcomed and entertained as guests, the conversation relating to general as well as religious topics. These visitors are very apt to come in the quiet and leisure of the evening. While they sip their tea and smoke their pipes, many subjects relating to foreigners and foreign customs, and the relations of the native teacher to the foreigners, are freely discussed; much interesting, novel, and important information is communicated; and from these social interviews there springs up a mutual confidence and attachment. Before the visitors take their leave, they are told of the custom of Christians to close the day with thanksgiving and prayer to God, and are invited to take part in these exercises. They listen with mingled feelings of curiosity and awe, while the Chinese Christian opens with reverence the volume of God's word and speaks of Him who is our Father in heaven, and has sent this book as a precious revelation of His will to His loved but erring children. Perhaps he chooses one from the parables of our Saviour, so wonderfully adapted to convey simple truth to the minds of the uninstructed, and unfolds the meaning of those precious lessons of Him who spake as never man spake. Then the whole company, Christian and heathen, bow together in the worship of the Great Unseen. To one and another the house of the native preacher becomes a favorite place for spending the evening, and in these evening exercises much religious truth is gradually imparted. Some of these visitors are found in process of time among the Sabbath worshipers. By degrees their eyes open to the light, and their hearts to receive the Lord Jesus as their Saviour and their King. They bring with them others in whom they are interested, and whom they can influence. Thus the work grows. A church is established. Living men and women, strong in the power of God's Spirit, stand up to do battle for Christ. A fountain of living and healing waters is opened, whose influence shall ever continue and increase.

The whole number of Protestant native Christians in China is at present about four thousand. These are to be found in the various stations along the coast—from Canton, in the south, to Pekin, in the north, but principally in the "five treaty ports," which have been occupied about twenty-five years. Most of the cities opened by the treaty of 1860 have also their native churches. I do not know of a single place in the Chinese Empire which has been occupied even but a few years as a missionary station which has not at present a Christian church. Indeed, it would be difficult to find a church or Christian community in the West which has increased in the same ratio as the Chinese churches. The annual report of the Board of Foreign Missions of the Presbyterian Church for 1868 shows an addition during the last year of one hundred and forty persons on profession of their faith to its eleven churches in China, which is more than one-third of the membership of these churches. This has been nearly their uniform rate of increase for several years past. How many churches in our own country give the same evidence of healthy growth and Christian activity?

To refer briefly to the missions with which I have been personally connected. When I reached Ningpo in 1854 we had there one church, numbering about twenty members. These were mostly from the city of Ningpo; all were pecuniarily dependent upon us; we had hardly a native assistant, and not a single out-station. That small and feeble church has grown into six regularly organized churches, with an aggregate membership of nearly four hundred persons. Several of these churches are situated thirty, fifty, and one hundred and twenty miles in the interior. Of the additions to them for several years past, only a very small proportion has any pecuniary connection with the mission whatever; on the contrary, a large majority suffer seriously in their temporal matters by becoming Christians. In connection with that one mission we have six native licentiates, four ordained ministers, and an efficient corps of catechists, Christian teachers, and candidates for the ministry. The most of the preaching and the pastoral work is now performed by natives, and our depleted band of foreign missionaries have almost more than they can do to superintend the work of natives, and instruct candidates for the ministry. The Chinese have proved themselves efficient laborers and church officers, and are generally disposed to contribute liberally of their means to support their own Christian institutions. Since my arrival in the United States I have received a letter from the native pastor of the church of Yu-yiao, in which he says, "Every member of this church, man, woman, and child, gives something for the cause of Christ. Most have adopted the rule of giving one-tenth of all their earnings or income, and some, not content with this proportion, give one-fifth." None of the members of this church are rich, and most of them are very poor. If Christians at home should adopt the same standard of giving, there would be no want of funds to carry on the benevolent enterprises of the Church. May I not add, How can we justify the adoption of any lower standard by the teachings of either the Old or the New Testament?

In 1861 I was engaged, together with Mr. Gayley, who died of cholera the next year, and Mr. Danforth, who was obliged to return home on account of illness about the same time, in establishing a mission on the promontory of Shantung. Here, though we commenced our work anew from the very foundation, we were permitted to receive converts into the church the first year; and we now have, as the result of the first seven years of labor of only three missionary families, two promising native churches, one at Tung-chow, and the other at Chefoo; each having a membership numbering more than thirty, and comprising several persons who give promise of being very useful as native helpers. In Tung-chow, the missionaries of the Southern Baptist Board, one of whom, the Rev. Mr. Hartwell, preceding us by several months in taking up his residence there, has met with equal success.

While in most places the work goes on quietly, gradually, and uniformly, God has shown us that he is able and willing to bring about more general and rapid movements, and is reproving us for our want of faith in not praying for, and expecting greater blessings. There have been several earnest religious awakenings in different parts of China North and South. One which has recently taken place in the villages of Lao-ling, near the northern border of the province of Shantung, is worthy of special notice. This place is about two hundred miles from any mission station, and had never been visited by a foreign missionary. About two years since, an old man living there, during a severe illness, was deeply impressed by a singular dream, suggested, perhaps, by serious thoughts of death and eternity; or should we not rather say, by the Holy Spirit, in connection with natural anxieties with regard to a future life? He thought he was conveyed to a most beautiful place which he denominated the "heavenly palace," and saw within it its happy inhabitants. Being desirous of entering himself, he was restrained by a guide or attendant, who directed his attention to his filthy garments, and his unfitness for entering such a pure and holy place. He awoke much distressed, and very anxious to obtain information as to how he could be prepared for admittance to this "heavenly palace," which even then he regarded as a reality. He was advised by a friend to make a journey to Tien-tsin as soon as he should be able to do so, to seek information from Roman Catholic missionaries who were known to be residing there. After a tedious journey he reached the city, and inquired in the street for some teacher who could tell him of the "heavenly palace." He was directed to a Protestant chapel, where he heard the preacher discoursing upon the text "Blessed are the pure in heart, for they shall see God." He felt at once that the presence of God was the glorious heavenly palace, and that impurity of heart was that which constituted his unfitness for it. He was cordially received by the missionaries of the English Methodist Church, and heard from them the truth as it is in Jesus. After a time he returned home, rejoicing in the knowledge of the Gospel and a Christian life, and taking with him the Bible and Christian tracts. His testimony and teachings awakened a general religious interest in the community where he lived, and he soon made a second journey to Tien-tsin, asking for a native preacher to return with him to instruct his people in the ways of God more perfectly. When a native preacher had labored there for several months, the place was visited by two foreign missionaries, who, after a careful examination of applicants for church membership, administered the rite of baptism to about forty persons. This was about one year after the first appearance of the old man in Tien-tsin. The work has since been steadily progressing; and more than one hundred persons have been received into the Church. The interest is spreading into adjoining villages, the inhabitants of which are asking for religious teachers and providing places for worship. These Christians in the interior have already met with opposition and persecution, but they have stood firm, and have not denied the faith. The work seems to be deep and thorough. The Sabbath is strictly observed, and the converts are growing in grace and knowledge.

What encouragement do such facts as these give us to pray for a general outpouring of God's Spirit upon the nations! There is, as far as I am aware, nothing peculiar in the character of the villages of Lao-ling, and there is no good reason why similar scenes may not be witnessed in any part of China. We need more faith, more zeal, more love, and more self-sacrificing labor to gather in the rich harvest. Much has already been accomplished which we ought gratefully to acknowledge; but the work is only begun.

CHAPTER XXIV.

CHARACTER AND EXPERIENCES OF NATIVE CHRISTIANS AND INQUIRERS.

Comparative Absence of pungent Convictions of Sin in Chinese Converts, and a Reason for it.—The Apathy of the Chinese with Respect to Death is removed by a Knowledge of Christianity.—Experience of Teacher Du.—Disadvantages and Compensations in the Condition of Chinese Christians.—Their Simplicity of Faith.—Their Views of Prayer.—Going up into a Mountain to pray.—Mercenary Inquirers.—"Stony-ground" Hearers.—Disappointed Expectations.—The Buddhist Devotee of Tsi-hia.—The Case of one who was almost persuaded to be a Christian.—Temptations and Defections of Church Members.—Differences and Estrangements among Christians.—Temptations overruled for Good.—Experience of two Native Preachers.—Difference of Views with Reference to the Admission of Inquirers to full Church Membership.—Cases of Discipline, and their comparative Frequency.—Trials and Temptations of Native Christians.—Eating Food offered to Idols.—Complicity with Idol Worship in other Ways.—Difficulties connected with the strict Observance of the Sabbath.—Experience of *Deo-vu Ah-san*.—Standard of Sabbath Observance in our Out-stations.—The History and Character of Jun-Kao.

WHILE the Spirit of God, operating in and through His Word, always produces the same general results, the religious life and experience of Christians in China are marked by some characteristic features which naturally grow out of their peculiar condition and circumstances.

One of these peculiarities which was often brought before my mind during seven years of pastoral supervision and frequent examinations of candidates for baptism, occasioned me for a time some solicitude and doubt. This was the general absence of those pungent convictions of sin which so frequently, though not necessarily, are connected with conversions in our own country. I have accounted for this fact satisfactorily to my own mind in the following manner. The Chinese, when enlightened by God's Spirit and made acquainted with their true moral character and relations to God, do not feel that they are sinners to the same extent and degree as we do, simply because they are not. They sin in a great measure through ignorance; we against light and knowledge. When a person of mature years in Christian lands is convinced "of sin, of righteousness, and of judgment," and looks back over perhaps a score or two of wasted years, memory brings up with appalling distinctness, time after time, when he has stifled the warnings of conscience; steeled his heart against convictions of duty; done despite unto the Spirit of grace; turned a deaf ear to the invitations of a preached Gospel; and perhaps to a mother's prayers and pleadings and tears; and trampled under foot the blood of the Son of God. These facts, when practically apprehended and felt, present an array of guilt from which the awakened conscience may well start back with dread and apprehension. Not so with the heathen Chinese. They wonder at their stupidity in having worshiped as gods the workmanship of their own hands, and been blind to the evidences which their senses and their consciousness furnish of the presence and universal providence of an unseen God; but they say, and say truly, in the matter of religious worship, "I did as I was taught from infancy, and had no knowledge of the true God and the better way." They soon learn, however, the lesson of the sinfulness of their nature, and their weakness and imperfections; and their humble confessions of sin and remissness in duty and ill-desert show that, when once they become Christians, their religious experience runs parallel with that of others.

That the peculiarity above mentioned is due to circumstances and education, rather than to any difference of race or mental constitution, is evident from the effect of religious knowledge and training upon the mental exercises and religious feelings of the people. Young men trained in Christian schools, who become Christians in after life, present the same phases of religious experience which are generally known among us. An intellectual knowledge of Christianity produces a thorough change in the religious feelings even of those who are unwilling to embrace it. I have known several illustrations of this fact, one of which I will mention. The person whom I first employed in Ningpo to teach my wife and myself the vernacular of that place was a pleasing and interesting man of the family name Du, between whom and us there sprang up a strong attachment. He expressed his belief in the truths of Christianity; always spoke of the Christian religion with great respect, and could hardly read the story of our Saviour's sufferings and death without showing deep feeling. He felt, however, that it was impracticable and impossible for one in his circumstances, and with his associations in life, to become a Christian. When he had been with us a little more than a year, I heard on my return from an itinerating tour that he was very ill. Going to his house, I met his son at the door—a bright, intelligent lad of about nineteen, an earnest student, and ambitious of literary preferment. He seemed more surprised than pleased to see me; and told me that his father was alarmingly ill, and was not himself; that his mind wandered, and he talked incoherently. Entering his room, I soon found that the evidences (to the son's mind) of mental aberration were, as I had inferred from his statement, of such a character as to give occasion for rejoicing rather than sorrow. Those lips from which I had learned that language, almost as dear to me as my mother-tongue, were speaking for the first time the "language of Canaan." He said to me, "This disease generally proves fatal, and I feel that it will be so in my case. I have been a great sinner. I ought long ago to have obeyed the commands and taken up the cross of Christ. During the last three days, while my family, contrary to my wishes, have been chanting Buddhist prayers, burning incense, and worshiping idol gods and evil spirits, I have constantly been praying to Jesus; and last night Jesus heard my prayer and sent me an answer in peace. He knows me, and I know Him." His conversation was perfectly rational, but his feelings were entirely unintelligible to his heathen family and friends. The Chinese generally view death with apathy and stoical indifference. It is not uncommon for old people to profess to desire and long for it; saying that life has no attractions, and that it is time for them to die. They expect to go to the land of spirits, and after a time to return to inhabit another body; and they simply resign themselves to their fate and take their chances. If they are filled with alarm, it is from the conviction that they are suffering the inflictions of demons or evil spirits. It was the knowledge of God, to whose character belongs the attribute of inflexible justice as well as infinite love, and the knowledge of the fixed and unending state of the redeemed and the lost, which gave rise in Du's mind to those new and strange exercises and anxieties, and to those importunate cries to "the only name given under heaven whereby we must be saved." I can not but hope that those cries and prayers were answered, and that from that room, filled with the symbols of idolatry and superstition, a soul went up to join the company of the redeemed around the throne of God. I offered to bear all the expenses of the funeral if the family would consent to have Du buried with Christian rites, but the offer was refused. I could mention several other persons who have been employed by foreigners as teachers, whose death-beds were marked with the same anxieties and forebodings, but not with the same hope.

The circumstances under which native Christians are placed in China are attended with peculiar trials and privations, and also with their compensations. They are in a great measure without a Christian literature, but, for this very reason, give more attention to the study of the pure Word of God. Scattered among a heathen population, they are drawn closer to each other in Christian sympathy and love. The trials, opposition, and persecution to which they are subject, have the effect of keeping false professors out of the Church, and developing and strengthening the character of true believers.

Their lives are often marked by a beautiful unquestioning faith. There are few doubting Christians; they have not yet reached the point of skeptical misgivings. To them there seems little room for doubt. They have set before them in bold contrast the reasonable, consistent, and soul-satisfying doctrines of Christianity, and the confused, baseless, and irreconcilable teachings of idolatry. They feel and know that they have passed from darkness to light; "Old things are passed away, and all things are become new."

Their prayers have often a practical and child-like simplicity. I have frequently heard them relate remarkable instances of deliverances, and providential interferences, and recovery from serious sickness and disease, in direct answer to prayer. I have hardly ever known a Chinese Christian who has manifested any indisposition or inability to take a part in social prayer-meetings. These peculiarities are principally due, it is to be hoped, to genuine piety and simple faith, but they may also result in part from their old habits and associations. They have all been accustomed to worship idols in the presence of others without shame or hesitation; and shall they be ashamed or backward, when they know it is their privilege to do so, to worship the true God? They have been accustomed to include in their petitions to false gods a great variety of matters connected with their every-day life, some of them comparatively trivial; and shall they not bring before their omniscient, loving Heavenly Father all their cares and sorrows, when they are encouraged and commanded to do so?

A beautiful instance of faith and earnestness in prayer occurred not long since in the province of Shantung. During a season of great suffering from drought, when the people were everywhere thronging the temples and praying to various deities for relief, a few native Christians who had but recently been received into the Church, and lived in the country at a considerable distance from their foreign teacher, met together to consult as to what they should do. They felt not only pained but rebuked by seeing their heathen countrymen worshiping gods which were no gods, while they had neglected to offer up their earnest and united prayers to Him who controls the elements of nature, and sends rain on the just and on the unjust. Without advice, hint, or suggestion from any one else, they determined to go up into a mountain and spend the whole night in prayer to God; influenced, perhaps, by the recorded example of our Saviour, or possibly by the example of Elijah under circumstances similar to their own. The next day, before those who lived at the greatest distance from the hill had reached their home, they were overtaken by a copious shower.

I am reminded that I may be giving to the reader too favorable an opinion of the Christian character of Chinese converts, and too bright a coloring to our missionary experiences. It is natural and right to dwell with delight and wonder on the "plants of righteousness" springing up in heathen wastes, unfolding into life and beauty, and bearing fruit to the glory of God. But here, as elsewhere, the enemy sows tares, and God's servants are often sorely tried.

Not a few of the natives who have no means of livelihood, and no social position to lose, and are wholly ignorant of the character and requisitions of Christianity, apply for baptism from mere mercenary motives. The withdrawal of such persons from us, if they continue to show no regard for the Gospel except as a means to a worldly end, occasions us comparatively little regret.

There are many others who are honestly and deeply impressed by the truth, and desirous and determined for a time to be Christians. These are the stony-ground hearers of the parable, who receive the word with joy, and endure for a season, but in time of persecution fall away. It is one of the principal trials of the missionary to see the zeal of these grow cold, until, one after another, they walk no more with us.

There are others who seem willing to endure trials apparently from love to Christ, and, through much difficulty, reach the very door of the church, when the adversary, as if by a violent assault, drags them back to the world, and they become our enemies. These cases occasion a disappointment like that felt by the husbandman when his luxuriant fields, just ripe for the harvest, are prostrated and desolated by the hail and tempest. Such instances stand out with painful distinctness in the lives of most missionaries.

I well remember the case of a noted Buddhist devotee in the district of Tsi-hia, in the province of Shantung, who was regarded with great veneration by the inhabitants of the surrounding country. He spent most of his time in a sitting posture, engaged, as it was supposed, in religious meditation and prayer. He lived on a purely vegetable diet, and, it was believed, on almost nothing. He had a great influence over the people, being regarded by them almost as an incarnation of Buddha, and the personification of holiness. He was visited several times by our native catechists, and seemed to evince a real desire after religious knowledge and happiness in the future state, and confessed that his religion and mode of life were not altogether satisfactory to him. After several conversations, he consented to read religious books, and was much interested in them. By degrees he became convinced of the truth of Christianity, and expressed a desire to be a Christian. During one of the visits of our catechists he went so far as to take down his idols from their shrines, remove his pictures of gods and goddesses from the walls of his sanctum, and to eat meat with his guests; thus formally renouncing his faith, and repudiating the merit which it was supposed he had acquired by his austere life. We began to hope that he would soon declare himself a Christian, and prove a "chosen instrument" for preaching the Gospel to the thousands whom he had "bewitched with his sorceries," and who had looked up to him as a religious oracle. A time was appointed for him to make a visit to Tung-chow, where he was to be my guest with a view to further instruction in preparation for receiving Christian baptism. To our surprise, he suddenly changed his plans, influenced we know not by what motives, and went back to his old course of life, representing us as deceivers and seducers, and himself as having been almost led away and ruined by us. Here again the adversary triumphed, and our hopes were blasted.

I find recorded in my journal, with a good deal of detail, the history of another case in which I was greatly interested; and notwithstanding its disproportionate length in such a chapter as this, I will give the greater part of it, as it illustrates many points of Chinese character and social life, as well as missionary experience, which I could not present so clearly in any other way.

"TUNG-CHOW, *Jan.* 14, 1862.—My teacher Suen is in a very interesting state of mind; and the dealings of God with him have been of such a character that I wish to make a record of them.

"Being very desirous of employing a finished Chinese scholar who could assist me in preparing books for the press, I made it a special subject of prayer on coming here that I might obtain such a one. I first saw Suen about the 1st of September in the chapel at Mr. Gayley's. He came in with a company of well-dressed young men, all appearing remarkably well-bred and intelligent. I was particularly struck with Suen's quickness, and polite, easy manners. When he left the chapel, I had little idea that I should see him again. More than a month after Tsao told me that a very respectable and gentlemanly scholar had offered his services as a Mandarin teacher. When he made his appearance, I recognized the same Mr. Suen whom I had seen in the chapel. He, with his family, had left Tai-nganfu, where he had been employed in the yamun of a relative, and came to this place to get away from the rebels. I told him that the wages which we are in the habit of giving teachers would not be sufficient to support his family; but I would be glad to have him while he was without other employment, and that when he could obtain a more lucrative position, I would expect him to leave me to avail himself of it. At first he regarded Christianity as differing little from Buddhism, and evidently had no great respect for it or its adherents. While we were revising a book for the press (the 'Native Assistant's Guide'), I saw that he was much struck with some thoughts contained in it, and his curiosity and interest were quite apparent. From this time he always seemed pleased to converse on the subject of Christianity in a general way, and rapidly acquired correct ideas of it.

"About three weeks ago I presented to him the subject of his practical interest in the Gospel, and pressed upon him the importance of giving it his most earnest consideration, and securing for himself the benefits which it offered. He frankly told me that his mind was full of doubts, and that he even doubted the veracity of the Christian revelation. I saw, however, that he was more interested than he was willing to acknowledge. After a long conversation he left me. It was evident that a clear apprehension of the truth had aroused both his sense of responsibility and the natural opposition of his heart.

"When he came the next day he told me that he had thought all night on the subject we had talked about, and that, the more he thought, the more his doubts and difficulties increased. I requested him to write them out and let me see them. This he promised to do. As he brought his papers from day to day, I said nothing in reply, as I wished him first to express freely all he had to say. Before he had finished writing, however, one of his papers was so blasphemous that I told him, that while I wished him to use the utmost frankness, presenting every thing without reserve, he must at least speak of the name of Christ with respect, remembering that he himself might some day find that he had been sinning against the Majesty of heaven and earth. His objections as thus enumerated amounted to twenty in number; and indicated a thinking mind, and close application and study. I occupied three days in answering them. It was evident that his intellect was satisfied as far as most of them were concerned. He was now becoming intensely interested; still he did not regard himself as an inquirer, nor did I address him as such. As many of his difficulties resolved themselves into doubts of the divine origin and truthfulness of the sacred Scriptures, I urged him to read carefully several chapters in the '*Tien tao su yuen*'* on this subject. The next day he said that he had read these chapters, and that after our conversations, the truths presented in them appeared in a new light. He had read the book through carefully before, but could not understand it; now it was, as it were, a new book. He said, however, that he had met with another difficulty; that he could not believe in the resurrection of the dead; that it could not be that the Bible taught such a dogma, and we must have misinterpreted it. I told him it was one of the most clearly revealed doctrines in the Scriptures, and read with him carefully our Lord's reasonings with the Sadducees, and the 15th chapter of 1st Corinthians. The most of the day was spent in conversations relating to these fundamental but mysterious doctrines of Christianity. He listened with fixed attention, and was much impressed, though he said but little. At this time his mind was opened to the beauty and power of the Scriptures, and he had evidently 'tasted of the word of God.' For several days subsequent to this we read the Scriptures regularly. He now had little interest in any thing but religious subjects, and studying the Bible was no irksome task. The righteousness of God by faith, as presented in the first part of Romans, struck him with great power. It was evident, from his conversation, that he was spending all his leisure time at home in reading the Scriptures and other religious books, and that he was making rapid advances in the knowledge of divine things.

"I had not as yet said much to him about the practical duties of Christianity, for he would not acknowledge his belief

* A work on the "Evidences of Christianity," by Rev. W. A. P. Martin.

in the existence of the Holy Spirit, nor of Satan, nor in the reasonableness and efficacy of prayer, nor in Scripture views of sin, nor in the justice of God's plan for saving sinners. I was satisfied, however, that his heart was sufficiently enlightened to furnish the ground for a direct appeal to his sense of duty and obligation, and urged him immediately to submit himself to God, and to attend earnestly to things which relate to his eternal peace. Four days ago I reminded him that this was probably the turning-point in his life, and would determine his weal or woe for time and eternity, and affect the condition not only of himself but of his family. I told him that God was calling him by his Spirit, and that he must now decide the question for himself, whether he would serve God or Satan. I told him further that I was exceedingly anxious about him, since he could not long remain in his present position, as he must either advance or recede. I urged him to commence immediately the practice of private prayer, to submit himself to God, and enter with Him into a solemn covenant to be His forever.

"When Suen came yesterday, he seemed more depressed than ever. He was not disposed to say much, but appeared pleased to have me talk on religious subjects. I was very greatly encouraged by some incidental remarks which gave evidence that he felt not only an interest in, but a love for the truth. He remarked once with earnestness, 'Oh, if my country as a whole would embrace Christianity, it would be blessed indeed!' We spent an unusual proportion of the day in talking on religious subjects. When he left me, I feared that I had said too much, and that I might have given a wrong direction to his thoughts, or in some way interfered with the work which it was evident that God's Spirit was carrying on in his mind. I determined to-day to spend the time usually employed in conversation in reading the Scriptures, leaving the Holy Spirit to apply the truth in His own way.

"This morning when I opened the Bible to read I saw that he had something to say. Taking a long breath, he commenced the conversation in these words: 'These few days Satan and the Holy Spirit are struggling in my heart. Something says, "The Gospel is false; have nothing to do with it;" and something says, "It is true; you must not reject it." Sometimes I have harsh thoughts of God, and feel that he has treated me unjustly; and again I think that I am indebted to him for many blessings.' I asked him in what respect he sometimes thought God had been unjust to him. He replied, 'My ancestors for several generations have been officers; of my fellow-students in early life, many who are not at all superior to me in talents and acquirements now occupy high positions of rank and affluence, while I have been frustrated in all my schemes, and disappointed in all my hopes.' I answered, 'God has been better to you than you think, and has done more for you than you desired. He has hedged up all ways but one; that way is now opened before you, and God's Spirit is beckoning you to enter; not to obtain the short-lived honors and pleasures of this life, but the gift of eternal life and blessedness.' He replied, 'There are many hinderances to my becoming a Christian.' I asked him to name them. He drew a paper from his pocket, on which he had them written. It reads as follows:

"'(1.) My old mother is opposed to my being a Christian. (2.) I can not bear to give up the reverence which the customs of my country require me to pay to ancestors. (3.) I dread the scorn of my former associates, who will say that, having failed in my former plans, I became a Christian because I could not do any better. (4.) My becoming a Christian will cut me off from sympathy with my former acquaintances, as St. James says, '"The friendship of the world is enmity with God."' (5.) If I become a Christian, I know of no way by which I can honestly and consistently, with the teachings of the Bible, support my family.'

"I replied, 'The claims of God upon you are paramount to those of your mother; and besides, your filial duty to your mother requires you to take a firm stand, and endeavor, with the blessing of God, to save her soul before she dies. As to the friendship of the world, how can we hesitate in choosing between it and the love and favor of God?' Fearing that he had incorrect views as to the requirements of Christianity with reference to ancestors, I remarked, 'Christianity does not do violence to any of the right feelings and impulses of our nature. It is our privilege and duty to remember, love, and revere the memory of our departed parents; and it is our privilege to visit and ornament their graves, and to give any proper outward expressions to the feelings of our hearts.' 'Yes,' he said; 'but my case is different from yours. When you become a Christian, you enter the religion of your fathers, and look forward to a reunion with them in heaven.' This was the tender point. I replied, 'With reference to your ancestors, you must leave them in God's hands. They died as you never can, "without the law." God is a God of infinite love and infinite justice, and will do just what is right. If they could speak to you, they would probably say, '"Flee to Christ for your life, and lay hold of Him as your only Saviour."' I added, 'Think of what may be the feelings of your son in future years if you refuse to become a Christian. Your trouble is that your ancestors did not know of Christ, and could not believe in Him; your son's would be, '"My father knew of Christ, and was urged to believe in and be saved by Him, but would not."' I acknowledged that his difficulties were real and serious, but said that, while I sympathized with him deeply, I could do little for him. I pointed him to Christ for the fullest sympathy and help. He went away apparently with a burden heavier than before, and left me oppressed with a weight of sympathy, anxiety, and responsibility.

"*Wednesday*, 15*th*.—To-day, when Suen came, he asked whether prayer were indeed efficacious? I answered that it most certainly was. He replied, 'I have tried to give myself to God, and have prayed three days, but have obtained no answer.' I told him I feared he did not pray aright, and endeavored to instruct him in the nature of acceptable prayer. I found that he had not depended as he should on the mediation and sacrifice of Christ, but had offered his prayers too much in his own name. I told him, moreover, that though his prayers might be scriptural and acceptable, God would answer them and give him peace in His own time and way, and that he must pray with earnestness, importunity, and faith, assured that God will be true to his promises. I exhorted him never to doubt God, but to look well to his own deceitful heart, and guard against the insidious attacks of Satan. The change in his feelings is remarkable. He has conversed again with his mother, and it is evident that his family know the state of his mind, so far as they can understand and appreciate it. A few days ago when he was writing his objections against Christianity, his wife opposed him, saying that he should not do so, for Christianity is true. He says that his wife is still of the same opinion, though she evidently does not now sympathize with, and can not understand him. We talked much to-day of the work of the Spirit and the new birth.

"*Thursday*, 16*th.*—When Suen came this morning, I saw that his countenance was less sad. I inquired how he was getting on. He answered, 'My confidence is becoming stronger, and my doubts weaker. I feel that I am progressing.' I questioned him as to his views of the nature of sin, and was glad to find that they were scriptural. His account of the way in which he had consecrated himself to God was also very interesting and encouraging. I read with him the description which Hopeful gives of his conversion in the 'Pilgrim's Progress,' and the 7th and 8th chapters of Romans. He now seems to love the Scriptures. After reading with him, I had a long conversation on the sacraments and Christian duties. In speaking of God's providential care over his people, he remarked, 'I read some passages in the Scriptures yesterday which have in a great measure relieved my anxiety.' I asked him what they were. He repeated, with evident delight, the verses which refer to the ravens and the lilies. Just before he left I said to him that I had not hitherto suggested our praying together, because I felt that this was a duty which he must begin unaided, and that I thought it would now be well for us to seek God's blessing together; and asked him if, after my prayer, he would follow in one of his own. To this he assented. His prayer was broken, but simple, unaffected, and scriptural. He spoke of himself as one who had known nothing, who now knows very little, but desires to know more. He prayed for the enlightening influence of the Spirit, the pardon of his innumerable sins through Jesus Christ, and for his family. Also, that God would assist him in passing the new year without sin.

"*Saturday, 25th.*—More than a week has elapsed since my last entry. During this time Suen has learned much of the difficulties of the narrow way, and much also of his own heart. Last Sunday he came for the first time to spend the Sabbath with us. This change from his ordinary habits increased the opposition of his family. He has had occasion several times to reproach himself for not being able to exercise a meek and loving spirit while they were opposing him. He was surprised that he had so little strength, and also to find it so difficult to lead a Christian life. Last Thursday, in answer to my inquiries, he told me that he was having a great deal of difficulty; that he had been led into sin, and was feeling very sadly about it. The night before was the time for worshiping the 'God of the Kitchen,' and he was expected to perform the act of worship. His mother spoke to him about it several times, but he put her off, saying, 'Wait a little.' At last, when she asked him again, he said, 'I have worshiped;' thus deceiving her, and so the matter dropped. He felt that he had done wrong, and asked forgiveness in prayer, but was still much troubled. After he had retired for the night, he told his wife more particularly of his determination to be a Christian, and she became so angry that she threatened to leave him and go west to Tsi-nan. I told him that I was sorry, but he had only one course to pursue, and that was to obey God at all hazards, and leave the result with Him. I said, moreover, that he need not expect God's blessing till he undeceived his family with reference to the affair of the 'Kitchen God' and confessed his fault. I urged him too to declare more decidedly his determination with reference to all idolatrous services, so as to avoid similar difficulties in the future. He seemed to be much depressed in spirits, and I feared that he might not have strength to stand the trial. Yesterday he did not come, and I was not a little anxious. To-day he told me that night before last he informed his family clearly of his determination to have nothing more to do with idolatry in any form, and confessed the sin of deception the night previous. They were so much distressed that they all began to cry and lament, and he cried with them. His mother spoke more harshly to him than ever before, and said some things which made him feel very sadly. His wife is the most severe of all, and he feels his case a very trying one. He says that his family have not at all given up the idea of reclaiming him (as they regard it). They look at him as out of his mind, and think that I have given him some mysterious potion, by which I have gained a great power over him. I am delighted to see evidences that he is being taught of the Spirit how to pray. I have this evening received a note saying that his family have laid a trap to keep him from coming to the service to-morrow, and that it is uncertain whether he can get away or not. May God give him grace to do his whole duty, and overrule these trials for his good.

"*Tuesday*, 28*th*.—Day before yesterday Suen did not attend the Sunday service. The means which his family employed to keep him at home was that of hiding his clothes in the night, so that he had nothing to dress himself with in the morning. I fear that he is altogether too yielding and irresolute. Tsao tells me that Suen was at his place yesterday, and produced the same impression on him. I can but commit him into the hands of Christ, who alone can keep him from falling. He has asked leave of absence for the holidays. May God give him strength to withstand temptation.

"*Saturday, Feb. 1st.*—Yesterday Suen came to make a New Year's call. I am happy to write that I am in a measure relieved from the anxiety I had felt about him. In the first place, he met me with an affectionate warmth which I have not noticed in him before. Many of his remarks also indicated that his interest was not abated. Judging from my exhortations that I had some fears respecting the state of his mind, he said, 'I am sorry that you have so much anxiety and trouble about me. I assure you I have not given up my resolutions; God has not forsaken me, and my purpose is still fixed.' I cautioned him not to trust in self, and that when he thought he was doing well, he might be but following the suggestions of Satan. He is now finding indeed that his enemies are they of his own household. His old mother is very much distressed, feeling that her son is being led away by a false religion. His sister, who was disposed to sympathize with him at first, has fallen in with the prevailing opposition of the family. His wife is violent. The night before the Chinese New Year, while he was talking with her and declaring his determination to be a Christian, she made a vow or oath that she would in that case kill herself; and, in attestation of it, endeavored to cut off her finger, and injured it very severely. His little boy is entirely under the influence of his mother. Suen hardly knows what to do. I urged upon him the duty of a strict observance of the Sabbath. He fears that if he attends church on the coming Sunday, his wife may do something desperate, but positively promises that he will come out the Sunday after."

Here the subject is discontinued in my journal. The New Year holidays, with their varied temptations, proved a disastrous season for poor Suen. When they were over, he returned to his regular employment, continuing to profess an undiminished interest in personal religion, but he had now little disposition to converse on the subject, and his manner was constrained. He had shrunk back from bearing the cross, and his course was from that time backward and downward. The work in which he was engaged with me, and which he before so much enjoyed, was now distasteful, and was carelessly performed. In the course of a few weeks his connection with me became as irksome to him as it was unsatisfactory to me, and he left my employment. It is hardly necessary to add that I parted from him under these circumstances with deep regret and disappointment.

But there are still greater trials than such as I have described above. They come from the defections of those who have formally taken upon themselves the vows of the Lord Jesus; who have been loved and trusted as brethren; who have run well, and borne a decided testimony for the Gospel for months and years; but have afterward fallen under the power of temptation, and brought reproach upon the cause of Christ. It was only to be expected that in China, where Satan has held undisputed sway over the minds of men for so many centuries, the few native Christians and churches that are initiating aggressive movements against his supremacy would be the objects of his bitterest malignity and most violent assaults. Perhaps we should not wonder that the fold is sometimes unexpectedly entered, and the sheep, or some whom we had thought the sheep of Christ, destroyed. The temptations of native Christians are varied and numerous. In China, the world, the flesh, and the devil seem each to have an additional power, and the condition of Christ's people as a "church militant" is strikingly illustrated. Young converts, ignorant of themselves and the devices of Satan, are almost unconsciously led into temptation, and frequently become discouraged and disheartened. Still oftener, seeing the faults of others more clearly than their own, and adopting a high standard of Christian duty, they become censorious, and strifes and contentions spring up in the church. But the wiles of the adversary are often overruled to defeat his own purposes. Nothing is more consolatory and inspiring than to see the young, inexperienced, and self-confident Christian, after having yielded to temptation, cling closer to the Saviour with a truer humility and more earnest faith, and rise to renew the contest with new resolution and assurance.

I have known repeated instances in which misunderstandings and estrangements between Christian brethren have in the end resulted in strengthening and cementing their friendship, as well as increasing their influence. About ten years ago our mission in Ningpo was just establishing out-stations in Yu-yiao and San-poh, in both of which places we now have vigorous and growing churches. A misunderstanding arose between the two natives who had charge of these out-stations; their wives, both most estimable Christian women, taking an active part in the inception and continuance of the dispute. Each party felt itself aggrieved, and that the other was the sole offender. The breach became wider, so that there was very little intercourse between the two families, though they labored in adjoining districts. This state of feeling interfered seriously with their happiness and usefulness, and began to be talked about by the few converts whom they had gathered. In visiting the out-stations, I had several conversations with them about this matter, but their difficulties seemed to them insurmountable, and neither was disposed to yield. In the course of a few months I told them very seriously that I thought there was no just cause for this estrangement, and that they were sinning against each other, and against Christ; and that they could not expect a blessing upon themselves and their work until these differences were adjusted, urging them both to think and pray over the matter. I told the assistant at Yu-yiao that, when I came round again, he must go with me to San-poh and see his brother face to face, and if possible, then and there, put an end to these differences. He made no reply, but his silence and manner showed that he felt the importance of such a step, and was willing and desirous to do what was really his duty. About a month afterward we were slowly wending our way in a native boat, through the populous plain of San-poh, toward the little village of Siao-gyiao-deo. Arriving at the house of the native assistant there, after the customary salutations and a few inquiries about his work, I said to him, "Do not trouble yourself to entertain me to-day, for I have been a more frequent guest in your house of late than your old friend whom I have brought with me;" and, leaving the two together, I retired. In a few hours one of them made his appearance from the room where they had been closeted together, and I asked him, "What success?" He answered, "First we prayed together, and then I commenced saying to him that it was my fault that we had been so long separated. He interrupted me, insisting that the fault was his. He would not let me make any confessions, nor could I him; and I assure you we have had a 'good time.'" Under the power of grace, each had been led to see a beam in his own eye, and only a mote in his brother's; their difficulties vanished, and their old friendship revived with new force, and has, I think, never since been interrupted.

The views of missionaries differ somewhat as to the principles by which they should be governed in admitting inquirers to full church membership; some receiving them at an early period, and others keeping them a longer time on trial. It is a difficult matter to determine practically the best course to take in each case as it arises, and there seems to be danger of going to one extreme or the other. Of course, the number and the character of the native Christians in different stations will depend much on the view which is adopted as to this matter, and the equally important one of *church discipline.* On the whole, the number of defections is smaller than, under the circumstances, might be expected. In the missions connected with our own church, the proportion, as near as I could estimate it, was about seven per cent. of the whole number admitted; and other missions have reported about the same result. In some cases, the administration of discipline is immediately followed by the happiest effects; in others, persons suspended or excommunicated are brought back after a period of months or years; others seem to be given over to Satan; and the final result of their defection is veiled in the depths of the future.

Some of the principal difficulties of native Christians grow out of the social idolatrous customs of the country. The question as to eating things offered to idols comes up in precisely the same form in which it was presented to the Apostles in early times. In the case of the funeral of a relative of a native Christian in families all the other members of which are idolaters, it is difficult to determine precisely what course the Christian should take. He must endeavor to avoid complicity with idolatry, on the one hand, and the appearance of disregard for deceased relatives, on the other. Again, we sometimes go into the house of a native Christian, and find a representation of the Kitchen God in its accustomed place, with incense burning before it, and perhaps other objects of worship exposed to view. This fact is necessarily calculated to excite suspicion. But the native Christian may happen to have a strong-minded wife, who will restore the Kitchen God to its shrine as often as it is removed, and insists on her right to adhere to the customs of her people and worship what she chooses. Here, too, it is difficult to determine how far a Christian man ought to rule in his own house, and what concessions may be made on the plea of peace and necessity.

Perhaps the principal difficulty which Chinese Christians meet with relates to the observance of the Sabbath. A laborer is in danger of being thrown out of employment if he will not work whenever his employer wishes him. A shop-keeper may lose his customers if he does not keep his doors open at all times. When I went to China, it was an occasional subject of discussion among missionaries whether we had the right, under the circumstances, to insist upon the strict observance of the Sabbath as a necessary condition of church membership. The matter seems, however, to be one in which we have no discretion. If this duty is of divine obligation, we must require it at all hazards. I believe that a strict adherence to it will always be found practicable, and is not only desirable, but absolutely necessary to the existence of a pure Christianity in any country.

An experience of one of our church members in Ningpo will illustrate this subject, as well as some important phases of Chinese life and character to which I have not referred. I commenced my first attempts at chapel preaching in what is called the Bing-gyiao-deo chapel at Ningpo. I noticed almost every day a man in working dress, who would come in with a very accustomed air, take his seat in one corner, and listen quietly, while he smoked his pipe. I learned that he was the proprietor of the adjoining bean-curd shop, and that he was familiarly called *Deo-vu Ah-san*—"Bean-curd Ah-san." He had been acquainted with our operations in the chapel from its first erection, and came in to see how the young missionary succeeded. Sometimes when conversations with visitors led me into regions of the Ningpo dialect, which I had not thoroughly explored, having at that time been in China less than a year, he would come to my help, and render me very opportune assistance. One day, after dismissing the audience, I asked him to stay a while, as I wished to talk with him. I told him I was delighted to notice his knowledge of Christianity, and his disposition to defend it, and asked him why he did not become a Christian. He replied, with his characteristic promptness and frankness, "I do believe Christianity, and I would like to be a Christian; but I'll tell you what the difficulty is. I sell bean-curd for a living; and when I weigh it out to customers (and here he balanced his long pipe-stem nicely over his finger), I always feel a disposition to make the bean-curd side of the scale the lighter, and I know that is not consistent with Christianity. I don't feel ready to change my practice yet; I know what the Bible requires; and if ever I make a profession of my faith, I mean to live up to it. Besides, there is the Sabbath question. The bean-curd which I prepare in the morning must be sold the same day or early the next morning, or it will spoil, and be a dead loss; and shutting up shop the whole day would ruin me." In the course of a year I became pastor of the native church, and Ah-san not long after applied for baptism. His love for the truth had grown, and he had resolved to try to obey his convictions of duty. From the time of his application for baptism until he was received into the church, a period of several months, the shop was shut every seventh day. A few months after his public profession of Christianity, native church members noticed that his door was left ajar on Sunday, and an occasional customer was seen entering it. When spoken to about this, he said that the neighbors would come to him and ask if he had any bean-curd left over; and if he had, he let them take it as a matter of accommodation, and to keep it from spoiling. But the applicants for bean-curd on Sunday became more numerous, and Ah-san was less careful not to make too much on Saturday, and soon opened his shop on Sunday outright. The native elders expostulated with him to no effect, and I sent for him to come to see me. He told me he had thought the matter over deliberately and seriously, and he did not believe that God required him to close his shop on Sunday. It was very well for us to theorize about it; but he must provide for his family, and the customers were falling off, because they would buy where they could do so whenever they wished to, and there was danger of his coming to want. He said further, "I am very sorry to give you so much trouble, but I can not help it. If you feel it your duty to suspend me from the privileges of the church, or to excommunicate me, I will not complain; I shall do what I think is right, and so must you. I mean to live and die a Christian. I will never deny my Saviour, but I have determined to open my shop on Sunday. I hope the brethren who live in my neighborhood will come into my shop every evening as before, to unite with us in our evening service of reading the Scriptures and prayer; I will read (as I can do so better than they), and explain a little, and then I will call on them to pray."

This was Ah-san's fixed resolution; and, as he anticipated,

he was suspended from the communion of the church. In carrying out his purpose, he met with a difficulty in his family. His wife had united with the church in company with him. She was as decided a character as he, and as firmly set in her ways. I remember a complaint against her which he once made to me as her pastor. Said he, "I believe my wife is a true Christian, but she will not leave off some of her old heathen habits. When she becomes warm and earnest in her private devotions, she kneels down and strikes her head against the floor just as she used to do when she worshiped idols. When I am in the shop here, I often hear her up stairs, bump—bump—bump; I wish you would speak to her about it." This woman declared that she would never have any thing to do with making or selling bean-curd on Sunday. A daughter, who assisted her parents somewhat in the work, sided with her mother, and poor Ah-san was obliged to do what he could on Sunday alone.

Another difficulty arose which neither he nor any one else had anticipated. The week following his suspension, he had, as he told me afterward, an unpleasant pricking sensation on the back of his neck, with a slight swelling. In a few days it became a very painful boil, and the next Sunday he was from necessity obliged to shut his shop. Some of the native Christians called on him and suggested that there might be a providence in this. He replied, "Oh, I have had boils before; it will all be over in a day or two." But the boil grew more painful, and proved to be a carbuncle; week after week it gave him hardly a moment's sleep; but he kept up his courage, hoping that every week would be the last. He spent a large sum of money in employing physicians, but to no purpose. He became very weak and emaciated, and we began to fear that his sickness might terminate fatally. At last a change came over his feelings; he acknowledged that he felt that God's hand was in his sufferings, and declared his determination that, if God would spare his life and restore him to health, his shop should never be opened again on Sunday. Very soon after this he was relieved from pain, and recovered his health. When I last heard from him, he was still to be found in his bean-curd shop by the side of the Bing-gyiao deo chapel; his shop is strictly closed on Sunday, and he has not come to want.

Just before leaving China, I had practical evidence of the strictness with which the Sabbath is observed in our out-stations. After a pleasant visit in San-poh, Mr. Dodd and myself arrived at Yu-yiao on Friday evening, to spend some time in that station. Most of Friday evening, Saturday, and Saturday evening till a late hour were spent in examining candidates for baptism. On Sunday fifteen were received into the church—ten women and five men, and sat down with us for the first time at the Lord's table. It was a time long to be remembered by us. The scene we then witnessed was almost enough to satisfy a missionary for a life of labor and trial, and one on which angels might look with delight. It was ten o'clock at night before all the native Christians had left the chapel for their homes. Being very desirous of returning to Ningpo as soon on Monday as possible, as I was busily engaged in preparing to return to this country, I suggested to Mr. Dodd that we might take our bundles to our boat, which was lying about a quarter of a mile from the chapel, and sleep there, taking advantage of the ebb-tide, by which the boatmen could leave for Ningpo at twelve in the night. The native preacher, Kying Ling-yiu, hearing of our plan, requested us not to do so for the following reason. Said he, "Our people here are very stiff on the Sabbath question. Some time since a letter came here from Mr. Rankin, at Ningpo, to be forwarded in haste to San-poh. It arrived on Saturday. A passenger and mail boat was to leave the next day, but there would be none on Monday, and I feared that the detaining of the letter till Tuesday might be attended by serious inconvenience. So I handed it to Jun-kao, requesting him on his return home to give it to the boatman to take by the first opportunity. 'Why,' said he, 'the boat starts on Sunday. I will do no such thing!' and the letter was not sent till Tuesday. Now I know that what you propose to do is perfectly right, but I fear that it would give rise to remark and misapprehension, and might do some harm." We thanked him for his frankness, and, to prevent lowering in any degree the standard of Sabbath observance already established in this infant church, we waited till Monday P.M.

And now, with a few words respecting the man Jun-kao above referred to, I will close this long chapter and this subject. When our native assistant first went to Yu-yiao, Jun-kao was known there as one of the most notoriously wicked men in the place. We little imagined that he would be among the first converts there; but God had chosen him. He became an earnest and out-spoken Christian, and, as was evident to all, a truly reformed man, though he still felt it allowable for him to take his wine, and sometimes took it rather too freely. (He has since given it up altogether.) In order to be able to observe the Sabbath, he relinquished a comparatively easy and lucrative employment and took up the carpenter's trade, which he learned in his youth. At the time of my visit above referred to, he had been instrumental in bringing about fifteen persons, members of his family, relatives, and friends, into the church. He was by no means a perfect character, and probably gave more trouble to his pastor than almost any other member of the church, by his eccentricities, impulsiveness, and self-will; but it was equally true that no other church member was a more efficient helper. He has more than once stumbled and fallen, but he has never been utterly cast down, and his course has on the whole been a very consistent one.

These chapters on missions have far exceeded the bounds which I at first intended. I trust they may have the effect to satisfy the reader that there are in China true, earnest, and self-sacrificing native Christians, and native churches full of promise. My testimony is, and I speak of what I know from personal experience and observation, having been as familiarly and intimately acquainted with many of these native Christians as a pastor at home can be with the members of his flock, that the work of missions in China is in no sense "a failure." The Gospel of Christ there, as elsewhere, has proved itself to be "the wisdom of God and the power of God unto salvation."

CHAPTER XXV.

ROMAN CATHOLIC MISSIONS IN CHINA.

The Manner in which the early Missionaries of Rome gained an Entrance into the Chinese Empire.—Their Compromise of the Truth, and the Controversies and Dissensions between different Religious Orders.—Secular Employments.—The Mode of prosecuting their Missionary Work.—Character of the Missionaries.—Statistics of Missionary Results.—Their Improvement of the Advantages of the late Treaties.—Character of the Native Christians.—A Reference to the Religious Literature of the Church of Rome in China.—The Excellences and Defects of the System.—Its probable Influence on the Future of the Empire.

THE present and prospective influence of the Church of Rome upon the Chinese Empire renders the consideration of the missions of that Church a matter of much interest and importance. It is unnecessary to repeat the statements which were made in Chapter XX. respecting the first introduction of this faith into the East.

The labors of the early founders of the Roman Catholic missions in China were attended with many practical difficulties. Matteo Ricci gained an entrance into the country, and a favorable consideration for his new religion, by teaching astronomy and Western sciences, and thus conciliating the favor of the Emperor. In retaining his position at court and making converts from the natives, he compromised the truth of Christianity, and made concessions to idolatry to such an extent as to call forth the most decided protest and opposition of his own Church, a writer of which gives to him the following character: "Ricci was active, skillful, full of schemes, and endowed with all the talents necessary to render him agreeable to the great, or to gain the favor of princes; but at the same time so little versed in matters of faith that, as the Bishop of Conon said, it was sufficient to read his work on the true religion to be satisfied that he was ignorant of the first principles of theology. Being more of a politician than a theologian, he found the secret of remaining peacefully in China. The kings found in him a man full of complaisance; the pagans a minister who accommodated himself to their superstitions; the Mandarins a polite courtier, skilled in all the trickery of courts; and the devil a faithful servant, who, far from destroying, established his reign among the heathen, and even extended it to the Christians. He preached in China the religion of Christ according to his own fancy; that is to say, he disfigured it by a faithful mixture of pagan superstitions, adopting the sacrifices offered to Confucius and ancestors, and teaching the Christians to assist and co-operate at the worship of idols, provided they only addressed their devotions to a cross covered with flowers, or secretly attached to one of the candles which were lighted in the temples of the false gods."*

Ricci, in tolerating the worship of Confucius and of ancestors, justified himself in taking this course on the ground that these ceremonies were civil rather than religious in their character, being an expression of respect for the memory of worthy men, rather than of divine worship paid to gods. When a warm controversy arose on this subject between Ricci, together with the order of Jesuits to which he belonged, and the Dominicans, the Chinese Emperor took sides with the Jesuits, and granted toleration to the religion of Rome only in the form in which they taught it.

When the Pope's assumption of supreme authority over all kings and their subjects, and the contentions of the different religious orders had excited the suspicion and strict surveillance of the government, the teachers of Rome could retain their position in the empire only by exercising duplicity, and redoubling their efforts to make themselves useful to the Emperor in a secular way. Their employments were at this time

* "Anecdotes de le China," tome i. pref. vi. vii.

diversified by teaching and superintending the casting of cannon, and planning and constructing water-clocks and fountains for the Emperor's palace. It is said, on the authority of the missionaries themselves, that in 1636 Schaal cast a number of cannon for the Emperor Shunchi, and "Verbiest at one time cast one hundred and thirty pieces for Kanghi with wonderful success: he afterward cast three hundred and twenty more, which he blessed in a solemn manner, and gave the name of a saint to every piece."*

Yung-ching, the successor of Kanghi, issued an order in 1724 prohibiting the propagation of the Roman Catholic religion, and commanding all the missionaries not required at Pekin for scientific purposes to leave the country. Some of them succeeded in secreting themselves; and others who were sent away, stealthily found their way back to their flocks. During the period of more than a hundred years of persecution which ensued, many of the native Christians and some of the foreign teachers suffered death for their devotion to their religion. The manner in which the missionaries were accustomed to prosecute their labors previous to the recent treaties of toleration is given in the following extracts from Williams's "Middle Kingdom" and Edkins's "Religious Condition of the Chinese:"

"When a new missionary arrives, he is lodged with his brethren until a trusty guide comes from the country to conduct him to his appointed place. He adopts the Chinese garb; and with little or no knowledge of the language, commits himself to the care of the courier. 'Sometimes on foot, sometimes in boats, sometimes like a rich man in his sedan, and sometimes under the guise of an officer in his chariot, he pursues his course. If suspected, which is often the case, from the blue color of his eyes, the length or turn of his nose, or the fairness of his skin, he turns his face to the wall; if addressed with impertinent questions, he either feigns deafness, or professes not to understand the dialect of the ques-

* Williams's "Middle Kingdom."

tioner. If the case become an extreme one, and his conductor can not browbeat or evade the challenger, he declares him an idiot, whom he is conducting to his friends in another part of the empire; or the party seek safety in sudden flight, and come together again under cover of darkness.' When they reach their field of labor, the new missionaries are placed under the direction of their associates, spending some of their time in learning the language, and in hearing confessions with the aid of a manual prepared for that purpose. As they advance in knowledge of the language and of their charge, they go from one *Christianity* (as the separate circles of converts are called) to another, hearing confessions and masses, administering baptism and extreme unction, and performing the various duties belonging to a pastor's office. They are constantly changing their residence, which both diminishes the chances of their detection, and tends to the preservation of their health."

"The numbers of the native Catholic community in China are kept up chiefly at present by teaching within the community itself. Few converts, comparatively, are made from the surrounding heathen. The successive persecutions instituted by the government checked the aggressive efforts of the missions, and chilled the zeal of those who were contemplating the adoption of the Catholic faith. As the missionaries arrive from Europe, they are conveyed secretly into the interior under the care of converts, and pass their time afterward entirely in the society of the members of the community. Strangers are not permitted to know of their presence. The boatmen or chair-bearers who conduct them from place to place are native Christians. So also are their servants at the residences provided for them. On their reaching any station to perform their official duties, information is quickly communicated to all the residents who regard them as their spiritual guides, and they then assemble to receive their blessing. It is indispensable when they enter the room where the European priest is seated that they should perform a prostration before him. No one outside of the community is allowed to see the foreign priest till he has gone through a course of instruction under the native catechists and priests. When a heathen is ready for baptism he may have an interview with the 'spiritual father from the Western ocean,' but not usually sooner. This circumspection is rendered necessary by the state of the laws in China, which have hitherto not permitted the entrance of foreigners into the interior of the country. Very irksome is the restraint under which foreign priests are placed, for it is not considered safe for them to be noticed by any eyes except those of trusted friends. Sometimes when a rumor is spread of their presence in a walled city, they are conveyed in a sedan chair out of the gate, and brought in again by the gate on the opposite side of the city. This is done to induce the belief that they have taken their departure. They usually, however, avoid cities altogether and remain in the country, where accommodations are provided for them under the superintendence of the converts. They are liable to ejection at any moment from their temporary lodging-place, should suspicion be excited and inquiry be made for them. Huc speaks in his 'Travels in Tartary and Thibet' of the enjoyment occasioned to him and his companion by their sense of freedom when they had passed beyond the Great Wall into Tartary, because there they could allow themselves to be seen without fear of capture. In these circumstances, the gathering in of new converts is left to the zeal and efficiency of the native converts."

Many of the early Romish missionaries of China were men of decided ability and learning, and of earnest zeal and devotion. Those of the present day, though not wanting in the latter qualities, are, judging from those whom I have met, from the comparative want of literary works of a high order of recent date, and from the character of native converts, inferior in ability and culture to their predecessors.

The following statistics, taken from Williams's "Middle Kingdom," will give some idea of the state of Roman Catholic missions soon after the treaty which opened the "five ports:" "The summary for the year 1846 gives twelve bishops, seven or eight coadjutors, about eighty foreign missionaries, and ninety native priests. The number of converts in the whole is now not far from 400,000. The number of schools is not given; in Sz-chuen alone there are fifty-four for boys, and one hundred and fourteen for girls. There are six colleges for educating native priests, including that at Naples, but we can not learn the total number of pupils. The amount of funds received from Europe for them all in 1846 was about $59,000."

Under the protection of the recent treaties the missions of the Romish Church are being carried on openly, and with renewed activity and very decided results. The number of foreign priests has been greatly increased; new schools and foundling asylums have been established; and many female assistants have entered the field, and are busily employed in connection with foundling asylums; visiting from house to house, dispensing medicine, conciliating the good-will of the people, and baptizing the children. Under the provisions of the late treaties, land and important building-sites which were taken from the Roman Catholics during the persecutions of former years have been restored, thus giving them prestige among the people, and furnishing them with additional means for extending their operations.

The comparatively large number of converts connected with the Romish Church is readily accounted for by the length of time during which its missions have been prosecuted; the striking resemblance, described in Chapter VIII. between its doctrines and rites and those of Buddhism; by the fact that very little knowledge or evidence of a change of heart and life is deemed requisite to church membership; and the freedom accorded to native converts in allowing them to work on Sunday, and to conform in many respects to the superstitious practices of their countrymen. Their religion consists in being baptized, and attending regularly the mass and the confessional, and believing that their souls are safe in the keeping of the Church and the priest. In order to participate in the benefits conferred by the Church, they are taught that they must abjure all connection with the worship of Chinese gods, and never deny, on pain of eternal punishment, the religion which they have adopted. The result is, that they generally keep aloof from the idolatrous worship of Buddhism and Tauism, bear testimony to the universal duty of worshiping one God and believing in one Saviour, and will generally adhere to their religious professions to the death. But in renouncing idolatry as taught by Buddhism, they still practice it in another form; worshiping saints and intercessors, pictures, images, and crucifixes; believing in works of merit and supererogation; exercising blind faith in their religious teachers, and carrying about with them some engraving of our Saviour, or the cross, or other symbol, which is regarded with superstitious reverence, and sometimes as possessed of a talismanic charm.

An idea of the character of Romanism in China may be derived from their literature written for the instruction and admonition of the faithful. While it contains many works full of Christian truth and of sterling literary merit, it includes others as full of superstition, fables, and pious frauds as the works of Buddhism; thus presenting another strong resemblance to it. Before leaving China, I made a collection of many of their books, which I spent some time in reading. Some of them have left an impression on my mind which I can never forget; showing how well they are calculated to arrest the attention and impress the memory. I remember one in particular, which comprised several volumes, and had for its special object the explaining, illustrating, and enforcing of the different dogmas and practices of the Romish faith; such as celibacy, the celebration of the mass, making pilgrimages to holy places, etc. The Ten Commandments professedly form the basis of the book, and each doctrine or practice, in order to give it a divine sanction, is, by some means or other, associated with one of the commandments. The peculiar feature of this work is found in the alleged historical facts and experiences which are cited to prove the truth, and establish the importance of the rites and usages of the Church. These facts are evidently intended for those who are ignorant and uninformed, and are remarkably adapted to work upon their religious or superstitious fears. Some of them I will give from memory.

A whole community of the faithful are about to be massacred by an unbelieving king, and his soldiers are in attendance for this purpose, when he offers them life on the one condition that they shall verify the statement of their sacred book by causing a mountain before them to move by means of their prayers. A priest quiets the fears and trepidation of his followers, appears before the king, calls upon God to move the mountain, and it moves! and the astonished king becomes a true believer and propagator of the faith!

A young girl, who had devoted herself to a life of celibacy, is sought in marriage by the son of a person of wealth and rank, and is urged and tempted in a variety of ways to break her vow. In one of these efforts to shake her constancy, a person is struck dead in her presence, and then through her prayers he is immediately restored to life. She is then, on account of her exercise of mysterious and miraculous powers, accused of being a witch, and condemned as such to be burned; but the fire refuses to do its work, and the funeral pile is consumed to ashes, while she sits quietly and unconcerned, without even the smell of the flames on her garments. She afterward dies voluntarily, and reappears as a beautiful virgin clothed in white to console her mourning parents. It might be interesting to learn which of the Ten Commandments this book refers to as enjoining celibacy. The story of the girl just given is connected with the third commandment, "Thou shalt not take the name of the Lord thy God in vain." This is done in a manner something as follows: "It is a solemn thing to make a vow to God. Breaking such a vow is 'taking the name of God in vain;' therefore the vow of celibacy must never be broken."

A man in time of persecution was urged to deny his Saviour, but refused, asseverating that the name of Jesus was deeply engraven on his heart. He was immediately killed, his heart extracted, and the name was actually found clearly represented on it!

A company from Germany who had visited the Holy Land were just about going on board ship on their return. As mass was about to be performed in a church near by, one of the company declared that he could never neglect or turn away from this solemn ceremony, and determined to attend, even though he should lose his passage. The vessel sailed without him, and he started on his pilgrimage home on foot. He was soon overtaken by a person on horseback, who asked him to ride. In the course of a few hours, during which the time was beguiled with delightful religious conversation, he found himself at his cottage door in Germany; and his conductor, who proved an apparition of some celestial being, vanished. The less pious and scrupulous of the party arrived at home in the ordinary course of travel in about two months.

An earnest believer who determined to go regularly to mass, though his employer insisted on his keeping busy at the plough, was relieved by an angel in the form of a farm laborer, who attended the plough while the laborer was absent at the service.

Scoffers and unbelievers are dealt with in this book in a very summary and frightful manner. Once upon a time, when a "good Catholic" was going somewhere on a pilgrimage to obtain sacred ashes, he was told by a person with whom he was stopping by the way that he could get enough ashes in his kitchen without going any farther; whereupon the heap of ashes in the kitchen was lifted up by a furious wind and blown into his eyes, ears, and nose, tormenting and frightening him to such an extent that, in his frenzy, he jumped into the canal and drowned himself. On another occasion, a person unfriendly to the holy religion was ridiculing the elevating of the host among a company of friends at dinner by going through the forms connected with that ceremony by way of amusement. When his hands were uplifted in the act of blessing the host, to the horror of all present, they were immediately fixed in that posture, and remained so through life; so that when he was buried, a coffin was made of a peculiar shape adapted to accommodate this unnatural position of the body!

These are samples of the kind of matter of which this book is full. From the foregoing statements and representations taken from the Roman Catholic literature of China, the reader can draw his own inference respecting the character of the missionaries and native Christians of that Church. I would not be understood, however, as presenting this book as a fair sample of their literature generally, though many others have a strong resemblance to it. That one such book is sanctioned and tolerated in this enlightened age by the adherents of any religion, Christian or pagan, may well excite our wonder. That there are many persons among the missionaries and converts of the Romish Church in China who are honest and sincere in their religious convictions, I do not doubt. I rejoice to hope and believe also, that the truth of God, though held by them in a corrupted form, and with a large admixture of the commandments of men, has, by the blessing of God, been the means of the spiritual regeneration and salvation of many. In the language of Dr. Williams, to whose admirable work on China I have so often had occasion to refer, "The letters of some of the missionaries to their own friends breathe a spirit of pious ardor and true Christian principle worthy of all imitation. * * * * Many of their converts also exhibit the greatest constancy in their profession, suffering persecution, torture, imprisonment, banishment, and death, rather than deny their faith, though every inducement of prevarication and mental reservation was held out to them by the magistrates to avoid the necessity of proceeding to extreme measures. If suffering the loss of all things is an evidence of piety, many of them have proved their title to it in many ways. But until there shall be a complete separation from idolatry and superstition; until the confessional shall be abolished, and the worship of the Virgin, wearing crosses and rosaries, and reliance on ceremonies and penances be stopped; until the entire Scriptures and Decalogue be given to the converts; and until, in short, the great doctrine of justification by faith be substituted for the many forms of justification by works, the mass of converts to Romanism in China can hardly be considered as much better than baptized pagans. Their works and influence upon their pagan countrymen show how little leaven of godliness there has been in the lump, and both priest and people can not well refuse to be judged by evidence furnished by themselves."

That such a religion, holding, though imperfectly, the great truths of the unity of God and salvation through a Redeemer, and thus contrasting favorably with the gross forms of Chinese idolatry, while, at the same time, it adapts itself to the customs and prejudices of the people, should speedily gain currency among such a people as the Chinese, is not surprising. It will no doubt have a powerful influence in co-operating with other causes to subvert and overthrow the existing systems of idolatry; but we may not look to it to supply the Chinese with a pure, vital, and aggressive Christianity. It may spread rapidly at first, but it can not bear the ordeal of free discussion, which it must ere long meet with. At present, in so wide a field, the representatives of the Romish and the Protestant Churches labor apart. But when the influence of both shall have extended, and the reign of Buddhism and Tauism shall have passed away, the struggle will ultimately be in the East, as in the West, between the two forms of Christianity, Protestantism and Popery. The appeal will be to the sacred Scriptures, the common ground of our faith. Our confidence as to the result is in the power of God's truth, accompanied by the blessing of His Spirit.

CHAPTER XXVI.

THE TAI-PING REBELLION.

The Interest which has been felt by Western Nations in the Tai-ping Rebellion.—Early Life of Hung-sew-tswen.—He receives the Bible and Tracts from Missionaries.—His Sickness and fancied Revelations.—His Attention is directed anew to the Christian Books.—He constructs from them a new System of Religion, commences propagating it, and gains many Converts.—The Steps by which the Adherents of this corrupt Form of Christianity became an Insurgent Army.—The long Struggle for Empire, and the final Defeat and Overthrow of the Tai-ping Rebellion.

Few events connected with China have within the last twenty years excited as much interest in Western lands, or been as often referred to in our public prints, as the rebellions and civil wars which are desolating different parts of the country, and producing the impression in the minds of some not familiarly acquainted with the character and history of the government that a state of strife and anarchy is its normal condition. The great Tai-ping Rebellion is of special interest to us on account of its religious, or, rather, Christian character; and for this reason, as well as on account of its great influence on the present condition and future prospects of China, it merits a special consideration.

This remarkable movement originated with a man named Hung-sew-tswen, who was born in a small town near Canton in the year 1813. Though of a poor family, as he gave early evidence of a bright intellect and aptness for study, his parents and friends gave him the advantages of a Chinese education; and when about twenty years of age, he is found taking part in the literary examinations at Canton. Some time between the years 1833 and 1836, while attending these examinations, he received from the native preacher Liang-a-fah some Christian tracts, and portions of the Old and New Testament Scriptures. These seem to have been carelessly read, and to have produced at the time but little effect upon his mind. In 1837 he returned home from the literary examinations, in which he had been again unsuccessful, seriously ill, and in a desponding state of mind. During his sickness, which continued for more than a month, he was subject to mental aberration, and regarded himself as being favored with supernatural manifestations and revelations. He thought that he was washed from the impurities of his nature; that he had a new heart given to him; and was introduced into the presence of an august being, who exhorted him to lead a virtuous life and exterminate demons. During his sickness he also "often saw a man of middle age, whom he called his elder brother, who instructed him how to act, accompanied him in his wanderings to the uttermost regions in search of evil spirits, and assisted him in slaying and exterminating them." These fancied revelations seem to have produced a deep impression on his mind, and to have changed his character and outward demeanor, though, after his recovery, he returned to his quiet occupation as a student and village school-teacher.

In the year 1843, just after the war with England, and the establishment of new relations with Western nations, when it was natural for the minds of the natives to be directed toward foreigners, a friend of Hung, whose name was Le, was led to read the foreign books in Hung's library, which it appears had been disregarded for years. He became much interested, and through him they were again brought before the attention of Hung, and were the means of giving a new shape to his life, and opening before him a new and remarkable career. "He was greatly astonished to find in these books the key to his own visions which he had six years before. He now understood the venerable old man who sat upon the highest place, and whom all men ought to worship, to be God, the Heavenly Father; and the man of middle age who had instructed him, and assisted him in exterminating the demons, to be Jesus, the Saviour of the world; the demons were the idols."

The conviction now fixed itself upon his mind that he had held real communications with the God of Heaven, and had been intrusted by Him with a special mission. He and his friend Le studied carefully, and thought deeply on the subjects treated of in these books. By degrees they developed a system of religion containing a modicum of Christian truth, together with many singular misconceptions, and vagaries of their imaginations. They baptized each other, and commenced propagating among their friends and neighbors this new and remarkable form of Christianity. The first converts were made in the vicinity of their own home, including several literary men or teachers, and the parents, brothers, and relatives of Hung. Among the teachers was one, Fung-yun-san, who afterward became a prominent actor in the history of this new movement. He and Hung, after losing their pupils in consequence of having removed the tablet of Confucius and abolished the religious rites paid to him in the school, left their home in the beginning of 1844 to preach in other parts, hoping to support themselves by selling ink and writing-pencils. After visiting numerous places in the province of Kwang-se, they spent some months with a relative of Hung living in the southern part of the province, and made there more than one hundred converts. Fung-yun-san, fearing to be burdensome to Hung's relatives, left with the intention of returning home. On his way, he met some workmen with whom he was acquainted, and remained with them, assisting in their occupation of carrying earth, and at the same time propagating his religion among them. "Ten of them soon became his converts; and having introduced him to the notice of their employer, the latter engaged him as a teacher, and was shortly after himself baptized. Fung-yun-san was thus enabled to remain several years in the neighborhood, preaching with great zeal and such success that whole families of various surnames and clans were baptized, formed congregations among themselves, and became extensively known under the name of the 'Society of God-worshipers.'"

Hung-sew-tswen, soon after Fung had left him, also returned home, and spent his time studying and writing on religious subjects and teaching others. In the summer of 1847 he went to Canton, where he formed the acquaintance of Mr. Roberts, an American missionary of the Baptist Church, and received instruction from him for two months. He then applied for baptism, and for a position in connection with Mr. Roberts as a native preacher or assistant. Both of these proposals Mr. Roberts declined, probably fearing, from his asking a place, that he was actuated by mercenary motives. Foreign missionaries frequently meet with applications of this kind; and Mr. Roberts seems to have regarded this case as not differing particularly from others, little dreaming of the bold undertaking which this poor and obscure country school-teacher was about to initiate.

Leaving Canton, he went into Kwang-se to visit his relatives, through whom he learned of the movements of Fung-yun-san, and of his success in propagating the new faith. He immediately visited the converts there, and found that they had increased to about two thousand persons, and that accessions were constantly made to their numbers from the surrounding districts. He was welcomed by these co-religionists as the founder of their sect, and his presence and superior knowledge and ability gave a new impulse to the movement. The God-worshipers soon attracted the attention of the people, and their known and avowed purpose to destroy idolatry excited suspicion and alarm. It was not long before complaints were made against them as a corrupt, dangerous, and rebellious sect; and Fung-yun-san and another person who had been a prominent iconoclast were cast into prison. The latter died in jail, and the local authorities determined to send the former, in charge of two policemen, to his native district. "During the journey, Fung-yun-san, in his usual manner, spoke with great eloquence and in persuasive language about the doctrine, and they had not walked many miles before the two policemen were won as converts. They not only agreed to set him at liberty instantly, but declared themselves willing to abandon their own station and follow Fung to the congregation at Thistle Mount, where he soon after introduced them as candidates for baptism."

While the prime actors in establishing this new religion were travelling hither and thither on different missions, new developments were taking place among the God-worshipers in Kwang-se. In their congregations for worship persons would sometimes fall down in a fit or trance, and give utterance to alleged revelations, prophecies, etc. Records were made of many of these utterances, which seem to have varied so much in their character that some were regarded as coming from God, and some from the devil. Particular persons became noted for their revelations, and were regarded as the acknowledged instruments for communicating the Divine Will.

It was impossible for such a community to exist long without coming to an open outbreak with the authorities, and such an event took place in the autumn of 1850. The position of the God-worshipers now became perilous in the extreme. They were in danger of being sought out and exterminated as a corrupt and dangerous element in the body-politic. While they were obliged to sacrifice their lives or fight in self-defense, their rapid increase in numbers, and the fancied favor and protection of the God they worshiped, encouraged them to undertake aggressive movements, with the object not only of propagating their faith, but also of establishing an independent empire.

The members of this religious society, converting their property into ready-money, cast it into a common fund or treasury. Hung-sew-tswen organized them into an army, and introduced the strictest discipline. They first attacked individuals and towns which had opposed and persecuted them on account of their religion, and obtained without difficulty all needed supplies of food and clothing. The disaffected of the people flocked to their standard, and numerous bands of robbers and banditti gave in their adherence, were instructed in some degree in the doctrines and forms of the new religion, and incorporated as a part of the army. The troops sent by the government to suppress this insurrection were scattered like chaff before the wind; city after city fell before the triumphant march of these God-worshipers, and the whole empire was struck with surprise and terror.

Hung-sew-tswen, elated with success, and confirmed in his belief of his divine commission, aspired to higher prerogatives, and projected bolder plans. He proclaimed himself the head of a new kingdom styled *Tai-ping tien kwoh*—"The Peaceful Heavenly Kingdom," and assumed the title of Son of Heaven. Christ was familiarly spoken of as his brother, and he professed to have frequent communications from the Heavenly Father. Many views of his character and mission seem to have been derived from the Pentateuch. As Moses was called of God to be his medium of communication with the Israelites, and to found a new religion and kingdom, exterminating the Canaanites and destroying every vestige of idolatry, so he regarded himself as the chosen instrument of God to declare his will, and establish a new Chinese dynasty; driving out the Manchus, and introducing the worship of the living and true God in the place of the false gods of Confucianism, Buddhism, and Tauism.

Religious worship was kept up in the camp. The Sabbath was observed, the day chosen by them being our Saturday, or the Jewish Sabbath. The Scriptures were read and expounded according to their understanding of them; prayers were offered; hymns and doxologies sung in honor of the Triune God; and eloquent preachers exhorted the multitude, urging them to honor and obey God, to be faithful to his vicegerent the new Emperor, and to fight bravely for the establishment of the "heavenly dynasty;" promising positions of honor and influence in the new state, as well as eternal blessedness in heaven. It is said that before battle they often knelt down under the open heaven and invoked the protection and assistance of the Heavenly Father, and then charged upon their enemies with the assurance of success. The strong bond of union produced by common dangers, mutual dependence, common religious sympathies, and a common aim, with a faith in their destiny, and their strong religious or fanatical zeal, gave them a power which the imperial armies could not withstand. When towns or cities submitted to their authority without opposition, they were treated with leniency; when they denied and resisted their claims, they were regarded as acting in opposition to the will of Heaven, and consequently as having forfeited their lives, and were devoted to indiscriminate slaughter.

Such, in general, was the character of this remarkable organization which spread terror and desolation through the interior provinces of the empire. Their course from Kwang-se was to the north. Traversing the northern part of the province of Kwang-se, the whole of the province of Ho-nan and part of Hoo-peh, a distance of about six hundred miles, they reached the largest trading-mart of China, Wu-chang, situated on the Great River. Capturing and plundering this place with its suburbs, and destroying a considerable part of it, they proceeded down the river by boats, and, after taking other less important cities, possessed themselves of Nankin, which Hung-sew-tswen determined to make the capital of his new kingdom. So terrified were the Tartar garrison of this great and powerful city that they gave up all hope of resistance and plead for mercy. Belonging, however, to a race which the insurgents regarded as usurpers, and which, when they conquered China, slaughtered millions of its inhabitants, they were all put to death, men, women, and children, to the number of about twenty thousand.

When the Tai-pings had established themselves in Nankin, they addressed themselves to the work of subjugating the empire. A very important expedition started north for the purpose of taking Pekin. The entire failure of this enterprise gave to the rebellion a serious check, and encouraged the reigning dynasty in putting it down. Other expeditions in different provinces were more successful, and many districts and parts of provinces were obliged to submit for a longer or shorter time to the control of the dreaded Chang-mao.*

For some years there seemed to be much reason to fear that the reigning dynasty would be exhausted and overpowered, and that the rebels would establish their rule over the eighteen provinces. Some foreigners hoped that the rebels might possess themselves of the empire, found a beneficent government, enter into more friendly relations with Western nations, and adopt modern ideas and a Christian civilization.

These hopes, however, were doomed to disappointment. Camp-life was not found favorable to the cultivation of religion and morality. Many of the better class of the rebels died on the battle-field or in the camp, and their places were supplied by persons of a very inferior character. Their form of religion became more and more corrupt, and the religious element, which was their principal source of strength, became weaker and weaker.

Hung, while continuing to profess great respect and friendship for Christian nations, calling foreigners brethren, and seeming desirous of entering into cordial relations with them, assumed a pre-eminence and arrogance almost exceeding that of the Emperors of the reigning dynasty. He spoke of his own revelations from heaven as having the same authority as those in the Scriptures, and as being of more importance, and, in some instances, superseding those of the Bible on account of their being more recent. His religious views became more

* *Chang-mao*, or "Long-haired," was the name almost universally given to the rebels by the Chinese. The shaving of the front part of the head is a Manchu custom, and was imposed upon the Chinese after their subjugation as a token of allegiance. The rebels, throwing off their allegiance, allowed the hair to grow, and so were called "Long-hairs," this being a synonym for rebels.

and more erratic and fanatical, and naturally suggested the idea of a certain degree of mental aberration. Some of our most intelligent missionaries succeeded in reaching his capital several years after his establishment in Nankin, and were kindly received, but were able to exercise no influence over him. Mr. Roberts was invited to take an office under the new government, which he accepted; but finding that he could accomplish nothing, and that his position was far from being a desirable or comfortable one, left Nankin in disgust.

The character and acts of the military chiefs deteriorated even more rapidly than that of their leader. They began to act independently of their head, and to quarrel among themselves. Corruption and disaffection spread among the subordinate officers and soldiers. The Tai-pings were still able to ravage and desolate the provinces, but they showed very little ability for reorganization and pacification. The more wealthy and influential classes refused to trust them, or to recognize in them the future rulers and tranquilizers of the empire.

In the mean time, hoping to retrieve their waning fortunes, the rebels endeavored to take possession of the coast provinces, and avail themselves of the advantages of the commerce of their ports. They were driven back, however, from Shanghai by English forces, aided by the Chinese. They succeeded in taking Ningpo with very little opposition and very little bloodshed, and seemed desirous of continuing on friendly terms with us and engaging in foreign trade. They were, however, soon driven out from that city by English troops; and chiefly by the aid of the English, the capital cities of Su-chow and Hang-chow, with others of less note, were wrested from them. It is due to them to say that, notwithstanding their intercourse with and treatment by foreign nations was calculated to embitter their minds and give rise to resentment and retaliation, foreign residents in Ningpo and foreign travellers who visited them in the interior were almost invariably received with cordiality and respect, and treated with kindness.

Driven out of their strongholds in the Kiang-su and the Che-kiang provinces, they retired to Nankin. Here they were reduced to great straits; but having experienced relief and succor in similar circumstances before, they still kept up an obstinate defense, hoping that the tide of fortune would again turn in their favor. The Chinese authorities were so sure of capturing this city and crushing out the rebellion that they insisted on finishing the work alone, and the English troops withdrew.

In the summer of 1864 an immense besieging army could be seen from the decks of foreign steamers which were constantly traversing the great river, completely surrounding the doomed city of Nankin. It had for years been emptied of its numerous and cultivated inhabitants, tens of thousands of whom, reared in luxury, had wandered about as refugees, and died of exposure, grief, and starvation. It was now a military camp, and a scene of desolation. Many of the rebels, anticipating the result of the siege, had escaped, and joined insurgent and predatory bands in other parts. Some of those who remained might be seen fishing on the banks of the river, secure from the occasional shots of the enemy, who kept at a safe distance on the opposite side of the stream. It was evidently the intention of the besieging army to reduce to starvation those whom they knew would expect no quarter, and would sell their lives as dearly as possible.

In July, 1864, Nankin, the last stronghold of the Tai-ping rebels, who had struggled for the empire for fourteen years, was taken, and, with its fall, the last hope of the Tai-ping dynasty perished. Hung-sew-tswen committed suicide, but many of his officers and soldiers were captured and executed.

A movement of such vast proportions, and continuing for so many years, though failing in its special object, could not but produce great changes and results.

It effected foreign nations, in cutting off in a measure the supplies and closing up the channels of trade. It has devastated some of the richest and most beautiful portions of the

Chinese Empire, leaving behind it tracts of desolation, marked for hundreds of miles by blackened walls and heaps of ruins, uncultivated fields, and depopulated towns and cities. The present dynasty has received a blow from which it will not soon recover. Its treasury has been exhausted, its resources drained; its people have become accustomed to the idea of rebellion, and various independent insurrections have been and still are springing up in different parts of the empire.

CHAPTER XXVII.

PRESENT CONDITION AND PROSPECTS OF THE CHINESE EMPIRE.

The Present of China a Period of Transition.—Her Aversion to Change.—Various Causes conspiring to introduce a new Order of Things.—General Principle of Development and Decline.—The History of China a Succession of Dynasties.—Local Insurrections and Rebellions.—Influences brought to bear upon China from foreign Lands.—Wars with England and France.—The necessary Effect of a Knowledge of the Modern Arts and Sciences, and of Christianity.—The Influence upon China of the Chinese who return Home from California.—The Government adopts Western Rules of International Law.—Chinese Youths studying Foreign Languages with a View to being Interpreters.—The Policy of the Empire principally influenced by the Exigencies of her present Position, and the Advice of Foreign Ministers and Employés in Pekin.—A University for teaching the Modern Sciences has been established.—The Origin, Character, and Results of the Chinese Embassy.—The Party of Progress, and the Objects for which they are striving. —The present Status of Missionaries.—China irrevocably committed to Reform and Progress.

The present of China is emphatically a period of transition. As seen by a superficial observer, she appears the same now that she has been for ages. The philosophy of Confucius still sways the minds of her inhabitants. The system of competitive examinations is strictly observed, as in former times. No idol temples have been destroyed, no ancient rites discontinued, no national usages or social customs changed. Still, there are causes in operation, and changes being wrought beneath the surface, which must result in a complete revolution of ideas, and affect the whole aspect of the nation. The present condition of China may be compared to that of a river covered with ice in the early spring. The genial sun shines upon it, and the warm winds breathe upon it, but it resists every softening influence, and retains the stern and unchanging aspect of winter. In a few favored spots, the sun has melted its congealed surface, and the limpid water reflects the beauties of sky and landscape, or leaps and sparkles under the passing breeze. Still, the great river, day after day, and week after week remains, to outward appearances, as it was. But the influences at work above and beneath can not be resisted, and that impenetrable covering, spread over so vast an extent, must either be swept away by the flood, or silently dissolve and disappear.

To bring about a new order of things in China, different causes are co-operating from within and from without. It must be remembered that civil wars and rebellions have been doing their work there for more than fifteen years. These protracted and exhausting struggles generally mark the decline and termination of individual dynasties, of which the whole history of China is made up. It is firmly believed by the people that national life, like vegetable and animal, has its period of growth and development, and then of decline and decay. It is not, however, the nation that dies, but the dynasty, while the nation lives on through the dynasties; just as a tree passing every year through the same succession of development and decay, still continues to grow in size and strength. This idea, which may be called a national one, has been strikingly expressed in an antithetical sentence found in a celebrated historical novel, and familiarly quoted even by many who can not read—"The great power of the empire, when long divided, will be reunited; when long united, will be divided."

The present, which is a Tartar dynasty, has ruled the empire for about two hundred years. It has furnished several noted Emperors, and established a proud record. The reigning house has still noble and patriotic men connected with it, but corruption in the capital and in the provinces is sapping the very foundations on which it rests. The people and their rulers have, in a great measure, mutually lost confidence in each other; and as the great Chinese sage has truly said, "A nation may more easily exist without an army and without provisions, than without *faith*." Wars have exhausted the treasury; the officers, being almost obliged, in order to support themselves, to resort to exaction, and to receive bribes, have become unblushingly familiar with these practices, and not a few make use of them to the extent of amassing immense fortunes. Thus the poverty and demoralization which are regarded as an excuse for extortion and oppression are constantly increasing. Offices are sold in order to replenish the public coffers, and disappointed scholars, who are thus shut out from the hope of preferment, help to spread discontent among the people. Ill-disposed, turbulent, and ambitious persons organize bands of robbers, which are recruited from those who are pinched by want, or outraged by oppression, or those who have been taken captives by violence, but choose to cast in their lot with their captors rather than return to desolated homes and a life of privation. One of these predatory bands but a few months since approached very near to the capital, and threatened to cut off its communication with the coast. The numerous independent rebellions which are springing up in different parts of the empire, while they are evidences of the weakness of the government, tend to weaken it still further, and matters have been proceeding from bad to worse.

The people are evidently not expecting the immediate return of peace, order, and good government. In the central provinces, multitudes of villages and cities which were devastated by the Tai-ping rebels are being rebuilt in an imperfect manner, and with less regard to permanency than to supplying the imperative wants of the present. In portions of the northern provinces which have been ravaged by predatory bands, the people employ the respite of temporary quiet during the intervals of invasion in providing means of defense for the future. In the province of Shantung, I have passed in one day's journey of thirty miles within sight of nearly twenty villages surrounded by high mud walls or embankments. These works of defense were the result of the labor of one summer. They were built by the inhabitants of a number of surrounding villages, who united in fortifying in this way a large central town, into which they might flee in time of invasion for mutual protection and defense. Occasionally one of these cities of refuge is seen on a high hill or mountain top, suggesting to the passing traveller scenes of rapine and terror through which the inhabitants of adjacent villages have passed, and the constant dread occasioned by the anticipation of their recurrence.

This state of things, in other times and under other circumstances, would be very apt to lead to a change of dynasty, the government remaining the same. But there are now new and powerful influences emanating from foreign lands which have never before been felt—at least to the same extent—and which must greatly affect the issue. It is for the present rulers of China to determine whether they will ignore or resist these influences, and thus make the downfall of their government more certain and rapid, or whether they will find in them new sources of strength and recuperation. There is reason to hope that they are disposed to pursue the latter course, and that by availing themselves of the assistance which may be drawn from abroad, they may retrieve their fortunes, reassure their people, and perpetuate their dynasty, by reforming it, and adjusting it to their new relations with the world, and the necessities of the present age.

The Chinese have for many centuries rested in the conclusion that their form of government and civilization was the best that could be devised; that the teachings of their sages were complete; and that there was nothing to be learned from other nations. This one comprehensive conclusion, to doubt which would almost have been regarded by them as an evidence of stupidity or insanity, has been an insuperable barrier in the way of development and progress, and one which it has been very difficult to remove. Intercourse with foreign nations has been gradually, but in a variety of ways, correcting this error.

The foreign wars with China, especially the last one with England and France, the influence of which was felt in the very seat of the Chinese Empire, has shown the abject helplessness of that nation in the face of a foreign force vastly inferior in numbers. Still they may, and do, say that an ability to fight is no evidence of a superior race and civilization, but rather the contrary. It is a quality which results from brute force and courage, and naturally belongs to uncultivated barbarians and savages.

They have been accustomed to point with pride to the arts of peace as evidences of China's greatness and superiority, to her internal improvements, vast resources, public works, commerce, and manufactories. Our descriptions of the modern arts as practiced in our own country, of our superior architecture and ship-building; our railroads, steam-boats, telegraphs, newspapers, postal arrangements, and public schools, do not produce the impression upon them that we might expect. Of many of these arts they do not fully appreciate the advantages, while they think it is but natural for us to speak well of our own country; and may still imagine that an intelligent eye-witness from among them, who would be able to make a just comparison, would bring a very different report. They have seen some articles of foreign manufactures, such as watches and clocks, sewing-machines and steam-engines, and are willing to concede that in some respects we have a remarkable mechanical skill, and give evidence of a great deal of ingenuity and cleverness. They freely admit that we are an intelligent and curious people, who have distinguished ourselves by our proficiency in some of the mechanic arts; but they pride themselves upon their acquaintance with the mysterious sciences of astrology, divination, geomancy, ontology, necromancy, etc., treated of in their extensive literature—branches of learning esteemed by them as hardly second to any others in importance.

This inner wall of the defenses of national pride and prejudice is beginning to be undermined. A slight acquaintance with modern science is sufficient to shake the confidence of the people in those false and imaginary sciences which have had such an influence on their minds for ages. For instance, the production and effects of electricity are referred by them to a particular deity called the God of Thunder. Now, by the use of a small electrical machine, we can show them how this fluid is generated, and thunder and lightning produced; and can explain how electricity may be used for the purpose of the rapid communication of information. They believe that there are five simple elements in nature—*metal*, *wood*, *water*, *fire*, and *earth*—and they have no idea of any analysis by which any of these substances can be resolved into simpler ones. These *five elements* lie at the basis of different systems of astrology, geomancy, divination, and medicine; and the prominence and mysterious influences of these great powers in nature are often referred to as well-established and important conclusions of science.

To illustrate this subject, I will refer to the application of these fundamental ideas to the practice of medicine. It is supposed that these "five elements" have some mysterious connection with and relation to the different parts of the body, such as the heart, the lungs, the stomach, the liver, etc. If a disease is found to be in the part or organ of the body connected with the element *metal*, then the medicine must be drawn from the mineral kingdom; if in a part connected with the element *wood*, it must be drawn from the vegetable kingdom, and so on indefinitely. This will give a general idea of the wide application of these "first principles" of the Chinese, and of the revolution of ideas which must result from a slight knowledge of chemistry, showing, as it does, that the basis on which these various systems rests is unscientific and foolish in the extreme. These superstitious notions and theories of imaginary sciences are connected, as may be seen from the examples given above, with the Chinese systems of idolatry and philosophy, and with their social life; and the obliteration of one prominent doctrine of their system tends to produce distrust of the whole, and to disenthrall the mind, and send it forth on a new search for truth.

But the principal ground of the Chinese belief in their own superiority is to be found in the ethical and political teachings of Confucianism. This is the stronghold of their confidence and pride. Yet even here their minds are becoming seriously and painfully exercised. They listen with surprise to the propagators of a new religion, who, while speaking with great respect of Confucius and the system to which he has given his name, and confirming and reasserting many of the truths which he taught, dare to point out the defects of his system, and to present another with a superior character and claims. They find that, instead of the baseless assumptions and vague surmises which are connected with the religions with which they have heretofore been acquainted, this one from Western lands asks for no blind faith, appeals to no popular prejudice or superstition, but presents its irrefragable evidences and proofs. It comes not to corrupt and delude the people, but to instruct and elevate them, and to lay broader and deeper the foundations of social order and permanent prosperity and peace. It explores regions of truth into which their sages have not ventured; it brings to view a purer morality, a more disinterested love, a more spiritual and intense devotion, and a new and higher life. The careful and candid Chinese student opens his eyes to a new world of intellectual and spiritual light, and is reluctantly forced to acknowledge that a greater than Confucius is here.

The new ideas and influences referred to above have not yet become general and operative among the masses, but they have taken strong hold of individuals, and are extending in ever widening spheres, and with ever increasing power.

In this connection, it is proper to speak of the influence we are exerting upon China from our Western coast through the thousands of Chinese emigrants who are visiting our shores, and returning in great numbers to their homes. The influence of these emigrants is less than might at first be supposed.

Though their numbers seem large to us, they are, in proportion to the population from which they come, almost as nothing. They are principally from the province of Kwang-tung; and a single city of that province, Canton, might have furnished every emigrant which has ever come to our country from China without any appreciable loss or diminution of its inhabitants. Moreover, the great body of these emigrants are persons of very little position and influence in China. They go back to their homes in the city or country, and entertain their friends and neighbors with the story of their adventures for a short period; and then it loses its novelty, and they settle down to the quiet routine of their every-day life. The fixedness of custom and power of inertia in China are too great to be readily affected by such slight influences. Moreover, there is reason to fear that the Chinese do not carry back as favorable an impression of our country as we could wish. Many of them are treated with a great deal of severity and injustice, and have met with representatives of our race not at all calculated to make them any better, or to prepare them to exert a good influence on their own people on their return. I would not by any means be understood as saying that no good has resulted from this California immigration, but only that there is a tendency to overrate its importance. A decided impression has been produced, and in some respects a good one. While it is to be regretted that very few of the Chinese emigrants become Christians in this country, it is at the same time true that few go back with the same superstitious and idolatrous notions which they brought with them. It is often remarked by ship-captains that they are constantly engaged in idolatrous worship while going to California, but are comparatively very careless about such matters on their return.

Is it not strange that, with sixty thousand or more Chinese idolaters living among us, and entirely accessible to our influence, so little has been attempted by American Christians to enlighten and evangelize them? It is true that there are some disadvantages in laboring for them here, as compared with laboring for them in China, growing out of their wandering and unsettled life, separation from home influences and associations, their demoralized condition, and their absorbing interest in making money, but this by no means excuses our neglect. There are peculiar advantages also in having them so near us, and so much under our influence. The Presbyterian Board is, I believe, the only one which has established a permanent mission among these emigrants, and the experience of its earnest and devoted missionaries who have been laboring there for more than ten years is full of encouragement.

The future influence of the Chinese upon our Western coast is probably destined to be very great. Their quiet habits and industry are gradually winning the esteem and confidence of our people; and it is to be hoped that they will receive such treatment from our government and citizens as to attract to our shores a large number of persons from the more intelligent and influential classes. The increasing demand for labor in our country, the overburdened population of China, and the present unsettled state of the empire, are facts which conspire to stimulate and increase immigration to our shores. Should the tendency become general, a tide of population would pour over our Pacific States and down the eastern slope of the Rocky Mountains unprecedented in the history of nations; and the effect of such an immigration, or we might almost say inundation, no human foresight can now determine.

There are other causes tending to produce a change in the views, relations, and policy of the Chinese of a still more pressing and imperative character. Their liability to misunderstandings, and consequent collisions and wars with Western nations, resulting from their ignorance of our usages, and the determination of European powers to apply the same laws and regulations which prevail among other nations to China only with more rigor, have produced a disposition on her part to become acquainted with, and to adopt our conventional rules of international law. A work on this subject has been translated by Dr. Martin, of Pekin, and printed at the expense of the Chinese government, and has no doubt been perused with much care and profit by persons high in position and influence in the empire.

A special clause of the last English treaty provided that its authoritative form should be the English rather than the Chinese text; so it is thus made desirable and almost necessary for at least some of the Chinese to become familiar with our language. Consequently, classes were formed in Pekin and other parts of China soon after the ratification of the late treaties, composed of intelligent and promising Chinese and Tartar youths, with a good ground-work of their own literary training, who have undertaken the study of the English language and literature with a view to becoming government interpreters.

The present exigencies of the empire have also directed the attention of its rulers to the desirableness, if not the absolute necessity, if they would not let the sceptre of government slip from their grasp, of possessing themselves of a knowledge of the military science of the West. They can not fail to see that an aspirant for the throne who should take the initiative in obtaining foreign gun-boats and acquiring the ability to use them, and raising an army disciplined under foreign drill and furnished with foreign weapons, would be irresistible on sea or land.

The various reasons given above for adopting a more liberal and enlightened policy would be sufficiently evident to the Chinese, without any special explanation, information, or advice from others. But they are made still more so by the presence of the ministers of Western powers and intelligent foreigners in the employ of the government who reside in Pekin, and have constant and familiar intercourse with the chief men of influence in the empire. Through this intercourse, much reliable information is communicated respecting

other countries, tending to produce enlightened views, a mutual understanding, and a mutual confidence. The Chinese are learning to understand their own position and relations to other powers, and their own interests; also to discriminate between the characters, peculiarities, and policies of different nations.

Under these circumstances the government has lately inaugurated two movements, as desirable as they were unexpected, which show how rapidly its policy is being changed, and furnish ground for expecting still more rapid changes in the future.

A few months since we were startled by the intelligence that a university was about to be established at Pekin, having for its avowed object the teaching of foreign sciences, under the superintendence of professors from America and Europe. As was to be expected, this new movement met with a determined opposition from the old conservative school of China. It was urged by one of this class, who is a person of great prominence and influence, that if it were necessary to have such an institution, they could of course furnish better teachers from their own literati than could be obtained from abroad. He was effectually answered by being called upon to supply the men, which, failing to do, the university was founded without further opposition.

The fact of the establishment of such a school in Pekin will in time have a great moral effect throughout the empire. Scholars in the provinces will have their curiosity excited to know what this new learning from the West is, and a powerful stimulus will be given to free thought and inquiry. The young men who will here receive a thorough training will be influential officers at home, and foreign embassadors to other powers, and the authors of Chinese works on the modern sciences.

The other significant fact just alluded to is the appointment by the Chinese government of the Embassy which has recently left our shores. This Embassy may justly be regarded as introducing a new era in the history of China. Starting out to visit the various "*Western* Powers," it takes its journey toward the *East*, and reaches first the United States, its nearest neighbor. The extremes of the East and the West have met. The oldest nation of the earth has come to make overtures to the youngest. She came on an errand of amity and good-will, to establish more intimate relations, to seek mutual advantages. She came, laying aside her long-cherished pride and assumption of superiority, with true humility (and not without an acknowledged dignity and self-respect) as a learner; to find that she is living in a new world, and to ingraft the ideas and the civilization of the nineteenth century upon an old but still vigorous stock, which has witnessed the vicissitudes and withstood the storms of more than twenty centuries.

The origin of this Embassy is peculiar and full of interest. Our minister, Hon. Anson Burlingame, during his residence of about six years in Pekin as United States Minister, had acquired to an unusual degree the confidence and esteem of the present rulers of China. His just appreciation of the character of their people and government; his sympathy with them in their trials; and, above all, his evident desire to accord to them fully their national rights, awakened in them a hearty and affectionate response. When about to return home, they expressed their deep regret and sense of loss at his leaving them. They had already begun to feel the necessity of entering into closer relations with other powers, and the desirableness of doing it speedily; but from their long isolation, and ignorance of Western languages and customs, foreign travel and foreign courts, they could at present hardly find a suitable person from among their own people to take the lead in such a movement. It occurred to their minds that Mr. Burlingame might be induced to become their official representative, and undertake this mission for them. When they were told that there was nothing impracticable in such a plan, they made to him, as soon as it could be done in a regular and formal manner, the proffer of this high position and trust, which proffer was accepted.

Placing him at the head of the Embassy, they associated with him two Chinese officials of high rank, *Chi-kang* and *Sun-kia-ku;* the former a Tartar, and the latter a Chinese. The Embassy has connected with it two foreign interpreters or secretaries, one English and one French; also six Chinese student interpreters—young men between twenty and twenty-five years of age, two of whom speak French, two English, and two Russian. Besides, there are twenty others, who are subordinate officers, Chinese secretaries, valets, physicians, and servants.

The cordiality and enthusiasm with which these representatives of China were received were not more remarkable than the happy impression which they have left behind them. It was evident to all that they were men of a high degree of intelligence and culture. Whether in the public assembly, or the fashionable *soirée*, or in the domestic circle, they were everywhere at ease. Their gracefulness of manner, their unpretending and cordial politeness, their careful and discriminating observations and inquiries, and their ready wit and pleasantry were subjects of general remark. It was also observed that the English of the student interpreters was remarkably free from a foreign accent.

The treaty concluded in Washington between our government and the Chinese is rather one-sided, nearly all its provisions being in favor of the Chinese. For this reason, it is all the more honorable to Mr. Burlingame and to our government. Instead of being dictated by selfishness and secured by intimidation, it presents the rare excellence and beauty of a great and powerful nation giving to a weaker one her rights from motives of impartial justice and generosity. The substantial evidence thus afforded of genuine friendship will be of greater advantage to both parties than the provisions of the treaty themselves. The Chinese seem to have left us more than satisfied, and will go back to their homes to impart to their countrymen different views from those which have heretofore been entertained, and to give a broader meaning to the familiar saying of their great teacher, "All within the four seas are brethren."*

PRINCE KUNG.

The members of this Embassy represent the party of progress, which is now, and has been for years in the ascendant. At its head is Prince Kung, who, during the minority of the

* Further information respecting the origin, objects, and results of this Embassy may be obtained from a speech of Mr. Burlingame in New York, and from the treaty agreed upon in Washington, both of which may be found in the Appendix.

Emperor Tung-che, now about thirteen years old, virtually wields the power of Regent. This party fully appreciates the true position and interests of China in the present crisis, and is introducing foreign ideas and new measures as fast as the state of public opinion and feeling among their countrymen will allow. The changes which they are effecting may seem slow to us, but they are rapid and radical beyond all former precedent. Besides admitting the ministers of foreign powers to their capital, establishing a foreign university of learning, and sending forth to Western nations its first Embassy, it is building gun-boats, introducing foreign drill and discipline and warlike weapons into the army, and employing a large number of foreigners to aid them in effecting the changes which they desire. The Chinese members of the Embassy were constantly making notes of their journey, which will probably be published on their return with the official sanction of the government, and will give a new impulse to the cause of progress. We will no doubt hear of ministers and consuls being sent from China to foreign nations, and of the construction on her soil of telegraphs and railroads as soon as the carrying out of these measures is practicable.

In the mean time enlarged advantages for prosecuting the work of missions are being granted faster than we are appropriating them. Missionaries, in accordance with the treaties of 1858, not only reside in the open ports, and travel and teach wherever they please throughout the empire, but are allowed to rent houses for permanent residence in places not named in the treaty. Protestant missionaries are fast acquiring a character of their own, in distinction from the representatives of the Church of Rome, and are constantly gaining to a greater degree the confidence of the people and their rulers.

There are evidences of a change of feeling with regard to the idolatrous rites practiced by the people. The following information, derived from missionary sources, is being extensively copied and circulated in our religious periodicals: "The Emperor of China has issued an edict forbidding the rebuilding of destroyed, and the repair of decayed temples, except the temples of Confucius. The principal judge of Suchow has prohibited the people of that large city from worshiping in the temples, or burning incense, candles, or silver paper before the idols." We are hardly warranted in inferring from these facts that there is a decided disposition among Chinese officers to favor Christianity. They would probably explain the origin of these edicts by attributing them to a desire to husband the resources of the empire, and to avoid all unnecessary waste of funds during the exigencies of the present time. The fact remains, however, that the building of temples and the worship of idols is regarded at least as a matter of secondary and trivial importance, and that, for some cause or other, heathen temples are likely to fall into decay. These indications of change are certainly significant, and point unmistakably to the period when "idols shall be utterly abolished."

Enough has been said to confirm and illustrate the general statement that the present is for China a period of transition, and marks a new and most important epoch in her history. She has loosed from her ancient moorings, and, under influences hitherto unfelt, is moving slowly but surely in a course in which the star of science leads, and the pressure of necessity urges her. What storms and trials she may meet none can tell. In her new and untried career, shall we not give her our cordial sympathy and co-operation, hoping that her future may be full of blessings to her vast population and to the world?

CHAPTER XXVIII.

CONCLUSION.

The Presence and Agency of Christ among the Nations.—He rules the World in the Interest of the Church.—Different Influences conspire to prepare the Way for the Establishment of His spiritual Kingdom.—The Responsibility of the Church in the present Juncture.—Evidences of low and unscriptural Views with Regard to Missions.—The true Standard of Christian Duty.

THE present condition of China will be viewed in different lights by different individuals. The merchant will see in it an opportunity for supplying the new-felt wants of the people, and introducing, as there is a demand for them, the manufactures, machinery, and mechanical implements of the West. Statesmen of different nations will be on the alert to secure political and commercial advantages for their respective countries. Scholars will look for freer access to the public libraries and general literature of China, and hope for additional light upon history, chronology, ethnology, and other departments of science. These will generally be considered as the principal and most important ends to be secured in our intercourse with that great nation. Not a few who seem to think that the great end for which Eastern nations exist is to minister to and enrich the West, will regard it as but reasonable and right that those countries which have labored, expended, and suffered most for the purpose of opening China, should be compensated by commercial and political advantages, the securing of these objects having been from the first the principal and avowed motive which led to these expenditures.

But the intelligent Christian who reads aright the book

of Revelation, of History, and of Providence, will take another and widely different view of this whole matter. Behind these second causes he will recognize the mighty workings of Him who has all power in heaven and in earth, and who rules all nations in the interests of His Church. Those solemn and sublime, though mysterious, words addressed by Jesus of Nazareth to the Roman governor, "I am a king," present a practical reality which some Christians as well as others are too apt to lose sight of. Yes, high above all earthly potentates, Jesus sits the *Universal King*. As in former times He used the sword of the Assyrian as the rod of his anger, and for "Jacob his servant's sake" called even Cyrus by His name, and said of him "He is my shepherd, and shall perform all my pleasure," so at present He makes use of England and France, and other nations which He has raised up for His own purposes, as unconscious instruments to do His will. They pursue their own ends, which are often unworthy and sinful, but He overrules their acts, bringing good out of evil. His purposes, at first concealed from mortal view, are gradually unfolding; and His comprehensive plan of providence and grace will surely be accomplished when the petty schemes of men and nations, through which they have been developed, are forgotten.

Now among the clearest facts of God's revelations of the future are these: The kingdom of which Christ is the head shall be universal; it shall rise upon the ruins of idolatry and superstition, and, in its final triumph, establish here in our world a millennium of peace and glory. "All kings shall fall down before him, all nations shall serve him."

"It is not for us to know the times and the season which the Father has put in His own power," but who can fail to see that the leading events of the present are pointing to the consummation of the divine purposes? The tendency of our race after the confusion of tongues and the dispersion was to the constant multiplication and separation of numerous nations speaking different languages. This tendency has been reversed, and the opposite one is now most marked. Tribes and races hitherto segregated and comparatively unknown are now joining the brotherhood of nations. India, China, and Japan, with their teeming millions, are waking from the sleep of ages, to respond to the impulse of new ideas, and to join in the march of modern civilization. Men are running to and fro, and knowledge is being increased. While the sons of Japheth are dwelling in the tents of Shem, and disseminating Western ideas, Eastern nations are coming to us, not only by embassies and immigrants, but through travellers whose express object is to gain information. Young men of the ruling classes in Japan, full of intelligence, zeal, and energy, are laying aside official rank and dignity, and coming to our shores, entering our primary schools and colleges, and are making remarkable progress in knowledge; burning with a desire to go back and inform and elevate their countrymen. Some of them, under a strong conviction of duty, and with the true spirit of martyrs, are taking upon themselves the vows of Christ, though they know that by the laws of their country such a course is threatened with death.

It is also a most significant fact that the influence of Christian nations is everywhere predominant throughout the world. The common language of the two great Protestant powers, England and the United States, the language in which are garnered the richest treasures of sanctified learning and Christian thought, is taking the precedence of all others, and is now spoken to a greater or less extent in almost every nation under the whole heaven. Old systems of error and superstition are crumbling and falling, and idolatry, whose reign has been so protracted and so nearly universal, seems to be passing from the earth. With the increased facilities for communicating ideas and for locomotion, nations are practically brought nearer together. In a few years almost all of them will, through the magnetic wire, be within speaking distance of each other, and the traveller will be able to pass round the world in less than three months.

Christ is indeed doing a great work in the earth. In his hands, all agencies, national and individual, commercial, diplomatic, and scientific, tend to the same result. We should not depreciate these powerful auxiliaries to the establishment of His kingdom, much less regard them as antagonistic. They are important in their several spheres, and to accomplish their appropriate ends. They may do much in undermining old systems of idolatry, though they can not substitute any thing better in their place; and, without the Gospel, they may prove a curse rather than a blessing.

Under these circumstances, how sublime the mission, and how great the responsibility of the Church in the present age! Of this responsibility I desire, in conclusion, to speak plainly and earnestly. I know that, while missionaries are generally listened to with interest and attention as long as they can tell an interesting story, or while they communicate important information respecting the countries from which they come, they are often complained of when they take the liberty of "*preaching* on missions." I acknowledge that this does not seem the most appropriate work for them to do, but there would be less necessity for it, and disposition to attempt it, if it were generally attended to by pastors at home.

Most Christians agree that the work of missions is important; but this acknowledgment is with many rather the expression of an inoperative sentiment than a practical truth. They admire the missionary zeal of the Apostle Paul, but would perhaps regard a person manifesting the same zeal at the present day, though with equal or greater reason, a visionary enthusiast. Their sympathies may perchance be excited when an eloquent preacher pictures to their imagination the condition of Athens eighteen hundred years ago as a city filled with idols; but the present spectacle of whole nations filled with idols, and brought into the closest relations with us, affects them but little. The same religious views, feelings, labors, and sacrifices which were very appropriate in apostolic times, seem to them rather out of place in these modern days.

How persons who believe the Bible can entertain such views, is to me a mystery! It may be said of them, with reference to the New Testament, as it was of the Jews, with reference to the Old; even to this day, when the words of Christ and His Apostles are read, "the veil is upon their heart." The duty of missions is the burden of the New Testament. From Matthew to Revelation, it is written on almost every page; and the glorious theme is frequently referred to in some of the most glowing and sublime passages of ancient prophecy. How strange that the ministers of the New Testament, who are appointed to speak as the oracles of God, should, after preaching to a Christian congregation for years, leave them in doubt as to the authoritative teachings of the Bible on this fundamental and vital matter! Surely there *is* need of preaching on missions, not as a subject to be treated of on special and extraordinary occasions, and distinct from the usual ministrations of the sanctuary, but as a necessary part of Gospel preaching; till every professed disciple feels that this work is as much a part of Christian duty as any other which is commanded in the Scriptures; and that to be out of sympathy with it is so far to be out of sympathy with Christ.

It is a lamentable fact, that a large proportion of the theological students who are willing to engage in missionary work meet with opposition from Christian parents or friends. In certain cases, there are good and sufficient reasons which evidently make it the duty of those who earnestly desire to go abroad to remain at home. In other instances, the obstacle is simply the unwillingness of parents to allow them to go. A theological student said to me not long since, "I am very willing to be a missionary, but our family has never yet been broken up; our parents like to have their children about them, and are averse to my leaving." It is not a matter of regret that such persons do not go, but rather that such a low standard of duty and Christian consecration should prevail in the Church of Christ, and especially in the ministry. These are the same difficulties which are often presented to us by inquirers in heathen lands: "I would like to be a Christian, but my parents are opposed to it. The peace and quiet of our family has never yet been disturbed, and I do not like to go contrary to their wishes." The only proper answer to such objections and excuses, whether among the heathen or in the Church, is the words of Christ, "He that loveth father or mother more than me is not worthy of me."

The contributions of Christians to the cause of missions also show how inadequate their efforts are to meet the demands of the case, and are the best outward index of the interest which is really felt. The Protestant Church, with her scriptural faith, her professions of love to Christ, and the numerous claims of His cause upon her at home and abroad, gives a much smaller proportion of her means to the cause of Christ than Roman Catholics and pagans do for the support of their forms of religion and idolatry. The average of the contributions of the members of the Presbyterian Church, including those of the few who give largely and generously, is about seventy cents each annually; not more than one-twentieth of the amount expended by many a poor laboring man for the single and unnecessary item of tobacco! The Church needs another reformation to establish the doctrine of the necessity of "good works," as the Reformation in the time of Luther did that of justification by faith. Faith without works is dead, and this dead faith and covetousness, which is idolatry, threaten to destroy the life and energy of the Church. On this important Christian duty, so prominently presented, and so often urged upon Christians in the Bible, there is also great need of plain and pungent expounding of the Scriptures in our churches. I find that some pastors are afraid to preach on this subject, though they feel that nothing is more urgently required. The fact is that their people, for want of scriptural teachings on this point, have become so confirmed in covetousness that they "will not endure sound doctrine." It is encouraging to find some Christians, and I rejoice to believe that their number is every year increasing, who act and live on the principle that they are stewards, and solemnly consecrate to God such a proportion of their incomes as they are not ashamed to look at on their account-books.

But let us ever remember that while God makes use of His Church and her offerings, still, with the fullest supply of men and means, we would, without the presence and aid of His Spirit, be utterly powerless to do any good, or to convert one soul.

Fellow-Christians, the Master, from whom you have received so freely of spiritual and temporal blessings, calls upon you for your best offerings for His cause: your sons, your daughters, your gold and silver, your warmest sympathies, and earnest prayers. SHALL HE CALL IN VAIN?

THE END.

APPENDIX.

SPEECH OF THE HON. ANSON BURLINGAME, THE HEAD OF THE CHINESE EMBASSY TO THE WESTERN POWERS, DELIVERED IN NEW YORK JUNE 23, 1868.

MR. PRESIDENT, AND CITIZENS OF NEW YORK,—Our first duty is to thank you for this cordial greeting; to say to you that it is not only appreciated by us, but that it will be appreciated by the distant people whom we represent; to thank you for this unanimous expression of good-will on the part of the great city of New York; to thank you that, rising above all local and party considerations, you have given a broad and generous welcome to a movement made in the interests of all mankind. We are but the humble heralds of this movement. It originated beyond the boundaries of our own thoughts, and has taken dimensions beyond the reach of our most ardent hopes. That East which men have sought since the days of Alexander now itself seeks the West. China, emerging from the mists of time, but yesterday suddenly entered your Western gates, and confronts you, by its representatives, here to-night. What have you to say to her? She comes with no menace on her lips. She comes with the great doctrine of Confucius, uttered two thousand three hundred years ago, "Do not unto others what you would not have others do unto you." Will you not respond with the more positive doctrine of Christianity—"We will do unto others what we would have others do unto us?" She comes with your international law. She tells you that she is willing to come into relations according to it; that she is willing to abide by its provisions; that she is willing to take its obligations for its privileges. She asks you to forget your ancient prejudices, to abandon your assumptions of superiority, to submit your questions with her as she proposes to submit her questions with you—to the arbitrament of reason. She wishes no war; she asks of you not to interfere in her internal affairs; she asks you not to send lecturers who are incompetent men; she asks that you will respect the neutrality of her waters and the integrity of her territory; she asks, in a word, to be left perfectly free to unfold herself precisely in that form of civilization of which she is the most capable to judge. She asks you to give to those treaties which were made under the pressure of war a generous and Christian construction. Because you have done this, because the Western nations have reversed their old doctrine of force, she responds; and in proportion as you have done that, in proportion as you have expressed your good-will, she has come forth to meet you. And I aver that there is no spot on this earth where there has been greater progress made within the past few years than in the empire of China. She has extended her business and reformed her revenue system. She is changing her military and naval organizations, and is establishing a great school, where modern science and the foreign languages are to be taught. She has done this under very adverse circumstances. She has done this after a great war, lasting through thirteen years—a war out of which she comes with no national debt. You must remember how dense is her population, and how difficult it is to introduce radical changes in such a country as that. The introduction of your own steamers threw out of employment one hundred thousand junkmen, and the introduction of several hundred foreigners into her civil service embittered, of course, the ancient native employés. The establishment of a school was firmly resisted by a party led by one of the greatest men of the empire. Yet, in spite of all this, the present government of China has advanced steadily along the path of progress, sustained, it is true, by the enlightened European and Western Powers now at Pekin, and guided largely by a modest and able man—Mr. Hart, the Inspector-General of Customs, at the head of the foreign employés of China. Yet, notwithstanding this manifest progress, there are people who will tell you that China has made no progress; that her views are retrograde; and they tell you that it is the duty of the Western Treaty Powers to combine for the purpose of coercing China into reforms which they may desire, and which she may not desire, to undertake to say that these people have no rights which we are bound to respect. In their coarse language they say, "Take her by the throat," using the tyrant's plea. They say that they know better what China wants than China herself does. Not only do they desire to introduce new reforms born of their own interests and of their own caprice, but they tell you that the present dynasty must fall, and that the whole structure of Chinese civilization must be overthrown. I know that these views are abhorred by the governments and the countries from which they come, but they are far away from their countries. They are active, brave, and unscrupulous, and, if they happen to be officials, it is in their power to complicate affairs, and to involve ultimately their distant countries in war. Now it is against the malign spirit of this tyrannical element that this mission was sent forth to the Christian world. It was sent forth that China might have her difficulties stated. That I happen to be at the head of it is, perhaps, more an accident than any design. It is perhaps because I had been longer there than my colleagues. It was because I was about to leave it. It was because, also—and probably more than all—because my humble name was associated with the establishment of the co-operative policy which, co-operating with abler men than myself, was established not many years ago. It is to sustain that policy—which has received the warm approval of all the great Treaty Powers, and which is cherished by China—that we are sent forth; and it is in behalf of that generous policy, founded upon principles of eternal justice, that I would rally the strongest thing on this earth—the enlightened public opinion of the world. Missions and men may pass away, but the principles of eternal justice will stand. I desire that the autonomy of China may be preserved; that her independence may be maintained; that she may have equality, and that she may dispense equal privileges to all the nations. If the opposite school is to prevail, if you are to use coercion against that great people, then who is to exercise the coercion? Whose forces are you to use? Whose views are you to establish? You see, the very attempt to carry out any such tyrannical policy would involve not only China, but would involve you in bloody wars with each other. There are men of that tyrannical school who say that China is not fit to sit at the council-board of the nations, who call them barbarians, who attack them on all occasions with a bitter and unrelenting spirit. These things I utterly deny. I say, on the contrary, that that is a great and noble people. It has all the elements of a splendid nationality. It has the most numerous people on the face of the globe; it is the most homogeneous people in the world; its language is spoken by more human beings than any other in the world, and it is written in the rock; it is a country where there is a greater unification of thought than any other country in the world; it is a country where the maxims of the great sages, coming down memorized, have permeated the whole people until their knowledge is rather an instinct than an acquirement. It is a people loyal while living, and whose last prayer when dying is to sleep in the sacred soil of their fathers. It is a land of scholars and of schools — a land of books, from the smallest pamphlet up to voluminous encyclopedias. It is a land, sir, as you have said, where the privileges are common; it is a land without caste, for they destroyed their feudal system two thousand one hundred years ago, and they built up their great structure of civilization on the great idea that the people are the source of power. That idea was uttered by Mencius more than two thousand years ago, and it was old when he uttered it. The power flows forth from that people into practical government through the co-operative system, and they make scholarship a test of merit. I say it is a great, a polite, a patient, a sober, and an industrious people; and it is such a people as this that the bitter boor would exclude from the council-hall of the nations. It is such a nation as this that the tyrannical element would put under its ban. They say that all these people (a third of the human race) must become the weak wards of the West; wards of nations not so populous as many of their provinces; wards of people who are younger than their newest village in Manchuria. I do not mean to say that the Chinese are perfect; far from it. They have their faults, their pride, and their prejudices like other people. These are profound, and they must be overcome. They have their conceits like other people, and they must be done away; but they are not to be removed by talking to them with cannon, by telling them that they are feeble and weak, and that they are barbarians. No; China has been cut off by her position from the rest of the world. She has been separated from it by limitless deserts and broad oceans. But now, when the views of men expand, we behold the very globe itself diminishing in size; now, when science has dissipated the desert, and when it has narrowed the ocean, we find that China, seeing another civilization on every side, has her eyes wide open to the situation. She sees Russia on the north, Europe on the west, and America on the east; she sees a cloud of sail on her coast; she sees mighty steamers coming from every quarter; she feels the spark from the electric telegraph falling hot upon her, and she rouses herself, not in anger, but for argument. She finds that by not being in a position to compete with other nations for so long a time that she has lost ground; she comprehends very well that she must come into relations with those civilizations which are pressing all around her; and feeling that, she does not wait, but comes out to you, and extends to you her hand. She tells you she is ready to take upon her ancient civilization the graft of your civilization; that she is ready to take back her own inventions, with all their developments; that she is willing to trade with you, to buy of you, to sell to you, to help you strike off the shackles from trade. She invites your merchants, she invites your missionaries, and tells them to plant the shining cross on every hill and in every valley, for she is hospitable to fair argument. She offers you almost free trade to-day. Holding the great staples of the earth—tea and silk, she charges you scarcely any tariff on the exports you send out to exchange for them. She is willing to meet the interior questions which are arising now as to transit dues; and if you will only have patience with her and right reason on your side, she will settle these to your satisfaction. The country is open; you may travel and trade where you like. What complaint have you to make of her? Show her, I say, fair play; exhibit that to her, and you will bless the toiling millions of the world. That trade, which has in my own day in China risen from eighty-two millions to three hundred millions, is but a tithe of the enormous trade that may be carried on with China in the future. Let her alone, give her her independence; let her develop herself in her own time and in her own way. She has no hostility to you. Let her do this, and she will initiate a movement which will be felt in every workshop in the civilized world. She says now, "Send us your wheat, lumber, gold, silver, goods from everywhere. We will take as many of them as we can; we will give you back our tea, silk, and free labor, which we have sent so largely out into the world, which is overflowing upon Siam, the British possessions, Singapore, Manilla, Peru, Cuba, Australia, and California. What she asks is, that you will be as kind to her people as she is to yours. She wishes simply that you will do justice. She is willing not only to exchange goods with you, but to exchange thoughts; she is willing to give you her intellectual civilization for your material civilization. Let her alone, and the caravans toward the North and Russia will swarm larger than they are now. Let her alone, and the great steamers of the "Peninsular and Oriental Co." and the "Messagerie Imperiale" may multiply their coming; let her alone, and that great line which is the pride of New York —the Pacific Mail—may increase, or as many other lines as you choose to form, may increase their tonnage tenfold, and they will still have to leave their freight uncarried, as at present, on the wharf at Hong-kong and Yokohama. The imagination kindles at the future which may be, and will be, if you will be just and fair to China.

THE LATE TREATY WITH CHINA, SUPPLEMENTARY TO THE TREATY OF 1858.

ART. 1. His Majesty the Emperor of China, being of the opinion that in making concessions to the citizens or subjects of foreign powers of the privilege of residing on certain tracts of land, or resorting to certain waters of that empire for the purposes of trade, he has by no means relinquished his right of eminent domain or dominion over the said land and waters, hereby agrees that no such concession or grant shall be construed to give to any power or party which may be at war with or hostile to the United States the right to attack the citizens of the United States or their property within the said lands or waters; and the United States, for themselves, hereby agree to abstain from offensively attacking the citizens or subjects of any power, or party, or their property, with which they may be at war, on any such tract of land or waters of the said empire; but nothing in this article shall be construed to prevent the United States from resisting an attack by any hostile power or party upon their citizens or their property. It is further agreed, that if any right or interest in any tract of land in China has been or shall hereafter be granted by the Government of China to the United States or their citizens for purposes of trade or commerce, that grant shall in no event be construed to divest the Chinese authorities of their right of jurisdiction over persons and property within said tract of land, except so far as that right may have been expressly relinquished by treaty.

ART. 2. The United States of America and His Majesty the Emperor of China, believing that the safety and prosperity of commerce will thereby best be promoted, agree, that any privilege or immunity in respect to trade or navigation within the Chinese dominions which may not have been stipulated for by treaty shall be subject to the discretion of the Chinese Government, and may be regulated by it accordingly, but not in a manner or spirit incompatible with the treaty stipulations of the parties.

ART. 3. The Emperor of China shall have the right to appoint consuls at ports of the United States, who shall enjoy the same privileges and immunities as those which are enjoyed by public law and treaty in the United States by the consuls of Great Britain and Russia, or either of them.

ART. 4. The twenty-ninth article of the treaty of the 18th of June, 1858, having stipulated for the exemption of Christian citizens of the United States and Chinese converts from persecution in China on account of their faith, it is further agreed, that citizens of the United States in China of every religious persuasion, and Chinese subjects in the United States, shall enjoy entire liberty of conscience, and shall be exempt from all disability or persecution on account of their religious faith or worship in either country. Cemeteries for sepulture of the dead of whatever nativity or nationality shall be held in respect, and free from disturbance or profanation.

ART. 5. The United States of America and the Emperor of China cordially recognize the inherent and inalienable right of man to change his home and his allegiance, and also the mutual advantages of the free migration and immigration of their citizens and subjects respectively from the one country to the other for purposes of curiosity, trade, or as permanent residents. The high contracting parties, therefore, join in reprobating any other than an entirely voluntary immigration for these purposes. They consequently agree to pass laws making it a penal offense for a citizen of the United States or a Chinese subject to take Chinese subjects either to the United States or to any foreign country, or for a Chinese subject or a citizen of the United States to take citizens of the United States to China or to any other foreign country without their free and voluntary consent respectively.

Art. 6. Citizens of the United States visiting or residing in China shall enjoy the same privileges, immunities, or exemptions in respect to travel or residence as may there be enjoyed by the citizens or subjects of the most favored nation; and, reciprocally, Chinese subjects visiting or residing in the United States shall enjoy the same privileges, immunities, and exemptions in respect to travel or residence as may be enjoyed by the citizens or subjects of the most favored nation; but nothing herein contained shall be held to confer naturalization upon the citizens of the United States in China, nor upon the subjects of China in the United States.

Art. 7. Citizens of the United States shall enjoy all the privileges of the public educational institutions under the control of the Government of China, and, reciprocally, Chinese subjects shall enjoy all the privileges of the public educational institutions under the control of the Government of the United States which are enjoyed in the respective countries by the citizens or subjects of the most favored nations. The citizens of the United States may freely establish and maintain schools within the empire of China at those places where foreigners are by treaty permitted to reside, and, reciprocally, Chinese subjects may enjoy the same privileges and immunities in the United States.

Art. 8. The United States, always disclaiming and discouraging all practices of unnecessary dictation and intervention by one nation in the affairs or domestic administration of another, do hereby freely disclaim any intention or right to intervene in the domestic administration of China in regard to the construction of railroads, telegraphs, or other material internal improvements. On the other hand, His Majesty the Emperor of China reserves to himself the right to decide the time and manner and circumstances of introducing such improvements within his dominions. With this mutual understanding, it is agreed by the contracting parties, that if at any time hereafter His Imperial Majesty shall determine to construct or cause to be constructed works of the character mentioned within the empire, and shall make application to the United States or any other Western power for facilities to carry out that policy, the United States will, in that case, designate and authorize suitable engineers to be employed by the Chinese Government, and will recommend to other nations an equal compliance with such application, the Chinese Government in that case protecting such engineers in their persons and property, and paying them a reasonable compensation for their services.